COMPUTER GAMES

AND IMMERSIVE

ENTERTAINMENT

Next Frontiers in Intellectual Property Law

SECOND EDITION

Chrissie Scelsi and
Ross A. Dannenberg
Editors

ABA Section of
Intellectual Property Law
AMERICAN BAR ASSOCIATION

Cover design by Jill Tedhams/ABA Design

Printed in the United States of America.

23 22 21 20 19   5 4 3 2 1

Library of Congress Cataloging-in-Publication Data
Names: Scelsi, Chrissie, editor. | Dannenberg, Ross A., editor. | American
    Bar Association. Section of Intellectual Property Law, issuing body.
Title: Computer games and immersive entertainment / edited by Chrissie
    Scelsi and Ross A. Dannenberg.
Description: Second edition. | Chicago : American Bar Association, [2018] |
    Includes bibliographical references and index.
Identifiers: LCCN 2018037990 (print) | LCCN 2018038489 (ebook) | ISBN
    9781634251198 (ebook) | ISBN 9781634251181 (print : alk. paper)
Subjects: LCSH: Computer games—Law and legislation—United States. |
    Video games—Law and legislation—United States. | Virtual reality—
    United States. | Shared virtual environments—Law and legislation—
    United States. | Copyright—Computer programs—United States. |
    Intellectual property—United States. | Computer games—Law and
    legislation. | Video games—Law and legislation. | Virtual reality. |
    Shared virtual environments—Law and legislation.
Classification: LCC KF3024.C6 (ebook) | LCC KF3024.C6 C625 2018 (print) |
    DDC 346.7304/8—dc22
LC record available at https://lccn.loc.gov/2018037990

www.ShopABA.org

Contents

How to Use This Book   ix

Introduction   xi

Contributors   xvii

CHAPTER 1
Contracts as Private Law in Video Games and
Immersive Entertainment   1
Michael Bombace, Brian D. Sites, Curtis A. Peele, Joshua A.T. Fairfield

Introduction   2

I.   Purpose and Scope of Agreements   4
    A.   History of EULAs, TOS, and TOU Agreements   4
    B.   Common Provisions in Modern Agreements   10
    C.   Scholarly Criticisms of Terms: One Brief Example   14
    D.   The Future of EULAs, TOS, and TOU   17

II.   Current and Potential Limitations on Terms and
    Agreements in Digital Games   19
    A.   Unconscionability   19
    B.   Modifications   39
    C.   Privity of Contract   43
    D.   Minors   48

III.   Potential Resolutions to TOU Limitations in Digital Games   51
    A.   Industry Practices   52
    B.   Judicial Intervention   56
    C.   Legislative Action   58

Conclusion   60

CHAPTER 2
Copyright Law   **61**
Marc E. Mayer

Introduction   62
I.   Basic Requirements for Copyright Protection   64
     A. Literal and Nonliteral Aspects of Computer Games   64
     B. Originality   72
     C. Fixation   75
     D. Limitations on the Scope of Copyright Protection   80
II. Authorship and Ownership   89
     A. Works for Hire   91
     B. Joint Works and Contributions   95
     C. EULAs and Ownership of Game Mods
         and Virtual Property   97
III. Copyright Infringement   101
     A. Copycat or "Clone" Games   104
     B. Your Game Stole My Movie/Screenplay/Book!   108
     C. Streaming, Twitch, Machinima, and "Let's Play"
         Videos   111
Conclusion   117

CHAPTER 3
Patents: Real-World Issues in Mixed Realities   **119**
Steve Chang and Sanford Warren

Introduction   120
I.   A Brief Overview of U.S. Patent Protection   120
     A. Utility Patents: U.S. Patentability Requirements   120
     B. Design Patents: U.S. Patentability Requirements   128
     C. Obtaining a Patent for Inventions on Video Games
         and Virtual Worlds   129
II. Patent Protection for Video Games and Virtual Worlds   130
     A. Utility Patents   130
     B. Design Patents   138
III. Using a Patent in a Virtual World   146
     A. Enforcement Avenues   146
     B. Infringement Issues   157

    C. Damages Issues   160
    D. Video Game Lawsuits   164
Conclusion   172

CHAPTER 4
Implications of Video Games and Immersive
Entertainment in Trademark Law   **173**
William K. Ford and Anna L. King

Introduction   174
I.   Overview of Trademark Protection   176
II. Trademark Issues in the Video Game and Virtual
     World Contexts   184
    A. Traditional Uses: Physical Products   185
    B. In-Game Uses: Direct Liability   187
    C. In-Game Uses: Secondary Liability   191
III. Analysis of Trademark Issues in Video Games
     and Virtual Worlds   192
    A. Nominative Fair Use   202
    B. The First Amendment   208
IV. Secondary Liability   216
V. Unfair Competition: Trademark Infringement and
     Misappropriation   219
Conclusion   222

CHAPTER 5
Implications of Video Games and Immersive
Entertainment and the Law of Trade Secrets   **225**
Thomas J. Mihill, Steven M. Kushner, Adam C. Losey

Introduction   226
I.   Trade Secrets Generally   226
    A. What Is a Trade Secret and What Can Be Protected?   226
    B. The Competitive Advantage Requirement   230
    C. The Secrecy Requirement   232
    D. Trade Secret Information Protected by Other IP Laws   236
II. Trade Secrets in Video Games and Virtual Worlds   239
    A. Gameplay: What Players/Users See   239
    B. Game Design: Behind the Scenes   245

III. Applying the Traditional Analysis to Video Game
     and Virtual World Issues   249
IV. What Remedies Are Available for Trade Secret
     Misappropriation?   251
     A. Injunctive Relief   251
     B. Damages   253
     C. Criminal Actions   253
Conclusion   254

CHAPTER 6
Rights of Publicity   **255**
Lynne Boisineau and Ben Manevitz

Introduction   256
I. The Development of Right of Publicity Protection
    in the United States   258
    A. Elements   259
    B. Types of Potential Claims Overlapping
       with the Right of Publicity   264
    C. Variations in State Law   271
    D. Defenses   272
Conclusion   296

CHAPTER 7
International Considerations of Video Games
and Immersive Entertainment   **299**
Ken Cheney

Introduction   300
I. International Copyright Issues in Online Games
    and Virtual Environments   304
    A. Choice of Law and Conflict of Laws   305
    B. Territoriality of Copyright Infringement   314
    C. Proposed Copyright Reform in Europe and China   321

II. International Trademark Issues   324
    A. Ownership and Territoriality   325
    B. Difficulty in Protecting Marks Subject to Global
        Exposure   327
    C. Enforcement and the Special Case of Foreign
        Defendants   329
III. Comparative Patent Law Issues   330
    A. Eligibility of Inventions Directed to Online Virtual
        Environments and Computer-Related Subject Matter   332
    B. Filing Issues for Online Virtual Environments
        and Internet-Related Inventions   335
    C. Some Issues Involving International Inventorship   337
    D. Enforceability against Foreign Defendants   338
IV. Jurisdictional Issues in the International Enforcement
     of Intellectual Property Rights   340
Conclusion   345

TABLE OF CASES   **347**

INDEX   **373**

How to Use This Book

This book is intended for those in the legal field (e.g., practitioners, law students, and legal scholars), placing a heavy emphasis on statutes, case law, and established legal resources. If you are not a legal practitioner of some sort, and are instead looking for a higher level introduction to legal issues one may encounter during video game development, we recommend you read the *American Bar Association's Legal Guide to Video Game Development* (2d ed. 2016), edited by Ross Dannenberg.

In this book, the chapters address, in order, contracts, copyright, patents, trademarks, trade secrets, and right of publicity as addressed by U.S. law, and we conclude with a commentary on international issues stemming from the multinational user base and foreign operation of games and immersive entertainment. One need not read the entire book—unless of course you are interested in doing so—but rather we recommend that you read each chapter as needed, perhaps as a starting point for research, or as a primer on a particular area of the law.

If you find any errors or omissions that you believe should be fixed or topics that should be included in the next edition of this book, please reach out to us. The editors' contact information and biographies may be found in the Contributors section of this book.

Introduction

Chrissie Scelsi
Ross Dannenberg[1]

Entertainment media encompassed by video games and immersive entertainment has continued to grow and prosper since the publication of the first edition of this treatise. At the time of our first edition (2010), the games industry had a total combined dollar sales of $15.9 billion, with $9.4 billion from video game sales, $0.7 billion in computer game sales, and $5.8 billion from sales in other game delivery formats.[2] Nearly 11 years later, U.S. video game industry revenue has continued to grow to a total of $36 billion, with $6.9 billion in hardware sales and $29.1 billion in software.[3] The impact of the industry on the U.S. gross domestic product is $11.7 billion in value, and the industry now employs more than 220,000 Americans. Immersive entertainment media such as augmented and

---

1. Ross Dannenberg is a senior partner with Banner & Witcoff, Ltd. Chrissie Scelsi is U.S. general counsel for Wargaming (USA), Inc. For full biographies, see the Contributors section of this book. The editors would also like to thank Andrew Thomas, a rising 3L at American University Washington College of Law, for his invaluable research assistance, bluebooking, and cite checking during final preparation of this book.

2. Entertainment Software Association, 2011 Essential Facts about the Computer and Video Game Industry (2011), https://isfe.eu/sites/isfe.eu/files/attachments/esa_ef _2011.pdf.

3. Press Release, Entertainment Software Association, Two-Thirds of Parents Embrace Video Games as a Family Pastime (May 14, 2018), http://www.theesa.com /article/two-thirds-parents-embrace-video-games-family-pastime/8.

virtual reality are also on the cusp of mainstream adoption, with the global market for these technologies estimated to reach $215 billion by 2021.[4]

Gaming and immersive entertainment have also grown in terms of widespread adoption. The 2018 Entertainment Software Association (ESA) report *Essential Facts about the Computer and Video Game Industry* illuminated a number of interesting statistics about the growth of the gaming audience, as well as significant indicators about how the face of gaming is changing. First, the ESA found that 65 percent of American households are home to someone who plays video games regularly, and that 64 percent of them own at least one device on which video games can be played.[5] The report also noted that 70 percent of the video game playing population is over the age of 18, and that the average video game player is 34 years old.[6] It further illuminated a significant demographic change in the gaming audience, with adult women representing a greater portion of the game playing population (33 percent) than boys under the age of 18 (17 percent).[7] This finding runs counter to the traditional gamer stereotype that is typically portrayed in the media. The report also notes that more than half of the most frequent gamers in a typical household play multiplayer video games with others at least once a week, and more than two-thirds of American parents play video games with their children at least once a week.[8]

Much as the demographics of the gaming audience have changed and expanded, the report's editors noted how the changes and advances in technology in gaming and immersive entertainment have changed the vernacular of the space as well. An interesting example that emerged was the question of how to address

---

4. Statista, *Forecast Augmented (AR) and Virtual Reality (VR) Market Size Worldwide from 2016 to 2022 (in Billion U.S. Dollars)*, https://www.statista.com /statistics/591181/global-augmented-virtual-reality-market-size (last visited July 25, 2018).

5. ENTERTAINMENT SOFTWARE ASSOCIATION, 2018 ESSENTIAL FACTS ABOUT THE COMPUTER AND VIDEO GAME INDUSTRY (2018), http://www.theesa.com/wp-content/uploads/2018 /05/EF2018_FINAL.pdf.

6. *Id.*

7. *Id.*

8. *Id.*

the topic of virtual worlds. At the time of this book's first publication, virtual worlds such as *Second Life* were gaining in popularity and grabbing headlines. Since then, the concept of a virtual world has changed and become even more immersive with the advent of virtual reality rigs like the *Oculus Rift, PlayStation VR, HTC Vive,* and more recently the *Oculus Go.* The technology has also caught the imagination of the mainstream audience with the release of the movie version of *Ready Player One,* with audiences buzzing about whether and how soon people will be able to immerse themselves in the Oasis. Similarly, we recognized the need to update the title to include the term "immersive entertainment" to encompass the advent of augmented reality. This technology went mainstream with the launch of *Pokémon GO,* which at its peak had more than 28.5 million people playing, and became a global phenomenon with crowds of players swarming parks and other locations to catch rare Pokémon. The popularity of the game also prompted legal precedent, as some states and municipalities proposed new laws to prevent large groups of players from damaging parks and other public places while playing games, though the ordinance put in place by Milwaukee County requiring that publishers get consent before releasing similar games in county parks was eventually struck down by a court on First Amendment grounds.[9]

The platforms on which games are played have also greatly expanded since the first edition of this book was published. The ESA study found that 41 percent of U.S. households play games on personal computers, 36 percent play on smartphones, 36 percent play on a dedicated game console, 24 percent play on a wireless device such as a tablet, 14 percent play on a dedicated handheld gaming system, and 8 percent play on virtual reality devices.[10] The formats have also evolved, as the split between digital and physical sales of games has shifted from 31 percent digital and 69 percent physical in 2010 to 79 percent digital and 21 percent physical in 2017.[11] Popular genres of games have in some ways stayed the same, with shooter, sports, action, and role-playing games still

---

9. Candy Lab Inc. v. Milwaukee County, 266 F. Supp. 3d 1139 (E.D. Wis. 2017).
10. *Id.*
11. *Id.*

the top sellers in 2017, but have also evolved to include the wildly popular genre of battle royale games like *PUBG* and *Fortnite* attracting millions of users.[12]

Another interesting trend that we have noted in the preparation of this second edition of the treatise is the change in how legal aspects of games and immersive entertainment are viewed by players. While end-user license agreements (EULAs), terms of service (TOS), game rules, and privacy policies may have seemed somewhat arcane to players at one time, the advent of smartphones and the widespread usage of applications and games have now put such documents and updates to them on the regular radar of users.

Intellectual property law has continued to play a prominent role in the gaming and immersive entertainment space, which is not surprising given the interesting issues that often emerge as technologies race well beyond the reaches of established case law and force lawyers working in the space to find creative solutions to protect companies while still engaging players. U.S. patent law has changed significantly since the first edition of this book with the passage of the Leahy-Smith America Invents Act in 2011, which saw the United States shifting in 2013 from a "first to invent" system to a "first to file" system. Copyright continues to play an important role in the gaming space, particularly with the explosion in popularity of mobile games that has resulted in a number of lawsuits over alleged game clones. The same is true for trademark law, as game developers continue to grapple with the question of how to depict or simulate reality without running afoul of the trademark and brand rights of real-world companies and people. This challenge not only applies to the realm of trademark law, as right of publicity issues have been increasingly litigated in recent years, particularly with respect to sports games. The Internet's ability to make a game available globally also presents interesting matters of international law, as Chapter 7 illuminates.

---

12. *Id.*; *see also* Max A. Cherney, *"Fortnite" More Important Than Cryptocurrency to Large Companies During Earnings Season,* MARKETWATCH, June 6, 2018, https://www.marketwatch.com/story/fortnite-more-important-than-cryptocurrency-to-large-companies-during-earnings-season-2018-06-05.

Video games and immersive entertainment continue to evolve at a staggering pace, and we can only imagine what this landscape will look like in another eight years. Will augmented reality technology simply be an add-on when you buy your next set of prescription glasses? Will contact lenses be augmented-reality ready?[13] Will top-of-the-line virtual and augmented reality headsets reach sub-$50 levels, or even be given away using a freemium model? Perhaps augmented reality bionic lenses will be included as an option when you get Lasik eye surgery. Whether future technological advances look more like something from *Minority Report* or *The Expanse* remains to be seen, but the legal issues these new technologies present will certainly be complex and require considerable thought. We can't wait to see what's next!

---

13. Amir Iliaifar, *iOptik Contact Lenses Augment Your Eyes and Allow for Futuristic Immersive Virtual Reality*, DIGITAL TRENDS, Jan. 19, 2012, https://www.digitaltrends.com/cool-tech/ioptik-contact-lenses-augment-your-eyes-and-allow-for-futuristic-immersive-virtual-reality.

Contributors

Editors

Ross Dannenberg (@GameLawyer)—Ross Dannenberg is an intellectual property (IP) attorney and senior partner with the law firm Banner & Witcoff in Washington, D.C. Ross handles a wide range of IP issues, including patents, copyrights, and trademarks, working primarily with software developers of all types. Ross has been working extensively with the video game industry since 2005, when he started PatentArcade.com, the web's only blog dedicated to the cross section of video games and IP law. Since that time, Ross has helped protect well-known game franchises, including *Halo®, World of Tanks®, Guild Wars®, The Witcher, Dying Light, Blue Dragon, Letterpress, Entranced, Perfect Dark®, Flight Simulator®, Project Gotham Racing, Midtown Madness, Bowl-O-Rama®*, and *RuneScape®*, among others.

In addition to his work protecting video games and mobile apps, Ross has extensive experience with enforcing those rights against infringers, including experience enforcing and defending legal rights involving claims of patent infringement, copyright infringement, trademark infringement, Digital Millennium Copyright Act (DMCA) violations, computer fraud and abuse, unfair competition, and related business torts. Ross also assists clients with business and development-related issues, including licensing third-party content and music; preparing website terms of use, end-user license agreements, and copyright and DMCA policies; as well as ensuring that game publishers are compliant with the Children's Online Privacy Protection Act (COPPA).

Ross was the founding chair of the American Bar Association's Committee on Computer Games and Virtual Worlds in the Intellectual Property Section, a position he held from 2005–2008; he was the 2011–2012 vice-chair of the IT Division and the division chair from 2012–2014. Ross is a member of the International Game Developers Association, a founding member of the Video Game Bar Association, a former member of the Lawyer Pilots Bar Association, and fellow of the American Bar Foundation. Ross has also served as an adjunct professor of patent and copyright law at George Mason University School of Law. He earned a bachelor's degree in Computer Science from the Georgia Institute of Technology in 1994 and a Juris Doctor from the George Washington University Law School in 2000, where he was a member of the *Environmental Lawyer* legal journal.

In addition to a wide variety of articles and interviews appearing in publications such as *USA Today*, *ABC News*, *Bloomberg*, *PC Magazine*, and *Gamasutra*, Ross is also the editor of the American Bar Association's *Legal Guide to Video Game Development*, and has been recognized multiple times as a SuperLawyer (by Thomson Reuters) and as an IP Star (by *Managing Intellectual Property*). Ross is also a member of Mensa.

For more information, visit https://bannerwitcoff.com and http://www.patentarcade.com, or follow @GameLawyer on Twitter. Ross can be contacted at rdannenberg@bannerwitcoff.com.

Chrissie Scelsi (@PunkLawyer)—Chrissie Scelsi is U.S. general counsel for Wargaming, an award-winning online game developer and publisher that is a leader in the free-to-play MMO market across PC, console, and mobile platforms. She is responsible for legal and business matters for the company's operations in the United States, including copyright, trademark, advertising, privacy, compliance, e-sports, licensing, events, and answering basically any question related to what can be done with a tank. Prior to joining

Wargaming, Chrissie practiced entertainment and new media law in private practice and was in-house counsel for game-based simulations company Bohemia Interactive Simulations, where she was responsible for advising on software licensing matters, government contracting and regulatory compliance, trademarks, copyright, and corporate issues.

Chrissie served as a co-editor for the first edition of this book, *Computer Games and Virtual Worlds: A New Frontier in Intellectual Property Law*, and is a chapter contributor to the ABA's *Legal Guide to Video Game Development*, both of which were published by the ABA Section of Intellectual Property Law. Chrissie is a former chair of the Entertainment, Arts, and Sports Law Section of the Florida Bar and is a member of the Video Game Bar Association and of the board of the Esports Bar Association. She is a member of Council for the ABA Section of Intellectual Property Law and serves on the section's Landslide® magazine board, as well as the CLE Board and Copyright Reform Task Force. She has been named as one of the top eight Central Florida attorneys with Twitterati status by the *Orlando Business Journal* based on the number of follows of her @PunkLawyer handle. Chrissie received her Bachelor of Business Administration in Marketing from Loyola University New Orleans, a Juris Doctor from Saint Louis University School of Law, and a Master of Laws in Entertainment and Media Law from Southwestern School of Law.

For more information, follow @PunkLawyer on Twitter, or Chrissie can also be contacted at c_scelsi@wargaming.net.

Authors

Lynne Boisineau (Chapter 6: Rights of Publicity)—Lynne Boisineau is a former partner and head of McDermott Will & Emery's Orange County trademark and right of publicity practice, and founding partner of Boisineau Law (as of July 2018). Lynne speaks and writes on the topics of trademark, copyright, and right of publicity as they apply to video games, social media, and virtual/augmented reality, including an article for the ABA's *Landslide Magazine* entitled "Giving the Right of Publicity a Much-Needed Makeover for the Social Media Revolution" and for the ABA's *GPSolo Magazine* entitled

"INTELLECTUAL PROPERTY LAW: The Right of Publicity and the Social Media Revolution." Lynne also counsels clients on all trademark, copyright, right of publicity, social media, and domain name issues, as well as managing numerous U.S. and global IP portfolios. Lynne has been ranked in the World Trademark Review 1000: The World's Leading Trademark Professionals (2014–present).

Michael Bombace (Chapter 1: Contracts as Private Law in Video Games and Immersive Entertainment)—Michael Bombace is counsel and director of legal and emerging technologies at Abaxx, a professional services firm advising clients in the government and commercial space on financial data and payments. Michael focuses on regulatory, compliance, and risk with emphasis on cryptocurrencies, Blockchain, and tech startups. Michael is also general counsel for the Government Blockchain Association in a pro bono capacity where he oversees global legal needs. Michael has spent time at Booz Allen, Citi, and Ripple, and volunteered at Bitcoin.org. He also writes on a variety of issues, such as financial crimes, virtual worlds, cybersecurity, cryptocurrencies, and legal and regulatory developments in these spaces.

Michael received his Juris Doctor from Washington and Lee University School of Law.

Steve Chang (Chapter 3: Patents: Real-World Issues in Mixed Realities)—Steve Chang is a principal shareholder in the Washington, D.C., office of Banner & Witcoff. Steve's practice focuses on assisting clients with managing their domestic and foreign utility and design patent portfolios. He works with clients to encourage (e.g., via developing inventor incentive programs), collect, and cultivate invention disclosures from busy inventors, to help identify core concepts for patentability, and to guide the preparation and prosecution of the corresponding patents with an eye towards compact prosecution and broad patent scope. In addition to patent prosecution, he is experienced in evaluating the strengths and weaknesses of patents for litigation and/or licensing, and his litigation work includes district court trial and appeals to both the U.S. Court of Appeals and the U.S. Supreme Court.

Steve has handled utility patents in a wide range of computer and electrical technologies, including Internet services, video games, content delivery networks, user interfaces, wired (e.g., DOCSIS, MoCA, etc.) and wireless (e.g., cellular, Wi-Fi) communication systems, and many others.

He has also handled hundreds of design patent applications to help his clients protect the novel ornamental appearances of their physical hardware and software user interfaces. Sample representations include work to protect operating system user interfaces, computing hardware, and user input devices used by millions of people today.

Outside of work for clients, Steve is an adjunct professor at Georgetown University Law School, teaching its course on IP Pretrial Litigation Skills. Steve has also given speeches and presentations for a variety of organizations, such as the Institute of Electrical and Electronics Engineers, ABA, Entertainment Software Association, Triangle Game Conference, and U.S. Navy Office of the General Counsel, and has authored various articles and book chapters in the IP field.

Steve received his Bachelor of Science degree in Electrical Engineering from the Ohio State University in 1995, and has been with Banner & Witcoff since receiving his Juris Doctor from the Temple University School of Law in 1998.

Steve is a member of the District of Columbia Bar, and is admitted to practice before the U.S. Patent and Trademark Office, the U.S. Court of Appeals for the Federal Circuit, the U.S. District Court for the District of Maryland, and the U.S. Supreme Court.

Ken Cheney (Chapter 7: International Considerations of Video Games and Immersive Entertainment)—Ken Cheney is a partner at Morgan, Lewis & Bockius LLP, and is experienced in all aspects of IP. Ken's patent practice includes patent portfolio management and counseling (domestic and international) in various technical areas including computer hardware and software systems, networking, analog and digital technology, integrated circuits, and medical devices. He also represents clients in post-issuance patent challenges before the U.S. Patent and Trademark Office Patent Trial and Appeal Board, and his litigation experience has involved patent and trademark infringement, trade secrets, fraud, and breach of contract.

Ken received his Juris Doctor from Loyola Law School, Los Angeles, and his bachelor's degree in Computer Engineering from the University of California, Irvine. While in law school, he was a senior production editor of the *Loyola International and Comparative Law Review* and a moot court competition semifinalist. Prior to law school, Ken worked as a software engineer for high tech startup companies and in the aerospace industry, integrating and testing power systems and mixed-signal technologies in spacecraft applications. Ken is also a musician and enjoys playing video games with his wife and four kids.

Joshua A.T. Fairfield (Chapter 1: Contracts as Private Law in Video Games and Immersive Entertainment)—Joshua Fairfield is an internationally recognized law and technology scholar, specializing in digital property, electronic contract, big data privacy, and virtual communities. He has written on the law and regulation of e-commerce and online contracts and on the application of standard economic models to virtual environments. Joshua's current research focuses on big data privacy models and the next generation of legal applications for cryptocurrencies. His articles on protecting consumer interests in an age of mass-market consumer contracting regularly appear in top law and law-and-technology journals, and policy pieces on consumer protection and technology have appeared in the *New York Times*, *Forbes*, and the *Financial Times*, among other outlets. Before entering the law, Joshua was a technology entrepreneur, serving as the director of research and development for language-learning software company Rosetta Stone.

Joshua consults with U.S. government agencies, including the White House Office of Technology and the Homeland Security Privacy Office, on national security, privacy, and law enforcement within online communities as well as on strategies for protecting children online. From 2009 to 2012, he provided privacy and civil liberties oversight for Intelligence Advanced Research Projects

Activity research programs in virtual worlds. In 2012/2013 he was awarded a Fulbright Grant to study trans-Atlantic privacy law at the Max Planck Institute for Research on Collective Goods in Bonn, Germany. He was elected a member of the American Law Institute in 2013.

William K. Ford (Chapter 4: Implications of Video Games and Immersive Entertainment in Trademark Law)—William K. Ford is an associate professor at the John Marshall Law School in Chicago. He teaches courses in contract law and IP, including a course on video game law. He has published articles and book chapters on copyright issues in the early video game industry, the right of publicity and games, trademark issues and games, and restrictions on minors' access to violent video games. William received his Juris Doctor from the University of Chicago in 2003.

Anna King (Chapter 4: Implications of Video Games and Immersive Entertainment in Trademark Law)—Anna King is a shareholder with the law firm Banner & Witcoff in its Chicago office. She currently concentrates her practice on trademark, domain name, and copyright prosecution and counseling matters. She manages worldwide portfolios including prosecution of applications, enforcement, oppositions, and cancellations, as well as counseling and licensing.

Anna currently serves as a board member and chair of the Trademark Committee of the Intellectual Property Law Association of Chicago and is an active member of the Harmonization of Trademark Law and Practice Committee of the International Trademark Association (INTA) and the Trademark Relations with the USPTO Committee of American Intellectual Property Law Association. Anna has written several articles for such organizations as INTA, Practicing Law Institute, and the Bureau of National Affairs, as well as World Trademark Review.

Anna was awarded her Juris Doctor degree from Indiana University School of Law–Bloomington. There she was involved in the Intellectual Property Association, Sports and Entertainment Law Society, and Sherman Minton Moot Court. Anna earned a Bachelor of Arts degree in Anthropology, cum laude, from Connecticut College. Anna is admitted to practice before the Supreme Court of Illinois and the U.S. District Court for the Northern District of Illinois.

Steven M. Kushner (Chapter 5: Implications of Video Games and Immersive Entertainment and the Law of Trade Secrets)—Steven M. Kushner is a partner of the firm Fellows LaBriola LLP. Steven is a trial lawyer with an emphasis in business disputes, business torts, and IP. Steven began trying cases with the DeKalb County solicitor's office in Georgia, prosecuting misdemeanors in 1991 as a third-year law student. Since graduation, Steven has been representing multinational and domestic companies, as well as individuals, in commercial disputes through mediation, arbitration, and trials in state and federal courts throughout Georgia and the United States.

In the business/commercial area, Steven represents and advises both local and national clients in resolving contract disputes and business torts, including actions to enforce, and actions seeking relief from, restrictive covenants, the protection of trade secrets, shareholder disputes, and commercial landlord and tenant matters.

In the IP area, Steven assists his clients in protecting their copyrights and trademarks, and prosecuting and defending against infringement.

Steven was admitted into the undergraduate honors program at the University of Michigan in 1985. Upon graduation in 1989 with a Bachelor of Arts in English Literature, Steven entered the Emory University School of Law, where he received his Juris Doctor in 1992. While at Emory, Steven was awarded the American Jurisprudence Book Award for Oral Advocacy and, upon the university's nomination, was listed in Who's Who Among America's Colleges and Universities for 1992. Steven served as the director-in-chief of the Emory Moot Court Society and was selected a national member of the Order of Barristers.

Steven has attained the Martindale-Hubbell AV rating, indicating very high to preeminent legal ability and very high ethical standards, as established by confidential opinions from members of the bar.

Steven has been included in *Georgia Trend's* Legal Elite for 2006, 2007, 2009, and 2013. Steven has also been included in Super Lawyers for the 2005 through 2017 editions and has been listed in the top 100 lawyers in Georgia for each consecutive year since 2008. Most recently, Steven was selected by his peers for inclusion in the Best Lawyers in America© 2016 in the field of commercial litigation.

Adam C. Losey (Chapter 5: Implications of Video Games and Immersive Entertainment and the Law of Trade Secrets)—Adam Losey represents companies and individuals in high-stakes litigation across the country. In addition to his litigation practice, he routinely advises clients on a variety of information security, privacy, electronic discovery, technology contracting, social media, and Internet-related matters. He has been selected among the leading commercial litigation and electronic discovery lawyers in the world by Who's Who Legal®. He has also been selected for inclusion in the Best Lawyers in America© in the area of electronic discovery and information management law. He is both Peer Review Rated and Client Rated as AV® Preeminent™, the highest performance rating in Martindale-Hubbell's peer review and client review rating system. Adam is a partner of the firm Losey PLLC. He also knows the Konami Code by heart, and is an avid video game enthusiast. He can be reached at alosey@losey.law.

Ben Manevitz (Chapter 6: Rights of Publicity)—Principal of the Manevitz Law Firm, Ben counsels individuals and businesses in the fashion, art, and other creative industries, with a particular eye to the prosecution and enforcement of trademarks and copyrights. He holds a bachelor's degree in English from Cornell (1991), a Juris Doctor from the University of Pennsylvania Law School (1997), and a Master of Laws in IP from Cardozo School of Law (2006).

Marc E. Mayer (Chapter 2: Copyright Law)—Marc Mayer is a partner in the Entertainment and IP Litigation Group and co-chair of the Video Game and Interactive Entertainment Group at Mitchell Silberberg & Knupp LLP. His work is at the forefront of IP and copyright law, especially as it relates to new and emerging technologies.

He concentrates his practice in the areas of copyright, trademark, trade secret, and right of publicity disputes in the entertainment and technology industries. Ranked among the nation's leading IP litigators, Marc has been an indispensable member of lead counsel teams in many of the most important copyright and trademark cases to have been litigated in recent years.

Marc regularly represents the leading interactive game developers and publishers, motion picture studios, broadcast and web-based content providers and publishers, and record companies in copyright, trademark, anti-piracy, and related matters. Among many video game clients, Marc has represented clients such as Blizzard Entertainment, Riot Games, Activision Publishing, Valve Corporation, Nexon Korea, and Take-Two Interactive in a variety of copyright, trademark, and IP-related matters. Some notable matters include successfully defending Blizzard from copyright and right of publicity claims involving characters in *World of Warcraft*, successfully defending Activision against trademark claims arising from the use of logos and symbols in its *Call of Duty* games, representing Blizzard and Valve in a copyright action involving the unauthorized use of the games *Warcraft III*, *World of Warcraft*, and *Dota 2*, and obtaining multimillion dollar judgments on behalf of Riot Games, Blizzard, and Nexon against makers of unlawful cheating and botting software. Outside the video game space, Marc has represented major record labels in their battle with Sirius XM and Pandora over the use of pre-1972 sound recordings, Internet service providers sued for the distribution of user-uploaded content, and motion picture companies in their fight against online piracy.

Marc is a frequent author and speaker, and serves in a number of leadership roles in professional organizations. In 2014, Marc spoke at the Game Developers Conference in San Francisco regarding the use of copyrights and trademarks in virtual worlds, and was featured in the *Daily Journal* cover story "Hired Guns Hunt Hackers for Video Game Makers." He also serves on the board of directors of the New York Videogame Critics Circle, a nonprofit organization that provides scholarships, workshops, and mentoring for children in underserved communities interested in pursuing careers in the video game industry.

Marc has been recognized by the *Los Angeles Business Journal* in their "Most Influential Intellectual Property Attorneys" list in 2017. He was also named an "Intellectual Property Trailblazer" by the *National Law Journal* in 2017. Marc has repeatedly been named as a "Recommended Attorney" in the category of IP–copyright by Legal 500.

Thomas J. Mihill (Chapter 5: Implications of Video Games and Immersive Entertainment and the Law of Trade Secrets)— Thomas J. (T.J.) Mihill is a partner with Owen, Gleaton, Egan, Jones & Sweeney, LLP. T.J. practices primarily in IP, business law, and litigation. He has represented individuals and corporations in the registration of copyrights and trademarks, as well as handling trademark and copyright infringement claims, trade secret violations, and cybersquatting actions. T.J. is particularly active in Internet and video game law, and is on the board of directors and secretary for the Georgia Game Developers Association. In addition to representing video game designers and game design companies, he has litigated infringement actions, licensing claims, and royalty disputes in state and federal courts on behalf of authors, artists, and musicians. T.J. has spoken and written on legal issues concerning privacy and First Amendment rights; IP; video games, virtual worlds, and digital entertainment; Internet law; and social networking sites.

Curtis A. Peele (Chapter 1: Contracts as Private Law in Video Games and Immersive Entertainment)—Curtis Peele is general counsel at CareerArc Group LLC, an emerging human resources technology company, where he is responsible for all of its legal functions, including commercial contracts, compliance, corporate governance, IP, privacy/data security, enforcement, strategic partnerships, and mergers and acquisitions.

Previously, Curtis was legal counsel at Myspace, Inc. where he advised senior management on technology transactions involving information technology, digital advertising, and content distribution. Prior to Myspace, he worked in the IP, Media, and Technology Group at Latham & Watkins LLP where he counseled new media companies and traditional media companies on commercial and corporate transactions involving the development, registration, and licensing of IP for television, online, and mobile media.

Curtis received his Juris Doctor from the Duke University School of Law and his Bachelor of Arts in Government from Dartmouth College.

Brian D. Sites (Chapter 1: Contracts as Private Law in Video Games and Immersive Entertainment)—Brian Sites is an associate professor at Barry University School of Law in Orlando, Florida. His primary research area is law and technology. His published works and presentations primarily address the intersection of evolving technology and the law, fair use, and criminal law topics. His Master of Laws is from Columbia Law School, and his Juris Doctor is from Florida State College of Law. He is a member of the Florida Bar and is admitted to practice before the U.S. Court of Appeals for the Sixth Circuit.

Sanford E. Warren, Jr. (Chapter 3: Patents: Real-World Issues in Mixed Realities)—Sanford E. Warren, Jr. is a name partner at Warren Rhoades LLP located in Irving, Texas. Sanford practices IP litigation in the manufacturing, medical device, electronic, chemical, semiconductor, telecommunications, retail, and construction fields. Sanford has prosecuted hundreds of patent applications to issuance as well. Sanford has also managed worldwide trademark portfolios in the aviation, chemical, entertainment, and health fields.

Sanford is a member of the State Bar of Texas and its Litigation and Intellectual Property Sections, the Dallas Bar Association and its Intellectual Property Section, and the INTA. He is also a member of the American Chemical Society. Sanford is a former member of the editorial board of the Trademark Reporter of the INTA. He is also the former IP counsel for American Airlines. Sanford is a lifetime fellow of the Dallas Bar Association Foundation and the Texas Bar Foundation.

Research Assistant

Andrew F. Thomas—Andrew F. Thomas is a third-year law student at American University Washington College of Law and a research intern for Banner & Witcoff, staying abreast of new developments in video game law, researching nuances of IP as it applies to video games, and writing blog posts for PatentArcade.com. Andrew's area of focus at American University is in IP and entertainment law. He is looking forward to contributing to the Glushko-Samuelson Intellectual Property Law Clinic in his final year of law school. Before attending law school, Andrew earned a Bachelor of Fine Arts in Theatre from New York University, Tisch School of the Arts. He worked for four years on a variety of film and television sets in New York City, including Martin Scorsese's "Vinyl." Andrew also produced the short film "Spiders," a 2016 Festival de Cannes selected short film. When he is not studying, Andrew is saving Hyrule from Ganon in *Zelda* or launching rockets in *Kerbal Space Program*. Andrew can be reached at andythomas93@gmail.com.

Contracts as Private Law in Video Games and Immersive Entertainment

1

Michael Bombace
Brian D. Sites
Curtis A. Peele
Joshua A.T. Fairfield[1]

Takeaways

- *End-user license agreements (EULAs), terms of service (TOS), and terms of use (TOU) are contractual agreements between game players and the companies that operate the games. These agreements can overlap and have important differences.*

---

1. Michael Bombace is counsel and director at Abaxx and general counsel at Government Blockchain Association. Brian D. Sites is assistant dean and associate professor at Barry University School of Law. Curtis A. Peele is general counsel at CareerArc. Joshua A.T. Fairfield is professor of law at Washington and Lee University School of Law. For complete author biographies, see the Contributors section of this book.

- *Such agreements are highly customizable governing tools and are widely used in regulating and protecting digital games and their content, whether game operator or player generated.*
- *These agreements are subject to the traditional limitations under contract law, including unconscionability, modification, privity, and limited enforcement against minors.*
- *These agreements are favored by digital game operators in regulating most online disputes and will continue to evolve as a result of judicial and legislative developments in the digital games industry.*

Introduction

"There are gods, and they are capricious, and [they] have way more than ten commandments. Nobody knows how many because everyone clicked past them."[2]

Video game users are generally constrained in their actions by the programming of the game. In the landscape of a digital world[3] life is ubiquitously governed by contract law. Speech, conduct, and existence—in fact, everything that a player does or says—is constrained by a contract accepted prior to accessing the digital

---

2. Raph Koster, *What Are the Lessons of MMORPGs Today?*, Raph Koster's Website, Feb. 24, 2006, http://www.raphkoster.com/2006/02/24/what-are-the-lessons-of-mmorpgs-today; *see also* David P. Sheldon, Comment, *Claiming Ownership, but Getting Owned: Contractual Limitations on Asserting Property Interests in Virtual Goods*, 54 UCLA L. Rev. 751, 751 (2007); Lydia Pallas Loren, *Slaying the Leather-Winged Demons in the Night: Reforming Copyright Owner Contracting with Clickwrap Misuse*, 30 Ohio N.U. L. Rev. 495, 497 (2004) (discussing the use of humor in a website's provisions for failure to register software downloaded through their web pages and the threat of a leather-winged demon of the night seeking recourse).

3. For brevity, references herein may be made to "digital games," "digital worlds," "video games," and "virtual worlds" to broadly refer to all types of digital games including the evolving space of virtual and augmented reality. The title of this treatise and this specific chapter references "immersive worlds," a term to capture video games, virtual worlds, virtual reality, and augmented reality. While they all differ in meaningful ways, they are equally governed by contracts. Additionally, reference is made to players, users, and residents. These are used interchangeably throughout this chapter and should be viewed under the same umbrella when assessing legal obligations.

game itself.[4] Such contracts are commonplace today. Most computer or smartphone users who have installed any software have confronted an installation screen requiring them to agree to specified terms of use as part of the software's installation. These agreements are often referred to as "end-user license agreements" (EULAs), "terms of service" (TOS), or "terms of use" (TOU), along with the privacy policy and other legal documents. These labels are sometimes used interchangeably though the various types of agreements often differ in practice.[5] These contractual agreements are the foundation of modern digital world governance. For example, EULAs typically govern an intellectual property license transaction such as a software license. TOU or TOS generally govern a broader set of issues including the software, use and access of a website, mobile app, chat forum, and any other services related to the user's interaction with the game company.

This chapter addresses some of the most relevant legal issues that all three types of agreements currently present. Where different agreements raise distinct issues, they will generally be referenced by their discrete names. Otherwise, this chapter relies on more general wording by referring to them simply as "terms" or "TOU."

---

4. *See* Bragg v. Linden Research, Inc., 487 F. Supp. 2d 593 (E.D. Pa. 2007); Joshua A.T. Fairfield, *Anti-Social Contracts: The Contractual Governance of Virtual Worlds*, 53 McGill L.J. 427 (2008). The question of contract-governed online communities is increasingly important because community-governing contracts (end-user license agreements (EULAs), codes of conduct, terms of service (TOS), or terms of use (TOU)) have become the tool of choice for companies seeking to govern multimillion-member online communities, from Facebook to YouTube to *World of Warcraft*. Millions of people worldwide live significant parts of their lives in communities governed by these contracts. The law of contract is the only law consistently employed to govern these communities. *See also* Gerri L. Dreiling, *Online Gaming Runs Afoul of Click-Wrap Contract and Federal Law*, Mo. Law. Wkly., Sept. 26, 2005 ("In order to play the game, the user must click through 'I agree' boxes on both an End User License Agreement (EULA) and Terms of Use (TOU)."); Bettina M. Chin, Note, *Regulating Your Second Life—Defamation in Virtual Worlds*, 72 Brook. L. Rev. 1303, 1317–18 (2007) ("Before a user is allowed to access the services that the web site provides, she must assent to the terms of the agreement.") (citing E. Allen Farnsworth, Farnsworth on Contracts § 3.1 (2d ed. 1998)).

5. *See, e.g.*, MDY Indus., LLC v. Blizzard Entm't, Inc., 629 F.3d 928, 937–42 (9th Cir. 2010) (discussing distinctions between contract law and copyright law as they pertained to Blizzard's various contractual agreements with *World of Warcraft* subscribers and a third-party software company).

I. Purpose and Scope of Agreements

A. History of EULAs, TOS, and TOU Agreements

Digital worlds are numerous and heavily populated. They can also be quite profitable.[6] They are used for countless purposes, including entertainment, academics, military training, medical treatment, legal advice, and commerce.[7] Those who inhabit digital worlds often spend tremendous amounts of time within them—upwards of 20 hours a week on average by one estimate.[8] That time is increasingly spent on mobile devices, which are now ubiquitous throughout society.[9] Some players also have a financial stake in

---

6. The video game industry is a multibillion-dollar industry. *See* Kevin Anderton, *The Business of Video Games: A Multi Billion Dollar Industry [Infographic]*, FORBES, Aug. 29, 2017 12:59 p.m., https://www.forbes.com/sites/kevinanderton/2017 /04/29/the-business-of-video-games-a-multi-billion-dollar-industry-infographic /#219756536d27. In 2013, it was estimated that the massively multiplayer online (MMO) industry alone earned about $3 billion of revenue. *See* Matthew Handrahan, *The Old Republic Earned $165 Million Last Year—Report*, GAMESINDUSTRY.BIZ, July 18, 2014, https://www.gamesindustry.biz/articles/2014-07-18-the-old-republic-earned-usd 165-million-last-year-report. Despite the impressive numbers, *World of Warcraft*, the most popular MMO, has seen a decline of subscribers, going from about ten to 15 million subscribers to about five million subscribers. *See* Andy Chalk, *This Is the Last World of Warcraft Subscriber Report You Will Ever Read*, PC GAMER, Nov. 3, 2015, 10:33 p.m., https://www.pcgamer.com/this-is-the-last-world-of-warcraft-subscriber -report-you-will-ever-read/. *World of Warcraft* still maintains a subscriber-based business model, while other MMO games have shifted toward a microtransactions business model. *See* Paul Tassi, *"World of Warcraft" Still a $1B Powerhouse Even as Subscription MMOs Decline*, FORBES, July 19, 2014, 1:26 p.m., https://www.forbes .com/sites/insertcoin/2014/07/19/world-of-warcraft-still-a-1b-powerhouse-even-as -subscription-mmos-decline/#33eb14b66db7.

7. Joshua A.T. Fairfield, *Virtual Property*, 85 B.U. L. REV. 1047, 1059–61 (2005) (discussing uses of virtual worlds).

8. Nick Yee, *The Demographics, Motivations, and Derived Experiences of Users of Massively-Multiuser Online Graphical Environments*, 15 PRESENCE: TELEOPERATORS & VIRTUAL ENV'TS 309 (2006), *available at* http://nickyee.com/pubs/Yee%20-%20 MMORPG%20Demographics%202006.pdf (concluding that individuals spend approximately 22 hours each week in their chosen MMO role playing games).

9. Alison Murdock, *Consumers Spend More Than 1 Billion Hours a Month Playing Mobile Games*, VERTO ANALYTICS, May 17, 2016, http://www.vertoanalytics.com /consumers-spend-1-billion-hours-month-playing-mobile-games/.

the world above and beyond subscription fees.[10] For example, some individual players, including corporations, collect substantial sums of money from operating businesses within the economy of virtual worlds.[11] Given the time and money invested in digital worlds by players, it is not surprising those players often place great economic and emotional value in the characters, property, or other items they have acquired or created within that world.[12]

Similarly, digital world creators and operators have a significant investment in the world itself.[13] The world's creators and operators have spent many hours designing, programming, testing, implementing, operating, and supporting the digital world, often at a cost of tens to hundreds of millions of dollars.[14] The intersection of players', creators', and operators' investments produces a common desire for the game to succeed. However, the respective investments of each stakeholder also create a prime opportunity for conflict and disagreements. How a digital game creator addresses and prevents those disagreements—in other words, how the world operator governs the game—is therefore a question of great importance to many of these users.

---

10. *See, e.g.*, Jamie J. Kayser, Note, *The New New-World: Virtual Property and the End User License Agreement*, 27 Loy. L.A. Ent. L. Rev. 59 (2006) (discussing a player's purchase of a virtual island for $26,500, which the player reportedly recouped within a year).

11. *See* Chin, *supra* note 4, at 1305–07, 1313–15 (discussing virtual residents of *Second Life* who have made thousands of dollars in real currency using virtual sales; also discussing corporations that have established a virtual presence in *Second Life*).

12. In fact, some residents so value their investment in the virtual world that they have resorted to legal action to protect it. *See, e.g.*, *Online Gamer in China Wins Virtual Theft Suit*, CNN, Dec. 20, 2003, 1:51 p.m., http://www.cnn.com/2003 /TECH/fun.games/12/19/china.gamer.reut. Some players have also reported feeling deeper loss for virtual world theft than for real world theft. *See* Julian Dibbell, Play Money: Or, How I Quit My Day Job and Made Millions Trading Virtual Loot (2006).

13. *See generally Why Video Games Are So Expensive to Develop*, Economist, Sept. 25, 2014, https://www.economist.com/the-economist-explains/2014/09/24 /why-video-games-are-so-expensive-to-develop.

14. *See* Ben Fritz & Alex Pham, *Star Wars: The Old Republic—The Story Behind a Galactic Gamble*, L.A. Times, Jan. 20, 2012 5:32 a.m., http://herocomplex.latimes .com/2012/01/20/star-wars-the-old-republic-the-story-behind-a-galactic-gamble/ (noting that *Star Wars: The Old Republic* cost nearly $200 million to create).

Digital games are largely governed by contractual agreements between digital game players and the company that operates the game.[15] These agreements generally must be accepted electronically by players before they may gain access to the digital game.[16] The actual "signing" or acceptance of the agreement often occurs either during the installation process—such as by expressly clicking an "Accept" or "I agree" button[17]—or, more implicitly, such as by accessing the website or mobile app upon which the digital game is made available and upon which TOU are posted. If a user does not "accept" the agreement in the software installation model, the software or other registration process will abort and the digital game will remain largely if not wholly inaccessible to that individual.[18] Like many consumer contracts, these agreements are nonnegotiable—either as a practical matter or as a contractual matter.[19] Because the terms serve as gatekeepers to many digital

---

15. *See, e.g.*, Andrew Jankowich, *EULAw: The Complex Web of Corporate Rule-Making in Virtual Worlds*, 8 TUL. J. TECH. & INTELL. PROP. 1, 5 (2006) (describing EULAs as attempts to "'legally link' the online world and the physical world through the agreements that create private rules"). EULAs are also referenced as such colloquially by individuals outside legal fields. *See, e.g.*, Wikipedia, *End-User License Agreement*, https://en.wikipedia.org/wiki/End-user_license_agreement (last edited July 16, 2018).

16. *See* Chin, *supra* note 4, at 1317.

17. *World of Warcraft*, for example, requires players to agree to the contractual documents during installation of the initial software and as part of installing many of its subsequent updates to the game world.

18. *See* Chin, *supra* note 4, at 1317 ("Before a user is allowed to access the services that the website provides, she must assent to the terms of the agreement.") (citing E. ALLEN FARNSWORTH, FARNSWORTH ON CONTRACTS § 3.1 (2d ed. 1998)); *see, e.g.*, Blizzard Entertainment, *Blizzard End User License Agreement* [hereinafter *Blizzard End User License Agreement*], http://us.blizzard.com/en-us/company/legal/eula.html (last revised June 1, 2018) ("This Agreement sets forth the terms and conditions under which [the users] are licensed to install and use the [Game]."); Linden Lab, *Second Life Terms and Conditions* [hereinafter *Second Life Terms and Conditions*], https://www.lindenlab.com/legal/second-life-terms-and-conditions (effective July, 31, 2017) ("If you do not . . . agree [to the conditions in this TOS], you should decline this [agreement], in which case you are prohibited from accessing or using Second Life."); Linden Lab, *Terms of Service* [hereinafter Linden Lab *Terms of Service*], https://www.lindenlab.com/tos (effective July 31, 2017).

19. Jankowich, *supra* note 15, at 7 ("Proprietors construct rules with little or no regard for the negotiating powers of prospective entrants. New entrants must either agree to the terms written by owners or decline to participate. When existing participants find these rules unsatisfying, their only option is to quit.").

games, users either take them in the form presented or forfeit access to that game's world.[20]

EULAs, TOS, and TOU are not, however, the only conceivable method of managing and protecting digital games and virtual worlds. For example, some early virtual worlds attempted to rely on self-governance by the world's residents.[21] Under a self-governance model, disputes are resolved by the residents them-selves and overarching authorities appointed by the digital world operators are less prevalent.[22] This model is found in some modern games.[23] While aspects of these models are successful, there are structural issues to address, such as the speed of clearing back-logs of cases filed.[24] Alternative structures still depend on the game provider, however, to issue deeper and full bans.[25]

Another example of alternative tools to combat toxicity in games is that of Blizzard with *Overwatch*. Blizzard uses traditional tools to ban players as well as reporting by players. The newest

---

20. *See, e.g.*, *Second Life Terms and Conditions*, *supra* note 18 ("If you do not . . . agree [to the conditions in this TOS], you should decline this agreement, in which case you are prohibited from accessing or using Second Life.").

21. *See* Viktor Mayer-Schönberger & John Crowley, *Napster's Second Life?: The Regulatory Challenges of Virtual Worlds*, 100 Nw. U. L. Rev. 1775, 1797–802 (2006) (discussing a failed attempt at allowing virtual world residents to self-govern).

22. *Id.*

23. Riot Games, *League of Legends: The Tribunal Policy* [hereinafter *League of Legends: The Tribunal Policy*], http://na.leagueoflegends.com/legal/tribunal (last modified Apr. 12, 2011) ("The Tribunal identifies players who have been consistently reported by the community over a large number of games and builds a Tribunal case for them. These cases are presented to random community members who use the Tribunal who then review the case files and render a judgment—pardon or punish. Player Support then uses this information to help assign the right penalties to the right players."). Note, the Tribunal stopped operating in 2014 due to planned updates. Lyte, *League of Legends: Upgrading the Tribunal*, Riot Games, https://na.leagueoflegends.com/en/news/game-updates /player-behavior/upgrading-tribunal (last visited July 23, 2018).

24. *See* Steven Asarch, *"League of Legends": The Problem with Riot Being Judge, Jury, and Executioner*, Player.One, May 15, 2016, http://www.player.one/league -legends-problem-riot-being-judge-jury-and-executioner-533853 (discussing limits of the Tribunal for *League of Legends* such as lack of permanent bans and ease of abuse from players).

25. *See* Jeff Grubb, *"Toxic" League of Legends Player Responds to His 1-Year Ban*, Venture Beat, Dec. 5, 2012, https://venturebeat.com/2012/12/05/toxic-lol-player -responds/ (discussing the eight reviews of a particular top ranked player by the *League of Legends* Tribunal and final ruling by Riot Games).

element to this approach is the extent to which Blizzard goes to check for toxicity in the game, such as comments and postings to YouTube.[26] This is not without issue though. Toxicity is a significant impact to game enjoyment while also being incredibly difficult to combat, even with new efforts, such as those by Blizzard.[27]

Intellectual property regimes, such as copyright law, are another common source of protection for the actual content in the virtual world.[28] Unlike governance under a strictly contractual agreement, intellectual property law protects certain features of the digital world itself.[29]

While intellectual property law and self-governance both play a role in protecting and ordering virtual worlds,[30] contractual agreements remain the dominant management tool.[31] The ubiquity of

---

26. *See* Erik Kain, *Blizzard Courts Controversy with New "Overwatch" Anti-Toxicity Measures*, FORBES, Jan. 29, 2018, 12:00 p.m., https://www.forbes.com/sites/erikkain/2018/01/29/blizzard-courts-controversy-with-new-overwatch-anti-toxicity-measures/#6470c4163ad6 (discussing interviews with Blizzard and the extent Blizzard takes to police toxicity with a careful note that the review of players on others sites is for noted support of toxicity in *Overwatch* itself and not general toxicity).

27. *See* Matt Brian, *"Overwatch" Player Toxicity Is Delaying Game Updates*, ENGADGET, Sept. 14, 2017, https://www.engadget.com/2017/09/14/blizzard-overwatch-toxicity-developer-update/ (discussing the delays and cost associated with addressing toxicity).

28. *See, e.g.*, Micro Star v. FormGen, Inc., 154 F.3d 1107 (9th Cir. 1998) (involving use of copyright protection for derivative works); *see also* Sheldon, *supra* note 2, at 762 (discussing why contract law is relied on over intellectual property law to address virtual world property rights).

29. Patent law may also be used to protect inventions that make virtual worlds possible and inventions that are made possible or created within virtual worlds, as discussed in Chapter 3.

30. *See, e.g.*, Candidus Dougherty & Greg Lastowka, *Virtual Trademarks*, 24 SANTA CLARA COMPUTER & HIGH TECH. L.J. 749 (2008) (discussing recent developments and application of trademark law in virtual worlds); *see also* Erez Reuveni, *Authorship in the Age of the Conducer*, 54 J. COPYRIGHT SOC'Y U.S.A. 285 (2007) (discussing limits of copyright law in the context of modern, evolving virtual world creations); Bryan T. Camp, *The Play's the Thing: A Theory of Taxing Virtual Worlds*, 59 HASTINGS L.J. 1, 51 (2007) (noting that "EULAs arose out of the uncertainty about whether software developers were adequately protected by copyright law").

31. *See, e.g.*, Sheldon, *supra* note 2, at 762 (discussing why contract law is relied on over intellectual property law to address virtual world property rights).

EULAs, TOS, and TOU is not surprising.[32] With millions of residents interacting in real time, virtual worlds are dynamic communities that are multifaceted, ever evolving, and, by definition, difficult to manage.[33] Legal contracts offer numerous benefits as a method of governing such worlds.[34] First, they are an express agreement between parties that can clearly demarcate the boundaries of what is permissible conduct and what is not.[35] Second, they provide an enforcement mechanism should residents not comply with these rules—namely, termination provision(s).[36] A termination provision states that if a digital world resident breaches the agreement, his or her account can be terminated, resulting in the resident's exclusion from the game's world.[37] Third, the agreements offer companies

---

32. *See* Molly Stephens, Note, *Sales of In-Game Assets: An Illustration of Continuing Failure of Intellectual Property Law to Protect Digital-Content Creators*, 80 TEX. L. REV. 1513, 1521–23 (2002) (noting that standard theories of infringement are not stable, so EULAs are necessary); *see also* Sheldon, *supra* note 2, at 762 (arguing that contract law is relied on over intellectual property law both because contract law provides more flexibility and because intellectual property law is seen as inadequate by virtual world operators in addressing virtual world property rights).

33. *See, e.g.,* Steven Johnson, *Brave New World: Online Fantasy Worlds Put Our Democratic Ideals to the Test*, DISCOVER, Apr. 2, 2006, http://discovermagazine .com/2006/apr/well-intro ("[A]s the last 5,000 or so years of human civilization make clear, any time large numbers of human beings gather together in one shared space without laws governing their behavior, problems inevitably arise."); *see also* Julian Dibbell, *Griefer Madness*, WIRED, Feb. 2008, at 90 (describing "griefer culture" in virtual worlds and concluding that those who "grief," or harass, in virtual worlds are more interested in annoying other participants than playing the game under the terms of the EULA). *See also* Mayer-Schönberger & Crowley, *supra* note 21, at 1794–97 (discussing two examples of community governance that failed due to the challenges virtual world governance poses).

34. *See, e.g.,* Jankowich, *supra* note 15 (discussing the advantages and limitations of EULAs).

35. *See, e.g., Blizzard End User License Agreement, supra* note 18.

36. *See, e.g.,* Funcom, *Age of Conan Unchained End User License Agreement* [hereinafter *Age of Conan Unchained End User License Agreement*], http://www .ageofconan.com/corporate/license_agreement (last updated Apr. 8, 2011).

37. A point of contention between players and developers is when a player is banned or terminated, who owns the virtual goods and currency that the banned player has invested in in-game. Some argue that players have virtual property rights that are separate from the copyrights given to the developers. *See* Fairfield, *supra* note 7, at 1048. Normally, a person acquires property rights upon the transfer of ownership or title in a chattel. Virtual content in games like *World of Warcraft* or *Second Life* is typically licensed to players, with the ultimate

running digital games a buffet-style management approach: the game operators can pick whatever terms and restrictions they want and include them in the agreement. They might also attempt to dictate whether or how background legal principles, such as what is "property" and who owns it, will apply.[38] Thus, a EULA, TOS, or TOU can be both comprehensive in scope and customized to fit each unique digital world. The agreements can even be used to attempt to allocate rights to digital world creators that are not otherwise provided for by law. For example, by stating in a EULA or TOU that a particular act is forbidden, the digital game operators might persuade users not to engage in that act, notwithstanding the fact that the act is otherwise lawful. Even if that portion of the agreement is for some reason not valid—for example, if it is against public policy—the mere inclusion of such ultimately unenforceable language can discourage a digital game resident from engaging in the "forbidden" act for fear of being excluded from the game.

B. Common Provisions in Modern Agreements

In an effort to provide wide-ranging protection to digital world operators and a smoothly operating environment, EULAs, TOS, and TOU are typically long and comprehensive.[39] Some digital

---

ownership and discretion as to who can use (or not use) remaining with the operator/publisher. *See Blizzard End User License Agreement, supra* note 18; *see also Second Life Terms and Conditions, supra* note 18. Yet there are *Second Life* players who earn enough money selling virtual items that the Internal Revenue Service requires those players to report the income on their taxes. *See* Second Life Wiki, *Linden Lab Official: Required Tax Documentation FAQ*, http://wiki.secondlife .com/wiki/Linden_Lab_Official:Required_Tax_Documentation_FAQ (last modified Feb. 10, 2014); *see generally* Leandra Lederman, *"Stranger Than Fiction": Taxing Virtual Worlds*, 82 N.Y.U. L. REV. 1620 (2007). To a player who earns an income from selling virtual items, even a temporary ban from the game can have a deep impact on his or her life.

38. *See, e.g.*, Daniel C. Miller, Note, *Determining Ownership in Virtual Worlds: Copyright and License Agreements*, 22 REV. LITIG. 435 (2003) (discussing the flexibility of EULAs).

39. It is worth noting that, in addition to EULAs, virtual world creators and operators have a yet more powerful tool for controlling their worlds: the software code that creates the virtual world. When an individual inside a virtual world attempts to take any action, that individual necessarily faces the simple question of whether the virtual world software allows for such actions to occur. If the virtual world does not allow the action, the action will not occur. For example, if a user

game and virtual world operators go so far as to use multiple, over-lapping documents covering different aspects of the same over-arching game.[40] Given the multitude of digital games and virtual world types, the provisions of recent agreements vary. Some provisions are common. For example, most terms prohibit "harass[ing] or offend[ing] other participants, impersonating a staff member of the [virtual world] provider, defrauding other participants, and using [an] avatar to conduct illegal activity."[41] Many also contain arbitration and choice-of-forum provisions.[42]

Another common provision is the "end of the world" clause, which is intended to allow the operator to cease operation of the virtual world at any time without liability to the world's users.[43] This power works in conjunction with the agreement's termina-tion provisions, which state that the operator may terminate indi-vidual users' accounts. As noted previously, this power to exclude residents from the game is a powerful governance tool and thus a

---

attempts to take a book from a bookshelf in a virtual world, he or she will succeed or fail based on whether the software developer made that book movable or not. Similarly, if a user tries to say certain profane words or send a private message to certain people, depending on the profanity filters and communication settings of the virtual world, the profanity or private message will either appear on another user's screen or not. By using these virtual laws of physics, virtual world creators control users' behavior most directly and powerfully.

EULAs, on the other hand, can only exert indirect control. EULAs establish prohibitions that do not themselves prevent the prohibited act from occurring, but instead authorize a punishment—such as removal from the virtual world—if the act occurs and is caught. Thus, by using the virtual world's parameters, virtual world creators control users in a more powerful manner than EULAs ever will. *See generally* Lawrence Lessig, Code: And Other Laws of Cyberspace (1999); Lawrence Lessig, Code: And Other Laws of Cyberspace, Version 2.0 (2006).

40. *See, e.g.*, Blizzard Entertainment, *Blizzard Legal Documentation*, http://us.blizzard.com/en-us/company/legal/ (last visited July 23, 2018).

41. *See, e.g., Age of Conan Unchained End User License Agreement, supra* note 36 ("Dispute Resolution"). *See also* Sheldon, *supra* note 2, at 763–65 (reviewing provisions in the EULAs for 14 major online games).

42. *See* discussion *infra* Section II.A.

43. Sheldon, *supra* note 2, at 768–69. *See, e.g., Age of Conan Unchained End User License Agreement, supra* note 36 ("[T]he Service is provided by Funcom at its sole and absolute discretion and may be terminated or otherwise discontinued by Funcom at any time to time and from time to time without notice. . . ."); *Blizzard End User License Agreement, supra* note 18, § 9(B) ("Blizzard may change, modify, suspend, or discontinue any aspect of the [game]. . . .").

significant contractual right.[44] It is also a serious decision given the backlash that can ensue.[45] It is also often a broad right. For example, Daybreak's (makers of *EverQuest II*) TOS reads, "Daybreak reserves the right to suspend, restrict or terminate [player's] access to or use of any Daybreak Game(s), at any time for any reason, in its sole and absolute discretion."[46] These "spirit of the game" provisions leave much to the discretion of virtual world operators.[47]

In practice, game operators do indeed call on these termination provisions.[48] Another increasingly popular addition is provi-

---

44. As two commentators described it:

> Expulsion as an enforcement mechanism is effective because participants in virtual worlds for example incur significant social and financial costs when they are forced to leave. They not only have to leave behind a network of friends and their accumulation of social and other capital, but they are also forced to abandon the persistent narrative that they have constructed around their avatar. There are additional financial costs: the required use of credit cards for payment of the virtual world's monthly fees ensures that individual participants are linked to specific credit cards (and thus, by approximation, people), making it difficult for individuals to re-register for a virtual world from which they have been banished.

See Mayer-Schönberger & Crowley, *supra* note 21, at 1793.

45. *See* Emanuel Maiberg, *When a Cold-Hearted Corporation Takes Away Your Beloved (Virtual) Pet*, ATLANTIC, Aug. 12, 2013, https://www.theatlantic.com /technology/archive/2013/08/when-a-cold-hearted-corporation-takes-away-your -beloved- virtual-pet/278588/ (discussing activists of a shuttered game organizing a 32,000-person Facebook group to boycott Electronic Arts products).

46. Daybreak, *Daybreak Terms of Service* [hereinafter *Daybreak Terms of Service*], https://www.daybreakgames.com/terms-of-service?locale=en_US (last updated July 25, 2017). *See also* Sheldon, *supra* note 2, at 769 n.84 (quoting a previous incarnation of *EverQuest II*'s user agreement and software license); NC INTERACTIVE, GUILD WARS USER AGREEMENT § 14 (last modified Mar. 2008), http://legal .guildwars.com/en/gw-user-agreement-en.pdf ("NC interactive reserves the right to suspend or terminate this Agreement (including your Software license and your Account) immediately and without notice if you . . . [violate] the spirit of the Game(s) as described in the Rules of Conduct.").

47. *But see infra* Section I.C (discussing possible limitations on broad language in such provisions).

48. *See, e.g.*, Kayser, *supra* note 10, at 64 (discussing termination of University of Michigan professor Peter Ludlow's account in *The Sims Online* for a story— reported in virtual newspapers but then picked up by real-life newspapers—on virtual child prostitution occurring in *The Sims Online*) (citing Eric Goldman, *Symposium Review: Speech Showdowns at the Virtual Corral*, 21 SANTA CLARA

sions that govern the exchange of real money (e.g., dollars or euros) for an in-game currency. Such provisions are, at times, fairly restrictive.[49] A major reason for this is to limit the functionality of the in-game currency so as to not trigger deeper obligations of a fully open loop game currency with state money transmission laws or anti-money laundering obligations under the Bank Secrecy Act.[50]

There has also been a growing move toward a profit model driven by discrete transactions in the game instead of a monthly subscription fee model. Under recent free-to-play models,[51] instead of relying upon players paying a monthly subscription fee, the game is provided either free or at only a generally low initial cost (such as to buy the software and install it) and the players are then encouraged to spend real-world money to obtain benefits in the game world. For example, players might be able to buy powerful weapons, customize the appearance of their character in unique ways, obtain novelty items, or otherwise enhance their enjoyment in the game through the expenditure of real-world funds or "micro-transactions." These models often have accompanying terms provisions that govern such microtransactions.[52]

Finally, in the event that a game operator concludes that the aforementioned provisions are insufficient to govern the digital world, the terms frequently state that the game operators may modify the agreement at will.[53] Operators sometimes provide the

---

COMPUTER & HIGH TECH. L.J. 845, 847 (2005)); Evan V. Symon & Anonymous, *I'm Paid to Play World of Warcraft All Day (And It Sucks)*, CRACKED, Apr. 16, 2016, http://www .cracked.com/personal-experiences-2228-im-paid-to-play-mmorpgs-its-nightmare -5-realities.html (discussing the risks associated with the practice of gold farming).

49. For example, Blizzard's EULA provides that money in your "Blizzard Balance" "has no cash value" and "does not constitute a personal property right." *Blizzard End User License Agreement, supra* note 18, § 1(D)(i)(2).

50. *See generally* Michael Bombace, *Blazing Trails: A New Way Forward for Virtual Currencies and Money Laundering*, 6 J. VIRTUAL WORLDS RES. (2013).

51. Two classic examples of free-to-play companies are Zynga and PopCap, both of which contain a variety of free-to-play games that attract millions of players.

52. *See, e.g.*, Valve Corporation, *Steam Subscriber Agreement* § 3D, http://store .steampowered.com/subscriber_agreement/ (last visited July 23, 2018) (describing, e.g., "license rights to virtual items").

53. *See, e.g., Blizzard End User License Agreement, supra* note 18 (Blizzard reserves the right to modify the agreement at any time). For further discussion of this right, see *infra* Section III.B.

user with the opportunity to agree to the new terms. However, as with the user's initial consent, the user is typically faced with a "consent or don't play" decision when it comes to revisions.

C. Scholarly Criticisms of Terms: One Brief Example

The governance-by-contract model is not without critics. Commentators have expressed concerns with a variety of such agreements' features. One commonly debated provision of these terms is the allocation of virtual world property rights.[54] In virtual worlds, the residents can create a variety of virtual things, ranging from simple tools (e.g., swords or potions)[55] to complex works of art (e.g., paintings, fashion designs, and even buildings).[56] Some virtual worlds enable residents to exercise a marginal degree of creativity, such as by combining specific items in certain ways to create new products. For example, *World of Warcraft* gives players tools to combine certain plants to make potions or certain types of ore to make weapons. Generally though, *World of Warcraft* does not enable free-form combining of plants and ore. *Minecraft* and *Second Life*, on the other hand, enable and encourage substantially greater creativity. *Minecraft* actively promotes user creations on their website[57] while making sure to outline permitted types of use in their terms and conditions.[58] Linden Labs provides the players with tools to actually code and build their own assets in *Second*

---

54. *See, e.g.*, Reuveni, *supra* note 30, at 319–39 (considering models of intellectual property law and EULA law interaction).

55. For example, in *World of Warcraft*, virtual world residents have the ability to choose up to two primary "professions" such as blacksmithing, tailoring, engineering, or alchemy, through which they can create predefined objects. *See, e.g.*, Blizzard Entertainment, *World of Warcraft: New Player's Guide Part Four*, https://worldofwarcraft.com/en-us/game/new-players-guide/part-four.

56. *See, e.g.*, Linden Lab, *Creator Resources*, https://secondlife.com/destinations /howto/creator (last visited July 23, 2018).

57. Minecraft, *Homepage*, https://minecraft.net/en-us/ (last visited July 23, 2018).

58. Mojang, *Terms and Conditions* [hereinafter Mojang *Terms and Conditions*], https://account.mojang.com/terms?ref=ft#brand (last visited July 23, 2018) ("We are very relaxed about things you create for yourself. . . . We are also quite relaxed about other non-commercial things so feel free to create and share videos, screen shots, independently created mods (that don't use any of our Assets), fan art, machinima, etc. . . . We are less relaxed about commercial things. . . . [Y]ou many not sell any merchandise that uses any of our Brands or Assets. . . .").

Life.[59] Thus, there are at least two main approaches in virtual worlds to giving virtual residents creative control. Some, like *World of Warcraft*, enable limited creativity using game content.[60] Others, like *Second Life*, encourage creativity with nearly no bounds.[61]

Most terms purport to allocate all rights to virtual property to the virtual world owners or operators.[62] Many also do not allow users to freely transfer virtual items for real-world currency, thereby restricting the possibility of cashing in for real money the hours of work the virtual world resident might have invested in creating or obtaining an item.[63] Such allocations of rights to virtual

---

59. Second Life, *Creators*, http://go.secondlife.com/landing/creator/?lang=en (last visited July 23, 2018) (describing the tools *Second Life* players have to create in the game).

60. Notably, some portions of *World of Warcraft* are less restrictive. For example, players can exercise a greater degree of creativity in designing special shirts in-game, called "tabards," that represent a player's guild.

61. The great degree of creative control (or great lack of limits or policing) that *Second Life* provides permits residents to easily duplicate others' existing intellectual property within the world, whether with or without permission. For example, a user could design a logo that imitates or duplicates the Nike logo, without the consent of Nike, and without policing by *Second Life*. It would be up to Nike to enforce its own intellectual property rights in such a scenario. Another example of broad creativity in modern digital games is Minecraft, a digital world in which players can build objects, structures, and essentially worlds in a seemingly endless variety of incarnations. *See, e.g.*, Minecraft, *supra* note 57.

62. *See* Fairfield, *supra* note 7, at 1082–84. *See also, e.g.*, *Age of Conan Unchained End User License Agreement*, *supra* note 36 ("You have no interest, monetary or otherwise, in any feature or content contained in the Game."); *Blizzard End User License Agreement*, *supra* note 18, § 2(A)(vii) (establishing Blizzard's ownership in all accounts); *id.* § 1(D)(i)(4) ("[Users] hereby grant Blizzard a perpetual, irrevocable, worldwide, . . . right and license to exploit the User Content and all elements thereof. . . .").

However, some providers allow for retention of intellectual property rights by players. In *Second Life*, players actually create fundamentally new content in the world and make it available to other players. This aspect of *Second Life* is highly unique—in most other virtual worlds, players only have the power to create a comparatively limited number of predefined items, not fully customizable items as in *Second Life. See Second Life Terms and Conditions*, *supra* note 18, Part 1, Content Licenses and Intellectual Property Rights.

63. *See, e.g.*, Wargaming, *End User License Agreement (NEW!)* § 8.1, https://legal .na.wargaming.net/en/end-user-licence-agreement/ (last updated June 15, 2018) ("[Virtual goods] are not real-world currency, have no monetary value, and cannot be used, exchanged, or redeemed except as provided in this EULA, and cannot be transferred, in any case.").

world operators can be unpopular.[64] Even where the agreements allow users to own intellectual property rights, those rights[65] are limited by the very nature of both the terms and the technology that makes such intellectual property creations possible. A major reason for this is to avoid legal obligations of a system that is open loop where users can cash in and out of the game. Where this is present, game providers can trigger obligations under state laws concerning money transmission. Other concerns are increased fraud, money laundering issues, and a host of other issues.[66]

One particular concern is that games permitting users to cash out may receive the "Adults Only" (AO) rating from the Entertainment Software Rating Board, which specifies that rating category for content that includes "gambling with real currency."[67] The AO rating has far-reaching effects on a game's profitability: all major video game console manufacturers prohibit AO-rated games from their platforms, and many retailers refuse to stock AO-rated games.[68]

Currently, such creations often exist only within the server of a third party and are not able to be moved outside that environment. It is possible, however, that the migration towards microtransaction-driven financial models—transactions that are

---

64. It would be an oversimplification to state that EULAs that allocate virtual world property rights to virtual world operators are necessarily unfair. Some commentators have, however, argued that EULAs unfairly allocate rights. For further discussion by one of the most outspoken commentators in this area, see, e.g., Fairfield, *supra* note 7, at 1082–84 (arguing that "[b]y means of contract, virtual environment holders currently parlay their (legitimate) claim to the intellectual property in an environment into an illegitimate claim to all of the virtual property possessed by or developed by the inhabitants of the environment" and citing an example of a EULA that disclaimed virtual world resident property rights).

65. Linden Lab *Terms of Service*, *supra* note 18, § 2.5.

66. *See* Bombace, *supra* note 50, at 1; *The Money-Making World of Gaming Cybercrime*, TREND MICRO, Nov. 11, 2016, https://blog.trendmicro.com/money -making-world-gaming-cybercrime/.

67. *See* Entertainment Software Rating Board, *ESRB Ratings Guide*, http://www .esrb.org/ratings/ratings_guide.aspx (last visited July 23, 2018).

68. *See* Ben Kuchera, *Why the Adults Only Rating May Be Pointless and Harmful to Games as an Art Form*, POLYGON, Feb. 10, 2014, 8:01 a.m., https://www.polygon .com/2014/2/10/5362502/adults-only-rating-pointless-and-harmful-games-as-art -form ("Stores won't carry games rated Adults Only, nor will Sony, Microsoft or Nintendo give them an official release on consoles.").

often based on discrete sales of distinct digital goods—will also foster an increase in the rights a digital game player is allocated under the terms. Alternatively, the microtransaction model might continue to define such sales as merely an exchange of the player's real-world currency for a discrete license tied to the newly obtained specific digital good.

D. The Future of EULAs, TOS, and TOU

Contractual agreements remain the predominant method of controlling digital world behavior today, just as they did at the time of publishing the prior edition of this book. However, the state of digital and virtual world governance is always in flux as new worlds, games, game content, updates, hacks, and mischief-making techniques emerge.[69] Some commentators have suggested that the variance in these agreements' terms will decrease over time.[70] Different digital world terms may "eventually converge around the most permissive, least constrictive regulatory framework" because "participants in [virtual] worlds prefer a situation with more rights."[71] Under this theory, digital world residents would gravitate towards those worlds offering them the greatest freedom and the most rights.[72] Alternatively, some commentators have suggested convergence will occur not around the most permissive regulatory models, but around the most stable, predictable, and time-tested models that prior worlds have successfully used.[73] Still other commentators have suggested that neither model captures the likely evolution of EULAs, TOS, and TOU, and that the actual development of digital world governance will be an ever-shifting,

---

69. Notably, some virtual worlds require players to re-sign EULAs whenever a new update is released. For example, in *World of Warcraft*, updates to the virtual world are mandatory, and if a user declines to install the update he or she loses access to the virtual world. Along with such updates, the operators of *World of Warcraft* may include a new EULA to be signed.

70. Mayer-Schönberger & Crowley, *supra* note 21, at 1812 (discussing commentators who have offered different theories on regulatory competition among EULA provisions).

71. *Id.*

72. *See id.*

73. *See id.* (citing David Vogel, Trading Up: Consumer and Environmental Regulation in a Global Economy 248, 259–60 (1995)).

rich blend of resident preferences.[74] It is not clear if any of these theories is necessarily correct. Further, the move away from the subscription-based model is a meaningful change and it will be significant to see if the last few companies relying upon that model—most notably, Blizzard via *World of Warcraft*—will join in the migration to free-to-play or persist in a subscription-based framework. A more cynical theory might posit that the usual companies (e.g., Blizzard) will continue to dominate the virtual world field in the short term with players looking more toward video game content than to the details of that game's terms. Likely, all of these will work in tandem to shape future terms.

As new digital worlds evolve, they might follow the model cast by prior successful worlds such as *Everquest, World of Warcraft,* and *Second Life.* Or, just as some recent worlds have diverged from prior models by adopting innovative contractual provisions, future digital worlds might chart new territory in the realm of virtual world rights and restrictions.[75] Regardless of what comes of terms agreements in general, their importance in managing digital worlds cannot be overstated. They have thus far been, and will likely remain, a popular and effective tool for digital world governance. Given that importance and the underlying investments digital world creators, operators, and residents have in these games, their terms will remain a closely monitored area of the legal landscape. The remainder of this chapter thus addresses several recent developments in that arena, as well as issues likely to arise with the continued use of terms to govern digital and virtual worlds.

---

74. *Id.*

75. *Compare* Linden Lab *Terms of Service, supra* note 18, § 2.3 ("You retain any and all Intellectual Property Rights you already hold under applicable law in Content you upload, publish, and submit to or through [*Second Life*]. . . ."), *with Blizzard End User License Agreement, supra* note 18, § 2(A) ("Blizzard is the owner . . . of all right, title, and interest in and to . . . the Games that are produced and developed by Blizzard ("Blizzard Games"), . . . and all of the features and components thereof.").

II. Current and Potential Limitations on Terms and Agreements in Digital Games

This section addresses four primary concerns for terms and agreements in digital games: (1) the doctrine of unconscionability; (2) modifications of TOU; (3) privity of contract and its scope; and (4) enforcement of TOU with minors.

A. Unconscionability

The black letter law of unconscionability states that a contract that results from an unfair bargaining process (procedural unconscionability) that then leads to an unfair result (substantive unconscionability) can be unenforceable against the disadvantaged party.[76] Unconscionability is a common law limit on contract drafters and therefore varies by state, but most states use a sliding scale[77]— the more unconscionable one category is, the less is required in

---

76. *See* RESTATEMENT (SECOND) OF CONTRACTS § 208 (2008) ("If a contract or term thereof is unconscionable at the time the contract is made a court may refuse to enforce the contract. . . ."). Many courts require that unconscionability be both procedural and substantive: an unfair process leading to an unfair result. *See, e.g.*, Swift v. Zynga Game Network, Inc., 805 F. Supp. 2d 904, 915 (N.D. Cal. 2011) ("To be unenforceable, a contract must be both procedurally and substantively unconscionable."); Higgins v. Superior Court of L.A., 140 Cal. App. 4th 1238, 1248 (Cal. Ct. App. 2006) ("Unconscionability has both a procedural and a substantive element, the former focusing on 'oppression' or 'surprise' due to unequal bargaining power, the latter on 'overly harsh' or 'one-sided' results. 'The prevailing view is that [procedural and substantive unconscionability] must *both* be present in order for a court to exercise its discretion to refuse to enforce a contract. . . .'") (citation omitted). However, both are not necessary in the same degree. *Higgins*, 140 Cal. App. 4th at 1249.

77. *See* Davidson & Assocs., Inc. v. Internet Gateway, Inc., 334 F. Supp. 2d 1164, 1179 (E.D. Mo. 2004) ("The prevailing view is that both procedural and substantive unconscionability must be present, although not to the same degree, before a court may exercise its discretion to refuse to enforce a contract or clause due to unconscionability."). *But see* Brower v. Gateway 2000, 246 A.D.2d 246, 253–54 (N.Y. App. Div. 1998) (construing a standard form contract shipped with a computer, and noting that "[w]hile it is true that, under New York law, unconscionability is generally predicated on the presence of both the procedural and substantive elements, the substantive element alone may be sufficient to render the terms of the provision at issue unenforceable").

another to find a contract or provision to be unconscionable and therefore unenforceable.[78] Unconscionability is a central limit on contracts broadly.[79] Courts apply this well-established doctrine[80] to digital game terms and agreements.[81] An instructive example for digital game operators concerns two cases involving Linden Research, *Bragg v. Linden Research, Inc.*[82] and *Evans v. Linden Research, Inc.*[83] Both *Bragg* and the *Evans* cases (*Evans I* and *II*)

---

78. *See, e.g.*, Bragg v. Linden Research, Inc., 487 F. Supp. 2d 593, 605 (E.D. Pa. 2007) ("The two elements operate on a sliding scale such that the more significant one is, the less significant the other need be.") (internal citations omitted); Harrington v. Atl. Sounding Co., 602 F.3d 113, 118 (2d Cir. 2010) ("The district court found that the facts of this case satisfied New Jersey's 'sliding scale' approach to unconscionability. . . .").

79. *See* RESTATEMENT (SECOND) OF CONTRACTS § 208 (2008) ("If a contract or a term thereof is unconscionable at the time the contract is made a court may refuse to enforce the contract. . . ."). Although software licenses may be characterized as not constituting a sale of goods, many courts disagree, and will apply article 2 of the Uniform Commercial Code to purchases of software by analogy, no matter how characterized. *See also* ProCD, Inc. v. Zeidenberg, 86 F.3d 1447, 1450 (7th Cir. 1996) ("Following the district court, we treat the licenses as ordinary contracts accompanying the sale of products, and therefore as governed by the common law of contracts and the Uniform Commercial Code. Whether there are legal differences between 'contracts' and 'licenses' (which may matter under the copyright doctrine of first sale) is a subject for another day."). Thus, article 2's unconscionability provision may be invoked. *See also* U.C.C. § 2-302 (pre-revision) (permitting the court to enforce part or none of a contract on the grounds that terms are unconscionable).

80. *See* David Horton, *Unconscionability Wars*, 106 NW. U. L. REV. COLLOQUY 387, 387 (2011) ("The unconscionability doctrine has emerged as the primary check on drafter overreaching. The Court has repeatedly acknowledged that lower courts can invoke unconscionability to invalidate one-sided arbitration provisions, and . . . judges have done exactly that.").

81. *See* Major v. McCallister, 302 S.W.3d 227, 232 (Mo. Ct. App. 2009) (Rahmeyer, J., concurring) ("[T]he same contract principles hold on the internet. When the consumer is presented with a contract of adhesion containing lengthy provisions and hidden terms, I believe courts should consider whether the process of assent or terms of the contract are unconscionable.").

82. *Bragg*, 487 F. Supp. 2d 593.

83. *See* Evans v. Linden Research, Inc., 763 F. Supp. 2d 735 (E.D. Pa. 2011) [hereinafter Evans I]; Evans v. Linden Research, Inc., No. C 11-01078 DMR, 2012 WL 5877579, at *17 (N.D. Cal. Nov. 20, 2012) [hereinafter Evans II]. *Evans I* took place in the same court under the same judge (the Honorable Eduardo C. Robreno) as *Bragg*. The *Evans I* court transferred the case due to a forum selection clause to California. The next iteration, *Evans II*, will continue as the California court certified a subclass, but denied the main class.

serve as anchor points for this section because they highlight the novel issues of digital games, application of unconscionability to digital games, and the changes a digital game operator can make to prevent a finding of unconscionability.

The following sections address how courts apply black letter unconscionability law to the unique cases of digital games. The first two sections are procedural unconscionability followed by substantive unconscionability. The third section is the Federal Arbitration Act (FAA) because of the pervasiveness of arbitration agreements in digital game contracts, and recent case law defining the relationship of arbitration under the FAA with the doctrine of unconscionability. The fourth section covers federal and state consumer protection limitations on terms and agreements. States are heavily influenced by federal law, and state efforts to protect consumers may be in flux in light of the preemption of the FAA over conflicting state law.[84] The analysis of the Linden cases is coupled with the U.S. Supreme Court case of *AT&T Mobility LLC v. Concepcion*.[85] Emerging trends are noted where they differ from the Linden cases and *Concepcion*.

1. Procedural Unconscionability

The first prong in unconscionability analysis is procedural unconscionability. Procedural unconscionability arises from (1) imbalances in bargaining power, as in "take it or leave it" contracts, or (2) a finding of surprise, such as where the contract is confusingly worded.[86] Two central factors for procedural unconscionability

---

84. *See* AT&T Mobility LLC v. Concepcion, 563 U.S. 333, 339–41 (2011) (detailing the question before the court whether § 2 of the FAA preempts California's *Discover Bank* rule, which classified most collective arbitration waivers in consumer contracts as unconscionable). *See also* Horton, *supra* note 80, at 14 ("[I]n *AT&T Mobility LLC v. Concepcion* Justice Scalia's majority opinion . . . earned the support of only three other Justices. . . . Because Justice Thomas provided the swing vote in *Concepcion*, and invited parties to address the link between § 2 and 4 [of the FAA] in the future, he ensured that unconscionability viability will become a flashpoint in the arbitration wars.").

85. *See Concepcion*, 563 U.S. 333.

86. *See, e.g., Bragg*, 487 F. Supp. 2d at 605 ("The procedural component can be satisfied by showing (1) oppression through the existence of unequal bargaining positions or (2) surprise through hidden terms common in the context of adhesion contracts.").

analysis are the manner in which a contract is (1) presented, or (2) negotiated. An animating question for contract presentation in negotiation is the presence of a market alternative. The two cases of *Bragg* and *Davidson & Associates, Inc. v. Internet Gateway Inc.* are instructive.[87]

The *Bragg* court found an arbitration provision contained in Linden Research's TOU procedurally unconscionable.[88] The court found that the TOS containing the arbitration provision was a contract of adhesion[89] and that a contract of adhesion is procedurally unconscionable under California law.[90] The court found that the "take it or leave it" nature of the contract[91] and the lack of market alternatives available to consumers added to the procedural unconscionability of the TOS.[92] Considering the question of surprise, the court concluded that the arbitration agreement was hidden in a lengthy paragraph labeled "General Provisions"[93] and that

---

87. *Compare Bragg*, 487 F. Supp. 2d at 606 ("Moreover, there was no 'reasonably available market alternatives [to defeat] a claim of adhesiveness.'") (citations omitted), *with* Davidson & Assocs., Inc. v. Internet Gateway, Inc., 334 F. Supp. 2d 1164, 1179 (E.D. Mo. 2004) ("[T]he defendants had the choice to select a different video game . . . the court finds that the licensing agreements were not procedurally unconscionable.").

88. *See Bragg*, 487 F. Supp. 2d at 607 ("Here . . . procedural unconscionability is satisfied.").

89. *See id.* at 606 ("The TOS are a contract of adhesion."). Contracts of adhesion are "standardized contract[s], which, imposed and drafted by the party of superior bargaining strength, relegates to the subscribing party only an opportunity to adhere to the contract or reject it." Neal v. State Farm Ins. Co., 188 Cal. App. 2d 690, 694 (Cal. Ct. App. 1961).

90. *See Bragg*, 487 F. Supp. 2d at 605 ("[T]he Court will apply California state law to determine whether the arbitration provision is unconscionable . . . [a] contract or clause is procedurally unconscionable if it is a contract of adhesion.") (citations omitted). The *Bragg* court used California state law as both parties agreed California law applied. In addition, the TOS at issue contained a California choice-of-law provision.

91. *See id.* at 606 ("'When the weaker party is presented the clause and told to "take it or leave it" without the opportunity for meaningful negotiation, oppression and therefore procedural unconscionability, are present.' . . . Linden presents the TOS on a take-it-or-leave-it basis.") (citations omitted).

92. *See id.* ("Moreover, there was no 'reasonably available market alternatives [to defeat] a claim of adhesiveness.'").

93. *See id.* ("In determining whether surprise exists, California courts focus not on the plaintiff's subjective reading of the contract, but rather, more objectively, on 'the extent to which the supposedly agreed-upon terms of the bargain are

the TOS failed to note the costs and rules of arbitration or provide a hyperlink with this information.[94]

Bragg remains at odds with national trends, in which standard form documents—especially online contracts—are routinely enforced.[95] Because of this disparity, *Bragg* remains instructive because of how it compares with other cases, for example *Davidson*, which upheld similar take-it-or-leave-it agreements. The Blizzard TOS and EULA in *Davidson* required users to click buttons confirming they agreed to both contracts before they could install the software. The *Davidson* court emphasized two factors in its decision: market alternatives and notice of terms. A finding of procedural unconscionability failed in large part because the defendants in *Davidson* could simply select another video game and had notice they were subject to the relevant terms.[96] For *Bragg*, the outcome was a stark contrast as the court determined there were no reasonable alternatives to *Second Life* because no other virtual world grants property rights to its users. *Bragg* also determined that the plaintiff did not have sufficient notice of terms as they were hidden and inconspicuous in a "General Provision" heading.[97]

Standard form contracts can avoid a finding of unconscionability due to surprise if the consumer is provided with the terms and is given a chance to reverse the purchase if unsatisfied.[98] Contracts are generally not deemed one-sided where the consumer has the

---

hidden in the prolix printed form drafted by the party seeking to enforce the disputed terms.' . . . Here, although the TOS are ubiquitous throughout *Second Life*, Linden buried the TOS's arbitration provision in lengthy paragraph under the benign heading 'GENERAL PROVISIONS.'") (citations omitted).

94. *See id.* at 607 ("Linden also failed to make available the costs and rules of arbitration in the [International Commercial Court (ICC)] by either setting them forth in the TOS or by providing a hyper-link to another page or website where they are available.") (citations omitted).

95. *See, e.g.*, Evans I, 763 F. Supp. 2d 735 (E.D. Pa. 2011); Swift v. Zynga Game Network, Inc., 805 F. Supp. 2d 904 (N.D. Cal. 2011).

96. Davidson & Assocs., Inc. v. Internet Gateway, Inc., 334 F. Supp. 2d 1164, 1179–80 (E.D. Mo. 2004).

97. *See Bragg*, 487 F. Supp. 2d at 606–07.

98. *See* ProCD, Inc. v. Zeidenberg, 86 F.3d 1447, 1452 (7th Cir. 1996) ("ProCD proposed a contract that a buyer would accept by *using* the software after having an opportunity to read the license at leisure.").

option to go to a competitor, as is usually the case with digital games at the time of registration.[99]

To prevent a finding of procedural unconscionability, digital game operators need to review their drafting carefully, and their game offerings. The design of a game could be so unique as to have no market alternative.[100] Unfortunately, *Bragg* is an outlier and the extent of market alternatives has not been fully defined or addressed by other courts.[101]

2. Substantive Unconscionability

The second prong in unconscionability analysis is substantive unconscionability, which focuses on overly harsh or one-sided results.[102] Courts may focus on one term or terms in the aggregate to find substantive unconscionability.

The *Bragg* court focused on four factors in finding the arbitration provision at issue substantively unconscionable: lack of mutuality, cost of arbitration, the forum selection clause, and the

---

99. *See* Dean Witter Reynolds, Inc. v. Superior Court, 211 Cal. App. 3d 758 (Cal. Ct. App. 1989) (finding contract not unconscionable as contract of adhesion where other institutions offered differing terms). *But see* Shroyer v. New Cingular Wireless Servs., Inc., 498 F.3d 976, 985 (9th Cir. 2007) ("Although there is clearly some disagreement among the California Courts of Appeal over this issue . . . we have consistently followed the courts that reject the notion that the existence of 'marketplace alternatives' bars a finding of procedural unconscionability. . . . '[A]bsent unusual circumstances, use of a contract of adhesion establishes a minimal degree of procedural unconscionability notwithstanding the availability of market alternatives. . . .'") (quoting Gatton v. T-Mobile USA, Inc., 152 Cal. App. 4th 571, 585 (Cal. Ct. App. 2007)).

100. *See Bragg*, 487 F. Supp. 2d at 606 ("Although it is not the only virtual world on the Internet, Second Life was the first and only virtual world to specifically grant its participants property rights in virtual land.").

101. The *Bragg* court did not discuss the extent of market alternatives. *Second Life* was the only virtual world on the market, in the United States or overseas, but how is the market defined? If a digital game in the United States were to offer a real money auction house (like Blizzard's *Diablo III*) complete with a banking license for the game operator (Like Sweden's award to Entropia Universe), could that constitute a game with no market alternatives (as there are none with that combination), or would the existence of other games with real-money trading and a bank license (though in different countries) balance out?

102. *See* Evans I, 763 F. Supp. 2d 735, 740 (E.D. Pa. 2011) ("The substantive component can be satisfied by showing overly harsh or one-sided results that 'shock the conscience'") (citing *Bragg*, 487 F. Supp. 2d at 605).

confidentiality provision.[103] First, it noted that the contract was void for lack of mutuality.[104] Lack of mutuality exists when the stronger party has a choice of forums available and the weaker party is forced into arbitration.[105] The court found that the TOU lacked mutuality because it provided Linden with several remedies, such as the right of self-help[106] (i.e., terminating a user's account) and the right to unilaterally modify the agreement,[107] while Bragg's only remedy was arbitration.[108]

Second, the court found that the cost of arbitration was prohibitive.[109] Courts have issued a variety of decisions on cost-sharing arrangements and arbitration.[110] Some courts find fee-sharing agreements unenforceable when the cost of arbitration is greater than the cost the customer would bear if the complaint were filed in court.[111] The *Bragg* court joined that trend by holding that the

---

103. *See Bragg*, 487 F. Supp. 2d at 607–10.

104. *See id.* at 608 ("This lack of mutuality supports a finding of substantive unconscionability.").

105. *See id.* at 607 ("Under California law, substantive unconscionability has been found where an arbitration provision forces the weaker party to arbitrate claims but permits a choice of forums for the stronger party.").

106. *See id.* at 608 ("In effect, the TOS provide Linden with a variety of one-sided remedies to resolve disputes, while forcing its customers to arbitrate any disputes with Linden.").

107. *See id.* ("Linden's right to modify the arbitration clause is also significant. 'The effect of [Linden's] unilateral right to modify the arbitration clause is that it could . . . craft precisely the sort of asymmetrical arbitration agreement that is prohibited under California Law as unconscionable.'") (quoting Net Global Mktg. v. Dialtone, Inc., 217 Fed. Appx. 598, 602 (9th Cir. 2007)).

108. *See id.* ("'[F]or all practical purposes, a customer may resolve disputes only after [Linden] has had control of the disputed funds for an indefinite period of time,' and may only resolve those disputes by initiating arbitration.") (citations omitted) (quoting Comb v. PayPal, Inc., 218 F. Supp. 2d 1165, 1175 (N.D. Cal. 2002)).

109. *See id.* at 610 ("Accordingly, the arbitration costs and fee-splitting scheme together also support a finding of unconscionability.").

110. *See, e.g.*, Adkins v. Labor Ready, Inc., 303 F.3d 496, 503 (4th Cir. 2002) ("Nor are we moved to a contrary conclusion by the fact that [other courts] have found specific cost-sharing provisions in other arbitration agreements to be unconscionable"). *See also, e.g.*, Riensche v. Cingular Wireless, No. C06-1325Z, 2006 U.S. Dist. LEXIS 93747 (W.D. Wash. Dec. 27, 2006) (cost-sharing in cases where consumer filing violated Rule 11 not unconscionable).

111. *See, e.g.*, Martin v. Teletech Holdings, Inc., 213 Fed. Appx. 581, 583 (9th Cir. 2006) (citing Ingle v. Circuit City Stores, Inc., 328 F.3d 1165, 1178 (9th Cir. 2003) (finding a cost-splitting provision unconscionable because it "would sanction

arbitration provision was unconscionable because, even if the arbitration cost-sharing arrangement proffered by the defendant was adopted, it would still cost Bragg far more than filing his complaint in court.[112]

Third, the court found that the forum selection clause supported a finding of unconscionability.[113] The court's finding was supported by prior decisions holding that it is unconscionable for a business with consumers scattered across the United States to require those consumers to travel to one location to arbitrate claims involving minimal sums.[114] The court found the forum selection clause unconscionable both because Linden had millions of customers located across the United States and because the average transaction in *Second Life* involved a small amount of money.[115]

---

charging even a successful litigant for her share of arbitration costs")); Ferguson v. Countrywide Credit Indus., 298 F.3d 778, 785 (9th Cir. 2002) (arbitration provision requiring arbitration costs to be shared equally by the company and the employee shocked the conscience, and that "a fee provision is unenforceable when the employee bears *any* expense beyond the usual costs associated with bringing an action in court") (citing Armendariz v. Found. Health Psychcare Servs., Inc., 24 Cal. 4th 83 (Cal. 2000)); Circuit City Stores, Inc. v. Adams, 279 F.3d 889, 894 (9th Cir. 2002) (reasoning that an arbitration agreement's requirement that the employee split the arbitrator's fees with the employer "alone would render an arbitration agreement unenforceable"). *See also Bragg*, 487 F. Supp. 2d at 609 ("Such schemes are unconscionable where they 'impose [ ] on some consumers costs greater than those a complainant would bear if he or she would file the same complaint in court.'") (quoting Ting v. AT&T, 319 F.3d 1126, 1151 (9th Cir. 2003)).

112. *See Bragg*, 487 F. Supp. 2d at 609–10 ("Any of these figures are significantly greater than the costs that Bragg bears by filing his action in a state or federal court.").

113. *See id.* at 610 ("[L]imiting venue to [Linden's] backyard appears to be yet one more means by which the arbitration clause serves to shield [Linden] from liability instead of providing a neutral forum in which to arbitrate disputes.") (quoting Comb v. PayPal, Inc., 218 F. Supp. 2d 1165, 1177 (N.D. Cal. 2002)).

114. *See id.* ("California law dictates that it is 'not reasonable for individual consumers from throughout the country to travel to one locale to arbitrate claims involving minimal sums.'") (quoting *Comb*, 218 F. Supp. 2d at 1177).

115. *See id.* ("[T]he record in this case shows that Linden serves millions of customers across the United States and that the average transaction through or with *Second Life* involves a relatively small amount.").

Fourth, the confidentiality provision supported a finding that the arbitration clause was unconscionable.[116] The court noted that confidentiality provisions alone are not *per se* unconscionable. Taken together with other one-sided EULA provisions, however, they supported such a finding.[117] In support of its conclusion, the court noted that confidentiality provisions place the company in a superior legal position by ensuring that its opponents have no access to precedent, while the company is able to accumulate a wealth of knowledge through the arbitration process.[118]

These arguments are often made in arbitration-unconscionability cases, or in similar sister cases brought under the "unreasonableness" standard for determining whether a choice-of-forum clause is unenforceable.[119] Cost problems can be a contributing factor.[120] If the consumer bears so much cost that any potential recovery will be less than the cost of arbitration, courts are inclined to view arbitration clauses as a method of preventing, rather than adjudicating, consumer claims.[121] For example, courts seem

---

116. *See id.* ("Arbitration before the ICC, pursuant to the TOS, must be kept confidential pursuant to the ICC rules. . . . Applying California law to an arbitration provision, the Ninth Circuit held that such confidentiality supports a finding that an arbitration clause was substantively unconscionable.") (citations omitted).

117. *See id.* ("This does not mean that confidentiality provisions in an arbitration scheme or agreement are, in every instance, *per se* unconscionable under California law. . . . Here, however, taken together with other provisions of the TOS, the confidentiality provision gives rise for concern of the conscionability of the arbitration clause.") (emphasis added) (citations omitted).

118. *See id.* ("The Ninth Circuit reasoned that if the company succeeds in imposing a gag order on arbitration proceedings, it places itself in a far superior legal posture. . . .") (citations omitted).

119. *See, e.g.,* Carnival Cruise Lines, Inc. v. Shute, 499 U.S. 585 (1991); *see also* Belfiore v. Summit Fed. Credit Union, 452 F. Supp. 2d 629, 632 (D. Md. 2006) ("Choice of forum and law provisions may be found unreasonable if . . . the complaining party 'will for all practical purposes be deprived of his day in court' because of the grave inconvenience or unfairness of the selected forum. . . .") (quoting Allen v. Lloyd's of London, 94 F.3d 923, 928 (4th Cir. 1996)).

120. *See* Green Tree Fin. Corp.-Ala. v. Randolph, 531 U.S. 79, 90 (2000) (noting that prohibitive cost can render arbitration clause unconscionable).

121. *See id.; see also* Morrison v. Circuit City Stores, Inc., 317 F.3d 646 (6th Cir. 2002) (cost-sharing arbitration agreement rendered arbitration clause so expensive as to deny plaintiffs a forum); Gray v. Rent-A-Center West, Inc., 314 Fed. Appx. 15, 16 (9th Cir. 2008) ("A litigant is effectively denied access to the arbitral

willing to entertain the issue of whether adjudication of United States-based claims under the rules of the International Commercial Court (ICC) rather than the American Arbitration Association might be unconscionable because of the high costs in adjudicating ICC cases.[122]

The *Bragg* decision remains instructive for digital games as *Bragg* determined that Linden's arbitration provision was substantively unconscionable because Linden reserved the right to engage in self-help.[123] Linden's self-help was the reservation of the right to suspend or terminate Bragg's account at Linden's sole discretion. This was one reason under the finding of a lack of mutuality, and a lack of mutuality was one of four elements that went to the determination that the arbitration provision was substantively unconscionable.[124] *Bragg* therefore did not rely solely on Linden's reserved right of self-help in finding the arbitration provision unconscionable. Case law concerning self-help provisions is similar.[125] These

---

forum 'when the cost of arbitration is large in absolute terms . . . [and] . . . th[e] cost is significantly larger than the cost of a trial.'") (quoting Vasquez-Lopez v. Beneficial Or., Inc., 152 P.3d 940, 951 (2007)), *vacated*, Gray v. Rent-A-Center West, Inc., 295 Fed. Appx. 115 (9th Cir. 2008); Epic Sys. Corp. v. Lewis, 138 S. Ct. 1612, 1633 (2018) (Ginsburg, J., dissenting) ("Individually, their claims are small, scarcely of a size warranting the expense of seeking redress alone. . . . But by joining together with others similarly circumstanced, employees can gain effective redress for wage underpayment commonly experienced.").

122. *See* Brower v. Gateway 2000, 246 A.D.2d 246, 254–55 (N.Y. App. Div. 1998) (citing Filias v. Gateway 2000, No. 96-CV-75722-DT, 1997 U.S. Dist. LEXIS 7115 (E.D. Mich. Apr. 8, 1997) (unreported)) (court inclined to find arbitration under ICC rules unconscionable).

123. *See Bragg*, 487 F. Supp. 2d at 608 (finding that Linden's termination provision that provided "Linden has the right at any time for any reason or no reason to suspend or terminate your Account, terminate this Agreement, and/or refuse any and all current or future use of the Service without notice or liability to you" was *one* of the one-sided provisions that made the user agreement substantively unconscionable) (citing the TOS).

124. It is important to note that any unconscionability analysis of an arbitration clause varies state to state. The *Bragg* court was applying California law. *See, e.g.*, O'Shea v. Direct Fin. Solutions, LLC, No. 07-1881, 2007 WL 4373038, at *4 (E.D. Pa. Dec. 5, 2007) ("in Pennsylvania . . . lack of mutuality does not invalidate an arbitration agreement").

125. *See* Goodridge v. KDF Auto. Group, Inc., 209 Cal. App. 4th 325, 343 (Cal. Ct. App. 2012), *review filed* (Oct. 23, 2012) ("Repossession is one of the most important remedies from a car dealer's perspective. In turn, a buyer has no self-help remedies against a car dealer. Accordingly, by exempting self-help remedies

clauses appear enforceable when they are not part of a broader contract that is unconscionable. This may receive further augmentation from *Evans II* due to recent subclass certification and commonality question of whether Linden Research's new TOS is "unconscionable or otherwise unenforceable against Second Life users whose accounts Linden suspended or terminated."[126]

A determination that account suspension or termination provisions are *per se* substantively unconscionable on their own, or otherwise unenforceable, could seriously alter the balance of the legal landscape for digital game law, not to mention website operators in general that rely heavily on this remedy. The right to suspend or terminate a user's access to a digital game is the most important tool in the digital game operator's toolbox. Game operators police online communities with this tool. The endpoint options of compelling arbitration or pursing a lawsuit in court are costly and time intensive.

Account suspensions and terminations allow game operators to stop behavior in breach of terms and agreements and maintain a positive game experience.[127] This last rationale is a defense that may need to be explored more fully by game operators if and when

---

from arbitration, KDF has attempted to maximize its advantage over Goodridge by avoiding arbitration of its claims. . . . [W]e conclude the Contract's arbitration clause is unconscionable. . . ."). In both cases the reserved right of self-help plays a role in finding substantive unconscionability. Both courts applied traditional unconscionability analysis, finding procedural unconscionability and substantive unconscionability. Two points emerge. Account suspension and termination provisions can go to a finding of substantive unconscionability but are not as of yet by themselves enough to find substantive unconscionability.

126. *See* Evans II, No. C 11-01078 DMR, 2012 WL 5877579, at *17 (N.D. Cal. Nov. 20, 2012).

127. *See id.* at *3, 14 (citations omitted) ("Plaintiffs Carl Evans . . . participated in Second Life . . . and . . . had . . . accounts unilaterally terminated or suspended by Linden . . . Mr. Evans's conduct may not rise to the level of criminal activity, his lewd, profane, violent, and threatening language toward other users has drawn over 100 abuse reports. . . . [H]e has demonstrated a substantial record of abusive and hostile conduct."). *See also* MDY Indus., LLC v. Blizzard Entm̄t, Inc., 629 F.3d 928, 936 (9th Cir. 2010) ("Blizzard launched Warden, a technology . . . to prevent . . . bots. . . . Warden was able to detect Glider, and Blizzard immediately used Warden to ban most Glider users . . . Blizzard claims . . . it received 465,000 complaints about WoW bots, several thousand of which named Glider. Blizzard spends $940,000 annually to respond to these complaints. . . .").

they are in court. The *Bragg* court noted that California law provided Linden with the option of providing a business rationale for contract terms, which, while harsh, were necessary for a "margin of safety" because of "business realities."[128] Linden did not address this in its briefs to the court or at oral argument.[129] A prior case that *Bragg* cited heavily is *Comb v. PayPal, Inc.*[130] PayPal was found to have an unconscionable arbitration provision and to have also failed to justify a legitimate business reason for its one-sided provisions, in particular PayPal's ability to suspend, terminate, and procure funds from any account at its sole discretion.[131] While PayPal dealt with "real money," the underlying transaction is similar to the arguments advanced in *Evans II*,[132] and perhaps there is a broader shift in courts' perspective in both powers that digital game operators reserve to themselves, such as account terminations, and what is being transacted, for example value and investment in virtual property and currency.[133]

The legal landscape for digital games may receive revisions from *Evans II*. The original case transferred from Pennsylvania to California.[134] This is important for two reasons. First, Linden revised their TOS extensively in the years after the *Bragg* decision.[135] The

---

128. *Bragg*, 487 F. Supp. 2d at 610 ("Under California law, a contract may provide a 'margin of safety' that provides the party with superior bargaining strength protection for which it has a legitimate commercial need.").

129. *See id.* at 611.

130. Comb v. PayPal, Inc., 218 F. Supp. 2d 1165 (N.D. Cal. 2002).

131. *See id.* at 1173–75 ("PayPal has not shown that 'business realities' justify such one-sidedness.").

132. *See Evans II*, 2012 WL 5877579, at *11 ("Contrary to Defendants' assertions, Plaintiffs have alleged a theory of liability that is not dependent on the reasons for termination of the Second Life accounts. Rather, Plaintiffs allege that when Linden suspended or terminated the accounts—whether or not it had a good reason for doing so—Linden confiscated the virtual land, virtual items, and currency remaining in those accounts without remuneration.").

133. *See* discussion *infra* Section III.B.

134. *See* Evans I, 763 F. Supp. 2d 735, 738 (E.D. Pa. 2011) ("[T]he Court finds that the mandatory forum selection clause included in Defendants' current Terms of Service applies. Thus, Defendants' Motion to Dismiss is granted in part and denied in part, and the case will be transferred to the Northern District of California.").

135. *Evans II*, 2012 WL 5877579, at *2 ("Linden's decision to strip Second Life users of their ownership rights culminated in March 2010, when Linden modified its Terms of Service.").

soundness of these edits will be tested because the new revisions provide not only for arbitration, but also court for disputes over $10,000. Second, the court in *Evans II* will grapple with several fundamental issues for digital games, such as the unconscionability of account termination or suspensions, ownership in virtual land or items, and whether a digital game operator must reimburse accounts terminated for virtual land, items, or currency.[136]

3. The FAA

Congress enacted the FAA[137] in 1925 in response to widespread judicial hostility. Arbitration is now the dominant form of dispute resolution for consumer contracts, including digital game TOU.[138] The FAA is important to understand because of what it provides to digital game contract drafters and what it does not.

Digital game TOU routinely contain both arbitration[139] and choice-of-forum provisions.[140] One of the benefits of these provisions is that they limit the legal exposure of the game operator, and permit the operator to litigate in an accessible forum. These provisions are routinely tested in court for two reasons. First,

---

136. *See id.* at *12.

137. 9 U.S.C. § 1 *et seq.* (1947).

138. Arbitration is so favored by the FAA, and subsequent case law, that the FAA mandates that even questions of what issues are to be arbitrated must be submitted to the arbitrator. *See* Shaffer v. ACS Gov't Servs., Inc., 321 F. Supp. 2d 682, 685 (D. Md. 2004) ("[A]ny doubts concerning the scope of the arbitrable issues should be resolved in favor of arbitration. . . .") (citations omitted); *see also* Bragg v. Linden Research, Inc., 487 F. Supp. 2d 593, 605 n.15 (E.D. Pa. 2007) ("Bragg does not challenge enforceability by claiming that a provision of the arbitration agreement will deny him a statutory right, a question of interpretation of the arbitration agreement which an arbitrator is 'well situated to answer.'") (citation omitted).

139. *See, e.g.*, Electronic Arts, *Star Wars: The Old Republic End User Access and License Agreement*, http://www.swtor.com/legalnotices/euala (last visited July 23, 2018) ("YOU AND EA AGREE THAT EACH MAY BRING CLAIMS AGAINST THE OTHER ONLY IN YOUR OR ITS INDIVIDUAL CAPACITY, AND NOT AS A PLAINTIFF OR CLASS MEMBER IN ANY PURPORTED CLASS OR REPRESENTATIVE PROCEEDING.").

140. *Id.* ("Governing Law. If you reside in a Member State of the European Union: (a) the laws of England, excluding its conflict-of-law rules, govern this license and your use of the Application . . . If you reside elsewhere, the laws of the State of California, excluding its conflicts-of-law rules, govern this License and/or your use of the Application.").

plaintiffs and their lawyers often want to reach federal court in order to bring a class action and potentially win a bigger award of damages. Second, plaintiffs may not be willing to litigate small-dollar claims in faraway venues due to the high cost and inconvenience of doing so. The FAA directly impacts arbitration and choice-of-forum provisions.

A central component of the FAA is section 2,[141] which reflects the strong federal policy in support of arbitration and the core principle that arbitration is a matter of contract.[142] The latter principle is referred to as the "savings clause" because it allows for generally applicable contract defenses, for example unconscionability. It does not allow, however, for arbitration agreements to be invalidated by defenses that apply exclusively to arbitration or that rely on the fact that an agreement to arbitrate is at issue.[143] Unconscionability therefore remains as a central contract defense and can impact arbitration agreements and forum selection clauses within digital game TOU. The seemingly settled area of unconscionability remains in flux despite "clarification" by the Supreme Court.

The Supreme Court determined in *Concepcion* that the FAA preempted the *Discover Bank* rule; established by the California Supreme Court in 2005.[144] The *Discover Bank* rule found class waivers in consumer arbitration agreements unconscionable if (1) the contract was an adhesion contract; (2) disputes between the parties involved small sums; and (3) the party in the weaker position alleged "a scheme to deliberately cheat large numbers of consumers out of individually small sums of money."[145] *Concepcion*

---

141. *See* 9 U.S.C. § 2 (1947) ("[A] transaction involving commerce to settle by arbitration a controversy thereafter arising out of such contract or transaction, or the refusal to perform the whole or any part thereof, or an agreement in writing to submit to arbitration an existing controversy arising out of such a contract, transaction, or refusal, shall be valid, irrevocable, and enforceable, save upon such grounds as exist at law or in equity for the revocation of any contract.").

142. *See* AT&T Mobility LLC v. Concepcion, 563 U.S. 333, 339 (2011) ("[C]ourts must place arbitration agreements on an equal footing with other contracts. . . .").

143. *See id.*

144. *Id.* at 352.

145. *See* Discover Bank v. Superior Court, 113 P.3d 1100, 1110 (Cal. 2005).

determined the *Discover Bank* rule disfavored arbitration because it treated collective arbitration waivers in consumer contracts of adhesion as *per se* unconscionable, and therefore stood as an obstacle to the FAA.[146]

The California Supreme Court augmented unconscionability analysis in *Discover Bank* by not requiring the traditional approach based on procedural and substantive unconscionability. The *Discover Bank* rule did not require an analysis of the contract terms themselves, but rather the nature of the contract and the dispute.[147] *Concepcion* is therefore more a story about limiting the *Discover Bank* rule, and less a fundamental shift in unconscionability analysis.[148]

The Supreme Court revisited the issue of arbitration clauses in *Epic Systems Corp. v. Lewis*;[149] however, the Court focused on whether the National Labor Relations Act (NLRA) or the FAA prohibits the enforcement of individual arbitration clauses.[150] A group of employees were collectively trying to sue their employers for wage theft, but the employers claimed that the individual arbitration clause in the employment contracts barred any collective effort.[151] The employees presented two arguments against individual arbitration clauses: (1) the FAA's savings clause provides a basis for refusing to enforce for claims under the Fair Labor Standards Act and class action procedures for claims under state law;[152] and (2) because the NLRA guarantees workers the right to engage in collective activities, the NLRA displaces the FAA by outlawing collective action waivers.[153] The Court rejected both

---

146. *Concepcion*, 563 U.S. at 348.

147. *See Discover Bank*, 113 P.3d at 1110.

148. *See* Jerett Yan, *A Lunatic's Guide to Suing for $30: Class Action Arbitration, the Federal Arbitration Act, and Unconscionability After AT&T v. Concepcion*, 32 BERKELEY J. EMP. & LAB. L. 551, 553 (2011) ("Most courts interpreting Concepcion simply read the decision as having pruned one of the most far reaching forms of unconscionability doctrine, leaving the bulk of the unconscionability jurisprudence intact.").

149. Epic Sys. Corp. v. Lewis, 138 S. Ct. 1612 (2018).

150. *See id.* at 1619.

151. *See id.* at 1620–21.

152. *Id.* at 1622.

153. *Id.* at 1623–24.

arguments and instead found the collective action waivers to be valid under both the NLRA and FAA.[154] An important distinction from *Concepcion* is that the employees in *Epic Systems* did not raise an unconscionability argument, but instead framed the argument as an issue of labor law conflicting with contract law.[155]

The *Bragg* court avoided the FAA's mandate to uphold arbitration agreements by framing the issue before it as a question of whether the arbitration clause even existed in the first place or was, instead, void for unconscionability.[156] This approach squares with *Concepcion* and *Epic Systems*.[157] The core question presented to the *Bragg* court was whether an arbitration provision contained in the *Second Life* TOS was so one-sided as to be unconscionable. The *Bragg* court found that the applicability of the FAA was an issue not even reached when courts are presented with general contract defenses, such as unconscionability.[158] The court also opted to analyze whether the arbitration agreement itself denied

---

154. *Id.* at 1632.

155. *See id.* at 1622 ("[The employees] don't suggest that their arbitration agreements were extracted, say, by an act of fraud or duress or in some other unconscionable way that would render *any* contract unenforceable.").

156. *See* Bragg v. Linden Research, Inc., 487 F. Supp. 2d 593, 604 (E.D. Pa. 2007) ("While there is a presumption that a particular dispute is within the *scope* of an arbitration agreement, there is no 'presumption' or 'policy' that favors the *existence* of a valid agreement to arbitrate.") (emphasis in original) (citations omitted).

157. *See* AT&T Mobility LLC v. Concepcion, 563 U.S. 333, 339–40 (2011) ("[Section] 2 . . . permits arbitration agreements to be declared unenforceable 'upon such grounds as exist at law or in equity for the revocation of any contract.' This saving clause permits agreements to arbitrate to be invalidated by 'generally applicable contact defenses, such as . . . unconscionability,' but not by defenses that apply only to arbitration or that derive their meaning from the fact that an agreement to arbitrate is at issue.") (quoting 9 U.S.C. § 2); *see also Epic Sys. Corp.*, 138 S. Ct. at 1622 ("[The employees] don't suggest that their arbitration agreements were extracted, say, by an act of fraud or duress or in some other unconscionable way that would render *any* contract unenforceable.").

158. *See Bragg*, 487 F. Supp. 2d at 605 ("Thus, 'generally applicable contract defenses, such as fraud, duress, or unconscionability, may be applied to invalidate arbitration agreements without contravening § 2.'") (quoting Doctor's Assocs. v. Casarotto, 517 U.S. 681, 687 (1996)).

Bragg the ability to arbitrate because it required Bragg to bear certain costs of doing so.[159]

After the *Bragg* decision, Linden Research was left with the question of how best to draft contracts to prevent a finding of unconscionability. Linden Research made subsequent changes that were the subject of *Evans*.[160] The court in *Evans* found the revised TOS not to be unconscionable. The focus of the court was on a forum selection clause instead of an arbitration agreement. Linden Research updated its TOS in several ways, and notably with a bifurcated option available to both parties. Claims below $10,000 were subject to either party's initiation to binding, nonappearance-based arbitration.[161] *Evans* looked to *Bragg* as the same judge, the Honorable Eduardo C. Robreno, presided over both cases and both parties in *Evans* invoked *Bragg*. Unconscionability analysis remained the same in *Evans* with analysis of procedural and substantive unconscionability, and the outcome was different with substantial revisions by Linden Research. The outcome remains opaque because of a key question remaining—what is the enforceability of any particular self-help remedy for a digital game operator? For example, account suspensions and termination are central tools for a digital game operator. The law on point remains unclear because account termination and suspensions remain as central tools and have not been found to be substantively unconscionable in other cases.[162]

---

159. *See id.* at n.15 ("Rather, Bragg claims that the arbitration agreement itself would effectively deny him access to an arbitrator, because the costs would be prohibitively expensive, a question that is more appropriately reserved for the Court to answer.").

160. *See* Evans I, 763 F. Supp. 2d 735, 741 (E.D. Pa. 2011).

161. *See id.*

162. *Compare Bragg*, 487 F. Supp. 2d at 607–11 (finding substantive unconscionability based on lack of mutuality, cost of arbitration, venue, and confidentiality issues), *with* Goodridge v. KDF Auto. Group, Inc., No. D060269, 2016 WL 142216 (Cal. Ct. App. Jan. 12, 2016) (unpublished table decision) (court finds the arbitration clause in the sales contract of a car to be enforceable).

4. Federal and State Consumer Protection Limitations on Terms and Agreements

Online contracts govern the overwhelming majority of relationships between online businesses and consumers. These contracts give digital game operators significant control over the nature of that relationship. For example, terms routinely contain "no cheating" provisions to maintain an enjoyable experience for customers. To enforce this provision, terms also contain account termination provisions should end users be found in violation of the terms. Terms are not unlimited in their power. They are limited by federal or state statutes and common law, contractual defenses.

A central federal statute that checks corporate drafters is the Federal Trade Commission Act, which established the Federal Trade Commission's (FTC's) authority.[163] This act provides the FTC broad powers[164] and acts as a model for state statutes. Every state, as well as the District of Columbia and the commonwealth of Puerto Rico, has enacted statutes to protect consumers against unfair, unconscionable, deceptive, and fraudulent business practices; unfair competition; and false advertising.[165] While some state

---

163. Federal Trade Commission Act, 15 U.S.C. §§ 41–58 (2006) (granting the FTC the power to regulate unfair trade practices); *see also* FTC, *A Brief Overview of the Federal Trade Commission's Investigative and Law Enforcement Authority*, http://www.ftc.gov/ogc/brfovrvw.shtm (last revised July 2008) (describing the FTC's authority under section 5 of the Federal Trade Commission Act).

164. *See* Federal Trade Commission Act, 15 U.S.C. § 45 ("The Commission is hereby empowered and directed to prevent persons, partnerships, or corporations [except certain entities such as banks and several others] . . . from using unfair methods of competition in or affecting commerce and unfair or deceptive acts or practices in or affecting commerce.") (citations omitted).

165. *See, e.g.*, FLA. STAT. § 501.204 (2017):

> (1) Unfair methods of competition, unconscionable acts or practices, and unfair or deceptive acts or practices in the conduct of any trade or commerce are hereby declared unlawful.

> (2) It is the intent of the Legislature that, in construing subsection (1), due consideration and great weight shall be given to the interpretations of the Federal Trade Commission and the federal courts relating to s. 5(a)(1) of the Federal Trade Commission Act, 15 U.S.C. s. 45(a)(1) as of July 1, 2017.

consumer protection statutes give consumers a private right of action,[166] many also protect existing causes of action by rejecting the enforceability of clauses that might otherwise invalidate claims or remove cases to arbitration or different forums.[167] After *Concepcion*, these statutes remain largely untouched except where they target arbitration agreements specifically.[168] The following are examples of each sort of statute.

State consumer protection statutes may apply to activities governed by TOU.[169] For example, Florida's Deceptive and Unfair Trade Practices Act, which is patterned after the Federal Trade Commission Act, prohibits unfair methods of competition and unfair or deceptive acts or practices in the conduct of any trade or commerce.[170] It enables consumers to recover actual damages and reasonable attorneys' fees and provides for injunctive relief and declaratory judgments.[171] Florida's act is now called into question insofar as it stands as an obstacle to the FAA,[172] a clear reason that arbitration and the *Concepcion* ruling is so important to state consumer protection limitations on terms and agreements. The

---

166. *See, e.g.*, Va. Code § 59.1-204 (2006) ("Any person who suffers loss as the result of a violation of this chapter shall be entitled to initiate an action to recover actual damages, or $500, whichever is greater.").

167. *See* Fla. Stat. § 501.201 *et seq.* (2017).

168. The *Cruz v. Cingular Wireless* court found:

After careful consideration, we now hold that, in light of *Concepcion*, the class action waiver in the Plaintiffs' arbitration agreements is enforceable under the FAA. Insofar as Florida law would invalidate these agreements as contrary to public policy (a question we need not decide), such a state law would "stand[ ] as an obstacle to the accomplishment and execution" of the FAA . . . (quotation omitted), and thus be preempted. Accordingly, we affirm the district court's order dismissing the Plaintiffs' claims and compelling arbitration.

Cruz v. Cingular Wireless, LLC, 648 F.3d 1205, 1207 (11th Cir. 2011) (citations omitted).

169. *See* Complaint, Hernandez v. Internet Gaming Entm't, Ltd., No. 07-21403 (S.D. Fla. May 30, 2007).

170. *See id.*

171. *Id.*

172. *See Cruz*, 648 F.3d at 1207; *see also* McKenzie Check Advance of Fla., LLC v. Betts, 112 So. 3d 1176 (Fla. 2013) (holding that the FAA preempts state law, compelling the enforcement of an individual arbitration clause).

consumer protection statutes of the remaining 49 states, the District of Columbia, and Puerto Rico are similarly worded.[173]

Using the Florida act, the plaintiffs in *Hernandez v. Internet Gaming Entertainment*, subscribers to *World of Warcraft*, brought suit against Internet Gaming Entertainment (IGE), a corporation that purchases and resells in-game currency.[174] Plaintiffs claimed "unfair methods of competition," "unconscionable acts or practices," and "unfair or deceptive acts or practices in the conduct of any trade or commerce" resulting from IGE's breach of the EULA between the plaintiffs and the virtual world operators, Blizzard Entertainment.[175] The class action[176] asked the court to expand significantly the bounds of Blizzard's EULA and to name the plaintiffs as third-party beneficiaries even though no such language was found in the agreement.[177] The claim was eventually dismissed.

Likewise, plaintiffs have used state consumer protection statutes to limit or invalidate certain clauses in license agreements.[178] In *America Online v. Superior Court*,[179] the California court found that a forum selection clause in the petitioner's service agreement was not binding based on California's public policy.[180] The plaintiffs in the original suit filed claims under California's Consumers Legal Remedies Act (CLRA) and the state's Unfair Business Practices Act.[181] While the California claims would have allowed a class action, the consumer protections statute of Virginia—the

---

173. *See, e.g.*, 815 ILL. COMP. STAT. 505/2 (2008); GA. CODE ANN. § 10-1-393 (2008); N.C. GEN. STAT. § 75-1.1 (2005).

174. *See* Complaint, Hernandez v. Internet Gaming Entm't, Ltd., No. 07-21403 (S.D. Fla. May 30, 2007).

175. *Id.*

176. The legal landscape for class actions is clearly limited due to the inclusion of arbitration clauses and the *Concepcion* and *Epic Systems* holding. Of note to this section is the central role of contract drafting and what is granted. The emerging line of *Evans* cases demonstrates that where a class action option is available, it will be used and perhaps to the detriment of a digital game operator, here Linden Research.

177. Complaint, Hernandez v. Internet Gaming Entm't, Ltd., No. 07-21403 (S.D. Fla. May 30, 2007).

178. *See* Am. Online, Inc. v. Superior Court, 90 Cal. App. 4th 1 (Cal. Ct. App. 2001).

179. *Id.*

180. *Id.* at 5.

181. *Id.* at 4–5.

forum stated in the contract—did not appear to permit relief sought on behalf of others.[182] Based on Virginia's conflict of laws requirements (which forbade application of the CLRA) and the CLRA (which contained a "no-waiver" provision prohibiting state consumers from waiving their rights under the CLRA), the court invalidated the forum selection clause.[183]

B. Modifications

Digital game operators have tremendous powers in the online contracts they use. As noted earlier in this chapter, these contracts frequently contain provisions that give the game operator the power to unilaterally modify the contract at any time and at its sole discretion.[184] This right of modification is a powerful and useful tool for digital game operators for business needs or legal changes. For example, numerous game companies modified their online contracts after the ruling in *Concepcion* to include class arbitration waivers.

The method of notification is central to a review of modifications and their legality. Some operators notify their users of modifications and ask for an express acceptance of the newly modified terms upon login.[185] Others may post notice of the modifications on the digital game's website along with a statement to the effect that continued use of the game thereafter constitutes acceptance of the modified terms.[186] Other methods are available and may turn on business decisions and costs. The notification approach taken by a digital game operator is critical as it, and the modification itself, can raise issues of unconscionability, consideration, or illusoriness.

---

182. *Id.* at 16.

183. *Id.* at 17.

184. *See* Linden Lab *Terms of Service, supra* note 18; *see also Blizzard End User License Agreement, supra* note 18; *Daybreak Terms of Service, supra* note 46.

185. *See Daybreak Terms of Service, supra* note 46 ("We may amend this Agreement at any time in our sole discretion. Amendments shall be communicated to you at the time you log into your Account. Such amendments shall be effective whenever we make the notification available for your review.").

186. *See Blizzard End User License Agreement, supra* note 18, § 9 ("Blizzard may create updated versions of this Agreement (each a 'New Agreement') as its business and the law evolve.").

Modifications to TOU are limited by the doctrine of unconscionability. Modifications may be held procedurally unconscionable if done without proper notice or with no reasonable market alternatives. Digital game operators may reduce the risk of a court finding any modifications substantively unconscionable by not making significant changes to material terms. They can reduce the risk of a court finding procedural unconscionability by expressly reserving the right to change specific terms in the original TOU. By giving digital game users sufficient notice, modified terms are less likely to come as a surprise to the players.[187]

Courts may also find modifications to an existing TOU to be substantively unconscionable.[188] Given that substantive unconscionability is often tied to the materiality of the modified terms, any significant changes to virtual property or currency, termination, or arbitration (i.e., *Bragg*) may render such changes substantively unconscionable.

Modifications generally require additional consideration under the common law; however, additional consideration is likely not required for digital game operators. This is true regardless of whether courts treat sales of software as goods or as services. Many courts have assumed (without explanatory analysis) that software licensing and online games are governed under the Uniform Commercial Code (UCC) as a sale of goods.[189] The UCC

---

187. *See* Davidson & Assocs., Inc. v. Internet Gateway, Inc., 334 F. Supp. 2d 1164, 1179 (E.D. Mo. 2004). One factor the courts considered when determining that there was no procedural unconscionability with Blizzard's EULA was that there was no surprise about the contract terms. The company gave notice to buyers that the game contained a EULA with additional terms. If virtual world creators reserve the right to modify terms in the original EULA, they are providing virtual world players with notice, so when a modification does occur, there will be no surprise for the player.

188. *See* Bragg v. Linden Research, Inc., 487 F. Supp. 2d 593, 605–07 (E.D. Pa. 2007) (deciding that terms in *Second Life*'s EULA were substantively unconscionable because of one-sidedness and harshness, including the unilateral right to modify as one element in the finding of unconscionability).

189. *See Davidson & Assocs.*, 334 F. Supp. 2d at 1177 n.11 (stating "[t]he Court assumes, as have several other courts, that the games in question constitute goods under the UCC") (citing Specht v. Netscape Commc'n Corp., 306 F.3d 17, 29 n.13 (2d Cir. 2002), and I.Lan Sys., Inc. v. Netscout Serv. Level Corp., 183 F. Supp. 2d 328, 332 (D. Mass. 2002)).

requires no new consideration when modifying an existing contract.[190] Online digital games increasingly provide a range of services in addition to downloadable software.[191] For example, the virtual worlds of *World of Warcraft* and *Diablo III* have install discs or a downloadable option from Blizzard. Both virtual worlds also have an online service known as Battle.net,[192] an online gaming service that matches players to compete with each other based on player skill, and ability to purchase and save games (among many other services).[193] These services are governed by documents titled "Terms of Service," and therefore resemble a service more so than a sale of goods. This would result in the UCC not applying. Were this the case, TOU modifications would be governed by common law and thus would require additional consideration.[194] Most TOU can avoid this problem by reserving the right to modify their terms. This creates a bargained-for exchange for any modifications exercised in the future.[195] Another option used by several digital game operators is a revision of their terms and agreements in conjunction with new patches. The patch, or new content of the game, can act as consideration.

Digital game operators can stipulate that future access to the virtual world is valid consideration for acceptance of the

---

190. U.C.C. § 2-209(1) (1977) ("An agreement modifying a contract within this article needs no consideration to be binding.").

191. *See* MDY Indus., LLC v. Blizzard Entm't, Inc., 629 F.3d 928, 935 (9th Cir. 2010) ("The Wow software has two components: (1) the game client software that a player installs on the computer; and (2) the game server software, which the player accesses on a subscription basis by connecting to Wow's online servers.").

192. *See* Blizzard, *Blizzard Battle.net Desktop App*, https://www.blizzard.com /en-us/apps/battle.net/desktop (last visited July 23, 2018).

193. *Id.* An example includes the ability to design maps for other players in *StarCraft II.*

194. *But see* McCallum Highlands, Ltd. v. Wash. Capital Dus, Inc., 66 F.3d 89, 93 (5th Cir. 1995) (noting that under the "pre-existing duty rule," an agreement to do what one is already bound to do cannot serve as sufficient consideration for a modification of a contract).

195. *See* RAYMOND T. NIMMER, LAW OF COMPUTER TECHNOLOGY § 7:128 (2018) ("[I]f during [the] discussions it was said or at least mutually understood that the contract was subject to subsequent terms contained in the software box . . . the later terms are not a modification, but a part of the original agreement.").

modifications and that users who disagree with the proposed modifications to the TOU may simply cancel their services.[196]

Lastly, the ability for digital game companies to unilaterally modify contract terms begs a deeper question—is there even a promise made? The doctrine of illusoriness holds a contract as unenforceable where a party offers for consideration a promise so insubstantial as to not impose any actual obligations. All contracts require some form of consideration. Online contracts are no exception. In the digital game context, like online exchange generally, reserved rights to amend are widespread. A recent case suggests both a clear view of courts' negative view of unfettered amendment powers by companies in consumer contracts and an easy solution for companies that many already follow.

In re Zappos.com Inc., Customer Data Security Breach Litigation[197] is a 2012 case concerning e-commerce company Zappos. The case presents two points. First is the doctrine of illusoriness applied in the online context. This is a slightly surprising development as the doctrine is not widely used due to the fundamental guidepost that contracts ought to be enforced whenever possible. Second, browsewrap contracts[198] are more likely to trigger a finding of illusoriness because mere access of a website is found to be user assent.[199] The simple fix is to use a click-through setup, a step that is widely used and also gaining more traction.

Another concern with the modification of a TOU emerges when company employees communicate with users in a way that may

---

196. *See Blizzard End User License Agreement, supra* note 18 (*"Rejection.* If you decline to accept the New Agreement, or if you cannot comply with the terms of the New Agreement, you will no longer be permitted to use the Platform or Account(s).").

197. *In re* Zappos.com Inc., Customer Data Sec. Breach Litig., 893 F. Supp. 2d 1058 (D. Nev. 2012).

198. *See* Mark A. Lemley, *Terms of Use*, 91 MINN. L. REV. 459, 460 (2006) ("[B] rowsewrap licenses, in which the user does not see the contract at all but in which the license terms provide that using a Web site constitutes agreement to a contract whether the user knows it or not.").

199. *See* Pollstar v. Gigmania Ltd., 170 F. Supp. 2d 974, 981 (E.D. Cal. 2000) ("A shrinkwrap license appears on the screen when the CD or diskette is inserted and does not let the consumer proceed without indicating acceptance. By contrast, a browse wrap license is part of the web site and the user assents to the contract when the user visits the web site.").

clarify or define their contractual relationship. In a recent case, James Varga, a well-known broadcaster on the game streaming service Twitch, filed suit against Twitch alleging, among other causes of action, Twitch breached its contractual relationship with Varga by terminating his account for broadcasting content in violation of the terms of service, which had previously been discussed with a Twitch employee.[200]

C. Privity of Contract

Two shortcomings of TOU are that they do not create rights or obligations between or among gamers themselves, nor do they bind third parties who have not signed or agreed to any agreement.[201] The former scenario was recently before a U.S. court: players sued to enforce contractual promises made by other players to the virtual world creator in *Hernandez v. Internet Gaming Entertainment*.[202] The latter scenario was also before the Ninth Circuit Court of Appeals: MDY, a third-party software developer, sued Blizzard Entertainment, the creator of *World of Warcraft*, seeking a declaratory judgment on Blizzard's claim that MDY tortiously interfered with contracts between Blizzard and *World of Warcraft* customers.[203] The following is a discussion of the problems that privity causes when digital game operators attempt to govern their digital world populations by contract.

1. Privity in Digital Games

Privity has not commonly been discussed in relation to digital games because of the perception that everyone who interacts

---

200. *See* Complaint at 6–7, James Varga v. Twitch Interactive, Inc., No. CGC-18-564337 (Cal. App. Dep't Super. Ct. 2018).

201. For a complete treatment of the inherent problems when using contracts to govern virtual communities (upon which this section's analysis relies), see generally Fairfield, *supra* note 4, at 450.

202. *See* Complaint, Hernandez v. Internet Gaming Entm't, Ltd., No. 07-21403 (S.D. Fla. May 31, 2007); Joint Stipulation, Hernandez v. Internet Gaming Entm't, Ltd., No. 07-21403 (S.D. Fla. Aug. 26, 2008) (IGE U.S. agreed it "will not engage in the selling of [*World of Warcraft*] virtual property or currency . . . for [5 years].").

203. *See* MDY Indus., LLC v. Blizzard Entm't, Inc., 629 F.3d 928 (9th Cir. 2010) (holding that players directly infringed copyright despite the essential step defense; players' violation of the TOU by using a bot did not infringe Blizzard's copyright).

with a digital world must sign their terms and agreements with the game operator. The doctrine of privity provides that a contract may not impose obligations on persons who are not parties to it.[204] Because the corporations that create digital games use terms and agreements to regulate signatory obligations and entitlements, digital game members have traditionally been limited to the methods of recourse listed in the agreement when disagreements arise among them.[205]

However, there are currently two primary arguments available for parties wishing to address the "privity problem." The first concerns expressed or implied third-party beneficiary clauses. The second raises the issue of intentional or tortious interference of contract by third parties.

2. Third-Party Beneficiary Clauses

Third-party beneficiary terms allow parties to benefit from agreements to which they are neither obligors nor direct beneficiaries (e.g., persons to whom performance is to be rendered).[206] When identifying third-party beneficiaries, courts have differentiated between "direct" and "incidental" beneficiaries.[207] Direct beneficiaries are intended by the contracting parties to benefit from the contract, while incidental beneficiaries receive a benefit from the contract that is not expressly intended by the contracting parties.[208] For a plaintiff to have a cause of action, the current common law rule requires that an intention to benefit be indicated by the

---

204. *See* G.H. TREITEL, TREITEL ON THE LAW OF CONTRACT (11th ed. 2003).

205. *See, e.g., Blizzard End User License Agreement, supra* note 18; *see also* Linden Lab *Terms of Service, supra* note 18.

206. *See* BLACK'S LAW DICTIONARY 165 (8th ed. 2004) ("[T]hird-party beneficiary. A person who, though not a party to a contract, stands to benefit from the contract's performance.").

207. *See* A.E.I. Music Network, Inc. v. Bus. Computers, Inc., 290 F.3d 952, 955 (7th Cir. 2002) ("Against this conclusion the Board argues that A.E.I. was merely an 'incidental' and not a 'direct' beneficiary of the Board's contract with BCI. Third parties, that is, persons who are not parties to a contract, are permitted to enforce the contract if and only if the parties made clear in the contract an intention that they be permitted to do so.").

208. *See* Am. United Logistics, Inc. v. Catellus Dev. Corp., 319 F.3d 921, 930 (7th Cir. 2003) ("A direct third-party beneficiary is a person who, although not a party to the contract, the contracting parties *intended* to benefit from the contract.");

contract itself.[209] Therefore, only "direct third-party beneficiaries" may benefit from the rule.[210] It is against this standard that *World of Warcraft* players claimed to be intended, direct beneficiaries of promises not to gold-farm, and such claims would have been tested.[211] The case ultimately settled, with IGE agreeing to "not engage in the selling of World of Warcraft virtual property or currency (commonly referred to as 'gold,' 'gold farming,' 'real money trade' or 'RMT') for a period of five (5) years."[212]

Third-party beneficiary clauses might also be used to regulate behavior among players in virtual worlds.[213] For example, each player could contractually acknowledge every other player as a beneficiary of a promise not to engage in offensive conduct. In practice, however, there are several problems with the third-party beneficiary approach, which results in an aversion by most

---

see also id. ("By contrast, an incidental third-party beneficiary is a person who, not a party to the contract, receives a benefit from the contract unintended by the contracting parties.").

209. However, this intention can be inferred rather than explicit. *See* Michael Risch, *Virtual Third Parties*, 25 SANTA CLARA COMPUTER & HIGH TECH. L.J. 415 (2009).

210. *See, e.g.*, Lory v. Fed. Ins. Co., 122 Fed. Appx. 314, 317 (9th Cir. 2005) ("[I]n order for a person to recover as a third-party beneficiary of a contract, an intention to benefit that person must be indicated in the contract itself . . . The contemplated benefit must be both intentional and direct . . . and it must definitely appear that the parties intend to recognize the third party as a primary party in interest.") (quoting Nahom v. Blue Cross & Blue Shield of Ariz., Inc., 180 Ariz. 548 (Ariz. Ct. App. 1994)).

211. *See* Fairfield, *supra* note 4, at 453 ("Third-party beneficiary clauses require that the beneficiary be the intended, not just the incidental, beneficiary of a contractual promise. There was no language in the World of Warcraft EULA to support such a designation.").

212. *See* Benjamin Duranske, *Hernandez v. IGE Settles, IGE U.S. Confirms It Will Not "Engage in the Selling of WoW Virtual Property or Currency" for Five Years; Class Action Still Possible*, VIRTUALLY BLIND, Aug. 27, 2008, http://virtuallyblind. com/2008/08/27/hernandez-ige-settles/.

213. *See* Fairfield, *supra* note 4, at 449 ("It is, of course, possible for [the virtual world operator] to use its bottleneck status (everyone who enters the virtual world must, after all, sign a EULA with [it]; but, as will be shown, not everyone who affects virtual worlds must do so) to act as a clearing house for the legal obligations that most community members want. [The operator] might require that each signatory designate every other signatory as a third-party beneficiary of any promises to [the operator].").

operators to its use.[214] First, third-party beneficiary terms allow non-signatories to benefit from, but not be bound by, an agreement.[215] Next, the industry rarely uses third-party beneficiary clauses in TOU agreements because of the difficulty of limiting enforcement of such terms to nonfrivolous claims.[216] Digital game operators may not want their customers suing one another over offensive chat, for example. Finally, rights created by third-party beneficiary clauses are still contract rights and give rise to contract damages (i.e., money damages) at law. Contract damages are ineffective where injunctive relief would be most efficient (e.g., non-harassment).[217]

3. Circumventing Privity through Tort

Another unanswered question is whether and how a digital game creator might use tort rules in conjunction with its TOU to affect the behavior of other companies that may wish to sell to the creator's customers. Suppose a company, A, has a contract with its customer, B. Suppose C, a software developer, writes software that permits B to violate the terms of the A–B contract. Can A sue

---

214. *See id.* at 449–50 ("[A]s an industry-wide practice, virtual-world creators do not in fact include third-party beneficiary terms, and it is worth asking why. It may be that corporations simply do not, for example, want customers suing each other over a scandalous chat in virtual-world channels. Or, corporations may not want to lose any customers.").

215. *See id.* at 449 ("Third-party-beneficiary designations only come to the aid of parties who wish to benefit from other people's promises to the creator of the virtual world. But that represents merely half of the problem. There is no way to *bind* a party who is not signatory to a contract."); *see also* Thomas Merrill & Henry Smith, *The Property/Contract Interface*, 101 COLUM. L. REV. 773, 776–77 (2001) ("[C]ontract rights are *in personam*; that is, they bind only the parties to the contact.") (emphasis added).

216. *See Blizzard End User License Agreement, supra* note 18; *see also Second Life Terms and Conditions, supra* note 18; Linden Lab *Terms of Service, supra* note 18.

217. *See* Fairfield, *supra* note 4, at 450 ("Further, rights created by third-party beneficiary clauses are still contractual rights, and therefore give rise to contract remedies. Causes of action in contract law usually give rise to money damages. It would be impractical to use the law to keep someone off of your land, for example, if your only option was to bring a series of lawsuits to receive monetary compensation for actual damage to the trampled grass."); *see also* Adam Cohn & Stuart Meyer, *Open Source Business Models*, 916 PLI/PAT 83, 92 (2007) ("[S]pecific performance is an extraordinary remedy and contract law has a strong bias against injunctive relief.").

C, despite lack of privity between the two? One way to do so is to claim that C intentionally interfered with the A–B relationship, thus effectively extending to C the binding effect of the A–B contract. The preceding illustration is how Blizzard successfully bound MDY to its own EULA.[218]

Intentional or tortious interference claims allow for tort liability to compensate for pecuniary loss when the party suffering a loss can show that a third party interfered with a contract and induced a breach. The claim requires a showing that a valid contract existed, the third party had knowledge of the contract, and the third party intentionally and improperly interfered with that contract.[219] Unlike contract claims, a successful intentional interference claim allows the prevailing party to recover both compensatory damages (either from the tortfeasor or from the breaching party, but not both) and punitive damages.[220]

Claims of intentional interference suffer from many of the same deficiencies as third-party beneficiary theories. While intentional interference assertions allow plaintiffs to circumvent privity arguments, they also allow plaintiffs to assert claims against third parties despite the fact that such third parties never agreed to abide by the terms of the agreement with which they supposedly interfered. The *MDY* district court effectively bound MDY to the EULA Blizzard had entered into with its own users by granting Blizzard's motion for summary judgment on the tortious interference claim.[221] The court determined that MDY knowingly assisted Blizzard customers in violating the EULA, and profited thereby.[222]

---

218. This hypothetical is based loosely on the facts of MDY Indus., LLC v. Blizzard Entm't, Inc., 629 F.3d 928 (9th Cir. 2010).

219. Guidiville Band of Pomo Indians v. NGV Gaming, Ltd., 531 F.3d 767, 774 (9th Cir. 2008).

220. *See generally* Texaco Inc. v. Pennzoil Co., 729 S.W.2d 768 (Tex. Ct. App. 1987).

221. MDY Indus., LLC v. Blizzard Entm't, Inc., No. CV-06-2555-PHX-DGC, 2008 U.S. Dist. LEXIS 53988, at *51 (D. Ariz. July 14, 2008) ("Because the other requirements for tortious interferences have been satisfied, the Court will grant summary judgment in favor of Blizzard with respect to MDY's liability on this claim.").

222. *See id.* at *46–51 (determining whether MDY's conduct was proper, the court concluded that the nature of MDY's conduct was to knowingly assist other players to violate the EULA for MDY's own gain, and the motive of MDY's conduct was "clear[ly] profit").

On appeal, the Ninth Circuit overruled the grant of summary judgment due to a genuine issue of material fact.[223] Whether EULAs can be so broadly applied to third-party software developers who lack the requisite knowledge and intent appears to remain an open question.[224]

D. Minors

Children are a growing and important demographic for digital game operators. Companies responded with numerous themed digital games.[225] Children are a concern for game operators, though. For example, children increasingly use money within games, sometimes with unfortunate results.[226] Their status as minors poses limitations on a digital game operator's ability to enforce TOU provisions if they are under 18. Children also pose additional risks due to requirements imposed by federal law, such as the Children's Online Privacy Protection Act (COPPA).[227] These

---

223. *See* MDY Indus., LLC v. Blizzard Entm't, Inc., No. 09-15932, No. 09-16044, 2011 U.S. App. LEXIS 3428, at *63–64 (9th Cir. Feb. 17, 2011) ("Blizzard is entitled to summary judgment if there are no triable issues of material fact as to the fourth element of its tortious interference claim. . . . We conclude that summary judgment was inappropriate here, because [there is] . . . a genuine issue of material fact.") (citations omitted).

224. *See* MDY Indus., LLC v. Blizzard Entm't, Inc., No. CV-06-2555-PHX-DGC, 2011 U.S. Dist. LEXIS 68735, at *7–8 (D. Ariz. June 27, 2011) ("The Ninth Circuit specifically remanded for a trial on the tortious interference claim, finding that 'there are triable issues of material fact.' . . . The Court finds that a trial should be held on both the tortious interference claim and the issue of personal liability.") (quoting *MDY*, 2011 U.S. App. LEXIS 3428, at *63–64).

225. Often, purchasing a specific toy will grant the child entry into these virtual worlds by using an online passcode or a USB key. For example, Ganz, the creator of Webkinz, sells stuffed animals that each come with a unique identifier that enables the child to unlock virtual representations of these pets at http://www.webkinz .com. *See* Joseph Pisani, *Toys Take to the Web*, CNBC, Feb. 19, 2008, 11:15 a.m., http://www.cnbc.com/id/23235775.

226. *See* I.B. *ex rel.* Fife v. Facebook, Inc., No. C 12-1894 CW, 2012 WL 5303297 (N.D. Cal. Oct. 25, 2012) (discussing a class action on behalf of minors that used their parents credit and debit cards to purchase Facebook credits and the belief of the minors they were only buying virtual currency and not charging their parents cards repeatedly without their consent).

227. *See* 15 U.S.C. §§ 6501–6506 (2018). COPPA imposes requirements upon website operators or online services directed to children under the age of 13 or where there is actual knowledge they are collecting personal information online from children under 13.

contracts assume the user has the legal capacity to enter into the contract, something difficult to guarantee with online games.

The law on minors in online spaces remains in transition because of the novel issues of online environments: in-game monetization strategies, mobile developments,[228] and expansion of online tracking technologies. These concerns have serious implications for contractual governance and upcoming regulations from the FTC.[229] Game operators need to be cautious about current and future practices in contract drafting because of developing case law and upcoming updates to the central piece of legislation affecting minors and online activity.[230]

Courts are reluctant to enforce contracts against minors because of policy considerations. Children are believed to be less likely to understand what they are agreeing to and are more likely to make impulsive and unwise decisions. Accordingly, common law has firmly established—and state statutes have reaffirmed— that a minor may disaffirm a contract at any point up to and within a reasonable time after reaching the age of majority, thereby rendering the contract a nullity.[231] Notably, an agreement entered into by a minor is *voidable*, not *void*. Unless the child seeks to void the contract, the contracting parties are bound by its terms. However, some (but not all) courts hold that a child who "intentionally" misrepresents his or her age may not void his or her contracts.[232] These courts generally require the misrepresentation to be affirmative. The mere failure to give notice of infancy is usually not sufficient to defeat the minor defense.[233]

---

228. *See* Consent Decree and Order for Civil Penalties, Injunction, and Other Relief, United States v. W3 Innovations, LLC, No. CV11-03958 (N.D. Cal. Sept. 8, 2011), https://www.ftc.gov/sites/default/files/documents/cases/2011/09/110908w3order .pdf (finding W3 Innovations, a company that develops mobile phone games, violated COPPA by illegally collecting and disclosing personal information from tens of thousands of children under age 13 without their parents prior consent).

229. *See* News Release, FTC, FTC Seeks Comments on Additional Proposed Revisions to Children's Online Privacy Protection Rule (Aug. 1, 2012), http://www .ftc.gov/opa/2012/08/coppa.shtm.

230. *Id.*

231. *See* MacGreal v. Taylor, 167 U.S. 688, 696 (1897).

232. 43 C.J.S. Infants § 151 (2008).

233. *See* Woodall v. Grant & Co., 9 S.E.2d 95, 95 (Ga. Ct. App. 1940); *see also* Uhlmann Grain Co. of Tex. v. Wilson, 68 S.W.2d 281, 283 (Tex. Ct. App. 1933).

The enforceability of terms or agreements against a minor has not been extensively tested in the courts, particularly against minors who affirmatively misrepresent their age to gain access to virtual worlds, so its validity remains uncertain. However, existing case law suggests that although contracts signed by minors are generally voidable at the minor's discretion, courts will not allow a minor to take the benefits of a contract without the burdens of conditions or stipulations in the contract. For example, a minor who obtains medical treatment under an insurance contract cannot return the services he or she receives, but if the minor recovers the value of those services from a tortfeasor, he or she would be required to return the money upon disaffirmance of the contract.[234] Likewise, a minor cannot avoid obligations under a clickwrap agreement[235] for educational software while still maintaining the benefits of a passing grade in a class from use of the software.[236] Thus, EULAs are not *per se* unenforceable against minors, but instead focus on the individual facts of each case. Other factors that are likely to influence the outcome may include the nature of the affirmative act and misrepresentation, notice given to the minor, language and presentation of the EULA and what it purports to do, and the type of harm. For example, the exception may hold for a teenager who affirmatively clicks on a box that falsely claims he or she is 18 or older to gain access to a virtual world intended for adults only. However, a 12-year-old girl who gains access to a virtual world intended for children by simply clicking on a box that states she agrees to the EULA may not satisfy the requisite intentional and affirmative act if there is language buried in the agreement that requires a minor to seek parental consent before accessing the virtual world. Accordingly, game operators may not

---

234. *See, e.g.*, Hamrick v. Hosp. Servs. Corp. of R.I., 110 R.I. 634 (R.I. 1972); *see also* 5 WILLISTON ON CONTRACTS § 9.14 (4th ed. 2018).

235. *See* Lemley, *supra* note 198, at 459 ("[C]lickwrap licenses [where] an online user clicks 'I agree' to standard form terms.").

236. *See* A.V. v. iParadigms, Ltd. Liab. Co., 544 F. Supp. 2d 473 (E.D. Va. 2008) (holding that plaintiffs, who were high school students, a fact that the court focused heavily on, cannot use the infancy defense to void their contractual obligations under a clickwrap agreement for educational software while still maintaining the benefits of the agreement), *aff'd in part, rev'd in part*, 562 F.3d 630 (4th Cir. 2009).

be able to enforce a EULA against a child or the parent when the child successfully bypasses minimum parental control measures to gain access to the game.[237]

The ability of digital game operators to minimize liability and overcome the defense of infancy may depend on the level of safeguards in place intended to prevent unauthorized access by a minor. These may include security measures to verify age and ensure the parent remains actively involved during the registration process. The more difficult it is for a minor to circumvent these safeguards, the more likely the minor will be found to have affirmatively and intentionally misrepresented his or her age by bypassing such safeguards. As a result, a game operator may be able to avoid the defense of infancy by successfully arguing this exception to enforce the terms of its EULA.

III. Potential Resolutions to TOU Limitations in Digital Games

Digital game operators remain best equipped to regulate in-game disputes, which generally result from user misbehavior. However, a game operator's ability to effectively handle these disputes, which are numerous, is not without limits or inherent inequities. As these games continue to grow in popularity and attract more users, a system for online dispute resolution managed primarily by the players themselves may provide a novel, yet fair and cost-effective industry solution for regulating user behavior in gaming communities. It is also appropriate to examine industry solutions that properly balance the rights of operators and their users under

---

237. This leads to impacts beyond enforcement of a particular contract, collection of payment for virtual goods, or compliance under COPPA. For example, Facebook noted in its annual filings, "Our data limitations may affect our understanding of certain details of our business. For example, while user-provided data indicates a decline in usage among younger users, this age data is unreliable because a disproportionate number of our younger users register with an inaccurate age. Accordingly, our understanding of usage by age group may not be complete." *See* Facebook, Inc. Annual Report (Form10-K) (Dec. 31, 2015), *available at* https://www.sec.gov/Archives/edgar/data/1326801/000132680116000043/fb-12312015x10k.htm.

TOU, particularly with regards to a digital game operator's most powerful self-help remedy—the ability to suspend or terminate a user's account. The industry's continued reliance on terms and conditions that favor operators invites close scrutiny by the courts and risks these provisions becoming unenforceable as contracts of adhesion unless operators take steps to rebalance these one-sided terms. In many cases, it will be in a game operator's interest to adjust their terms in favor of transparency and balance prior to court scrutiny. Careful monitoring of user complaints, and complaints filed with consumer advocacy organizations such as the Better Business Bureau, as well as state attorneys general, may well prove worthwhile; both to prevent such complaints from being escalated to lawsuits, and as a guide to TOU improvements.[238]

While the industry is best positioned to continue regulating user misbehavior, it will still be necessary for the courts to step in when industry fails to address novel issues, particularly those issues concerning digital goods. Possible solutions to these issues may be found by applying familiar common law property protections to fairly allocate rights between users and digital game operators. Finally, a natural alternative to judicial intervention is legislative action that can build on consumer protection laws to enact rules and regulations that specifically address digital goods.

A. Industry Practices

TOU will continue to remain the digital game industry's preferred governance tool for resolving the vast majority of online game disputes even though users themselves have limited enforcement rights against other users under such arrangements.[239] This practice of TOU reliance is not unique to the game industry but is followed by website operators in general that prefer the ease of use of one legal document to govern a host of services performed online.

---

238. *See, e.g.*, Charlie Hall, *Star Citizen's Developers Met with Nation's Leading Consumer Protection Group*, POLYGON, Feb. 12, 2018, 3:30 p.m., https://www.polygon .com/2018/2/12/16997396/star-citizen-better-business-bureau-terms-of-service -changes ("[R]epresentatives from Cloud Imperium Games (CIG) and Roberts Space Industries (RSI) met with the Better Business Bureau (BBB) of Los Angeles and Silicon Valley. . . . They discussed, among other things, ways to improve transparency. . . . Changes have also been made to CIG's terms of service."). *See also* Kain, *supra* note 26.

239. *See* discussion *supra* Section II.C.

In the case of game operators, the vast majority of disputes that arise during a game are caused by user misbehavior (e.g., verbal abuse, cheating). As creators, managers, and experts of their own games, it follows that operators are in the best position to regulate user misbehavior. In doing so, these operators typically prescribe a code of conduct, often included in the TOU itself or incorporated by reference, to guide its users on appropriate behavior during gameplay. This code is enforced by an operator's most powerful self-help remedy—the ability to suspend or terminate a user's account.[240] However, an inherent limitation of this practice is that the players themselves cannot directly enforce their rights against other users because the TOU is an agreement solely between the player and the operator. Despite several attempts to assert third-party rights under a TOU,[241] players must still continue to rely on operators to enforce their rights against other users even though account suspensions or terminations may not properly vindicate the rights of a user victimized by deeply hurtful, or even defamatory, misconduct.

As these digital games continue to evolve and attract millions of players that demand a positive and enjoyable game experience, it is likely that the digital game industry will look to unconventional and alternative dispute mechanisms governed predominantly by the players themselves to effectively address inherent inequities of relying on game operators alone to resolve user behavior disputes, and perhaps reduce the high costs of enforcement in the process.[242] In 2011, Riot Games' Tribunal, which grew as a natural

---

240. *See, e.g.,* Charlie Hall, *PUBG Anti-Cheat Maker Banned a Million Players in January Alone,* POLYGON, Feb. 5, 2018, 12:15 p.m., https://www.polygon.com/2018/2/5/16973984/pubg-cheat-ban-1-million-january-china-battleye; Luke Plunkett, *PUBG Banned Over 1 Million Cheaters Last Month,* KOTAKU, Feb. 5, 2018, 6:20 p.m., https://kotaku.com/pubg-banned-over-1-million-cheaters-last-month-1822741674; *see also* Mark Langshaw, *Blizzard Suspends Over 5,000 Accounts,* DIGITAL SPY, Oct. 2, 2010, http://www.digitalspy.com/gaming/news/a279886/blizzard-suspends-over-5000-accounts/; Jason Schreier, *Blizzard Bans Starcraft II Player for Cheating Against AI,* WIRED, Oct. 10, 2010, 3:09 p.m., https://www.wired.com/2010/10/starcraft-ban/.

241. *See* discussion *supra* Section II.C.2.

242. *See* Eric Caoili, *Blizzard Awarded $6 Million in Glider Bot Case,* GAMASUTRA, Oct. 1, 2008, http://www.gamasutra.com/php-bin/news_index.php?story=20475#.UOczi2_5gX0 (reporting that Blizzard Entertainment was awarded $6 million in compensatory damages by a U.S. district court that presumably was intended

extension of its Code of Conduct, enabled its own *League of Legends* gamer community to self-regulate themselves through a form of online dispute resolution.[243] By equipping credentialed players with the ability to review evidence (e.g., chat logs), interpret and apply Riot's Code of Conduct, and subsequently vote on a course of action for Riot's representatives to take (e.g., "pardon" or "punish"), Riot tried to empower its players to act as arbitrators to handle the company's own disputes. Riot had hoped to introduce objective measures to improve the accuracy of a ruling for user misconduct by crowdsourcing a case with multiple voting recommendations by different players.[244] However, in 2014, Riot Games ended the Tribunal system because the system "was focused entirely on punishments," and moved too slowly.[245] There were reports that Riot may bring back the Tribunal system,[246] but has yet to formally do so.

While the TOU remains an effective vehicle for resolving user misbehavior, there still remain those unique disputes that expose one-sided TOU provisions (including termination and modification rights) and demand compromise by the industry. The *Bragg* court's close scrutiny of Linden Lab's overly broad termination provision provides a cautionary tale for digital game operators because it supported the court's substantive unconscionability holding.[247]

---

to compensate Blizzard for the enforcement costs it incurred to prevent MDY Industries from continuing to deploy its Glider bot software and enable *World of Warcraft* players to "cheat" through the use of automated, repetitive actions (e.g., scavenging loot)).

243. *See League of Legends: The Tribunal Policy, supra* note 23.

244. *See* posting by Pendragon (Director of Player Experience), *The Tribunal: The First Year*, RIOT GAMES, May 25, 2012, http://forums.na.leagueoflegends.com /board/showthread.php?t=2151902&page=1 (reporting that more than 47 million votes were cast in the Tribunal's first year, with 51 percent of cases resulting in a guilty verdict and only 5.7 percent leading to a permanent ban from the *League of Legends*, suggesting that such a large amount of votes lead to fair and equitable results).

245. *See* Yannick LeJacq, *League of Legends Is Bringing Back an Old System to Deal with Jerks*, KOTAKU, May 4, 2015, 6:15 p.m., https://kotaku.com/league-of -legends-is-bringing-back-an-old-system-to-dea-1702108970.

246. *See id.*

247. *See* Bragg v. Linden Research, Inc., 487 F. Supp. 2d 593, 608 (E.D. Pa. 2007) (finding that Linden's termination provision that provided "Linden has the right at any time for any reason or no reason to suspend or terminate your Account,

Even though the ability to terminate or suspend user accounts is perhaps the most useful and effective self-help tool available to game operators, the *Bragg* court's decision encourages operators to avoid overly broad provisions in their TOU that enable account termination for any reason. These actions by operators seem all the more necessary given the industry's shift from an emphasis on paid subscription models to microtransactions where consumer spending on digital goods continues to grow ever more robust. Consequently, account termination becomes a much more costly punishment for gamers whose account values continue to rise from these purchases.[248] An obvious response would be for operators to, at the very least, modify these provisions and provide specific grounds for account suspension or termination beyond the obvious and general reasons.[249] Perhaps taking a cue from the *Bragg* court's holding, as it likely did for revising its arbitration clause that now provides for more "neutral" rights between the parties,[250] Linden's TOS at least defines the grounds for account suspension but stipulates that any "Virtual Tender will automatically terminate."[251] Simi-

---

terminate this Agreement, and/or refuse any and all current or future use of the Service without notice or liability to you" was one of the one-sided provisions that made the user agreement substantively unconscionable).

248. *See* Rip Empson, *Study: U.S. Consumer Spending on Virtual Goods Grew to $2.3 Billion in 2011*, TECHCRUNCH, Feb. 29, 2012, https://techcrunch.com/2012/02/29/virtual-good-market-boom/ (reporting that consumer spending on virtual goods reached $2.3 billion in 2011, which is double the amount spent in 2009, and equates to an average of $64 spent by each gamer on virtual goods in 2011).

249. *See, e.g.*, Linden Lab *Terms of Service, supra* note 18, § 6 ("You agree to abide by certain rules of conduct, including any applicable community standards for portion of the Service you are using and other rules prohibiting illegal and other practices that Linden Lab *deems* harmful.") (emphasis added).

250. *See id.* § 10. Likely in response to the *Bragg* court's close scrutiny of its arbitration provision, particularly the high costs of arbitration it imposed, Linden Lab's current arbitration provision (1) states that its goal is to provide its users with a "neutral and cost-effective means" of resolving disputes quickly, (2) limits the application of arbitration to claims less than $10,000, and (3) enables either the operator or the user to elect arbitration through an alternative dispute resolution provider "mutually agreed upon by the parties." *Id.*

251. *See* Linden Lab *Terms of Service, supra* note 18, § 5.5. Linden Lab's TOU provides several grounds for account suspension or termination beyond those just for broad violations of its TOU alone, including protecting the "best interests" of *Second Life*'s community or if any user poses an "unacceptable risk" to this community (e.g., registered sex offenders).

lar concerns regarding the ability to unilaterally amend any TOU provision,[252] a practice followed by most web operators in general, can be resolved by ensuring users are properly notified of any *material* changes to an operator's TOU, such that any continued use by a gamer after receiving such notice is deemed a consent to such modified terms.[253] These approaches, while minimal, are certainly a step in the right direction for the industry to follow.

However, even in the face of mounting pressure for the digital game industry to rebalance one-sided TOU provisions, it is unlikely that game operators will ever voluntarily give up these broad, unilateral powers, unless specifically required by a court, or legislation, to do so. In fact, most game operators still retain broad termination rights despite the *Bragg* court's holding.[254] The industry's insistence on continuing this practice has the legal risk of inviting more aggressive judicial and legislative measures in the future. Perhaps this is a risk game operators are willing to take to preserve their most powerful self-help remedies.

B. Judicial Intervention

While digital game operators remain in the best position to regulate the vast majority of disputes that arise in their games, disputes over digital goods and currency will likely be resolved by the courts because of the unique issues raised. At present, there remains little legal guidance (both statutory and judicial) as to what rights a user has in "its" digital goods (if any) despite the digital game industry's heavy reliance on microtransactions. As a result, operators are free to determine who owns digital goods and, unsurprisingly, they choose to retain ownership. However, this practice will almost certainly be challenged by a court in the

---

252. *See* discussion *supra* Section II.B.

253. *See* Mojang *Terms and Conditions, supra* note 58 ("We may change these Account Terms from time to time, if we have reason to. . . . We'll inform you of the change before it takes effect, either by posting a notice on our Website or some other reasonable way.").

254. *See, e.g.*, Zynga, *Terms of Service* [hereinafter Zynga *Terms of Service*], http://company.zynga.com/legal/terms-of-service (last amended May 21, 2018) ("ZYNGA MAY, IN ITS SOLE DISCREATION, LIMIT, SUSPEND, TERMINATE, MODIFY, OR DELETE ACCOUNTS. . . .").

future and likely resolved by allowing a user to at least retain some rights to his or her digital goods.

One proposal to resolve disputes over digital goods is for judges to apply common law principles to conduct that "takes place" in digital games.[255] After all, many real-world property issues and land disputes also occur in digital games. Arguments in favor of this approach provide that familiar rules and guidance will lower information costs and create clear expectations when addressing digital goods issues.[256] Furthermore, the iterative, incremental, experimental features of judicial decision making are well suited to solve rapidly emerging technological issues that arise from digital goods and that may go unforeseen and lost in a body of technology legislation.[257] Currently, TOU that address digital goods do so in a licensing framework that does not actually grant users a property right in digital goods, only a license to use those items.[258] Little guidance exists for the treatment of digital goods because the law has not defined the relationship between TOU and users over digital goods, leaving it almost entirely to the game operators to determine what rights users have over digital goods.[259] For example, the *Bragg* court declared that the case was about virtual property, but it still remains unclear what rights users have to the digital goods they create, buy, or sell in *Second Life*.[260] In fact, what is clear is that users have little rights, if any, to these digital goods, evidenced by a game operator's ability to terminate a user's account with no obligation to refund the monetary value of the digital good.[261] It

---

255. *See* Fairfield, *supra* note 4, at 465–68.

256. *See id.* at 459.

257. *See id.* at 466.

258. *See* Linden Lab *Terms of Service*, *supra* note 18, § 5.5 ("All licenses granted by Linden Lab to use the Service, *including any Virtual Tender* will automatically terminate.") (emphasis added).

259. *See* Fairfield, *supra* note 4, at 465.

260. *See id.* Linden argued, pursuant to the terms of its TOU, that Bragg only held a license right to the virtual land held in his account, while Bragg contended that Linden was engaging in double-speak by publicly advertising that it was selling "ownership" of land while this licensing scheme remained buried in the fine print of its TOU.

261. *See, e.g., Blizzard End User License Agreement*, *supra* note 18; *Second Life Terms and Conditions*, *supra* note 18, § 5.5 ("All licenses granted by Linden Lab to use the Service, *including any Virtual Tender* will automatically terminate.")

follows that a court applying common law property principles may determine that while it may be onerous to return the monetary equivalent of all purchased digital *items* in a user's account, the user should, at the very least, be entitled to receive the monetary equivalent of the digital *currency* held in an account that is terminated for reasons unrelated to a user's TOU breach (e.g., a game operator's discontinuation of services).

Accordingly, common law property principles that govern ownership and possession may be able to resolve these disputes by articulating the proper allocation of rights between digital game operators and their users over digital goods, and thereby establish clear expectations for both parties. Such expectations may even provide a financial incentive for operators who may be leaving money on the table by not granting users additional rights to their digital goods, evidenced by the strong demand for digital music files once anti-copying measures were removed and users were free to listen to their music files across multiple platforms.[262]

C. Legislative Action

The use of state consumer protection statutes to limit the enforceability of TOU forum selection and choice-of-law clauses suggests that a legislative response may be a workable solution for resolving digital game disputes, particularly those concerning virtual property. This solution may offer a response to concerns about (1) the competency of judges handling novel virtual property issues; (2) the length of time it takes to create and establish case

---

(emphasis added); Zynga *Terms of Service, supra* note 254 ("ZYNGA MAY, IN ITS SOLE DISCREATION, LIMIT, SUSPEND, TERMINATE, MODIFY, OR DELETE ACCOUNTS. . . .").

262. *See, e.g.,* Brad Stone, *Want to Copy iTunes Music? Go Ahead, Apple Says,* N.Y. TIMES, Jan. 6, 2009, http://www.nytimes.com/2009/01/07/technology /companies/07apple.html. On January 6, 2009, Apple announced a deal with the major music labels that enabled Apple to remove digital rights management (DRM) technology from its iTunes music downloads allowing users to freely copy and transfer songs to non-Apple devices. In exchange, Apple agreed to change its pricing from 99 cents for all songs to a sliding price scale that went from 69 cents a song to $1.29 a song depending on song popularity. *See also* Paul Resnikoff, *Apple Has Now Sold 15 Billion iTunes Songs . . .,* DIGITAL MUSIC NEWS, June 6, 2011, http://archive.is/N78H. After Apple announced its removal of DRM, its sales of iTunes songs nearly doubled in two years, increasing from eight billion in 2009 to 15 billion in 2011.

precedent suitable to properly address these unique issues; and (3) the narrow court holdings that leave many issues over virtual property unresolved and left to private settlement by the parties.[263] However, a legislative response is not without its own concerns given that existing state consumer protection laws that broadly prohibit unfair and deceptive trade practices are only a blunt tool in enforcing specific issues raised by rights to digital goods.

As a response to these overly broad and vague statutes, laws and regulations could be enacted and promulgated at the state or federal level to build or expand upon state consumer protection laws by specifically addressing digital game activities, including the purchase and sale of digital goods. Federal efforts to address privacy, specifically the creation of a Consumer Privacy Bill of Rights, may provide a model for digital goods because it builds upon an existing framework of fundamental privacy values, flexible and adaptable common law protections, and consumer protection statutes.[264] Likewise, efforts can be made by federal and state officials to build upon a similar framework that currently exists for an individual's fundamental property rights. However, unlike privacy law, which has attracted much more national attention, it will likely take years before Congress, state legislatures, or regulatory agencies specifically address issues related to virtual property even though a significant number of other countries' regulatory bodies have already done so.[265] During this time, it is critical that

---

263. *See* Fairfield, *supra* note 4, at 467–68.

264. *See* THE WHITE HOUSE, CONSUMER DATA PRIVACY IN A NETWORKED WORLD: A FRAMEWORK FOR PROTECTING PRIVACY AND PROMOTING INNOVATION IN THE GLOBAL DIGITAL ECONOMY (2012), *available at* https://www.hsdl.org/?view&did=700959 (describing the White House's issuance of a Consumer Privacy Bill of Rights as a blueprint for privacy in the digital age that builds upon "fundamental privacy values, flexible and adaptable common law protections and consumer protection statutes, Federal Trade Commission (FTC) enforcement, and policy development").

265. *See, e.g.,* Geoffrey A. Fowler & Juying Qin, *QQ: China's New Coin of the Realm?*, WALL ST. J., Mar. 30, 2007, 12:01 a.m., http://online.wsj.com/article /SB117519670114653518.html (reporting that Chinese regulators have barred users from trading virtual currency for real money). *See also* Cho Mu-hyun, *Korea Prohibits Trade of Online Game Items*, KOREA TIMES, June 13, 2012, 5:14 p.m., http:// www.koreatimes.co.kr/www/news/tech/2012/06/129_112964.html (reporting that the Korean Ministry of Culture, Sports, and Tourism had announced that it was planning to halt all virtual item trades through issuance of a law that would penalize violators up to 50 million won and five years in jail). *See also* Mikael

legal practitioners and members of the digital games community be active in providing lawmakers with input to ensure that laws and regulations governing digital games reflect the real concerns of those participants in the field, and not just theoretical concerns that are often prevalent in the academic and blogging discourse.

Conclusion

EULAs, TOS, and TOU are used throughout the digital game universe. Despite their inherent limitations, it is almost certain that these online agreements will continue to be used in the future because they remain a practical and effective tool for handling the vast majority of online game disputes. As courts continue to closely scrutinize these agreements, digital game operators will need to continue to refine and improve upon these contracts in parallel. With each new online game created, a new EULA, TOS, or TOU is forged. With each new game technology development (e.g., virtual reality, augmented reality, and Blockchain), these agreements get even more complex, and despite their ubiquity, the evolution of these agreements will likely remain uncertain because they raise complex questions about a user's rights in-game—in particular, with fundamental changes to technology underpinning these games, such as Blockchain.[266] Time will tell whether these online contracts will evolve in a manner that fairly allocates rights to gamers, or will strongly favor game operators as they have thus far. Under either outcome, these online agreements will likely continue to present novel challenges to the courts, perhaps better resolved by legislative bodies if industry self-regulation fails to work.

Ricknäs, *Online Game Company Approved for Real-World Bank*, PCWORLD, Mar. 20, 2009, 10:40 a.m., http://www.pcworld.com/article/161650/article.html (reporting that the Swedish Financial Supervisory Authority granted MindArk a license to run a traditional bank through its virtual world platform, Entropia Universe).

266. *See* Alexis Kramer, *Blockchain Games and Gambling Laws on Collision Course*, BLOOMBERG BNA, Jan. 18, 2018, https://www.bna.com/blockchain-games -gambling-n73014474273/.

Copyright Law

Marc E. Mayer[1]

2

Takeaways

- *Computer and video games are copyrightable works of authorship. However, they are unique in several significant respects. For example:*
  - (a) *Computer and video games are both "audiovisual works" and "computer programs." Thus, copyright may subsist both in the underlying code and in the audiovisual displays that result from the interaction of code with a personal computer, console, mobile device, or computer server.*
  - (b) *Computer and video games have both a static component (the software code, art, and music) and a dynamic component (the way that a game unfolds either through the interaction of game and player or game and multiplayer server). Thus, there are questions as to whether copyright subsists in dynamic virtual worlds and whether (or when)*

---

1. Marc Mayer is a partner in the Intellectual Property Practice Group at Mitchell Silberberg & Knupp LLP and chairs the firm's interactive entertainment practice. Marc thanks Mark Humphrey for his assistance with this chapter. This chapter is a revision of a chapter first written by John M. Neclerio and Matthew C. Mousley for the first edition of this book. For complete author biographies, see the Contributors section of this book.

player interactions with computer code or online servers create derivative works.

(c) Most computer and video games contain a set of underlying rules and gameplay mechanics that are expressed and manifested through visual representation and implemented via user interfaces and artificial intelligence. The interrelationship between rules, code, artwork, and user interface makes it extremely difficult to separate the difference between traditionally uncopyrightable game "rules" and copyrightable expression.

- *User-created video game content, such as game "modifications" ("mods"), custom levels, user-created "skins" or characters, or user-designed virtual spaces, are becoming a very important segment of video game content. They also are generally considered to be derivative works of the original computer game that cannot be exploited without the consent of the copyright owner. Courts have begun to address some of the ownership and infringement issues associated with game mods and collaborative game projects. These issues will continue to evolve as collaboration takes place in virtual spaces and as users seek to monetize their creations.*

- *The diversity of computer and mobile video games has spawned a broad and diverse body of infringement claims. These range from "traditional" claims of substantial similarity arising from the use of similar plots, storylines, and characters; to claims arising from the creation of "clone" or "copycat" games; to claims involving the manipulation of online games through disruptive and harmful software programs such as "bots" or "cheats."*

- *The growing popularity of e-sports, combined with the ease by which gameplay can be recorded, streamed, and disseminated online, has led to an enormous secondary market for the passive consumption of gameplay videos or live sports competitions. The recording and online broadcasting of video games implicates the rights of the owners of copyright in those games.*

Introduction

The application of copyright law to video game and interactive works is nothing new. Courts have applied copyright law with respect to video games as early as the late 1970s and 1980s in lawsuits involving early arcade games such as *Pong, Pac-Man,* and *Galaxian*. But as video games and virtual worlds have evolved, courts have grappled with an entirely new set of questions and issues that were never considered at the time the current Copyright Act was enacted in 1976.

The range of copyright issues facing the video game industry is wide-reaching. This is due in large part to the vast range of interactive electronic entertainment now being made available to consumers. Many games, such as those in the *Call of Duty* or *Uncharted* franchises, are nearly indistinguishable in relevant respects from major motion pictures in that they feature complex characters, detailed storylines, thousands of lines of dialog, and photorealistic graphics. Others such as *Minecraft* offer players an endless virtual sandbox where they are free to create their own virtual "worlds" and invite others to participate. Meanwhile, competitive games (or "e-sports") such as *League of Legends* and *Overwatch* have come to define an increasingly large segment of the video game world and have turned video games into spectator sports—and perhaps even an Olympic sport. And on top of everything is the massive and growing world of mobile games, which include casual puzzle and matching games, arcade-style games, complex adventure and role-playing games, and competitive collectible card games.

Courts are just beginning to address some of the copyright issues arising from contemporary computer and video games. These include, for example, copyright ownership of user-generated content, how to differentiate between game "ideas" and "expression," and whether copyright extends to the "dynamic" virtual worlds generated when a client interacts with a server.

This chapter discusses some of the key concepts of U.S. copyright law, and their application to some emerging issues in the video game industry. Specifically, I first discuss the basic requirements for copyright protection, including how video games are protected under the Copyright Act, as well as certain limitations on the rights of copyright owners, including the idea/expression dichotomy and its applicability to video game "rules." I then discuss concepts of authorship, ownership and joint authorship, including authorship of user-generated content. Finally, I discuss a few specific examples of copyright disputes that have arisen over the past several years.

I. Basic Requirements for Copyright Protection

Federal copyright law in the United States is governed by the Copyright Act of 1976, as amended,[2] which Congress enacted pursuant to the Copyright Clause of the U.S. Constitution.[3] The Copyright Act provides protection for "original works of authorship."[4] Works of authorship include the following: (1) literary works; (2) musical works, including any accompanying words; (3) dramatic works, including any accompanying music; (4) pantomimes and choreographic works; (5) pictorial, graphic, and sculptural works; (6) motion pictures and other audiovisual works; (7) sound recordings; and (8) architectural works.[5]

A. Literal and Nonliteral Aspects of Computer Games

Video games sit in an unusual place in the rubric of the Copyright Act. This is because video games exist at two levels and thus are effectively two types of works.[6] At one level, video games are computer programs, composed of thousands or tens of thousands of lines of computer code.[7] Though perhaps counterintuitive, computer code is considered a "literary work," including by the U.S. Copyright Office, which registers "computer programs" as "Tex-

---

2. 17 U.S.C. § 101 *et seq.* (2012).

3. U.S. CONST. art. I, § 8, cl. 8 ("To promote the progress of science and the useful arts, by securing for limited time to authors and inventors the exclusive right to their respective writings and discoveries.").

4. 17 U.S.C. § 102(a) (2018).

5. *Id.* § 102(a)(1)–(8). This list is illustrative and not exclusive. *See* Nat'l Conference of Bar Exam'rs v. Multistate Legal Studies, Inc., 495 F. Supp. 34, 36 (N.D. Ill. 1980) (holding that examination questions were "works of authorship" within the meaning of § 102), *aff'd*, 692 F.2d 478 (7th Cir. 1982). Within this list, the terms "architectural work," "literary works," "motion pictures," "phonorecords," "pictorial, graphic, and sculptural works," and "sound recordings" are defined at 17 U.S.C. § 101.

6. Miller v. Facebook, Inc., No. C 10-00264 WHA, 2010 WL 2198204, at *4 (N.D. Cal. May 28, 2010).

7. Broderbund Software, Inc. v. Unison World, Inc., 648 F. Supp. 1127, 1133 (N.D. Cal. 1986) ("[C]opyright protection is not limited to the literal aspects of a computer program, but rather . . . it extends to . . . its audiovisual displays.").

tual Works" (i.e., TX). For example, in *Apple Computer, Inc. v. Franklin Computer Corp.*,[8] the Third Circuit Court of Appeals considered various computer programs on an Apple computer. The court concluded that the term "literary works" includes "expression not only in words but also 'numbers, or other . . . numerical symbols or indicia.'"[9] The court therefore held that a computer program, written in programming code, was a literary work and (absent a defense to infringement) was "protected from unauthorized copying" under the Copyright Act.[10]

Video games also are "audiovisual works" that are protectable under the Copyright Act. For example, in *Tetris Holdings, LLC v. Xio Interactive, Inc.*,[11] the court noted that the copyright in a computer or video game extends to its "audiovisual display," including, for example, "game labels, design of game boards, playing cards, and graphical works."[12] The copyright in a video game also extends to characters embodied therein, as well as "shapes, sizes, colors, sequences, arrangements, and sounds."[13]

Thus, both the courts and the U.S. Copyright Office consider the source code that generates the images, sounds, and characters in a video game, and the resulting images, sounds, and characters, to be two embodiments of the same copyrighted work.[14]

---

8. Apple Computer, Inc. v. Franklin Computer Corp., 714 F.2d 1240 (3d Cir. 1983).

9. *Id.* at 1249 (citations omitted).

10. *Id.*

11. Tetris Holdings, LLC v. Xio Interactive, Inc., 863 F. Supp. 2d 394 (D.N.J. 2012).

12. *Id.* at 404.

13. *Id.; see also* Atari, Inc. v. N. Am. Philips Consumer Elec. Corp., 672 F.2d 607, 617 (7th Cir. 1982); Atari Games Corp. v. Oman, 979 F.2d 242, 245 (D.C. Cir. 1992) ("The hallmark of a video game is the expression found in 'the entire effect of the game as it appears and sounds,' its 'sequence of images.'") (quoting Stern Elecs., Inc. v. Kaufman, 669 F.2d 852, 857 (2d Cir. 1982)).

14. *See* U.S. COPYRIGHT OFFICE, CIRCULAR 61: COPYRIGHT REGISTRATION FOR COMPUTER PROGRAMS (2017), http://www.copyright.gov/circs/circ61.pdf ("You can register the audiovisual material for a videogame and the computer program that runs it with one application if the same party owns the copyright in the program and the audiovisual material.").

That means that it is possible for a later work to infringe the copyright in a video game's code without necessarily infringing the audiovisual work or screen display produced by the code. For example, a new work may use portions of source code that work "under the hood," though the artwork, music, and overall appearance of the game is different. Conversely, it is possible for a new work to infringe the audiovisual or screen display of a preexisting work without using the underlying source code. For example, a mobile version of a popular computer game might look and sound very similar to the original but do so using entirely new code. Either of these circumstances could give rise to a claim for copyright infringement.

As a recent decision illustrates, separating source code from an audiovisual work generated by that source code can be tricky, as the two are inextricably interrelated. In *Lilith Games (Shanghai) Co., Ltd. v. uCool, Inc.*,[15] a district court considered claims brought by the developer of a mobile game against a developer of a similar mobile game. Although the games were nearly identical in their appearance, the plaintiff elected to limit its claims for copyright infringement to approximately 240,000 lines of source code that it alleged had been misappropriated by the defendant. In analyzing whether the plaintiff was likely to succeed on the merits of its claim (and thus might be entitled to a preliminary injunction), the court analyzed *both* the "literal" (written source code) and "nonliteral" (audiovisual) elements of the game. It found that both were substantially similar, and that the "striking similarities between the games' protected elements such as the visual appearance of characters and settings further support the Court's conclusion that Lilith is likely to prove substantial similarity at trial."[16]

---

15. Lilith Games (Shanghai) Co., Ltd. v. uCool, Inc., No. 15-CV-01267-SC, 2015 U.S. Dist. LEXIS 128619 (N.D. Cal. Sept. 23, 2015).

16. *Id.* at *9.

1. Derivative Works, Mods, and Compilations

Compilations[17] and derivative works[18] also are copyrightable works of authorship.[19]

Derivative works. These are "works based upon one or more preexisting works," such as translations, motion picture versions, and other transformations or adaptations of previous works.[20] To qualify as a derivative work, the work must "exist in a 'concrete or permanent form,' . . . and must substantially incorporate protected material from the preexisting work. . . ."[21] Additionally, "a work will be considered a derivative work only if it would be considered an infringing work if the material that it has derived from a pre-existing work had been taken without the consent of a copyright proprietor of such pre-existing work."[22] This new work is subject to copyright protection, but protection will extend to the newly added copyrightable material, not to the "preexisting material employed in the work. . . ."[23]

---

17. "A 'compilation' is a work formed by the collection and assembling of preexisting materials or of data that are selected, coordinated, or arranged in such a way that the resulting work as a whole constitutes an original work of authorship. The term 'compilation' includes collective works." 17 U.S.C. § 101 (2012).

18. According to the U.S. Code:

> A "derivative work" is a work based upon one or more preexisting works, such as a translation, musical arrangement, dramatization, fictionalization, motion picture version, sound recording, art reproduction, abridgment, condensation, or any other form in which a work may be recast, transformed, or adapted. A work consisting of editorial revisions, annotations, elaborations, or other modifications which, as a whole, represent an original work of authorship, is a "derivative work."

Id.

19. *See id.* § 103(a).

20. *Id.* § 101.

21. Micro Star v. FormGen Inc., 154 F.3d 1107, 1110 (9th Cir. 1998) (quoting Lewis Galoob Toys, Inc. v. Nintendo of Am., Inc., 964 F.2d 965, 967 (9th Cir. 1992), and citing Litchfield v. Spielberg, 736 F.2d 1352, 1357 (9th Cir. 1984)).

22. 1 MELVILLE B. NIMMER & DAVID NIMMER, NIMMER ON COPYRIGHT § 3.01 (rev. ed. 2018).

23. 17 U.S.C. § 103(b) (2012). "If the underlying work is itself protected by copyright, then the copyright in the derivative work . . . neither nullifies nor extends the protection accorded to the underlying work." 1 NIMMER & NIMMER, *supra* note 22, § 3.04[A] (footnote omitted).

A troublesome "derivative work" issue that faces the owners of copyright in a computer game is the fact that games (especially modern computer games) are not "static" products but are regularly updated, resulting in numerous successive versions. While books and motion pictures are generally released in a "final" form, with revised versions separately published as "new editions" or "directors' cuts," that is not the case with software or video game products, which are constantly evolving. Indeed, it is increasingly common for games to be released to the public with "day 1 patches" that require the game to be updated and revised on the date of release. Many games, especially online games, are patched on a regular basis for a variety of reasons. Competitive multiplayer games may be patched weekly or monthly to address player complaints or improve a game's "balance" (that is, its fairness for all players). Other games may be updated or patched to fix bugs, to add new content or features, or to take advantage of new technology such as virtual reality headsets or ultra-high-resolution televisions. As a result, over the course of a game's life cycle it may encompass hundreds or thousands of versions, only the latest of which will be made available to the public at any particular time.

Both the Copyright Act and the Copyright Office have yet to squarely address the evolving nature of computer or video games. The Copyright Act provides that "where the work is prepared in different versions, each version constitutes a separate work."[24] But does that mean that in order to obtain the benefits of copyright registration the owner of a game must submit a new registration each time they update or patch a game to its latest version? Many developers register the first release build of a game and then submit additional registrations from time to time to ensure that all new content is protected. This dilemma is somewhat alleviated by the principle that "if the same party owns a copyright in both a derivative work . . . and the underlying work that is incorporated in the derivative work, registration of a copyright in the derivative work is sufficient to permit an infringement action on either the preexisting (unoriginal) material or on any newly contributed

---

24. 17 U.S.C. § 101 (2012).

material."[25] Nevertheless, it is generally good practice to periodically register additional versions of a game after a major update or patch, such as a new 2.0 or 3.0 version.

Mods. One notable category of derivative work is the video game "modification" (or "mod"). These are computer programs that "allow [users] to actually change the behavior of the game,"[26] by, for example, adding additional levels, changing game physics, and altering game artwork.[27] Game publishers often support mods because they encourage players to invest time and creative energy into a product and may also extend the "shelf-life" of a game by ensuring a flow of new and fresh content.

Mods vary greatly in scope and function.[28] "Full conversion" mods take the "building blocks" of the original game (such as its engine, artwork, sounds, and textures) and use them to create an entirely (or largely) new experience. The game *Counter-Strike*, initially created by independent players as a mod for the game *Half-Life*, became so popular among online players that the developers of *Half-Life* acquired rights in *Counter-Strike*.[29] More recently, the game *DayZ* began its life as a mod for the game *ARMA 2*. The new work eclipsed the popularity of the original and arguably spawned

---

25. R.W. Beck, Inc. v. E3 Consulting, LLC, 577 F.3d 1133, 1143 (10th Cir. 2009); *see also* Streetwise Maps v. Van Dam, Inc., 159 F.3d 739, 747 (2d Cir. 1998) ("[T]he registration certificate relating to the derivative work in this circumstance will suffice to permit [the plaintiff] to maintain an action based on defendants' infringement of the pre-existing work."); Xoom, Inc. v. Imageline, Inc., 323 F.3d 279, 283–84 (4th Cir. 2003) ("because Imageline owned copyright in SuperBundle and Master Gallery and in the underlying works of each, its registration of SuperBundle and Master Gallery was sufficient to permit an infringement action on the underlying parts, whether they be new or preexisting").

26. Cory Ondrejka, *Escaping the Gilded Cage: User Created Content and Building the Metaverse*, 49 N.Y.L. Sch. L. Rev. 81, 89 (2004).

27. *See generally* John Baldrica, Note, *Mod as Heck: Frameworks for Examining Ownership Rights in User-Contributed Content to Videogames, and a More Principled Evaluation of Expressive Appropriation in User-Modified Videogame Projects*, 8 Minn. J.L. Sci. & Tech. 681 (2007) (detailed evaluation of the intellectual property issues surrounding mods).

28. Rafi Letzter, *Online Communities Are Changing Video Games to Make Them Better, Weirder, and Much More Wonderful*, Bus. Insider, July 20, 2015, http://www.businessinsider.com/video-game-modding-2015-7.

29. *See* Ondrejka, *supra* note 26, at 86.

an entirely new type of game that has come to be known as a "battle royale" (a *Hunger Games*-style multiplayer game in which players compete to be the last to survive). Other types of mods may add new "skins" (appearances) to game characters, add new types of enemies, change dialog, or fix bugs. In one case, a passionate modder has continued to work on, patch, update, and improve a computer game released in 2004 (*Vampire: Bloodlines*), for more than a decade after its developer, Troika Games, dissolved and its publisher ended "official" support for the game.[30]

The issue of mods as derivative works was addressed in *Micro Star v. FormGen*.[31] FormGen, the creator of *Duke Nukem 3D*, allowed and encouraged players to build their own levels and to post them on the Internet for other players to download and use.[32] When Micro Star, a software distributor, began commercially selling a CD filled with 300 player-created levels, FormGen sued for infringement of its exclusive right to make derivative works of *Duke Nukem 3D*. The Ninth Circuit Court of Appeals held in favor of the plaintiff, finding that the game levels distributed by Micro Star would likely be found "'substantially similar in both ideas and expression'" to FormGen's copyrighted work because "the audiovisual displays generated when the player chooses the [new] levels comes entirely out of [*Duke Nukem 3D's*] source art library."[33] Additionally, the court found that "[t]he work that Micro Star infringes is the [*Duke Nukem 3D*] story itself," and that Micro Star's levels "telling new (though somewhat repetitive) tales of Duke's fabulous adventures" were infringing derivative works.[34] Thus, it is now fairly clear that mods are derivative works of the game on which they are based

---

30. Robert Zak, *One Man's Endless Quest to Fix Vampire: The Masquerade— Bloodlines*, PCGAMESN.COM, Nov. 6, 2017, https://www.pcgamesn.com/vampire-the -masquerade-bloodlines/vampire-the-masquerade-bloodlines-mods.

31. Micro Star v. FormGen Inc., 154 F.3d 1107 (9th Cir. 1998).

32. *Id.* at 1109.

33. *Id.* at 1112 (quoting Litchfield v. Spielberg, 736 F.2d 1352, 1356 (9th Cir. 1982)).

34. *Id.*

and cannot be created or distributed without the consent of the owner of the original game.[35]

Compilations. These are works formed by the collection and assembling of preexisting materials or of data that has been selected, coordinated, or arranged in such a way that the resulting work as a whole constitutes an original work of authorship.[36] An example of a compilation is a book that contains a listing of the values of used cars. For example, in *CCC Information Services v. Maclean Hunter Market Reports*,[37] the court considered the plaintiff's *Red Book*, a publication that contained a listing of such estimates based on expert valuations and other data.[38] The court found that, although the facts contained in the book were not themselves protectable, the *Red Book* as a whole could be protected because it was organized and arranged using the requisite amount of creativity: the information in the book was organized by region, state, mileage, make, and model of the cars valued, which the court found to be a sufficiently original organizational scheme.[39]

It is often the case that video games are the product of contributions made by several individuals, each of whom might make a different contribution to the overall project. This is especially true with respect to video game mods, which typically are made by volunteers who may contribute to the project and then move on. However, that does not make a video game (or video game mod) a "compilation." In *Blizzard Entertainment, Inc. & Valve Corp. v. Lilith Games (Shanghai) Co., Ltd.*,[40] the court considered whether a popular mod for the computer game *Warcraft III* was a "compilation"

---

35. *See* Blizzard Entm't, Inc. v. Lilith Games (Shanghai) Co., No. 3:15-CV-04084-CRB, 2017 WL 2118342, at *9–11 (N.D. Cal. May 16, 2017) (holding generally that mods are derivative works, and the copyright owner of such derivative may recover from someone who copies it).

36. 17 U.S.C. § 101 (2012).

37. CCC Info. Servs. v. Maclean Hunter Market Reports, 44 F.3d 61 (2d Cir. 1994).

38. *Id.* at 63–65.

39. *Id.* at 67.

40. Blizzard Entm't, Inc. v. Lilith Games (Shanghai) Co., No. 3:15-CV-04084-CRB, 2017 WL 2118342 (N.D. Cal. May 16, 2017).

of discrete elements because during the course of development of the mod, a number of individuals made contributions to the work. The defendant reasoned that because different people were responsible for conceptualizing different game characters, the final product should be viewed as a collection or "compilation" of discrete and separately authored content, rather than as a single, unified audiovisual work.[41] Judge Breyer of the Northern District of California rejected that argument:

> Movies, for example, almost always make up a "unitary whole" with "inseparable and interdependent parts," 17 U.S.C. § 101, because the direction, acting performances, cinematography, costume design, and all the rest merge into one integrated work . . . So too with video games. . . . [B]y [defendant's] logic, *Star Wars: The Force Awakens* (Walt Disney Studios 2015) would be a collective work because it arranged the most popular Star Wars heroes, settings, and one-liners into a new movie. The same might be said of *Love Actually* (Universal Pictures 2003), given its all-star cast and web of different storylines. But *Castaway* (20th Century Fox 2000), with its solitary protagonist and even more solitary plot, would presumably be a unitary work.[42]

Thus, while volunteer game development may raise interesting copyright ownership issues,[43] video games made through a collaborative process generally will not be considered compilations.[44]

B. Originality

A second prerequisite for copyright protection is that the work be original.[45] An author of a protectable work must have independently created it; he or she enjoys no protection in works that

---

41. *Id.* at *8.
42. *Id.*
43. *See infra* text accompanying notes 168–177.
44. *See Blizzard Entm't*, 2017 WL 2118342, at *8–11.
45. *See* Feist Publ'ns, Inc. v. Rural Tel. Serv. Co., 499 U.S. 340, 345 (1991) ("The *sine qua non* of copyright is originality.") (emphasis added).

were copied from another source.[46] However, the requisite level of creativity is extremely low—"even a slight amount will suffice."[47]

In most cases the issue of whether an author's contributions are sufficiently "original" for purposes of copyright protection will be relatively straightforward. Yet the unique, dual nature of video games (as computer programs and audiovisual works) can present interesting questions at the margins. For example, *M. Kramer Manufacturing Co. v. Andrews*[48] involved a video arcade poker game that was a variation on an existing, copyrighted poker video game with only some small changes. The new game had an additional "Hi-Lo" feature, a feature that allowed the cards to flash on screen, and the option of a split-screen mode.[49] The court found these changes, although minor, were sufficiently original contributions to justify separate and new copyright protection for the entire game.[50]

What about purely technical changes or modifications made to a game, such as porting a game to a new platform (for example, personal computer (PC) to Xbox or iPhone) or making an older PC game compatible with new operating systems or graphics cards? Courts have held that mere changes in a work's medium of expression alone is insufficient to confer copyright protection.[51] However, if changes involve alterations to the code base, to the user interface (particularly if a game is being ported to a mobile platform), or to the game's graphics, they might meet the "modicum" of creativity required for copyright protection.

---

46. *See* L. Batlin & Son, Inc. v. Snyder, 536 F.2d 486, 489–90 (2d Cir. 1976) (en banc) ("'[T]he one pervading element prerequisite to copyright protection' . . . [is] that the work be the original product of the claimant.") (quoting 1 M. NIMMER, THE LAW OF COPYRIGHT § 10, at 32 (1975)); *see also* Sherry Mfg. Co. v. Towel King of Fla., Inc., 753 F.2d 1565 (11th Cir. 1985) ("One who has slavishly or mechanically copied from others may not claim to be an author.") (quoting 1 NIMMER & NIMMER, *supra* note 22, § 1.06[A]).

47. *Feist*, 499 U.S. at 345.

48. M. Kramer Mfg. Co. v. Andrews, 783 F.2d 421 (4th Cir. 1986).

49. *Id.* at 425.

50. *Id.* at 440.

51. *See* Durham Indus., Inc. v. Tomy Corp., 630 F.2d 905, 910 (2d Cir. 1980) (holding that the mere reproduction of Disney characters in a different medium did not constitute originality); Agee v. Paramount Commc'n, Inc., 853 F. Supp. 778, 788 (S.D.N.Y. 1994) (holding that rerecording a sound recording onto an audiovisual work as background music does not create a derivative work).

An analogous issue arose in the context of sound recordings in *ABS Entertainment, Inc. v. CBS Corp.*[52] *ABS* involved a dispute over the scope of state law rights for sound recordings first fixed prior to February 1, 1972—and, specifically, whether California state law granted the owners of such sound recordings the exclusive right to publicly perform the recording over terrestrial radio.[53] (Through a quirk of history, only sound recordings fixed on or after February 1, 1972, are subject to federal copyright protection, while those created prior to that date are protected by a patchwork of state laws.[54]) In dismissing the plaintiff's California state law claims, the California district court found that when the pre-1972 recordings had been "remastered," substantive alterations had been made to the sound recordings, such as key changes, equalization adjustments, noise reduction, and the addition of reverberation.[55] As a result, when radio stations performed the recordings at issue, they had not performed a pre-1972 work, but a new, remastered work that was protected by the Copyright Act—which expressly *excludes* terrestrial performances of sound recordings from the scope of rights accorded to owners of such recordings. The Ninth Circuit Court of Appeals reversed, holding that the types of technical improvements and modifications made during the record remastering process did not sufficiently alter the original work to constitute a derivative work. Specifically:

> A remastered sound recording is not eligible for independent copyright protection as a derivative work unless its essential character and identity reflect a level of independent sound recording authorship that makes it a variation distinguishable from the underlying work. . . . If an allegedly derivative sound recording does not add or

---

52. ABS Entm't, Inc. v. CBS Corp., No. CV-15-6257 PA (AGRx), 2016 U.S. Dist. LEXIS 71470 (C.D. Cal. May 30, 2016), *rev'd*, – F.3d – (9th Cir. Aug. 20, 2018).

53. *Id.* at *6–8.

54. Capitol Records, Inc. v. Naxos of Am., Inc., 4 N.Y.3d 540, 544 (N.Y. 2005) ("Sound recordings produced after February 15, 1972 can be protected from infringement under federal copyright law but Congress did not extend statutory protection to recordings created before that date.").

55. *ABS Entm't, Inc.*, 2016 U.S. Dist. LEXIS 71470, at *12.

remove any sounds from the underlying sound recording, does not change the sequence of the sounds, and does not remix or otherwise alter the sounds in sequence or character, the recording is likely to be nothing more than a copy of the underlying sound recording and is presumptively devoid of the original sound recording authorship required for copyright protection.[56]

As a result, it is now clear that changes or modifications that simply improve the quality of a work but do not alter the fundamental character of the work are not eligible for independent copyright protection. Of course, video game "remasters" take many forms. A video game "remaster" that enables the preexisting work to run on a new platform but retains all of the visual and gameplay elements of the original is unlikely to be protectable as a derivative work. On the other hand, protection may still be available if the "remastered" version uses new textures and art assets. But even in that situation, the copyright may be a relatively "thin" one. Only those aspects of the game that differ between the original and the remastered version will be separately protectible. The new copyright in the derivative work will not extend to any sounds, dialog, characters, maps, or art assets that existed in the original work. Thus, in *ABS*, the owners of the pre-1972 works could still sue for misappropriation of the original pre-1972 masters, irrespective of whether there might be a separate copyright in the remasters.[57] It should be noted, however, that if there is commonality of ownership in the original and derivative work, the owner can sue for the entirety, irrespective of the contours of each derivative copyright. That will be the case for many video game ports or remasters.

C. Fixation

The third and last requirement for a work to be protectable by copyright is that it be "fixed in any tangible medium of expression" from which it can be "perceived, reproduced, or otherwise

---

56. *ABS Entm't, Inc.*, – F.3d –, No. 16-55917 (9th Cir. Aug. 20, 2018), at 20–22.
57. *Id.* at 38.

communicated, either directly or with the aid of a machine or device."[58] A work is considered "fixed" if it is sufficiently permanent or stable to permit it to be perceived, reproduced, or otherwise communicated for a period of more than transitory duration.[59]

Video games generally are considered "fixed" within the meaning of the Copyright Act as long as they are embodied in underlying computer code or audiovisual files (including any art assets or musical recordings) and those digital materials reside in a tangible medium, such as on a hard drive, a DVD-ROM, or a remote computer server.[60] In *M. Kramer Manufacturing Co. v. Andrews*, the court explained that the plaintiff's video game, an audiovisual work, was in fact fixed.[61] The computer program underlying the audiovisual elements of the game acted as the "form in which the audiovisuals are 'permanently embodied.' . . ."[62] The computer program thus fixed the audiovisual aspects of the game in a tangible medium of expression, satisfying the fixation requirement.[63]

---

58. 17 U.S.C. § 102(a) (2012). That a work must be fixed in a tangible medium of expression is a statutory requirement deriving from the Copyright Clause's express applicability to "writings."

59. *Id.* § 101. Transmitted works are deemed fixed if their fixation is simultaneous with their transmission. *Id.* Once a work is fixed, subsequent destruction of all copies of the work does not nullify copyright protection in the work. Pac. & S. Co. v. Duncan, 744 F.2d 1490, 1500 (11th Cir. 1984) (explaining that destruction of a work does not constitute abandonment, and seems to be the best way to ensure that no one else uses the work).

60. *See, e.g.*, M. Kramer Mfg. Co. v. Andrews, 783 F.2d 421, 441 (4th Cir. 1986); Stern Elecs., Inc. v. Kaufman, 669 F.2d 852, 855–56 (2d Cir. 1982) (finding that the sights and sounds of an electronic game were eligible for copyright protection because they were fixed in the memory devices of the game); Williams Elecs., Inc. v. Artic Int'l, Inc., 685 F.2d 870, 874 (3d Cir. 1982) (rejecting argument that images in video game were transient and unable to be "fixed").

61. *M. Kramer Mfg.*, 783 F.2d at 441.

62. *Id.* (citations omitted).

63. *Id.* An example of an original work of authorship that is not "fixed" and, therefore, is not protected is a live television news broadcast that has not been simultaneously recorded or videotaped. *See* 1 NIMMER & NIMMER, *supra* note 22, § 1.08[C][2]; H.R. REP. NO. 94-1476 (1976); *see also* Micro Star v. FormGen Inc., 154 F.3d 1107, 1111–12 (9th Cir. 1998) (explaining that supplemental computer code that describes audiovisual displays in a video game is a permanent or concrete form for purposes of determining that the audiovisual displays are a derivative work of the original computer code underlying the game); Trenton v. Infinity Broad. Corp., 865 F. Supp. 1416, 1423–25 (C.D. Cal. 1994).

While video game *software* plainly meets the "fixation" require-ment, there remains confusion as to whether the dynamic and interactive audiovisual screen displays created by game software are sufficiently fixed for copyright protection. In *Lewis Galoob Toys, Inc. v. Nintendo of America, Inc.*,[64] the Ninth Circuit Court of Appeals considered whether the use of a product that modified Nintendo games to give players extra lives or enhanced speed created a "derivative work" of the Nintendo games it modified. The court held that it did not, because the dynamic audiovisual screen displays created by the Nintendo system when combined with the Game Genie were not sufficiently concrete and permanent to constitute a derivative work.[65] The court reasoned, by analogy, that "although there is a market for kaleidoscopes, it does not necessarily follow that kaleidoscopes create unlawful derivative works when pointed at protected artwork."[66] Though not explicitly stated, *Lewis Galoob* might arguably be read to conclude more broadly that dynamic screen displays created by the interaction of computer software with hardware (such as a game console) were not "fixed" in a tangible medium of expression.[67]

More recently, a district court for the Northern District of Cali-fornia came to the conclusion that while "[t]here is no dispute that video games are generally copyrightable," the dynamic gameplay contained therein, including the game's avatars, are not "fixed" in a tangible medium of expression.[68] Thus, it refused to dismiss right of publicity claims asserted by a professional athlete against Elec-tronic Arts for use of his name and likeness in the *Madden* football game franchise.[69] The court explained its reasoning as follows:

> [G]ame play in the Madden games is dynamic, interactive, variable, and in the hands of the consumer. Plaintiffs contend the avatars allegedly representing their likenesses

---

64. Lewis Galoob Toys, Inc. v. Nintendo of Am., Inc., 964 F.2d 965 (9th Cir. 1992).

65. *Id.* at 968.

66. *Id.* at 969.

67. *Id.*

68. Davis v. Elec. Arts, Inc., No. 10-cv-03328-RS, 2017 U.S. Dist. LEXIS 216505, at *4–5 (N.D. Cal. Dec. 11, 2017).

69. *Id.*

even have performance characteristics representing plaintiffs' own capabilities in their time as active NFL players. While recordings of actual football games are subject to copyright notwithstanding the independent actions of players during the course of the games, such recordings satisfy the requirement of copyright that the work be "fixed" in a tangible medium of expression. The Madden games, in contrast, allow game play that is not fixed in a tangible medium of expression, and part of plaintiffs' claims is that their identities are reflected in that game play.[70]

What about the dynamic virtual worlds created by the interaction of client and server? In most multiplayer games, the "game" does not reside on a user's PC in any practical sense. Rather, players download (or purchase) and install a game "client." The client contains many of the building blocks that are used to play the game, such as art assets, animations, sounds, textures, and the game "engine." However, the game cannot be played (and does not really exist) until the player connects to an online server. The server connects players to each other and instructs the client how to use the various assets that reside on the user's computer. In *MDY Industries, LLC v. Blizzard Entertainment, Inc.*,[71] the Ninth Circuit appeared to hold that a dynamic multiplayer virtual world is, in fact, subject to copyright protection—even if the virtual world only comes into existence when a client and server interact. In that case, the court considered whether a system used by Blizzard (known as "Warden") to prevent players from accessing and playing the game *World of Warcraft* if they are running "bots" or other cheating software was a "technological measure that effectively controls access to a work protected under [the Copyright Act]."[72] MDY, the maker of a *World of Warcraft* bot known as "Glider," argued that because Warden did not prevent players from accessing the *World of Warcraft* client software—including all of the assets, sounds, and artwork contained within that client—it did

---

70. *Id.* at *4.
71. MDY Indus., LLC v. Blizzard Entm't, Inc., 629 F.3d 928 (9th Cir. 2010).
72. *Id.* at 942.

not actually control access to the copyrighted work (i.e., the *World of Warcraft* code, assets, or sounds). The Ninth Circuit agreed that Warden did not control access to those elements, but it *did* control access to *World of Warcraft*'s "dynamic non-literal elements."[73] These "dynamic non-literal elements" were defined by the district court (which definition was adopted by the Ninth Circuit) as the "real time experience of traveling through different worlds, hearing their sounds, viewing their structures, encountering their inhabitants and monsters, and encountering other players."[74] In other words, the Ninth Circuit held that, notwithstanding *Lewis Galoob*, the "dynamic" experience of a virtual world, created through the interplay of client and server, is itself a copyrighted work—and, moreover, the copyright in that virtual world is separate from the "literal" copyright in a game's code *and* the "nonliteral" copyright in the screen displays caused by that code. Surprisingly, however, the Ninth Circuit did not mention (far less distinguish) *Lewis Galoob* in its analysis.

The interplay between *MDY* and *Lewis Galoob* has yet to be addressed, and thus the contours of copyright protection for dynamic, ever-changing aspects of a virtual world remains unresolved. The consequences of this uncertainty are potentially far-reaching. For example, if a player uses a software product to reveal enemy locations or other hidden information on his or her computer screen, is that an infringing derivative work? What about using a "packet editor" to modify information being passed between the client and server to gain an advantage over an enemy or cause the online environment to act in an unintended manner?

Another interesting area yet to be fully explored is the copyrightability of works that are created through interaction with the real world, such as "augmented reality" games or apps that overlay real-world spaces with imaginary objects or spaces, or that create images that exist only at particular Global Positioning System (GPS) coordinates and exclusively through the lens of a mobile phone camera, headset, or augmented reality "glasses." While the software that creates the augmented reality would constitute a

---

73. *Id.* at 953–54.
74. *Id.* at 942–43.

copyrightable work, are images generated in a real-world space sufficiently "fixed" to give rise to a protectable copyright? As long as such images are stable and are not merely transitory in duration, they should be fully protectable under copyright law. As one commentator noted, although augmented realty "images are not actually in the physical environments in which they are made to appear, they nevertheless reside in a digital intermediary that is sufficiently 'tangible'—such as on the lens of a head-mounted mobile device or in a cloud-based computer server."[75]

It is likely that these issues will need to be revisited in the future with additional consideration given to contemporary technology and the relationship between video game clients and servers.

D. Limitations on the Scope of Copyright Protection

Several relevant doctrines limit the scope of protection for certain categories of works. I discuss three specific limitations that have particular relevance to video games and virtual worlds.

1. The Idea/Expression Dichotomy, Merger, and Game Rules

Perhaps the most important limitation on the scope of copyright protection is that a copyright does not extend to any "idea, procedure, process, system, method of operation, concept, principle, or discovery."[76] Related to this is the doctrine of "merger," which denies copyright protection to expression "that is inseparable from or merged with the ideas, processes, or discoveries underlying the expression."[77] For example, in the seminal case *Baker v. Seldon*,[78] the plaintiff had obtained a copyright in a book that taught readers how to perform a particular type of double-entry bookkeeping and included forms that readers could use to keep books according to the plaintiff's accounting method.[79] While the defendant produced forms similar to the plaintiff's and also

---

75. Brian D. Wassom, Augmented Reality Law, Privacy, and Ethics 14 (1st ed. 2015).
76. 17 U.S.C. § 102(b) (2012).
77. Gates Rubber Co. v. Bando Chem. Indus., Ltd., 9 F.3d 823, 838 (10th Cir. 1993); *see also* Civility Experts Worldwide v. Molly Manners, LLC, 167 F. Supp. 3d 1179, 1191 (D. Colo. 2016).
78. Baker v. Seldon, 101 U.S. 99 (1879).
79. *Id.* at 100–01.

utilized the plaintiff's method of bookkeeping, he did not in fact copy the plaintiff's book.[80] The U.S. Supreme Court held that this was not infringement of the plaintiff's copyright: the plaintiff could only obtain protection in his book, not in his idea for bookkeeping. Because the defendant had copied only the plaintiff's *idea* for a type of double-entry bookkeeping, not the book itself (i.e., his actual *expression*), there was no infringement.[81]

The idea/expression dichotomy sometimes rears its head in video game litigation in the form of a purported axiom that the rules of a game are not copyrightable; only the particular "expression" of those rules.[82] In its simplest form, this has been understood to mean that, for example, one cannot copyright the "rules" of a board game such as *Monopoly*—that is, rolling dice to move a piece around imaginary "properties" on a board, purchasing those properties, and paying others a fee when landing on their properties. But the "expression" of those rules, such as the design of the game pieces, the layout and colors of the game board, and the illustrations and text of cards used in the game, would be protectable. For example, in *Affiliated Hospital Products, Inc. v. Merdel Game Manufacturing Co.*,[83] the defendant copied the plaintiff's board game rulebook (making only small clarifications and improvements).[84] The Second Circuit Court of Appeals held that copying the rulebook was not copyright infringement because the content of game rules could not be copyrighted.[85] Rather, only the specific presentation and arrangement of the rules was protectable. The court feared that if game rules themselves (and not

---

80. *Id.*

81. *Id.* at 104–05.

82. *See, e.g.*, Chamberlin v. Uris Sales Corp., 150 F.2d 512, 513 (2d Cir. 1945) (finding that similarities between two sets of board game rules did not constitute infringement, where the similarities were due to derivation from the same source); Whist Club v. Foster, 42 F.2d 782, 782 (S.D.N.Y. 1929) (holding that publication of defendant's auction bridge rules that restated the same set of conventional precepts did not infringe copyright).

83. Affiliated Hosp. Prods., Inc. v. Merdel Game Mfg. Co., 513 F.2d 1183 (2d Cir. 1975).

84. *Id.* at 1188–89.

85. *Id.*

merely their visual arrangement) could be copyrighted, only one game maker could ever publish the rules to a particular game.[86]

In practice, distinguishing between uncopyrightable "rules" and copyrightable "expression" can be difficult. Oftentimes "rules" and "expression" are intertwined and it is not obvious whether a particular aspect of a game is or is not necessary to implementing its rules. This is particularly true in complex games such as video games, board games, and collectible card games. Games such as *Magic: The Gathering* and *Hearthstone* involve hundreds or thousands of individual cards, each with specific functions, strengths, weakness, and interrelationships. Certainly, the concept of a card game in which players attempt to defeat opponents by playing cards that require spending points is not protectable. But what if a competitor were to reproduce every one of *Magic*'s thousands of cards by copying each card's precise attributes, but with original artwork and text? The gameplay details and relationship between elements of a game often involve highly creative and subjective decisions that are the product of extensive thought by experienced game designers.

One court attempted to address these issues in the context of a card game in *DaVinci Editrice S.R.L. v. Ziko Games, LLC.*[87] DaVinci was the publisher of an award-winning card game called *Bang!*, which depicts a "Wild West" setting and themes.[88] The game involves players drawing cards that assigns them to the role of "Sheriff," "Deputy," "Outlaw," or "Renegade."[89] Each role is assigned a different winning condition; for example, the Sheriff wins if he survives until the Outlaws and the Renegade are killed, the Deputies attempt to protect the Sheriff, the Outlaws win if the Sheriff is killed, and the Renegade wins if he or she is the only

---

86. *Id.* This is also referred to as the "merger doctrine." When there is only one or a few ways of expressing a particular idea, the idea is said to merge with the expression, and no copyright protection is granted. Morrisey v. Proctor & Gamble Co., 379 F.2d 675 (1st Cir. 1967) (copyright in rules for Social Security account number sweepstakes limited under the merger doctrine).

87. DaVinci Editrice S.R.L. v. Ziko Games, LLC, 183 F. Supp. 3d 820 (S.D. Tex. 2016).

88. *Id.* at 823.

89. *Id.* at 823–24.

player left alive.[90] Players also draw a card that assigns them a particular character based on a Wild West figure (i.e., "Calamity Janet" or "Willy the Kid"), with its own unique ability that affects, for example, how they are able to attack other players.[91] Gameplay involves players attacking one another using "weapon cards" and "action cards" in order to deplete one another's "life points."[92] Depending on the outcome and who is left alive over the course of the game, different characters will be victorious.

Yoka, a Chinese company, created and released a "reskin" of the game titled *Legend of the Three Kingdoms*.[93] Yoka's game was nearly identical to *Bang!* in its rules and gameplay, but *Bang!*'s Western characters were replaced by characters from Chinese mythology, thus placing the game in a different setting, with different characters, and different player roles.[94] After first denying the defendant's motion to dismiss, the court later sided with Yoka on summary judgment on the grounds that none of the similarities urged by DaVinci constituted protectable expression.[95] For example, DaVinci claimed as an actionable similarity the fact that special abilities and life points, which were present in both games, could significantly affect gameplay.[96] The court disagreed, finding that these constituted game rules, procedures, or winning conditions that are not protectable by themselves, but that create "the environment for the expressive elements of the game."[97]

Notably, the *DaVinci* court did *not* rule out that a game could have a progression of events and a roster of developed characters that makes it expressive, similar to the progression of a book or movie plot (even where basic elements are common). But it also gave an example of games where the plot progressions and characters fall short of copyright protection, comparing them to sporting events where they are purely competitive and have no underlying

---

90. *Id.*
91. *Id.* at 824.
92. *Id.*
93. *Id.* at 825.
94. *Id.*
95. *Id.*
96. *Id.* at 822.
97. *Id.* at 828.

"script."[98] The court placed *Bang!* in this category because, other than particular character alignments, nothing is predetermined or scripted, meaning that there is no creative expression at work; the game is essentially no different than a game of basketball, where players are assigned positions, told the rules, and instructed to go compete.[99] Finally, *Bang!*'s characters were found to merely embody rules of gameplay given that their abilities affected, for example, their ability to attack from certain distances. The court found this no different than chess pieces having different movement abilities and restrictions—something quite obviously not copyrightable.[100]

DaVinci confirms that the analysis of what elements or aspects of a game are copyrightable is a highly nuanced one that must be done on a case-by-case basis. It also must be performed with a clear understanding of what elements or aspects of the game might be considered the author's creative expression as opposed to game mechanics that are and should be available to the public.

2. Scènes à Faire and "Stock" Expression

Much like big-budget movies or other popular media, video games tend to cluster around certain popular genres or settings, such as medieval "high-fantasy" worlds, far future space battles, or modern-day military combat. Several overlapping copyright doctrines allow creators to explore common settings or themes without violating the rights of those that came before.

The doctrine of *scènes à faire* limits copyright protection for "incidents, characters or settings which are as a practical matter indispensable, or at least standard, in the treatment of a given

---

98. *See, e.g.*, Nat'l Basketball Ass'n v. Motorola, Inc., 105 F.3d 841, 846 (2d Cir. 1997) ("Unlike movies, plays, television programs, or operas, athletic events are competitive and have no underlying script.").

99. *DaVinci Editrice S.R.L.*, 183 F. Supp. 3d at 832 ("[T]he events in a *Bang!* game are not predetermined because the interactions between the roles have no underlying script or detail and are not fixed . . . [l]ike basketball, *Bang!* has created a number of roles, defined their alignment with and opposition to other roles, and created rules for their interaction, but has not created a scripted or detailed performance for each game.") (citations omitted).

100. *Id.* at 834.

topic."[101] Some examples might include depictions of Winston Churchill in a game about World War II, skull and crossbones flags in a game about pirates, or spaceships in a game about intergalactic exploration. On the other hand, expression that is unique to a particular depiction of these settings is fully protectable, and thus a space combat game likely could not include the famous *Millennium Falcon* or *U.S.S. Enterprise* without authorization.

The doctrine of *scènes à faire* was applied to video games in the case of *Incredible Technologies, Inc. v. Virtual Technologies, Inc.*[102] The Seventh Circuit Court of Appeals, in considering a golf video game, concluded that to create a realistic golf game, the creator would need, at a minimum, "golf courses, clubs, a selection menu, a golfer, a wind meter, . . . [s]and traps and water hazards. . . ."[103] Because these basic elements were found to be necessary to the treatment of golf, the court held that they constituted *scènes à faire* that did not merit copyright protection.[104] Similarly, in *Data East USA, Inc. v. Epyx, Inc.*,[105] the court considered two karate-based video games to determine their similarity in an infringement analysis.[106] The court observed numerous game elements common to both games, such as a two-player option, forward and backward somersault moves, upper-lunge punches, and jumping sidekicks performed by the game characters.[107] The court determined that each of these elements was "inherent in the sport of karate" and thus "encompass[ed] the idea of karate" and were not protectable.[108]

Related to the doctrine of *scènes à faire* is that of generic or "stock" expression. This "doctrine" prevents copyright owners from claiming protection in elements of their work that are generic and common to all works in the genre. For example, in

---

101. Alexander v. Haley, 460 F. Supp. 40, 45 (S.D.N.Y. 1978). *See also* Incredible Techs., Inc., v. Virtual Techs., 400 F.3d 1007, 1011 (7th Cir. 2005).
102. *Incredible Techs.*, 400 F.3d 1007.
103. *Id.* at 1015.
104. *Id.* at 1014–15.
105. Data E. USA, Inc. v. Epyx, Inc., 862 F.2d 204 (9th Cir. 1988).
106. *Id.* at 209.
107. *Id.*
108. *Id.*

Bissoon-Dath v. Sony Computer Entertainment America, Inc.,[109] the court found that the plaintiff could not base a substantial similarity claim on the fact that his screenplays and the defendant's video game (*God of War*) included Greek gods such as Ares, Zeus, and Athena, as these are "stock figures not only of many contemporary stories, movies and video games, but also of the Western collective unconscious."[110]

In *Capcom U.S.A. v. Data East Corp.,*[111] the doctrines of *scènes à faire* and stock expression both came into play. Capcom, creator of the popular 1991 fighting game *Street Fighter II*, sued Data East, publisher of the 1993 game *Fighter's History*, for copyright infringement.[112] Capcom contended that Data East had copied fighting styles, appearances, special moves, and combination attacks of various *Street Fighter II* characters, in addition to the control sequences used to execute those moves.[113] Capcom sought a preliminary injunction against Data East.[114] The court denied the injunction, observing that the characters and moves in *Street Fighter II* largely consisted of stock characters and standard moves that were immediately recognizable and familiar to players.[115] The court also determined that the similar control sequences in the two games were not actionable under the merger doctrine (discussed previously), in part because there were a limited number of ways (i.e., joystick and button combinations) to express particular moves, particularly given that one of the aims of those control schemes was to imitate movements of the human body.[116]

3. Useful Articles and In-Game Items

Useful articles are items having "an intrinsic utilitarian function that is not merely to portray the appearance of the article or to

---

109. Bissoon-Dath v. Sony Computer Entm't Am., Inc., 694 F. Supp. 2d 1071 (N.D. Cal. 2010).

110. *Id.* at 1088–89.

111. Capcom U.S.A. v. Data E. Corp., No. C 93-3259 WHO, 1994 WL 1751482 (N.D. Cal. Mar. 16, 1994).

112. *Id.*

113. *Id.*

114. *Id.*

115. *Id.* at *14–15.

116. *Id.* at *7–8.

convey information," such as, for example, furniture, tools, and clothing.[117] A tiger costume for a child has been held to be a useful article because, although it is certainly creatively designed, it also serves as an article of clothing, protecting the wearer from the elements.[118] One may obtain copyright protection in the *design* of a useful article as a pictorial, graphic, or sculptural work, but "only to the extent that . . . such design incorporates pictorial, graphic, or sculptural features that can be identified separately from, and are capable of existing independently of, the utilitarian aspects of the article."[119] If the design aspects are not conceptually separable from the utilitarian elements, then no copyright protection will attach.[120]

For example, consider the copyright treatment of clothing. In the real world, clothing is generally classified as a useful article (e.g., to cover one's body and provide warmth) and, therefore, is not copyrightable subject matter.[121] However, certain aspects of certain kinds of clothing can be protected. For instance, in *Kieselstein-Cord v. Accessories by Pearl, Inc.*,[122] the Second Circuit held that the ornamental elements of a belt buckle were protectable because they were conceptually distinct from the utilitarian function of the buckle.[123] In contrast, the same court, in *Carol Barnhart, Inc. v. Economy Cover Corp.*,[124] found that the design

---

117. 17 U.S.C. § 101 (2012); *see also* Mazer v. Stein, 347 U.S. 201 (1954); Pivot Point Int'l, Inc. v. Charlene Prods., 372 F.3d 913 (7th Cir. 2004).

118. Celebration Int'l, Inc. v. Chosun Int'l, Inc., 234 F. Supp. 2d 905, 912 (S.D. Ind. 2002).

119. 17 U.S.C. § 101 (defining "pictorial, graphic, and sculptural works").

120. Leicester v. Warner Bros., 232 F.3d 1212, 1215–16 (9th Cir. 2000).

121. *See, e.g.*, Knitwaves, Inc. v. Lollytogs Ltd., 71 F.3d 996, 1002 (2d Cir. 1995) (noting that, as a general rule, items of clothing are not subject to copyright protection as "useful articles"); Whimsicality, Inc. v. Rubie's Costume Co., 891 F.2d 452, 455 (2d Cir. 1989) ("While the pictorial, graphic and sculptural aspects of useful articles may be copyrightable if they are separable from the article, physically or conceptually . . . clothes are particularly unlikely to meet that test—the very decorative elements that stand out being intrinsic to the decorative function of the clothing."); *but see* Star Athletica v. Varsity Brands, 137 S. Ct. 1002 (2017).

122. Kieselstein-Cord v. Accessories by Pearl, Inc., 632 F.2d 989 (2d Cir. 1980).

123. *Id.* at 993.

124. Carol Barnhart, Inc. v. Econ. Cover Corp., 773 F.2d 411 (2d Cir. 1985).

elements of life-sized breast forms on human torso mannequins were not conceptually separable from their utilitarian function (i.e., displaying clothing) and, thus, could not be protected.[125] The same analysis would also apply to utilitarian aspects of weapons (such as the shape of a gun's stock or barrel) or vehicles (such as the shape of a military tank).[126]

It may seem odd to discuss "useful articles" in the context of video games, which are purely virtual (and thus, perhaps, by definition, cannot be "useful"). But now a separate market exists for the purchase of "useful" (if not indispensable) items for game avatars. This includes not only purely cosmetic items (such as cosmetic avatar "skins" or clothing), but also functional items such as weapons and armor. So, for example, if a player can only effectively compete in a certain online environment with the purchase of a particular in-game weapon of generic and "functional" design, is that a useful or utilitarian item? Or, what if a player requires furniture in his or her virtual space so that other avatars can "comfortably" visit? Of course, this is all a fiction. The appearance of a virtual gun has absolutely no relationship to its function. One court, presented with the issue of whether "clothing" for a toy teddy bear is copyrightable subject matter, reasoned as follows:

> The clothing on a teddy bear obviously has no utilitarian function. It is not intended to cover embarrassing anatomical aspects or to protect the bear from exterior elements. Rather, it is intended and serves only to modify the appearance of the bear, to give the doll a different "look and feel" from others. Clothing on a bear replicates the

---

125. *Id.* at 418.

126. In the case of some objects where "shape is mandated by function . . . [i]f one manufacturer were given the copyright to the design of such an article, it could completely prevent others from producing the same article." Universal Furniture Int'l, Inc. v. Collezione Europa USA, Inc., 618 F.3d 417, 432 (4th Cir. 2010) (per curiam) (quoting Esquire, Inc. v. Ringer, 591 F.2d 796, 801 n.15 (D.C. Cir. 1978)). As a result, if and to the extent shape is indeed "mandated by function," then no copyright should be available for that shape no matter how aesthetically pleasing it may be. *Id. See, e.g.,* 11 NIMMER & NIMMER, *supra* note 22, § 924.1 (discussing that in the context of useful articles, "the serrated edge of a knife cannot be registered, even if the pattern of the serration is original").

form but not the function of clothing on a person. It does not constitute a "useful article" excluded from copyright protection.[127]

As a result, items that may be considered "useful" (and unprotectable) when they are tangible items might be entitled to copyright protection when depicted virtually. Or, the code that creates that virtual item may be entitled to protection. This protection, however, will be limited to the extent that the item merely mimics the same item as it exists in the real world. Otherwise, a game developer would be able to monopolize the depiction of real-life guns, clothing, or vehicles in its virtual world.

But conversely, the manufacturer of a useful article such as a weapon, vehicle, article of clothing, or item of furniture should not be able to assert a claim against a game developer for its depiction of a "virtual" version of that article in a video game. Rather, copyright protection would extend only to unique design or artistic elements that are conceptually separable from the utilitarian aspects of that article, such as a unique design painted on a vehicle.

II. Authorship and Ownership

The owner of a copyright possesses a "bundle" of specific, exclusive rights with respect to that work.[128] These exclusive rights include the right to reproduce the work (the "reproduction right"),

---

127. Boyds Collection, Ltd. v. Bearington Collection, Inc., 360 F. Supp. 2d 655, 661 (M.D. Pa. 2005).

128. *See, e.g.*, F. Gregory Lastowka & Dan Hunter, *The Laws of the Virtual Worlds*, 92 CAL. L. REV. 1, 30–31 (2004) ("The timeworn metaphor of property as a bundle of rights, chiefly the rights to use, exclude, and transfer, applies to virtual chattels as well."). *See generally* J.E. Penner, *The "Bundle of Rights" Picture of Property*, 43 UCLA L. REV. 711, 712–13 (1996) ("Any standard right in property is properly treated as a bundle of rights the owner holds against many others. Furthermore, the substance of the property right itself is subject to fractionation. . . . Properly understood, then, 'property is a bundle of rights' expresses the thesis that property constitutes a legal complex of various normative relations, not simply rights."); WESLEY NEWCOMB HOHFELD, FUNDAMENTAL LEGAL CONCEPTIONS AS APPLIED IN JUDICIAL REASONING AND OTHER LEGAL ESSAYS (David Campbell & Philip A. Thomas eds., reprint ed. 2002) (1919).

to create derivative works (the "adaptation right"), to distribute the work (the "distribution right"), to publicly perform the work ("the public performance right"), and to publicly display the work (the "public display right").[129] These rights, which come into existence at the time of the work's creation,[130] are independent of one another and can be disposed of or licensed together or separately.[131]

Under U.S. copyright law, ownership of a protectable work vests initially in the work's author.[132] Though there are philosophical differences as to what makes someone an "author," one of the most helpful (and frequently cited) definitions of the term can be found in *Aalmuhammed v. Lee*.[133] In *Aalmuhammed*, the Ninth Circuit analyzed the meaning of "authorship" in the context of whether an individual who provided some creative assistance with director Spike Lee's motion picture *Malcolm X* could claim an authorship stake in the film. In finding that the "author" of the film was director Spike Lee, the court held that an "author" is the person who "superintends" the work by exercising control.[134] This will likely be a person "who has actually formed the picture by putting the persons in position, and arranging the place where the people are to be—the man who is the effective cause of that," or "the inventive or master mind" who "creates, or gives effect to the idea."[135]

---

129. 17 U.S.C. § 106 (2012). Authors of works of visual art also enjoy the rights of attribution and integrity; however, under U.S. copyright law, unlike the rights set forth in § 106, these "moral" rights may not be conferred on anyone other than the work's author. *Id.* § 106A.

130. The copyright term typically endures throughout the author's life and for 70 years after his or her death. *See id.* § 302(a). For works created before January 1, 1978, there is a more complicated method for calculating the duration of the copyright. *See id.* §§ 303–304.

131. *See id.* § 201(d)(2) ("Any of the exclusive rights comprised in a copyright, including any subdivision of any of the rights specified by section 106, may be transferred . . . and owned separately.").

132. *See id.* § 201(a). If the work has more than one author, they take joint ownership of the work. *Id.*

133. Aalmuhammed v. Lee, 202 F.3d 1227 (9th Cir. 2000).

134. *Id.* at 1234.

135. *Id.* at 1232–33; *see also* Cmty. for Creative Non-Violence v. Reid, 490 U.S. 730, 737 (1989) (the "author" of a work is the person "who actually creates the work, that is, the person who translates an idea into a fixed, tangible expression

But the Copyright Act recognizes another way of becoming an author: via a "work-for-hire" relationship, either through employment or contract. In the case of works made for hire, the "employer or other person for whom the work was prepared" is deemed to be the author and thus the owner of the copyright.[136] Additionally, not every work has a single author. The Copyright Act specifically discusses "joint works," which are works "prepared by two or more authors with the intention that their contributions be merged into inseparable or interdependent parts of a unitary whole."[137]

I discuss both of these concepts in the context of video games, and then briefly discuss the unique situation of user-generated content in video games.

A. *Works for Hire*

Modern video games usually are made by teams of programmers, artists, designers, composers, and animators working for or on behalf of a development studio or publisher. As a result, most games are created as "works for hire," with the studio or publisher assuming the role as the game's "author." Under the Copyright Act, a work can be a work made for hire if either: (1) the work is prepared by an employee while performing duties that are within the scope of his or her employment; or (2) if the parties expressly agree in writing, and the work is specially ordered or commissioned for use as a contribution to a collective work, as a part of a motion picture or other audiovisual work, as a translation, as a supplementary work, as a compilation, as an instructional text, as a test, as answer material for a test, or as an atlas.[138] Both types of works for hire are common in the video game world. However, it should also be noted that "literary works" are *not* included as among the categories of "specially commissioned works." Thus, it

---

entitled to copyright protection"); Burrow-Giles Lithographic Co. v. Sarony, 111 U.S. 53, 61 (1884) (the author is "the person who has superintended the arrangement" of the work, and authorship involves "producing, as the inventive or master mind, the thing which is to be protected").

136. *See* 17 U.S.C. § 201(b) ("In the case of a work made for hire, the employer or other person for whom the work was prepared is considered the author. . . .").

137. *Id.* § 101 (defining "joint works").

138. *Id.*

is arguable that source code (in and of itself) cannot be a work for hire if created by an independent contractor, though if the code is part of an "audiovisual work" it should fall within the provision.

1. Employee-Created Works

The Copyright Act defines a "work made for hire" as including "a work prepared by an employee within the scope of his or her employment."[139] The act thus contemplates a two-part test: (1) is the creator an employee or independent contractor? and (2) if an employee, was the work prepared within the "scope" of the employee's employment? In *Community for Creative Non-Violence v. Reid*,[140] the U.S. Supreme Court held that both of these inquiries are to be determined using traditional principles of agency law.[141]

Many (if not most) game developers and publishers require employees to execute written work-for-hire agreements at the time of their employment. Doing so is a smart practice, because disputes can arise as to whether an employee's creative actions fall within the scope of his or her employment. That inquiry is generally approached using a three-part test set forth in section 228 of the *Restatement (Second) of Agency*.[142] Under that test, an employee's conduct falls "within the scope of employment if, but only if: (a) it is of the kind he is employed to perform; (b) it occurs substantially within the authorized time and space limits; [and] (c) it is actuated, at least in part, by a purpose to serve the [employer]."[143] In performing the test, courts look at facts such as where the work was created (at home or in the office), what computer equipment was used to create the work (the employee's or employer's), whether the employee was directed to create the work by his or her superior, whether (and how) the employee was

---

139. *Id.*

140. *Cmty. for Creative Non-Violence*, 490 U.S. 730.

141. *Id.* at 739–41, 751; *see also* 1 NIMMER & NIMMER, *supra* note 22, § 5.03[B][1][a][iii].

142. *See, e.g.*, U.S. Auto Parts Network, Inc. v. Parts Geek, LLC, 692 F.3d 1009, 1015 (9th Cir. 2012).

143. RESTATEMENT (SECOND) OF AGENCY § 228 (2010).

compensated for the work, and whether the employee received any assistance or input from the employer.[144]

In *Lewis v. Activision Blizzard, Inc.*,[145] the court addressed a dispute between the game developer Blizzard Entertainment and a former employee over ownership of voice-over recordings used for a *World of Warcraft* game character. The plaintiff had been employed by Blizzard as a *World of Warcraft* "game master"— defined as "customer service specialists with expert knowledge of the game who are [] present as characters within *World of Warcraft*'s epic fantasy setting to provide assistance and guidance to players while also coordinating world functionality" and who "are responsible for in-game customer support, helping manage our online community, and assisting with the creation of content during the ever ongoing development of the game."[146] While working for Blizzard, the plaintiff was invited to participate in a company-wide "open audition" for voice talent for *World of Warcraft* and was selected to have her voice recorded by Blizzard (at its internal recording studio) for a new "baby murloc" creature (a "cuter, smaller version of the original murloc").[147] Several years after her original voice recordings were created, the plaintiff filed a lawsuit against Blizzard, arguing that the performance of character voices was outside the scope of her job and thus she, not Blizzard, owned the copyright in the recordings.[148]

The court granted summary judgment for Blizzard, holding that "the baby murloc recordings fell squarely within the scope of her employment."[149] Among the facts that the court found persuasive were that the recordings were created on Blizzard's premises, using Blizzard equipment; the plaintiff had been paid her hourly wage for the work; she had accepted an opportunity that was only available to Blizzard employees; "assisting with content creation"

---

144. *Cmty. for Creative Non-Violence*, 490 U.S. at 751–52.
145. Lewis v. Activision Blizzard, Inc., No. C 12-1096 CW, 2013 U.S. Dist. LEXIS 149784 (N.D. Cal. Oct. 17, 2013), *aff'd*, 634 Fed. Appx. 182 (9th Cir. 2015).
146. *Id.* at *2.
147. *Id.* at *3–4.
148. *Id.* at *4–5.
149. *Id.* at *9–10.

was expressly included in her job description; and the purpose of her work was to further her employer's interests—namely, to improve *World of Warcraft*.[150]

2. Specially Commissioned Works

The second category of work for hire is a "specially commissioned work."[151] These are works created by nonemployees (i.e., independent contractors) pursuant to a written agreement.[152] Because video games typically are "audiovisual works," they should be among the types of works encompassed by the statute.[153] Thus, a work-for-hire agreement between a game developer and independent contractor (e.g., an individual hired to provide discrete artwork) will vest copyright authorship (and thus original ownership from inception) in the developer, without the need for an assignment of rights (where the work is owned initially by the contractor and only subsequently transferred to the developer).

The difference between ownership via "work for hire" and ownership via assignment can be critical, as author/assignors enjoy additional rights that are not enjoyed by those who perform work on a "for-hire" basis. One important right possessed by authors is the right to recapture a copyright under certain circumstances after 35 years via "termination of transfer."[154] Depending on the anticipated life span of a work (e.g., *Pac-Man* recently turned 38), the right of a game developer to terminate an assignment to a

---

150. *Id.* at *10–15.

151. *See* 17 U.S.C. § 101 (2012).

152. Generally the signed, written agreement "*must precede* the creation of the [commissioned] property. . . ." Schiller & Schmidt, Inc. v. Nordisco Corp., 969 F.2d 410, 413 (7th Cir. 1992) (emphasis added); Playboy Enters., Inc. v. Dumas, 53 F.3d 549, 558–59 (2d Cir. 1995). *See also* 1 NIMMER & NIMMER, *supra* note 22, § 5.03[B][2][b]. However, the Second Circuit and some other courts have also held that "the writing requirement of § 101(2) can be met by a writing executed after the work is created, if the writing confirms a prior agreement, either explicit or implicit, made before the creation of the work." *Playboy*, 53 F.3d at 559.

153. 17 U.S.C. § 101 (2012).

154. *Id.* § 203 ("In the case of any work *other than a work made for hire*, the exclusive or nonexclusive grant of a transfer or license of copyright or of any right under a copyright, executed by the author on or after January 1, 1978, otherwise than by will, is subject to termination under [certain] conditions.") (emphasis added).

publisher could be quite significant. As a result, it is generally beneficial for a game developer or publisher to contract for out-sourced work on a "for-hire" basis.

B. Joint Works and Contributions

Works created by more than one author "with the intention that their contributions be merged into inseparable or interdependent parts of a unitary whole" are known as "joint works."[155] As the definition makes clear, the mere fact that two people have collectively participated in the creation of a work is not sufficient to make it a "joint work." Instead, the putative joint authors must have intended the merging of their contributions and that such merging would result in a work of joint authorship.[156] Thus, for example, in *Childress v. Taylor*,[157] the court found that a woman who provided research, suggestions, and ideas to the lead writer of a stage play was not a joint author, including because "whatever thought of co-authorship might have existed in Taylor's mind 'was emphatically not shared by the purported co-author.'"[158]

An issue that is closely related to joint authorship is that of individual ownership of *contributions* made to an audiovisual work. This usually arises in circumstances where the putative author has made contributions to a work, but cannot prove the requisite intent for joint authorship or the contributions are insufficient to rise to the level of joint authorship. In such circumstances, the plaintiff may claim that while he or she is not a joint author of the entirety, he or she nevertheless is an author (and thus owner of copyright) in his or her specific contribution to the whole. This theory was rejected in *Garcia v. Google*.[159] In that case, the plaintiff, an actress, claimed that she had been "duped" into performing in

---

155. *Id.* § 101.
156. *See, e.g.,* Aalmuhammed v. Lee, 202 F.3d 1227, 1231 (9th Cir. 2000) ("The statutory language establishes that for a work to be a joint work . . . the authors must intend their contributions be merged into inseparable or interdependent parts of a unitary whole.") (internal quotation marks omitted).
157. Childress v. Taylor, 945 F.2d 500 (2d Cir. 1991).
158. *Id.* at 509.
159. Garcia v. Google, 786 F.3d 733 (9th Cir. 2015).

a film titled *Innocence of Muslims*.[160] The film was highly controversial and resulted in the plaintiff receiving death threats and other forms of harassment.[161] In an effort to have the film removed from platforms such as YouTube, the plaintiff claimed that although she was not a joint author of the film, she possessed a copyright in her five-second acting performance.[162] Thus, she could seek injunctive relief to prevent the distribution of that performance (and, by extension, the remainder of the film).[163] The Ninth Circuit, sitting en banc, rejected her claim, holding that her performance (even if copyrightable) was part of a "unified" audiovisual work.[164] Thus, she could not "own" her performance separately from the motion picture. The court's rationale was as follows:

> Garcia's theory of copyright law would result in [a] legal morass . . . splintering a movie into many different "works," even in the absence of an independent fixation. Simply put, as Google claimed, it "make[s] Swiss cheese of copyrights." Take, for example, films with a large cast . . . Treating every acting performance as an independent work would not only be a logistical and financial nightmare, it would turn cast of thousands into a new mantra: copyright of thousands.[165]

By the same token, those who contribute ideas, suggestions, and advice to the lead developer (or developers) of a video game will generally not be considered an "author" of the game. So, for example, those who participate in beta testing or bug fixing, post useful advice to a message board, or even provide some design work, may be useful contributors, but they are not "authors." This issue was addressed by the Northern District of California in the *Lilith* case.[166] There, the evidence was that three individuals (Eul, Guinsoo, and Icefrog) were the "masterminds" of versions of the

---

160. *Id.* at 736–37.
161. *Id.*
162. *Id.* at 737.
163. *Id.*
164. *Id.* at 743.
165. *Id.* at 742–43.
166. Blizzard Entm't, Inc. v. Lilith Games (Shanghai) Co., No. 3:15-cv-04084-CRB, 2017 U.S. Dist. LEXIS 74639 (N.D. Cal. May 16, 2017).

popular *Warcraft III* mod *Defense of the Ancients* (or *DotA*).[167] While these authors "took suggestions from others—some elaborate, some less so," they were the ones who decided which of those suggestions "made the cut."[168] "So just as Spike Lee was the author of the work at issue in *Aalmuhammed*, a reasonable jury could (and perhaps must) conclude that Eul, Guinsoo, and Icefrog are the authors of the various works at issue here."[169]

The thorny questions of authorship or joint authorship of collaborative or fan-made works such as mods are likely to become even thornier as works are collaboratively built in augmented reality or virtual reality spaces. It is not difficult to imagine collaborative virtual art or sculptural projects undertaken by several individuals working together in a real-world space or virtual reality space, either simultaneously or asynchronously. Much like graffiti or other public art, collaborative software could enable the creation of a virtual sculpture or mural in a public space, which could then be further modified or altered by later passersby. In that situation, it would be extremely difficult to determine who would be the "author" of any such work, and, indeed, it is possible that there is no single author of the work.

C. EULAs and Ownership of Game Mods and Virtual Property

End-user license agreements (EULAs) that govern the relationship between game publishers and their players play a critical role in defining the scope of rights in virtual property, and user-created content. A complete discussion of EULAs is contained in Chapter 1 of this book. Nevertheless, I briefly discuss the role that EULAs play in copyright ownership in the context of video games and virtual worlds.

One fascinating and often-debated issue is that of who owns the copyright in a game "modification" or custom game level created by a user. Without an express agreement to the contrary, an authorized derivative work is owned by its author (but only to the extent

---

167. *Id.* at *22.
168. *Id.* at *14.
169. *Id.* at *23.

of the author's contribution).[170] However, this is only a "default rule" and it can be modified by contract.[171] Thus, if the derivative work (or mod) was created pursuant to a license agreement (such as a EULA), the terms of the agreement will take precedence over the default rule.[172] So, for example, if the EULA provides that the creator of a derivative work does not own a copyright in the new work, that may be sufficient to vest ownership in the owner of the underlying work. In other words, the ownership of a mod is likely to be entirely governed by the terms of the EULA. If the EULA is silent, ownership of the mod will vest in its author, but only to the extent it consists of original expression.

EULAs differ substantially as to their treatment of mods or derivative works. For example, Mojang's EULA for its game *Minecraft* makes clear (in very plain English) that the users are the owners of their original content created using the game and its tools:

> *Any Mods you create for the Game from scratch belong to you* (including pre-run Mods and in-memory Mods) and you can do whatever you want with them, as long as you don't sell them for money/try to make money from them and so long as you don't distribute Modded Versions of the Game. Remember that a Mod means something that is your original work and that does not contain a substantial part of our code or content. You only own what you created; you do not own our code or content.[173]

Notably, however, the *Minecraft* EULA also prohibits the commercial use ("sell[ing] them for money") of user-created mods. Whether that restriction is a limitation on the scope of the

---

170. Schrock v. Learning Curve Int'l, Inc., 586 F.3d 513, 523 (7th Cir. 2009) ("[T]he [Copyright] Act provides that copyright in a derivative work, like copyright in any other work, arises by operation of law once the author's original expression is fixed in a tangible medium.").

171. *See, e.g.*, Liu v. Price Waterhouse LLP, 302 F.3d 749, 755 (7th Cir. 2002).

172. *See* L.A. Printex Indus. v. Aeropostale, No. CV 08-07085 DPP (Ex), 2010 U.S. Dist. LEXIS 46951, at *8 (C.D. Cal. May 5, 2010) (language authorizing the creation of derivative works entitled the creator to a copyright in the new material), *rev'd and remanded*, 676 F.3d 841 (9th Cir. 2012).

173. Mojang, *Minecraft End User License Agreement*, https://account.mojang .com/documents/minecraft_eula (last updated Sept. 20, 2017).

modder's copyright or is a purely contractual restriction is open for debate. Either way, it is a very common restriction found in most EULAs, and it likely is enforceable.

By contrast, the EULA for the game *Fallout 4* contains an unequivocal transfer of ownership of user-generated content to Bethesda Softworks and its parent Zenimax Media:

> If the Software makes available, as a separate downloadable installer, a level editor or other similar type tools, assets and other materials (the "Software Utilities") that permit you to construct or customize new game levels and other related game materials for personal use in connection with the Software ("Customized Game Materials"), then in the event you access such Software Utilities, the use of the Software Utilities is subject to the following additional terms, conditions and restrictions:
>
> *(a) All Customized Game Materials created by you are exclusively owned by LICENSOR and/or its licensors (as the case may be) and you hereby transfer, assign and convey to LICENSOR all right, title and interest in and to the Customized Game Materials* and LICENSOR and its permitted licensors may use any Customized Game Materials made publicly available to you for any purpose whatsoever, including but not limited to for purposes of advertising and promoting the Software . . .[174]

EULAs are enforceable contracts and they are routinely upheld by courts. As a result, the way in which a EULA delineates ownership generally will be the final word on ownership issues arising from the use of software or in-game tools.

Another issue commonly addressed by EULAs is that of "ownership" of virtual "property," such as in-game weapons, clothing, or even characters. This is no small matter. Many players spend hundreds or thousands of dollars each year on virtual goods, such

---

174. Steam, *Fallout 4 End User License Agreement*, https://store.steampowered .com/eula/377160_eula_0 (last visited July 25, 2018).

as "packs" of cards for computer collectible card games such as *Hearthstone* or *Gwent*, new characters or character skins for competitive multiplayer online battle arena (MOBA) games such as *League of Legends* and *Heroes of the Storm*, or new vehicles for racing games such as *Grand Turismo*. Other players might not spend cash on such items but may acquire them through many hours of play (i.e., "grinding"). In either case, a virtual good can be of enormous value to a player and may represent months of hard "work" or a significant monetary investment.

While acquiring a virtual good may give the player a strong feeling of ownership of that item, the reality is that the user has not actually "acquired" anything. Rather, the acquisition merely grants the player the ability to "use" the item, changing it from inaccessible (or "locked") to accessible ("unlocked"). Most EULAs make clear that all in-game content remains the property of the game developer or publisher. For example, Blizzard's EULA states as follows:

> The following components of the Platform (which do not include content or components of the Licensors' Games), are owned or licensed by Blizzard: All virtual content appearing within the Platform, including the Blizzard Games, such as . . . ***Virtual goods, such as digital cards, currency, potions, weapons, armor, wearable items, skins, sprays, pets, mounts, etc.***[175]

Moreover, since most EULAs give game publishers or developers the right to terminate or suspend user accounts, or to discontinue support for a game altogether, "ownership" of a virtual good is entirely in the control of the developer or publisher.[176]

---

175. Blizzard Entertainment, *Blizzard End User License Agreement* [hereinafter *Blizzard End User License Agreement*], http://us.blizzard.com/en-us/company/legal /eula (last revised June 1, 2018).

176. *See, e.g., id.,* ¶ 10[B][iii] ("In the event of a termination of this Agreement, any right you may have had to any pre-purchased Game access or virtual goods, such as digital cards, currency, weapons, armor, wearable items, skins, sprays, pets, mounts, etc., are forfeit, and you agree and acknowledge that you are not entitled to any refund for any amounts which were pre-paid on your Account prior to any termination of this Agreement. In addition, you will not be able to use the Platform.").

Likewise, peer-to-peer "transfers" of virtual goods are neither transfers of ownership nor (in most cases) acts of copyright infringement because the in-game item is neither being copied nor physically transferred.[177] As one author explains:

> Since the participants never have a right to physically possess either the virtual item or the data representing that item, . . . [i]t is more accurate to say that what participants possess is a license to enter the virtual world and to use items in connection with that access. Transfers of virtual items, avatars and accounts constitute not a transfer of possession of the virtual good itself, but instead a transfer of the license associated with use of the virtual good. . . .[178]

However, the sale of in-game goods will in many cases violate the game's EULA or terms of service.[179] Thus, they can result in termination of a user's account and forfeiture of any virtual items associated with that account.

III. Copyright Infringement

Copyright infringement occurs when one or more of the copyright owner's exclusive rights are exploited without the authorization of the copyright owner.[180] Knowledge or intent is not necessary to establish direct infringement, as even an innocent infringer may

---

177. See Molly Stephens, Note, *Sales of In-Game Assets: An Illustration of the Continuing Failure of Intellectual Property Law to Protect Digital Content Creators*, 80 Tex. L. Rev. 1513, 1520–29 (2002).

178. David P. Sheldon, Comment, *Claiming Ownership but Getting Owned: Contractual Limitations on Asserting Property Interests in Virtual Goods*, 54 UCLA L. Rev. 751, 774–75 (2007). The author also compares the relationship between virtual-world operators and players to that between an event promoter and ticket purchaser: "While [the ticket buyer] could be said to own the physical ticket, he does not own an absolute right to enter the venue during the event. Instead, the ticket represents a license to access the venue, subject to certain terms and revocable at the discretion of the venue." *Id.* at 775.

179. *See, e.g.*, *Blizzard End User License Agreement*, *supra* note 173, ¶ 1[C][iii] (prohibiting the gathering of in-game items for sale outside the platform).

180. *See* Baxter v. MCA, Inc., 812 F.2d 421, 423 (9th Cir. 1987) (discussing the elements of copyright infringement).

be held liable.[181] Since the owners of copyright possess exclusive rights to reproduce, adapt, distribute, publicly perform, and publicly display their works, copyrights may be infringed in a variety of ways. In the digital environment, copyright infringement can occur when works are uploaded to or downloaded from a computer server;[182] performed by means of a digital audio or audiovisual transmission (including a streaming transmission);[183] or adapted and modified via editing or other alterations.[184] However, to infringe a copyright, the act must be a "volitional" one;[185] purely passive and transitory copying (such as the passive transmission of a file through an e-mail pipeline) generally will not trigger copyright liability.[186]

In addition to "direct" copyright infringement, copyright law recognizes claims for "indirect" or "secondary" liability under two distinct but interrelated theories.

First, under the doctrine of *vicarious liability*, a defendant may be liable for another's infringement where it possesses "the right and ability to supervise infringing conduct" and has an "'obvious and direct financial interest in the exploitation of copyrighted materials.'"[187] Under this theory of liability, a flea market operator

---

181. Playboy Enters., Inc. v. Frena, 839 F. Supp. 1552, 1559 (M.D. Fla. 1993). *See also* Sega Enters., Ltd. v. Sabella, No. C 93-4260, 1996 WL 780560, at *7 (N.D. Cal. Dec. 18, 1996) (whether bulletin board system (BBS) operator "knew her BBS users were infringing on Sega's copyright, or encouraged them to do so, has no bearing on whether she directly caused the copying to occur").

182. *See* MAI Sys. Corp. v. Peak Computer, Inc., 991 F.2d 511, 518 (9th Cir. 1993) ("copying" within the meaning of the Copyright Act occurs whenever a computer program is transferred from a permanent storage device to a computer's random access memory); Creative Labs, Inc. v. Cyrix Corp., No. C 97-0912 CW, 1997 U.S. Dist. LEXIS 14492, at *13 (N.D. Cal. May 7, 1997) (defendant had "directly copied," and therefore had likely directly infringed, plaintiff's copyrighted software by placing an unauthorized copy on its website).

183. Am. Broad. Co. v. Aereo, Inc., 134 S. Ct. 2498, 2504 (2014).

184. Disney Enters. v. VidAngel, Inc., 224 F. Supp. 3d 957, 972–73 (C.D. Cal. 2016).

185. Perfect 10, Inc. v. Giganews, Inc., 847 F.3d 657, 666 (9th Cir. 2017).

186. ALS Scan, Inc. v. RemarQ Cmtys., Inc., 239 F.3d 619, 622 (4th Cir. 2001) (holding that an entity acting as a "passive conduit for copyrighted material . . . is not liable as a direct infringer").

187. 3 NIMMER & NIMMER, *supra* note 22, § 12.04[A][2] (footnote omitted) (quoting Shapiro, Bernstein & Co. v. H.L. Green Co., 316 F.2d 304, 307 (2d Cir. 1963)).

may be liable for sales of counterfeit CDs sold on its premises,[188] or the owner of a dance hall may be liable for infringing performances by a band paid to entertain and draw customers.[189] In the online context, the notorious Napster service was found vicariously liable for the infringing conduct of its users (namely, uploading and downloading MP3 music files) because it had the ability to control its system (including its online index), and the availability of free copyrighted music files on Napster's program was a draw for users, thus creating the necessary financial benefit.[190]

Second, a defendant will be liable for *contributory copyright infringement* when he or she knowingly contributes to the infringing conduct of another.[191] A classic example of contributory infringement in the online context is that of the online bulletin board operator who knowingly enables users to upload and download digital files to the system, such as in *Sega Enterprises v. MAPHIA*.[192] Other examples of contributory infringers include a "movie rental" business that encouraged the public to make use of its private rooms for the purpose of viewing copyrighted video cassettes,[193] sales representatives who were responsible for advertising and promoting infringing materials,[194] and the promoter of "pirate chips" that enabled the copying of computer programs.[195]

One subspecies of contributory liability (though sometimes framed as a separate basis for secondary liability) is that of

---

188. Fonovisa, Inc. v. Cherry Auction, Inc., 76 F.3d 259, 263–64 (9th Cir. 1996).

189. *See, e.g.*, Buck v. Jewell-LaSalle Realty Co., 238 U.S. 191, 198–99 (1931); Dreamland Ballroom, Inc. v. Shapiro, Bernstein & Co., 36 F.2d 354, 355 (7th Cir. 1929).

190. A&M Records, Inc. v. Napster, Inc., 239 F.3d 1004, 1023–24 (9th Cir. 2001).

191. 3 NIMMER & NIMMER, *supra* note 22, § 12.04[A][3][a]; *see also* Demetriades v. Kaufmann, 690 F. Supp. 289, 292–94 (S.D.N.Y. 1988); Gershwin Publ'n Corp. v. Columbia Artists Mgmt., Inc., 443 F.2d 1159, 1162 (2d Cir. 1971) ("[O]ne who, with knowledge of the infringing activity, induces, causes or materially contributes to the infringing conduct of another, may be held liable as a contributory infringer.").

192. Sega Enters. v. MAPHIA, 948 F. Supp. 923 (N.D. Cal. 1996).

193. Columbia Pictures Indus., Inc. v. Aveco, Inc., 800 F.2d 59, 62 (3d Cir. 1986).

194. Wales Indus. Inc. v. Hasbro Bradley, Inc., 612 F. Supp. 510, 518 (S.D.N.Y. 1985); Screen Gems-Columbia Music, Inc. v. Mark Fi Records, Inc., 256 F. Supp. 399, 403 (S.D.N.Y. 1966).

195. Cable/Home Commc'n Corp. v. Network Prods., Inc., 902 F.2d 829, 847 (11th Cir. 1990).

"inducement" to infringe a copyright.[196] This basis for liability was articulated in *MGM Studios, Inc. v. Grokster Ltd.*[197] In reversing a grant of summary judgment for the owners of peer-to-peer file-sharing networks, the U.S. Supreme Court held that the defendants had induced users to infringe plaintiff's copyrights by exhorting members of the public to use its system to copy and distribute copyrighted music files unlawfully, offering technical support, deliberately failing to employ any filtering tools to diminish the infringing activity, and making money by directing ads to the screens of computers employing their software.[198] These facts together, in the Court's words, were "unmistakable" evidence of an unlawful objective.[199]

Next I discuss a few of the most interesting examples of the types of copyright disputes that courts have recently addressed.

A. Copycat or "Clone" Games

In recent years, two major decisions have been issued concerning copycat or "clone" games.

First, in *Tetris Holding, LLC v. Xio Interactive, Inc.*,[200] in which Tetris Holding, LLC, the company that owns the intellectual property rights in and to the classic puzzle game *Tetris*, filed suit for copyright infringement against Xio Interactive, Inc., a developer that had created a multiplayer puzzle game for the iPhone called *Mino*.[201] Tetris Holding alleged that *Mino* was a direct knockoff of *Tetris* and brought a motion for summary judgment identifying multiple elements of *Tetris* Xio had allegedly copied with *Mino*.[202] (See Figure 2.1.) These included, but were not limited to:

---

196. MGM Studios, Inc. v. Grokster, Ltd., 545 U.S. 913, 930 (2005); 3 NIMMER & NIMMER, *supra* note 22, § 12.04[A][4] (discussing aspects of intent to induce infringement as distinguished from contributory infringement).

197. *MGM Studios*, 545 U.S. 913.

198. *Id.* at 937–38.

199. *Id.* at 940–41.

200. Tetris Holding, LLC v. Xio Interactive, Inc., 863 F. Supp. 2d 394 (D.N.J. 2012).

201. *Id.* at 396–97.

202. *Id.* at 397–98.

- The use of seven "Tetromino" playing pieces made up of four equally sized squares joined at their sides, identical to the pieces used in *Tetris*
- The bright, distinct colors used for each of the Tetromino pieces
- The use of a tall, rectangular playing field or matrix with identical dimensions to the *Tetris* playing field (i.e., ten blocks wide, 20 blocks tall)
- The display of a "shadow" piece beneath the Tetrominos as they fall
- Inclusion of a display near the playfield showing the next playing piece to appear in the playfield
- The appearance of individual blocks automatically filling in the playfield from bottom to top when the game is over
- The display of "garbage lines" with at least one missing block in a random order[203]

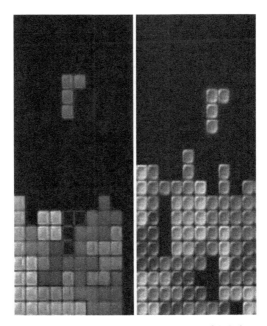

Figure 2.1 Tetris (left) versus Mino (right)

---

203. *Id.*

Xio essentially admitted that its game was a *Tetris* "clone," but argued that it meticulously copied only non-protected elements relating to the rules and functionality of *Tetris*, rather than the game's expressive elements inessential to gameplay.[204] The court agreed that Tetris Holding could not protect functional aspects of *Tetris*, but found Xio's argument legally incorrect and illogical.[205] For example, while Xio argued that all of *Tetris*'s expressive elements *Mino* had copied (essentially the entire game) were inextricably intertwined with the rules of *Tetris*, the court found that many of the elements that had been copied (including shapes and colors) were purely aesthetic choices.[206] The court also expressed concern that Xio's theory would "likely swallow any protection one could possibly have," given that "almost all expressive elements of a game are related in some way to the rules and functions of game play."[207] In fact, the parties apparently agreed that there are an "almost unlimited number" of ways to express the rules of *Tetris*, including myriad ways of designing pieces, the game board, and the playing field, which would still allow the game to function perfectly well.[208]

The second decision, *Spry Fox, LLC v. LOL Apps, Inc.*,[209] likewise involved two similar mobile games. Spry Fox, LLC, the creator of a mobile game called *Triple Town*, sued the maker of a game called *Yeti Town* for copyright infringement.[210] Both *Triple Town* and *Yeti Town* were played on a six-by-six grid.[211] In each game, players were provided with a series of objects to place in squares on the grid.[212] If the player placed three identical objects next to one another so that they connected, the matching objects disappeared and were replaced by an object higher in the game's hierarchy.[213] In *Triple*

204. *Id.* at 397.
205. *Id.* at 408.
206. *Id.* at 414.
207. *Id.* at 405.
208. *Id.* at 411.
209. Spry Fox, LLC v. LOL Apps, Inc., No. C12-147RAJ, 2012 U.S. Dist. LEXIS 153863 (W.D. Wash. Sept. 18, 2012).
210. *Id.* at *2–3.
211. *Id.* at *4.
212. *Id.*
213. *Id.*

Town, a player began with a patch of grass.[214] Under the game's progression system, three patches of grass became a bush, three bushes became a tree, three trees became a hut, and so forth.[215] *Yeti Town* followed the same three-object progression system with different items, including saplings, trees, tents, and cabins.[216] Both games also included antagonists that prevented the player from placing an object: a bear in *Triple Town* and a yeti in *Yeti Town*, both of which could be "trapped" by surrounding them with objects.[217] And, both games included a class of objects that could destroy other objects ("Imperial Bots" in *Triple Town* and campfires in *Yeti Town*).[218] The games, illustrated in Figure 2.2, also had several other similarities, including but not limited to similar player goals, similar reward systems, and similar in-game tutorials.[219]

Figure 2.2 Triple Town (left) versus Yeti Town (right)

As in *Tetris*, the defendant argued that the similarities between the two games were purely as to game "rules" or "ideas," and not the expression of those ideas.[220] The court found that both games embodied the idea of a "hierarchical matching game" in which players create objects higher in that hierarchy by matching three objects lower in the hierarchy; that both games had antagonists who would frustrate player efforts; and that both games

---

214. *Id.*
215. *Id.*
216. *Id.*
217. *Id.*
218. *Id.*
219. *Id.* at *5.
220. *Id.* at *16–17.

gave players objects that could destroy unwanted or ill-placed objects.[221] Copyright did not give Spry Fox a monopoly over this idea, and the court recognized that the defendants, or anyone else, was free to create a game of its own based on this idea of a hierarchical matching game.[222] However, the court also found that Spry Fox had chosen to express this underlying idea in its own way by selecting a particular object hierarchy, choosing the nature of its antagonist, designing a visual display, and placing everything on a field of play that it designed.[223] The court found each of these to be protectable expressive elements.[224] On that basis, the court found that Spry Fox's allegations were more than adequate to illustrate plausibly the objectively similar expression embodied in *Yeti Town*, and LOL Apps' summary judgment motion was denied.[225]

Together, *Tetris* and *Spry Fox* are good examples of how courts are likely to approach copycat or "clone" games. As might be obvious, the more complex and original the game, the greater protection it will be accorded. However, *Spry Fox*, in particular, illustrates that similarities do not have to rise to the level of a near carbon copy, as was the case in Tetris Holding, in order for infringement to be successfully alleged.

B. Your Game Stole My Movie/Screenplay/Book!

A second category of infringement claims involving video games are what one might consider "traditional" infringement claims in the vein of cases such as *Funky Films, Inc. v. Time Warner Entertainment Co., L.P.*[226] and *Litchfield v. Spielberg.*[227] In these cases, the plaintiff claimed that the defendant's video game was substantially similar to the plaintiff's screenplay, novel, or motion picture, in that the video game was similar in its plot, themes, dialog, mood, setting, pace, and characters. These cases have become more

---

221. *Id.* at *12–13.

222. *Id.* at *13.

223. *Id.*

224. *Id.*

225. *Id.* at *26.

226. Funky Films, Inc. v. Time Warner Entm't Co., L.P., 462 F.3d 1072 (9th Cir. 2006).

227. Litchfield v. Spielberg, 736 F.2d 1352 (9th Cir. 1984).

common over the past several years as technology has enabled video games to include complex plots, settings, and characters. Some examples of these cases follow.

In *Crawford v. Midway Games, Inc.*,[228] the plaintiff alleged that the defendant's military/action video game infringed the plaintiff's copyright in a military-themed screenplay.[229] The court found that the works shared only "the general idea that the United States government ha[d] created a special program aimed at employing soldiers . . . that possess[ed] paranormal or psionic powers."[230] The court found no other similarities "beyond this unprotectable general premise."[231] To the contrary, the court found many differences in plot, mood, and other aspects of expression. For instance, it observed that the protagonist in one work obtained training to develop psionic powers, whereas the protagonist in the other work possessed powers without any form of training.[232] As a result, the court held that there was no substantial similarity and thus no actionable copying.[233]

In *Capcom Co. v. MKR Group, Inc.*,[234] the court addressed the substantial similarity between two products (a motion picture and video game) involving a zombie apocalypse. The plaintiff owned the copyright in *Dawn of the Dead*, a movie involving zombies attacking people in a shopping mall.[235] The defendant produced a video game entitled *Dead Rising* that also involved zombies and was set in a shopping mall.[236] In analyzing substantial similarity, the court observed differences in plot, characters, theme, dialog, mood, setting, and pace.[237] For instance, the defendant's protagonist was a

---

228. *See* Order Granting Defendants' Motions for Summary Judgment at 1, Crawford v. Midway Games Inc., No. 2:07-cv-00967-FMC-JCx (C.D. Cal. Dec. 3, 2008), http://amlawdaily.typepad.com/Midway.pdf.

229. *Id.* at 1–2.

230. *Id.* at 14.

231. *Id.*

232. *Id.* at 15.

233. *Id.* at 18.

234. Capcom Co. v. MKR Group, Inc., No. C 08-0904 RS, 2008 U.S. Dist. LEXIS 83836 (N.D. Cal. Oct. 10, 2008).

235. *Id.* at *5.

236. *Id.* at *5–6.

237. *Id.* at *22–32.

"cynical and athletic young freelance photographer," whereas the plaintiff's protagonist was a "timid non-athletic middle aged television news helicopter pilot."[238] The court did acknowledge certain similarities between the works, such as the presence of zombies in a shopping mall, but held that these elements were too common and generic to merit protection.[239] Thus, the court held that there was no substantial similarity and therefore no actionable copying.[240]

One final example of this type of dispute is *Bissoon-Dath v. Sony Computer Entertainment America, Inc.*[241] Plaintiffs were the authors of treatments and screenplays that told stories set in ancient Greece about a struggle between Athens and Sparta in which several Greek gods, including Zeus and Ares, intervened.[242] Plaintiffs filed suit against Sony Computer Entertainment America and others, claiming that Sony's video game series *God of War*, which also took place in ancient Greece and involved conflict with and among the gods, infringed on their works.[243]

The court dismissed the action on the grounds that the court's substantial similarity inquiry revealed "far less similarity than would be required to overcome summary judgment, even if plaintiffs had proven access."[244] The court stressed that while plaintiffs' works and *God of War* had "some degree of similarity between the plots at an extremely generalized level[,]" plaintiffs could not own the basic idea for a story, because general plot ideas are not protected by copyright, and they "'remain forever the common property of artistic mankind.'"[245] The court further stressed that the foregoing is particularly true when, as in the case at hand, virtually all of the elements constituting the plaintiffs' works are stock elements (including concepts such as the "hero's journey") that had been used in literary and artistic works for "years, if not

---

238. *Id.* at *24–25.

239. *Id.* at *22–23.

240. *Id.* at *34.

241. Bissoon-Dath v. Sony Computer Entm't Am., Inc., 694 F. Supp. 2d 1071 (2010).

242. *Id.* at 1075–76.

243. *Id.* at 1076–77.

244. *Id.* at 1091–92.

245. *Id.* at 1091 (quoting Berkic v. Crichton, 761 F.2d 1289, 1293 (9th Cir. 1985)).

millennia."[246] And, indeed, the works were quite dissimilar beyond their very generalized plots; for example, the court found that while plaintiffs' works were thematically focused on peace, democracy, and the establishment of both, *God of War* was focused on "violence, the search for divine forgiveness, and the continuation of war," among several other dissimilarities.[247]

C. Streaming, Twitch, Machinima, and "Let's Play" Videos

Not only has the number of people playing video games grown exponentially over the past several years, so has the number of people *watching other people* play video games. Videos of people playing video games are among the most popular videos watched or searched for on video-sharing websites such as YouTube. These videos may include footage of a player's particularly skillful kill in a competitive action game, game tutorials, game reviews, or replays of professional matches. One popular category of video is known as a "Let's Play" video, in which someone plays a game from beginning to end while (sometimes) providing commentary while playing.[248] Another type of video is known as "machinima." In a machinima video, a person may use game assets, characters, or settings to create a sort of virtual puppet show or animated movie.[249] The popular web series "Red vs. Blue" is one example of a machinima production, using the characters and settings from the game *Halo* to tell new stories in an episodic format.[250]

Another way in which people consume media of people playing video games is via live streaming. In recent years, live streaming of games has been largely accomplished through the immensely popular Twitch platform.[251] Via Twitch, players can broadcast video feeds of games (known as "Twitchcasts") as they play them or

---

246. *Id.*

247. *Id.* at 1083.

248. *See generally* Let's Play Archive, *Frequently Asked Questions*, http://lparchive.org/faq (last visited July 25, 2018).

249. *See generally* Wikipedia, *Machinima*, https://en.wikipedia.org/wiki/Machinima (last edited July 16, 2018).

250. *See generally* Wikipedia, *Red vs. Blue*, https://en.wikipedia.org/wiki/Red_vs._Blue (last edited June 22, 2018).

251. Twitch, *Homepage*, https://www.twitch.tv/ (last visited July 25, 2018).

observe them. Perhaps most importantly, Twitch has become the primary platform for the broadcasting of professional "e-sports" matches.[252] Many Twitchcasts of professional matches are authorized by the e-sports league. But many other live streams are amateur streams that broadcast without a license.

The creation and distribution of gameplay videos without the authorization of the owner of copyright in the game often is a violation of the copyright owner's exclusive rights of reproduction and distribution.[253] Similarly, the unauthorized streaming (including "live streaming") of video games is often a violation of the owner's exclusive right of public performance and/or public display.[254] Thus, posting such videos or streaming such content might result in liability for the poster or streamer. It could also trigger an obligation by the service provider or video-sharing platform to remove the content, especially if the copyright owner has given formal notice of infringement pursuant to section 512 of the Digital Millennium Copyright Act (DMCA). Sometimes copyright owners will permit certain gameplay videos to be posted or streamed, such as those providing short tutorials or promoting a user-created mod.[255] However, any decision to permit a gameplay video to remain on

---

252. *See generally* Wikipedia, *eSports*, https://en.wikipedia.org/wiki/ESports# Internet_ live_streaming (last edited July 21, 2018).

253. *See* A&M Records, Inc. v. Napster, Inc., 239 F.3d 1004, 1014 (4th Cir. 2001) ("Napster users who upload file names to the search index for others to copy violate plaintiffs' distribution rights. Napster users who download files containing copyrighted music violate plaintiffs' reproduction rights."); Playboy Enters., Inc. v. Frena, 839 F. Supp. 1552, 1556 (M.D. Fla. 1993) (direct infringement by providing copyrighted images on Internet bulletin board: "Public distribution of a copyrighted work is a right reserved to the copyright owner, and usurpation of that right constitutes infringement.").

254. *See* Video Pipeline, Inc. v. Buena Vista Home Entm't, Inc., 342 F.3d 191, 197 (3d Cir. 2003) (streaming movie previews violated plaintiff's rights of public performance and display); Twentieth Century Fox Film Corp. v. iCraveTV, No. CIV.A 00-120, 2000 WL 255989, at *7 (W.D. Pa. Feb. 8, 2000) ("[P]laintiffs are likely to succeed in showing that defendants are unlawfully publicly performing plaintiffs' copyrighted works in the United States. Defendants do so by transmitting (through use of 'streaming' technology) performances of the works to the public. . . .").

255. *See* Aaron Swerdlow, *The Emerging Legal Battle over Video Game Streaming Rights*, VentureBeat, May 27, 2017, 6:00 a.m., https://venturebeat.com/2017/05/27 /the-emerging-legal-battle-over-video-game-streaming-rights/.

a video-sharing platform is within the discretion of the copyright owner, who may elect to enforce his or her rights at any time.

In some circumstances, uploaders of gameplay videos have sought to rely on the defense of "fair use,"[256] citing some scholarly or commentary purpose of the video. In some narrow circumstances, that defense might be applicable. For example, the uploader of a game review that includes a few small excerpts of game footage might be able to invoke the fair use defense.[257] However, videos that do no more than display game footage for the purpose of entertaining viewers, especially videos that contain the entirety of a game (such as "Let's Play" videos), are far less likely to be subject to a fair use defense.[258]

A related issue is the potential liability of a service provider such as YouTube or Twitch for its own acts of hosting, streaming, and distributing infringing content uploaded by users. Generally, such service providers have taken the position that they are protected from monetary liability for the storing and dissemination of infringing content uploaded by users pursuant to the "safe harbors" of the DMCA, 17 U.S.C. § 512. The scope of the DMCA safe harbors has been hotly litigated, and a complete discussion of the DMCA and its fairly complex provisions is outside the scope of this chapter, but a brief summary is useful in understanding the practicalities of dealing with unauthorized user-created or user-uploaded content on a video-sharing network.

---

256. 17 U.S.C. § 107 (2012).

257. Harper & Row, Publishers v. Nation Enters., 471 U.S. 539, 550 (1985) (citing Folsom v. Marsh, 9 F. Cas. 342, 344–45 (C.C.D. Mass. 1841) ("[A] reviewer may fairly cite largely from the original work, if his design be really and truly to use the passages for the purposes of fair and reasonable criticism. On the other hand, it is as clear, that if he thus cites the most important parts of the work, with a view, not to criticise, but to supersede the use of the original work, and substitute the review for it, such a use will be deemed in law a piracy.")).

258. *See* Twin Peaks Prods. v. Publications Int'l, 996 F.2d 1366, 1373–78 (2d Cir. 1993) (book containing plot summaries of popular television program did not make fair use of the source material). *But see* Nicholas Ribaudo, *YouTube, Video Games, and Fair Use: Nintendo's Copyright Infringement Battle with Youtube's "Let's Plays" and Its Potential Chilling Effects*, 6 Berkeley J. Ent. & Sports L. 114 (2017).

In broad terms, the DMCA insulates "Service Providers"[259] from monetary liability arising from engaging in four categories of activities undertaken in the ordinary course of their business: (1) transitory network communications (e.g., passive transmission of content, such as e-mail); (2) system caching, or temporary storage of material, to make content accessible to users; (3) "storage" of content "at the direction of a user" (e.g., storing user-uploaded content for later retrieval); and (4) providing information location or "linking" tools (e.g., search engines).[260] Cases applying the DMCA to video-sharing services such as YouTube generally have concluded that such services fall within the section 512(c) safe harbor (for storage at the direction of users).[261] Under this safe harbor, the service provider will not be liable for damages for hosting, indexing, and disseminating infringing content uploaded by users, as long as it meets a series of requirements.[262] Specifically, the service provider must

- have adopted, reasonably implemented, and notified users of a policy whereby it terminates the accounts of users who are "repeat infringers,"[263]
- accommodate and not interfere with "standard technical measures," such as digital fingerprinting or watermarking technology,[264]
- have designated an "agent" to receive notices of claimed infringement relating to content on its system, and registered that agent with the U.S. Copyright Office,[265]

---

259. A "service provider" is defined as "an entity offering the transmission, routing, or providing of connections for digital online communications, between or among points specified by a user, of material of the user's choosing, without modification to the content of the material as sent and received." 17 U.S.C. § 512(k) (2012).

260. *Id.* § 512(a)–(d).

261. *See, e.g.,* UMG Recordings, Inc. v. Veoh Networks, Inc., 718 F.3d 1006, 1018–19 (9th Cir. 2013); Viacom Int'l, Inc. v. YouTube, Inc., 676 F.3d 19 (2d Cir. 2012); Wolk v. Kodak Imaging Network, Inc., 840 F. Supp. 2d 724 (S.D.N.Y. 2012).

262. *See, e.g., UMG Recordings, Inc.,* 718 F.3d at 1018–20.

263. 17 U.S.C. § 512(i).

264. *Id.*

265. *Id.* § 512(c)(3) (2012).

- not have "actual" knowledge that material or activity using the material on its system is infringing or awareness of "facts and circumstances" from which infringing activity is apparent (i.e., "red flag" knowledge) and then fail to remove or disable access to that material,[266]
- not receive a financial benefit directly attributable to the infringing activity (e.g., charging for the content) and have the "right and ability to control" such activity,[267] and
- have an effective "notice and takedown" policy, whereby upon receiving a formal "notification" of claimed infringement, it responds "expeditiously" to remove or disable the infringing content.[268]

If these requirements are met, the service provider cannot face monetary liability for the conduct of its users.[269] That is a significant incentive for most service providers to comply with the statute, as large video-sharing services may host hundreds or thousands of infringing videos uploaded by users—thereby risking potentially enormous statutory damages. As a result, most service providers have adopted a "notice and takedown" policy and designated agents to receive such takedown notices. This means that copyright owners seeking to obtain removal of infringing content from services such as Twitch or YouTube need not necessarily file a lawsuit, but instead may serve a formal notice of infringement on the service provider's agent. If the service provider fails to remove the content in an expeditious manner, it risks exposure to monetary damages for the infringement. Additionally, the service provider must properly log infringement notices as "marks" or "strikes" against the uploader to determine whether the uploader is a "repeat infringer."[270] The failure to terminate an uploader who has received multiple infringement notices will cause the service

266. *Id.* § 512(c)(1)(A).
267. *Id.* § 512(c)(1)(B).
268. *Id.* § 512(c)(1)(C).
269. *Id.* § 512(c)(1).
270. *See id.* § 512(i)(1)(A).

provider to forfeit its safe harbor protection.[271] Courts have traditionally given a fair amount of flexibility to service providers to craft the terms of their repeat infringer policy.[272] However, the policy must be "effective," and service providers must take seriously their obligation to track repeat infringers and terminate them when appropriate.[273] For example, in *BMG Rights Management (US) LLC v. Cox Communications, Inc.*,[274] the Fourth Circuit recently denied safe harbor protection to an Internet service provider where it regularly reactivated terminated users, adopted an overly liberal "thirteen strike" policy, deleted DMCA notices sent by the plaintiff, and often made the deliberate decision not to terminate repeat infringers where it wished to avoid losing revenue from paying subscribers.[275]

While the DMCA provides copyright owners with a way to obtain the expeditious removal of content, many argue that it does little to actively deter infringement. This is in part because it does not incentivize service providers to actively police their system for infringing content or to screen content for infringement before it goes live on the system. (In fact, it arguably disincentivizes such activities.)[276] Thus, for content owners, the DMCA takedown process can feel like a game of "whack-a-mole," as new infringements appear almost as soon as the old ones are taken down. Nevertheless, courts have largely been unsympathetic to copyright owners in claims brought against services such as YouTube.[277] As a result,

---

271. Capitol Records, Ltd. Liab. Co. v. Vimeo, Ltd. Liab. Co., 826 F.3d 78, 83 (2d Cir. 2016) ("Service providers, however, forfeit entitlement to the safe harbor if they fail to expeditiously remove the infringing material upon receipt of notification of the infringement or upon otherwise becoming aware of it.").

272. BMG Rights Mgmt. (US) LLC v. Cox Commc'n, Inc., 881 F.3d 293, 303 (4th Cir. 2018).

273. *See, e.g., id.* at 303–05.

274. *BMG Rights Mgmt.*, 881 F.3d 293.

275. *Id.* at 303–05.

276. Service providers frequently cite 17 U.S.C. § 512(m) for the proposition that affirmative steps to police or screen content is not required under the DMCA. That provision provides: "Nothing in this section shall be construed to condition the applicability of [the DMCA safe harbors] on . . . a service provider monitoring its service or affirmatively seeking facts indicating infringing activity. . . ." 17 U.S.C. § 512(m)(1) (2012).

277. *See, e.g.*, Viacom Int'l, Inc. v. YouTube, Inc., 676 F.3d 19 (2d Cir. 2012).

the DMCA takedown process remains the primary means by which copyright owners ensure that infringing content is removed from video-sharing or streaming services.

Conclusion

The video game industry can hardly be said to be a new or young industry. Moreover, for decades, courts have dealt with how to apply copyright law to technologies that were not in existence, or even contemplated, at the time the law was drafted. But video games are unique and special in a variety of ways, among them being that advances in technology are rapidly changing the very concept of interactive entertainment in dramatic and unforeseen ways. The video games that came before the courts before the turn of this century bear only a passing resemblance to the interactive entertainment products available today. As a result, copyright decisions about arcade games and single-player console products are of limited use in analyzing some of the copyright issues surrounding multiplayer games, virtual worlds, user-generated content, and augmented reality.

The growing diversity, popularity, and complexity of video games and video game platforms means that courts will continue to tackle a host of issues—some unique to video games and virtual worlds, and others familiar to more traditional entertainment media. Fortunately, judges, legislators, and advocates have become quite sophisticated about the medium and increasingly willing to tackle the difficult issues that face the industry. As a result, it is likely that the law will continue to develop at a rapid pace, either through legislative action, judicial decisions, or industry self-regulation. Among the legal issues that are particularly ripe for development are those pertaining to the copyrightability and fixation of dynamic virtual worlds, the relationship between gameplay ideas and the expression of those ideas, and the relationship between computer code and screen displays generated by that code.

Patents: Real-World Issues in Mixed Realities

3

Steve Chang
Sanford Warren[1]

Takeaways

- *Software inventions, including video games and virtual worlds defined by computer software, are patentable when properly described and claimed in a patent application, provided the invention is new and nonobvious.*
- *Moving forward, unique claim strategy and careful attention to detail when drafting will be critical to successfully obtaining and enforcing patents in this field in light of recent developments in U.S. law regarding patent-eligible subject matter.*
- *Multiple avenues, with distinct damages and remedies, are available for patentees to enforce their patent rights.*

---

1. Sanford E. Warren, Jr. is a name partner at Warren Rhoades LLP located in Irving, Texas. Steve Chang is a principal shareholder in the Washington, D.C., office of Banner & Witcoff, Ltd. The authors wish to thank Nathan L. Levenson, an associate with Warren Rhoades, LLP for his assistance and contributions to this chapter. For complete author biographies, see the Contributors section of this book.

Introduction

As more and more real-world issues creep into video games and virtual worlds, it is inevitable that patents and patent disputes will arise as well. Those seeking to get or enforce patent rights for inventions protecting or practiced in a virtual world will inevitably encounter some unique legal questions that have not yet been squarely addressed. This will include both issues arising when obtaining patent rights on "virtual" inventions, such as the types of eligible inventions and claiming approaches, as well as issues confronted when actually exploiting or enforcing one's patent rights for virtual world inventions. For example, patent holders enforcing rights on "virtual" inventions may have to pierce the veil of anonymity offered by many virtual worlds and video games. Patent holders may also have to address jurisdiction and venue concerns exacerbated by the international nature and user base of online games.

I. A Brief Overview of U.S. Patent Protection

A. Utility Patents: U.S. Patentability Requirements

In the United States an inventor must demonstrate that his or her invention is useful, novel, and nonobvious before the U.S. Patent and Trademark Office (USPTO) will grant a patent. If a patent is issued, the term of the patent is 20 years from the filing date of the earliest U.S. patent application to which priority is claimed.[2] A patent owner then has the right to exclude others from making, using, selling, and offering to sell the patented invention in the United States, as well as importing the invention into the United States.[3] Since the right is one of exclusion, the patent owner may well be

---

2. 35 U.S.C. § 154(a)(2) (2006).
3. *Id.* § 271(a) (2006).

prevented from actually practicing its own invention if, for example, someone else owns a patent on a subpart of the invention. For example, a patent on a new video game may include a combination of a previously patented ray-tracing technique and a previously patented multi-user communication method. The owner of the patent on the video game may be unable to practice its own patented invention without a license from the patent holders on the ray-tracing technique and the multi-user communication technique.

The principle underlying the U.S. patent system is a *quid pro quo* between the inventor and the public where the inventor is afforded the right to exclude others from making, using, or selling the invention for a limited period of time in return for teaching the public how to practice a new, useful, and nonobvious invention.[4] The right to exclude provides the incentive to publish the invention's details, which in turn adds to the public knowledge, which in turn is intended to stimulate further innovation.

A useful invention is one that is operable to perform its intended function. It is also necessary for the invention to have a "useful purpose." The determination of what is "useful" in terms of patenting has been the subject of long-standing debate. In prior decades, this determination was imbued with moral overtones. For example, for some time inventions related to gambling were deemed not "useful" and therefore could not be patented.[5] While the determination of what constitutes a useful invention is important to the determination of patentability, it is now well established that video games and virtual worlds provide utility (e.g., entertainment, education, commerciality) and are therefore patentable. A useful invention must also fall within one of the four statutory categories of patent-eligible subject matter: processes, articles of manufacture, machines, and compositions of matter.[6]

---

4. *Id.* §§ 101–103, 112 (2017).
5. *See, e.g.*, Fuller v. Berger, 120 F. 274 (7th Cir. 1903) (invention for gambling purposes is not a useful device within the meaning of the patent law).
6. 35 U.S.C. § 101 (2018).

Historically, the courts have interpreted the statutory classes of patent-eligible subject matter broadly to include "everything under the sun made by man."[7] Indeed the United States has had one of the broadest standards of what types of inventions may be patented in the world. In 2014, however, the U.S. Supreme Court in *Alice Corp. Pty. Ltd. v. CLS Bank International*[8] further expanded on the analysis for determining patent subject-matter eligibility. In *Alice*, the Supreme Court reiterated a test by which patent claims that may arguably involve patent-ineligible concepts (i.e., "abstract ideas," "laws of nature," or "natural phenomena") will be found invalid under 35 U.S.C § 101 for attempting to claim patent-ineligible subject matter.[9] As a result, the Supreme Court's *Alice* decision undoubtedly impacted the realm of business method and software patents by limiting the scope of patent subject-matter eligibility under § 101.

In particular, the Supreme Court's decision in *Alice* provided district courts with a substantive legal test to assist in determining whether or not claims at issue involve patent-eligible subject matter under § 101. Specifically, *Alice* applied the two-prong test from *Mayo Collaborative Services v. Prometheus Laboratories, Inc.*[10] (a case involving laws of nature) to determine patent subject-matter eligibility for other patent-ineligible concepts. First, the trial court is required to "determine whether the claims at issue are directed to one of those patent-ineligible concepts."[11] Patent-ineligible concepts include laws of nature, natural phenomena, and abstract ideas.[12] If the claims at issue are found to be a patent-ineligible concept, the court must then apply the second part of the *Alice* test—whether or not the claims at issue pertain to "an inventive concept" to "'transform the nature of the claim' into a

---

7. Diamond v. Chakrabarty, 447 U.S. 303, 309 (1980) (quoting S. Rep. No. 1979, 82d Cong., 2d Sess., at 5 (1952)).

8. Alice Corp. Pty. Ltd. v. CLS Bank Int'l, 134 S. Ct. 2347 (2014).

9. *Id.* at 2354.

10. Mayo Collaborative Servs. v. Prometheus Labs., Inc., 566 U.S. 66, 71–72, 75–78 (2012); *see also Alice*, 134 S. Ct. at 2355.

11. *Alice*, 134 S. Ct. at 2355.

12. *Mayo Collaborative Servs.*, 566 U.S. at 79; *see also* Ass'n for Molecular Pathology v. Myriad Genetics, Inc., 569 U.S. 576, 587–89 (2013).

patent-eligible application."[13] *Alice* further reiterated the Supreme Court's previous definition in *Mayo* of an "inventive concept" as an "element or combination of elements that is 'sufficient to ensure that the patent in practice amounts to significantly more than a patent upon the [ineligible concept] itself.'"[14] In determining whether or not the claims involve an "inventive concept," the court is to "consider the elements of each claim both individually and 'as an ordered combination' to determine whether the additional elements 'transform the nature of the claim' into a patent-eligible application."[15] *Alice* made it clear that the two-prong test applies to all questions of patent eligibility under 35 U.S.C. § 101.[16]

Video games and virtual worlds are useful inventions, and are therefore patentable provided they are new, nonobvious, and meet the requirement of subject-matter eligibility set forth in *Alice*. Some examples of utility patent owners in the video game context include Activision,[17] Harmonix,[18] Konami,[19] and Gibson Guitars,[20] which each have patents on methods of interaction between a user and a music-based video game. Midway Games has a patent on "ghosting" in auto racing games, a process whereby a player races against a previously recorded best-effort of a previous player.[21] Sega has a patent on a floating directional arrow in auto racing

---

13. *Alice*, 134 S. Ct. at 2355 (citation omitted).
14. *Id.*
15. *Id.*
16. *Id.*
17. *See, e.g.*, U.S. Patent No. 9,452,358 (issued Sept. 27, 2016); U.S. Patent No. 9,061,205 (issued June 23, 2015); U.S. Patent No. 8,858,339 (issued Oct. 14, 2014); U.S. Patent No. 8,858,330 (issued Oct. 14, 2014); U.S. Patent No. 8,827,816 (issued Sept. 9, 2014).
18. *See, e.g.*, U.S. Patent No. 9,358,456 (issued June 7, 2016); U.S. Patent No. 9,024,166 (issued May 5, 2015); U.S. Patent No. 8,874,243 (issued Oct. 28, 2014); U.S. Patent No. 8,702,485 (issued Apr. 22, 2014); U.S. Patent No. 8,690,670 (issued Apr. 8, 2014).
19. *See, e.g.*, U.S. Patent No. 7,601,056 (issued Oct. 13, 2009); U.S. Patent No. 7,070,500 (issued July 4, 2006); U.S. Patent No. 6,905,413 (issued June 14, 2005); U.S. Patent No. 6,821,203 (issued Nov. 23, 2004); U.S. Patent No. 6,390,923 (issued May 21, 2002).
20. *See, e.g.*, U.S. Patent No. 5,990,405 (issued Nov. 23, 1999).
21. U.S. Patent No. 6,488,505 (issued Dec. 3, 2002).

games that helps users navigate the virtual world.[22] Microsoft has a patent on the feature of allowing users to select a car to race from a virtual showroom setting filled with a wide variety of cars in an auto racing game, in contrast to the conventional format of merely selecting a car from a list.[23] Nintendo has a patent on an adrenaline feature in sport-based games providing an adrenaline boost to the virtual athlete,[24] and another patent on a sanity feature in video games whereby a player-character becomes harder to control as the character's sanity decreases.[25] Nintendo also has a patent on a virtual world chat system whereby the radius to which a user's voice communications are transmitted depends on how loud the user speaks.[26] The Supreme Court's *Alice* decision has undoubtedly changed the game of patent practice, but companies are still actively pursuing utility patents related to video games and immersive entertainment due to the rising popularity of virtual reality and augmented reality technologies in the gaming and entertainment markets.[27] Some more recent examples of utility patent owners in the virtual world context (including both virtual reality and augmented reality) include Microsoft,[28] Oculus VR,[29] Apple,[30] and Nintendo,[31] and time will tell how future courts will treat these patents in view of *Alice*.

While the standards for patent-eligible subject matter have become more stringent and limited, the courts have still struggled with the boundaries of patent-eligible subject matter as science has ventured into areas such as cloning and computing. In

---

22. U.S. Patent No. 6,200,138 (issued Mar. 13, 2001).

23. U.S. Patent No. 7,670,220 (issued Mar. 2, 2010).

24. U.S. Patent No. 6,923,717 (issued Aug. 2, 2005).

25. U.S. Patent No. 6,935,954 (issued Aug. 30, 2005).

26. U.S. Patent No. 7,491,123 (issued Feb. 17, 2009).

27. *See generally* Press Release, ResearchAndMarkets, Augmented Reality and Virtual Reality Market—Global Forecast to 2023 (Mar. 8, 2018), https://www.businesswire.com/news/home/20180308006135/en/Augmented-Reality-Virtual-Reality-Market—Global.

28. *See, e.g.*, U.S. Patent No. 9,401,050 (issued July 26, 2016).

29. *See, e.g.*, U.S. Patent No. 9,063,330 (issued June 23, 2015).

30. *See, e.g.*, U.S. Patent No. 8,832,557 (issued Sept. 9, 2014); U.S. Patent No. 9,824,495 (issued Nov. 21, 2017); U.S. Patent No. 9,922,446 (issued Mar. 20, 2018); U.S. Patent No. 9,400,941 (issued July 26, 2016).

31. *See, e.g.*, U.S. Patent No. 8,922,588 (issued Dec. 30, 2014).

particular, as will be detailed in Section II.A.1, the courts have recently provided additional guidance on the patentability of business processes, which is particularly relevant to virtual worlds and video games.[32]

While, as discussed earlier, software may be patent-eligible subject matter under U.S. patent law, data structures and computer programs *per se* are not patentable. Software is considered a functional-descriptive item that imparts functionality to a computer onto which it is deployed, but which by itself has no inherent functionality. Software is therefore considered a mere descriptive item when separate from the computer, computer memory, or other computer readable medium on which the software is stored or executed.[33]

Once an invention is determined to meet the tests for patent-eligible subject matter and usefulness, the inventor must also show that the invention is novel[34] and nonobvious.[35] For an invention to be deemed novel, the exact same invention must not have been known or used by others or patented or described in a publication anywhere in the world prior to the date the patent application was filed.[36] Novelty is a relatively easy hurdle as compared to obviousness, because most inventors can identify *something* in their invention or some combination of features that has never been done before. The law may be summarized as follows: novelty means that as of the date you applied for your patent, your invention was not previously patented, published, publicly used, on sale, described in a patent application that was already on file, or otherwise publically known.[37] Everything except that last category (e.g., disclosures other than filed patent applications) is subject to a so-called "one-year grace period," which just means that an

---

32. *See In re* Bilski, 545 F.3d 943 (Fed. Cir. 2008).

33. *In re* Beauregard, 53 F.3d 1583, 1583–84 (Fed. Cir. 1995) (USPTO concedes that computer readable media storing computer executable instructions are patent-eligible subject matter under 35 U.S.C. § 101.); *see also* CyberSource Corp. v. Retail Decision Inc., 620 F. Supp. 2d 1068 (N.D. Cal. 2009) (interpreting the method claim analysis from *In re* Bilski as applying to Beauregard claims).

34. 35 U.S.C. § 102 (2017).

35. *Id.* § 103.

36. *Id.* § 102(a).

37. *Id.* § 102.

applicant's *own* public disclosures (e.g., if the inventor publishes a paper describing the invention) cannot be used against his or her application if the disclosure was less than a year before the application filing. The one-year grace period included in this latter requirement is more permissive than most other countries, which generally provide a so-called absolute bar to patentability for any invention that has been revealed at any time prior to filing the patent application (this is also known as "absolute novelty"). After this one-year period, inventors are barred from filing an application for their inventions even in the United States and this is referred to as a statutory bar to patentability. As a result of the new "first to file" regime of the America Invents Act (AIA), inventors who sell or disclose inventions need to promptly file an application because another invention may file within the one-year grace period and win the patent rights. In other words, although the one-year grace period still exists in the United States, its importance is much less than before the AIA was made into law.

Even though an invention might not have been described in a single prior publication or prior practiced invention, that invention still may be obvious in view of the prior art. An invention cannot be patented unless it is a sufficient advance over the prior art such that it would not have been obvious to a person having ordinary skill in the area of the relevant invention.[38] The determination of whether an invention is sufficiently nonobvious is generally the most difficult determination in patent law and it is one that has been the subject of recent U.S. Supreme Court consideration.[39]

For decades, the U.S. Court of Appeals for the Federal Circuit (CAFC) had been applying the so-called teaching, suggestion, or motivation (TSM) test to determine whether an invention is nonobvious in view of a combination of prior art references. The TSM test as applied by the CAFC required that an explicit or implicit teaching, suggestion, or motivation to combine references be found in the prior art in order to find an invention obvious based on a combination of those references. However, the Supreme Court

---

38. *Id.* § 103.
39. KSR Int'l Co. v. Teleflex Inc., 550 U.S. 398 (2007).

in *KSR International Co. v. Teleflex, Inc.*[40] held that the TSM test was being applied too rigidly, and that while looking for direct indicia supporting the combination of the prior art was certainly one way to determine whether an invention was obvious over the prior art, there are other tests that a court also could and should use in determining obviousness.[41] Those other tests include whether the invention is a variation of the prior art that is obvious to try, and whether the invention is merely a combination of known elements to achieve a predictable result (e.g., a combination of two known features of different video games, but that had never been used together in a single game).[42] The Court indicated that there may very well be other tests, and indicated that in order to aid each court's analysis, the USPTO should articulate a reasoned explanation in the record of the patent prosecution file why a person of ordinary skill in the art would combine the prior art references to arrive at the claimed invention.[43] In the aftermath of the *KSR* decision, the USPTO allowance rate noticeably decreased and the Board of Patent Appeals and Interferences[44] affirmed obviousness rejections at a rate of almost 2-to-1,[45] thereby making it more difficult to obtain and enforce patents on marginal inventions. From July 25, 2016, through January 7, 2017, the rate in which the Patent Trial and Appeal Board (PTAB) affirmed obviousness rejections increased to nearly 3-to-1.[46] However, the *KSR* decision has, over the long term, not changed the patentability of inventions where a

---

40. *Id.*

41. *Id.* at 415–18.

42. *See id.*

43. *See id.* at 426.

44. The Board of Patent Appeals and Interferences (BPAI) was an appellate board within the USPTO that heard appeals when a patent examiner rejected an invention and the applicant wanted to challenge that decision. Under the America Invents Act, the BPAI was replaced with the Patent Trial and Appeal Board (PTAB), effective September 16, 2012.

45. USPTO, *Board of Patent Appeals and Interferences—Receipts and Dispositions by Technology Centers for Ex Parte Appeals: Fiscal Year 2009*, http://www.uspto.gov /web/offices/dcom/bpai/docs/receipts/fy2009.htm (last modified Sept. 8, 2009); *see also* Dennis Crouch, *Board of Patent Appeals and Interferences (BPAI)*, PATENTLY-O, Mar. 4, 2008, http://www.patentlyo.com/patent/2008/03/board-of-patent.html.

46. *Obviousness Appeals before the PTAB*, ANTICIPAT BLOG, Jan. 11, 2017, https:// anticipat.wordpress.com/2017/01/11/obviousness-appeals-before-the-ptab/.

significant inventive advance has been made over the known art, and patent prosecution has become more consistent by using the dictates of the Court in the *KSR* decision.

In addition to novelty, nonobviousness, and usefulness, a patent application must meet certain descriptive requirements before a patent will be granted. A patent must be written with sufficient detail and clarity to ensure that it achieves its goal of teaching the public how to practice the invention. Specifically, a patent must provide a sufficient written description of the claimed invention and must also enable someone of ordinary skill in the art to make and use the invention.[47] Every patent must then conclude with one or more claims that define the scope of the invention protected by the patent.[48]

The enablement requirement allows an inventor to presume the level of knowledge of someone of ordinary skill in the art, and provide the details necessary for that person to make and use the invention. For example, in the software arts, a skilled programmer does not need to be given source code in order to replicate an invention. Rather, it is generally sufficient to provide software flow charts, data flow diagrams, network architectures and logic diagrams, object definitions, and the like, without having to provide the actual source code the inventor wrote.

B. Design Patents: U.S. Patentability Requirements

The foregoing discussion relates to utility patents, which apply to useful inventions. Patent protection is also available for "ornamental" inventions for any article of manufacture.[49] In the context of video games this may include game hardware (e.g., game controllers, game consoles, video displays), as well as surface ornamentation generated by video game software on a visual display.

---

47. 35 U.S.C. § 112(a) (2011) ("The specification shall contain a written description of the invention, and of the manner and process of making and using it, in such full, clear, concise, and exact terms as to enable any person skilled in the art to which it pertains, or with which it is most nearly connected, to make and use the same, and shall set forth the best mode contemplated by the inventor of carrying out his invention.").

48. *Id.* § 112(b).

49. *Id.* § 171 (2012).

For example, computer icons, graphical user interfaces, game characters, and scenery are all types of surface ornamentation that may be protected by a design patent, but only as that image is displayed on a physical display device, because the display device itself has historically been considered to be the "article of manufacture" by the USPTO. Indeed, if the design of a design patent is shown to have been dictated by utilitarian functionality, such as the basic shape of a fan blade for example, the design patent can be invalidated.

An object having a substantially similar design as the design claimed in a design patent may not be made, used, sold, offered for sale, or imported into the United States.[50] Note that the standard for infringement is not an identical design; rather, substantial similarity is sufficient to find infringement of a design patent.[51] As opposed to utility patents, which are valid for 20 years from the earliest filing date and require periodic payment of maintenance fees to remain in force, design patents are valid for 14 or 15 years from the date of issuance,[52] and require no maintenance fee payments.[53]

C. Obtaining a Patent for Inventions on Video Games and Virtual Worlds

In order to obtain a patent for inventions on video games and virtual worlds, one must first file a patent application for either a utility patent or design patent with the USPTO, where the application will be classified by technology area and assigned to an examiner. The examiner will evaluate the patent application to determine whether or not it complies with the legal requirements

---

50. *See* Gorham Co. v. White, 81 U.S. 511, 526–27 (1871); *see also* Egyptian Goddess, Inc. v. Swisa, Inc., 543 F.3d 665, 670 (Fed. Cir. 2008).

51. *See, e.g., Gorham Co.*, 81 U.S. at 531 ("whatever differences there may be between the [designs' details] . . . they are still the same in general appearance and effect. . . .").

52. The term of a design patent ultimately depends on its filing date. *See* 35 U.S.C. § 173 (2018). In particular, if a design patent application was filed on or after May 13, 2015, the term is 15 years from the date of issuance. *Id.* However, for design patent applications filed prior to May 13, 2015, the term is 14 years from the date of issuance. *Id.*

53. *Id.*

for patentability. In particular, the examiner will conduct a search for prior art including U.S. patents, published patent applications, printed publications, literature, and foreign patents. More often than not, an examiner will cite prior art against the application in an office action—rejecting some or all of the patent claims. For example, the office may state that the cited prior art anticipates the invention (i.e., there is no novelty) or renders the invention obvious.

A response to an office action typically includes persuasive arguments as to why the claims are patentable in view of the cited art or may include an amendment to the claims to overcome the cited prior art. An applicant should expect to go through a back-and-forth process with the examiner in an attempt to overcome the rejection to get the patent issued. If the examiner is not persuaded by the applicant's response or develops new reasons why the application does not comply with the legal requirements for patentability, an applicant will be notified of the continued rejection through a second office action. Because the USPTO cannot be expected to engage in this back-and-forth forever, this second office action is often declared "final." A final office action essentially means that the USPTO has decided that an impasse has been reached (e.g., the applicant's previous response was deemed unpersuasive, or the applicant's previous change to the claims still did not result in an allowable case). An applicant's choices after the final office action are essentially limited to: (1) appeal the rejection to the PATB; (2) pay a fee for another round of examination via a request for continued examination; or (3) abandon the application.

II. Patent Protection for Video Games and Virtual Worlds

A. Utility Patents

With the preceding background in mind, one can easily imagine a myriad of problems that may arise when obtaining a patent on an invention for a video game or virtual world, or even for an invention *within* a video game or virtual world. The types of inventions one can have in a virtual world will depend on the set of laws or rules used to define what is and what is not an invention. The following discussion is based on U.S. patent laws, which lists the following classes of invention eligible for patent protection: (1) processes; (2) machines; (3) manufacture; and (4) compositions of matter.[54]

1. Processes

Of the listed classes of invention, processes are perhaps the easiest type of invention to cross over into the virtual world of a video game. A "process" is defined as "an act, or a series of acts or steps. . . ."[55] One can easily imagine how a patented process could occur in both the "real" and "virtual" worlds. For example, a patented auctioning process for setting a minimum auction price applies equally well regardless of whether the item being sold is a "real world" item (like a book or car) or a virtual in-game item (like virtual gold in *World of Warcraft* or a special weapon in *EverQuest*), and regardless of whether the auction is held in person, via the Internet, or even "in-game" within a video game or virtual world.

Prior to *Alice*, business method patents were first rendered more difficult to obtain in the CAFC's decision in *In re Bilski*.[56] In *Bilski*, the patent applicant claimed a process that was squarely a business method—it created a middleman for a sales transaction between a buyer and a seller of a commodity (e.g., oil) having a fluctuating price, and set the prices to both at fixed levels, allowing both parties to hedge their bets on the fluctuating price.[57] The USPTO rejected this claim as being ineligible for patent protection, presenting a number of alternative arguments under various tests that had appeared in prior case law, and the CAFC addressed those various tests in affirming the rejection.[58] Following *Bilski*, the Supreme Court decision in *Alice* imposed stricter rules for determining what inventions are eligible for patenting. Although this area of the law is still developing, the Supreme Court's *Alice*

---

54. *Id.* § 101.
55. *See* Gottschalk v. Benson, 409 U.S. 63, 70 (1972).
56. *In re* Bilski, 545 F.3d 943 (Fed. Cir. 2008) (en banc), *aff'd on other grounds*, Bilski v. Kappos, 561 U.S. 593 (2010).
57. *Id.* at 949.
58. *Id.* at 950 (citing lack of useful result, pure mental steps).

decision has further restricted patent eligibility for business method patents.

The CAFC's holding in *Bilski* boiled down to a two-part "machine-or-transformation" test. Under that test, a claimed process is eligible for patent protection if it: (1) is tied to a particular machine or apparatus; or (2) transforms a particular article to a different state or thing.[59] In the virtual worlds context, the latter part of the test (the "transformation" part) seems to be the better argument for patentability of a process, because one can argue that most processes in a virtual world will transform some electronic data into a visual representation (the entire world being a visual representation). The *Bilski* decision expressly noted that the "transformation" of certain electronic data into a visual depiction can be sufficient.[60] The example cited in that discussion was *In re Abele*,[61] a case in which the patent applicant claimed a method of processing X-ray image data to generate a clearer X-ray image of a patient's body.[62] Because virtual worlds rely on generating visual simulations of objects, a virtual world process can conceivably be claimed as a transformation of electronic data that results in the simulated display, thereby possibly passing the "transformation" part of the test. Although the Supreme Court in *Bilski v. Kappos* held that the machine-or-transformation test is not the sole test for determining patent eligibility for processes,[63] it can still provide a "useful clue" in the second step of the *Alice* framework. Thus, this determination will likely be a close case for process claims in a virtual world's context both during prosecution at the USPTO and when proving validity during enforcement of the patent in court.

The first part of the machine-or-transformation test (i.e., the "machine" aspect) may also be applicable as well, because a virtual world process is arguably tied to the computer running the virtual world program; however, this aspect may be much more

---

59. *Id.* at 961. *See also* Ultramercial, Inc. v. Hulu, LLC, 772 F.3d 709, 716–17 (Fed. Cir. 2014).

60. *Bilski*, 545 F.3d at 962–63 (citing *In re* Abele, 684 F.2d 902 (C.C.P.A. 1982)).

61. *In re* Abele, 684 F.2d 902 (C.C.P.A. 1982).

62. *Id.* at 908–09.

63. Bilski v. Kappos, 561 U.S. 593, 604 (2010).

difficult to satisfy, if not impossible, with only claimed features to a generic computer in light of *Alice*.

Regarding video games and virtual worlds as patent-eligible subject matter, the process may no longer be the most easily identifiable type of invention that could apply in a virtual world, because at least one avenue of claiming a virtual world process (i.e., tying to a general computer) is a more difficult option after *Alice*. Although the process class of invention has become more stringent and limiting, courts have not yet addressed the issue of whether or not it is still possible to claim a virtual world process of transforming electronic data to a visual representation. This area of law is still developing and only time will tell the fate of process claims as they relate to the virtual worlds context.

2. Article of Manufacture

As noted previously, the process class of invention may be a bit more difficult in the wake of *Bilski* and *Alice*. There is, however, another option. Because all virtual worlds are run on computers, it is possible to claim a virtual world invention by claiming the computer on which that program runs. Specifically, a claim can be directed towards the physical medium (e.g., a hard disk, CD, memory chip, etc.) on which the computer program is stored. Such claims are commonly referred to as "Beauregard" claims, a name originating from the *In re Beauregard* decision in which the USPTO conceded (in a CAFC appeal) that claims directed to a computer-readable medium were eligible for protection as an article of manufacture.[64] Beauregard claims are still a viable option even after the *Alice* decision.[65] In fact, the CAFC, in *Alice*, did not even address the question of whether the type of claim (e.g., apparatus claims, method claims, Beauregard claims) affects patent eligibility.

There are drawbacks to *Beauregard*-style claims, however. The Beauregard claim is ideally suited for mass-distributed computer

---

64. *In re* Beauregard, 53 F.3d 1583 (Fed. Cir. 1995) (The commissioner of patents and trademarks conceded "that computer programs embodied in a tangible medium, such as floppy diskettes, are patent-eligible subject matter under 35 U.S.C. Section 101 and must be examined under 35 U.S.C. Sections 102 and 103.").

65. 2014 Interim Guidance on Patent Subject Matter Eligibility, 79 Fed. Reg. 74,618 (Dec. 16, 2014).

media, such as the CDs on which video games and virtual world software may be distributed, because that media is relatively easily identifiable (e.g., a single game publisher may have a warehouse containing hundreds of thousands of copies of the game disk, each a separate infringement), and each player has an infringing copy. However, for some virtual worlds, the majority of the software code may actually reside on a centralized computer server, if any, and players' own computers might only have a minimal or thin software client necessary to interact with that centralized server. For those types of virtual worlds, the Beauregard claim might only relate to one central server and present a smaller revenue stream to target in an infringement suit. Further, the centralized location may also limit the jurisdictional options available to the plaintiff, and can even thwart the plaintiff if that central server resides outside of the United States.

Accordingly, the article of manufacture approach is a viable alternative, and should be included in any claim strategy on a virtual world concept. Together with the process claim, these two classes of invention arguably provide the best options for claiming a virtual world or video game invention. The remaining classes, addressed in the following, may be a bit more difficult.

3. Machines

When it comes to evaluating an invention in a video game or virtual world, machines are more challenging in comparison to processes, but this class may eventually be more important in virtual worlds as the test for processes becomes more stringent and limiting. When one thinks of what a machine might be, one generally conjures up the image of some form of mechanical contraption: a car engine, household tools, or a mousetrap. There may be levers, gears, or bars, and maybe a motor or power supply, but it is generally envisioned as something *physical*. Can such a physical machine exist in a virtual world?

Putting aside the obvious example of a computer or server executing software, which clearly would meet the definition of a machine, one might also consider a "virtual" machine existing only within a video game or virtual world. This is a somewhat esoteric question that requires a definition of what it is to "exist." A common sense approach might define things as "existing" if those things can be perceived and observed in some way, and if they can interact with other objects that also exist. Under that approach, a "real" machine exists because it can be seen, and can be observed interacting with its environment. For example, one might confirm that a ball exists by seeing it, and by witnessing it bounce off the ground. All of that happens, however, because of the laws of physics. The ball can be seen because light reflects off of the ball and into the eye of the beholder. The ball bounces because gravity causes it to fall, and when it strikes the ground, the energy in the falling ball is transferred to, and reflected by, the ground, and the ball comes back up.

A virtual version of such a ball can exist as well, if all of the necessary laws of physics are simulated in the virtual world. If the computer defines the ball's properties (e.g., its shape, size, mass, and elastic properties), its location relative to the ground, and the force of gravity, then the computer can simulate the falling of the ball by calculating, at each moment in time, the ball's new position due to gravity. When the computer determines that the ball is in contact with the ground, it may then calculate the transfer of energy between the ball and the ground, given the ball's speed and elastic properties, and that calculation can then be used to determine how the ball should bounce from the ground. The behavior of this virtual ball can be "seen" on a computer display by having the computer generate images that illustrate the ball's position and shape over successive moments in time.

Such physics simulation in games has been around for many years. Take, for example, *The Incredible Machine*, a puzzle game from the early 1990s that simulated the behavior of various real-world objects, like balls, ramps, pulleys, levers, springs, rubber bands, and helium-filled balloons, and asked players to use those items to construct Rube-Goldberg-esque[66] contraptions for accomplishing some objective. The example puzzle in Figure 3.1[67] asks players to get the virtual basketball into the virtual basket.

---

66. Rube Goldberg was a Pulitzer Prize-winning cartoonist in the 1940s who was famous for drawing overly complicated contraptions for accomplishing simple tasks.

67. Screenshot from *The Incredible Machine*, version 3.0, published by Sierra Entertainment.

Figure 3.1 The Incredible Machine 3.0

The player is given a playfield (on the left side of the screen), which has a fixed arrangement of items (e.g., the basket, the backboard, the hamster cage, the basketball, etc.) that is "frozen" in time (e.g., paused, no gravity, no motion, etc.). The player is also given a limited collection of additional parts, such as belts, gears, and ramps (shown on the right side of the screen), which the player can add to the playfield in whatever arrangement the player wants. When the player is happy with his or her arrangement of parts, the player presses a button that "un-pauses" the scene (e.g., allowing gravity and simulated laws of physics to take effect), and the player can watch to see if the ball will successfully progress through the setup, and land in the basket. The puzzle's solution could involve something like attaching a conveyor belt to the hamster wheel so it moves when the hamster's cage is hit, and then having the pinball flipper at the end of the conveyor belt kick the ball up and into the basket. Whatever the solution, one can imagine that if someone had built that solution in real life, he or she could have patented that contraption (assuming it met the other requirements for a patent discussed previously).[68]

---

68. Interestingly, the developers behind *The Incredible Machine* received U.S. Patent No. 5,577,185 (issued Nov. 19, 1996), entitled "Computerized Puzzle Gaming Method and Apparatus" (claims were directed to the method of providing the game's puzzles).

But would such a patent, on a real-world machine, also prohibit someone from making a virtual version of the same machine? What if the claim literally recited the physical structural elements, like a spring and a bar in a mousetrap? Literal infringement of such a claim seems unlikely, unless the drafter took precautions to include virtual versions in the patent's description (e.g., by explicitly stating that the spring could be a physical spring, or a spring simulated in a virtual environment on a computer or other data processing device). The doctrine of equivalents, however, seems promising, because that doctrine allows a claim to cover accused devices that are not precisely the same as what the claim requires, and that amount of flexibility may be the launch point for a possible infringement claim. Generally speaking, the doctrine of equivalents expands a patent's scope to encompass devices that are "trivially" different from the patent's claimed invention.[69] Is a virtual version of a mousetrap only "trivially" different from a real-world mousetrap, because they both operate using the same application of the laws of physics? Does not the use of the term "virtual" in "virtual reality" suggest that the computer-generated simulations are close to, but not necessarily, the real thing? This also raises the reverse question: if a virtual machine is only a trivial variation from an actual machine, and therefore should be considered an infringement, would the virtual machine be rendered obvious by a pre-existing real-life version of the machine? The case law appears to suggest the answer is in the affirmative unless there is some hurdle or difficulty that needs to be overcome to make the virtual version of the machine work, in which case the invention might actually be overcoming the hurdle, rather than the virtual machine itself.[70]

4. Compositions of Matter

The last statutory class of invention seems less promising at the moment. A virtual object cannot, at least to the authors, fairly be

---

69. *See*, *e.g.*, Festo Corp. v. Shoketsu Kinzoku Kogyo Kabushiki Co., 535 U.S. 722, 733–34 (2002) ("The doctrine of equivalents allows the patentee to claim those insubstantial alterations that were not captured in drafting the original patent claim but which could be created through trivial changes.").

70. Dann v. Johnston, 425 U.S. 219 (1976) (stating that merely using a computer to automate a known process does not by itself impart nonobviousness to the invention).

considered a composition of matter. Of course, it is imaginable that if virtual reality and virtual worlds become prevalent enough, the common understanding of "matter" may at some time include virtual matter, but the law is not yet at that point. Significant case law decisions and/or law rewriting will likely be required before this statutory class of inventions becomes relevant to this field of virtual worlds.

B. Design Patents

The preceding discussion has focused on so-called utility patents, which are patents for "useful" inventions. Utility patents are not, however, the only type of patent that could be relevant to a video game or virtual world. Another type of patent is a design patent, set forth at 35 U.S.C. § 171. Instead of covering "useful" inventions, design patents cover the "ornamental appearance" of an item, such as the appearance of a Star Wars® character, depicted in Figure 3.2.[71]

Figure 3.2 U.S. Patent No. D265,754

The ornamental appearance has been defined to include both the shape of a physical article as well as any surface ornamentation that article may have. More recently, design patents have

---

71. Taken from U.S. Patent No. D265,754 (issued Aug. 10, 1982), assigned to Lucasfilm, Ltd. by inventors George Lucas et al.

been granted on on-screen display elements and icons, as well as on animated or transitional displays on a computer screen. Because virtual worlds are highly visual in nature, it should come as no surprise that design patents are an effective approach to protecting the visually distinctive elements in a virtual world. Often, this type of patent protection offers the best protection possible in view of the difficulties described previously with obtaining utility patent protection and in view of the most important aspects that a competitor wants to copy being wholly visual. Some game manufacturers are already pursuing this angle. Consider, for example, Konami's U.S. Patents D404,729,[72] D404,390,[73] D402,285,[74] and D402,282,[75] directed to the appearances of the on-screen characters shown in Figures 3.3 through 3.6.

Figure 3.4 U.S. Patent No. D404,390   **Figure 3.3 U.S. Patent No. D404,729**

---

72. U.S. Patent No. D404,729 (issued Jan. 26, 1999).
73. U.S. Patent No. D404,390 (issued Jan. 19, 1999).
74. U.S. Patent No. D402,285 (issued Dec. 8, 1998).
75. U.S. Patent No. D402,282 (issued Dec. 8, 1998).

Figure 3.5 U.S. Patent No. D402,285   **Figure 3.6 U.S. Patent No. D402,282**

Design patents, however, have not been merely limited to the ornamental appearance of on-screen characters found in video games or to visually distinctive elements found in virtual worlds. The recent implementation of virtual reality and augmented reality into wearable technology has also led companies to protect the ornamental designs of their electronic devices that provide users with these virtual world experiences. Compare, for example, Oculus VR's Design Patent No. D749,583[76] (Figure 3.7) with Samsung's Design Patent No. D764,466[77] (Figure 3.8).

Other examples of companies with design patents directed to virtual reality headsets include Apple,[78] Google,[79] Magic Leap,[80]

---

76. .U.S. Patent No. D749,583 (issued Feb. 16, 2016). *See also* Oculus VR's additional design patents—U.S. Patent No. D738,374 (issued Sept. 8, 2015) and U.S. Patent No. D701,206 (issued Mar. 18, 2014).

77. U.S. Patent No. D764,466 (issued Aug. 23, 2016).

78. U.S. Patent No. D757,003 (issued May 24, 2016).

79. U.S. Patent No. D750,074 (issued Feb. 23, 2016).; U.S. Patent No. D757,003 (issued May 24, 2016); U.S. Patent No. D792,398 (issued July 18, 2017).

80. U.S. Patent No. D758,367 (issued June 7, 2016).

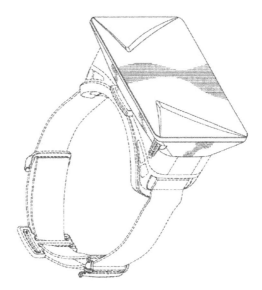

Figure 3.7 U.S. Patent No. D749,583

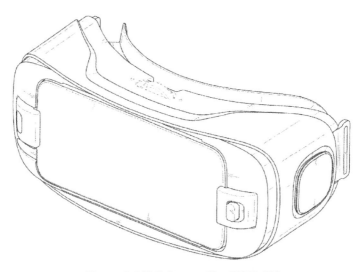

Figure 3.8 U.S. Patent No. D764,466

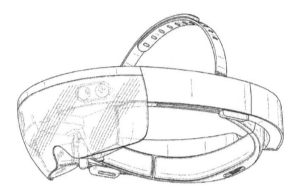

Figure 3.9 U.S. Patent No. D740,815

Huawei,[81] Intel,[82] and Ariadne's Thread.[83] Also consider Microsoft's Hololens, depicted in Figure 3.9,[84] which is usable for augmented reality applications.

1. Claiming Considerations

In design patents, the images in the patent form the "claim" of the design patent, which raises its own set of considerations (e.g., how much of a design to show, what portions of the design to claim, etc.).[85] However, once the types of potential classes of inventions for utility patents are identified, such as the process of a virtual world event, the article of manufacture of the CD containing the game program, a virtual object (e.g., a virtual mousetrap), and so on, a myriad of issues arise in determining how best to claim those inventions.

Claim strategy is of paramount importance because the claim language determines whether someone else infringes a patent, and thus determines the ultimate strength of the patent. A claim that is too broad might be susceptible to an invalidity attack based on prior art. Plus, the decisions surrounding claim strategy must be

---

81. U.S. Patent No. D803,213 (issued Nov. 21, 2017).
82. U.S. Patent No. D805,515 (issued Dec. 19, 2017).
83. U.S. Patent No. D761,257 (issued July 12, 2016).
84. U.S. Patent No. D740,815 (issued Oct. 13, 2015).
85. For regulations on design patents, see 37 C.F.R. § 1.152 (2000); *id.* § 1.153 (2012).

made when initially preparing a patent application, which is usually very early in the commercial process. A claim that is too narrow might be easy for others to design around and avoid infringement altogether. Drafting claims is therefore a delicate exercise in which the applicant (through its patent attorney) must exercise discretion, skill, and instinct in an attempt to obtain the broadest valid scope of protection. If even one claim term is given a meaning that the patentee did not intend, it may be difficult to subsequently enforce that patent as intended when the patent application was originally filed.

In *Activision Publishing, Inc. v. Gibson Guitar Corp.*,[86] Activision filed a declaratory judgment action asking the court for a finding of invalidity and noninfringement of Gibson's patent on a musical performance simulation, which Gibson alleged Activision infringed via its popular *Guitar Hero* games.[87] Gibson's claims required "participation of a user playing a musical instrument in a pre-recorded musical performance having audio and video portions, the musical instrument producing instrument audio signals at an instrument audio output when the instrument is played."[88] Gibson proposed a broad construction of the claims that would require that a "musical instrument" need only "indirectly produce music" and perhaps have no more than a mere appearance "that corresponds to a specific type of instrument used in the musical performance."[89] Activision argued for a much narrower construction, which the court largely adopted. The court, in its *Markman* ruling construing the claims, held that a "musical instrument" must be capable of: (1) making "musical sounds"; and (2) either directly, or indirectly through an interface device, producing an instrument audio signal representative of those sounds.[90] The court also held that the instrument must be capable of making musical sounds indepen-

---

86. Activision Publ'g, Inc. v. Gibson Guitar Corp., No. CV 08-01653-MRP (SHx), 2009 U.S. Dist. LEXIS 21931 (C.D. Cal. Feb. 26, 2009).

87. *Id.* at *4. The patent in suit is U.S. Patent No. 5,990,405, entitled "System and Method for Generating and Controlling a Simulated Musical Concert Experience," issued November 23, 1999.

88. U.S. Patent No. 5,990,405 col. 7, ll. 17–21 (filed July 8, 1998).

89. *See Activision Publ'g*, 2009 U.S. Dist. LEXIS 21931, at *17–19.

90. *Id.* at *20.

dent of the mechanism that outputs the instrument audio signal.[91] In view of the court's ruling, Activision filed a motion for summary judgment, which was quickly granted.[92] Gibson did not appeal the court's claim construction or the summary judgment ruling.[93]

As evidenced by the *Activision* outcome, the task of choosing claim terms should not be taken lightly. First and foremost, the various terms in the claims will be interpreted from the viewpoint of a hypothetical person of ordinary skill in the art. If the invention being claimed is a process or machine that ordinarily exists in the real world, then the patent drafter should be sure to include virtual versions of the invention in the specification. For example, when describing the mousetrap components, the drafter may wish to include in the description that the components may, if desired, be simulated in a virtual reality environment to have the properties described in the specification.

As another consideration, the drafter may wish to use the term "virtual reality" or "virtual" in the claim itself, to ensure that the reader will understand that the claim is intended to cover the virtual reality invention. But is such a term indefinite? Abstract? To use the mousetrap example again, would the term "virtual spring" be concrete enough that the hypothetical person of ordinary skill in the art would know what is covered by the claim, and how to avoid infringing it? Again, this will depend on the specification and the context of the claim. If the specification and claims provide enough assistance to that hypothetical person to understand what this "virtual spring" is, and is not, then there should not be a problem. In fact, there are already hundreds of issued U.S. patents describing virtual reality features and reciting "virtual" claim limitations. For example, U.S. Patent No. 7,337,410,[94] entitled "Virtual Workstation," includes terms like "virtual environment" and "virtual input device" in its claims. At a minimum, the USPTO felt

---

91. *Id.*

92. *Id.* at *44.

93. Gibson Guitar Corp. v. 745 LLC, No. 3:11-0058, 2012 U.S. Dist. LEXIS 4177, at *8–9 (M.D. Tenn. Jan. 11, 2012).

94. U.S. Patent No. 7,337,410 (issued Feb. 26, 2008).

these claim terms were sufficiently clear, at least under the then-accepted standards of patent-eligible subject matter.

Another type of claim that may present a challenge is a means-plus-function claim under 35 U.S.C. § 112(f). In a means-plus-function claim the claimed "means" for performing a function is to be interpreted as the corresponding "structure" described in the specification for performing the recited function, and equivalents to those means. But can that "structure" be virtual? It would seem so. The statute's only requirement refers to "structure," and the case law merely requires that the specification have a "clear association" between the structure in the specification and the recited function.[95] There appears to be no cases yet addressing "virtual means," where the corresponding structure in the specification is described as a virtual object, but it would seem that so long as the specification clearly describes a virtual (or potentially virtual) structure performing the recited function, then the means-plus-function approach would be acceptable as well. Of course, the claim as a whole would still need to comply with the usefulness, novelty, and nonobviousness requirements. Case law has indicated that where the means for performing the function recited in the claims is software, at least one specific software algorithm must be disclosed, even if the software algorithm would otherwise be within the level of knowledge of someone of ordinary skill in the art.[96]

It thus appears safest to take a more traditional approach to the claims, without using the terms "virtual" or "virtual reality." For example, the patent statute itself lists "processes" as subject-matter eligible for a patent,[97] so there may be less controversy if the virtual invention can be claimed as a process. Most features of a virtual invention can be broken down into the process steps the computer performs to simulate that invention, so the traditional

---

95. *See, e.g.*, Med. Instrumentation & Diagnostics Corp. v. Elekta AB, 344 F.3d 1205 (Fed. Cir. 2003); B. Braun Med. Inc. v. Abbott Labs., 124 F.3d 1419 (Fed. Cir. 1997).

96. *See* Aristocrat Techs. v. Int'l Gaming Tech., 543 F.3d 657 (Fed. Cir. 2008).

97. 35 U.S.C. § 101 (2018) ("Whoever invents or discovers any new and useful *process*, . . . may obtain a patent therefor. . . .") (emphasis added).

process claim structure appears to be the most solid approach so long as the claim can prove usefulness under the machine or transformation test.

III. Using a Patent in a Virtual World

A. Enforcement Avenues

The patent right is a negative one, as a patent merely gives the patentee the right to prevent others from making, using, or selling the patented invention. But how does one do that? There are a variety of avenues by which a patentee may enforce its patent right, and in the following paragraphs we provide a brief overview of each.

1. Federal District Courts

The first, and most traditional, avenue for enforcing a patent is in the courts. Subject-matter jurisdiction is vested in the federal district courts:

> The district courts shall have original jurisdiction of any civil action arising under any Act of Congress relating to patents, plant variety protection, copyrights and trademarks. No State court shall have jurisdiction over any claim for relief arising under any Act of Congress relating to patents, plant variety protection, or copyrights. For purposes of this subsection, the term "State" includes any State of the United States, the District of Columbia, the Commonwealth of Puerto Rico, the United States Virgin Islands, American Samoa, Guam, and the Northern Mariana Islands.[98]

District court patent litigation can be the most time-consuming, and costly, way to enforce a patent. Patent suits can take two to five years to get to trial, depending on the jurisdiction, and you can bet that the case will not end with the trial verdict, as the losing party more than likely will pursue appeals that can tack on another one to two years to the proceedings. In a recent study by

---

98. 28 U.S.C. § 1331(a) (1980).

the American Intellectual Property Law Association, average cost for a patent case having $10–25 million at risk, just to get through the discovery process, is $1.23 million, and average total cost through trial is $2.374 million.[99]

Aside from the cost and time, there are other notable issues with district court patent litigation. Of particular relevance to virtual worlds is the question of personal jurisdiction/venue, and two types of issues stand out. First is the basic question of *who* to sue. Many websites do not offer information identifying an actual human being or corporate entity responsible for the site, and it can be tough to figure out who to sue in the first place. Second, even if you have figured out who to sue, it is not always easy to determine where they may be subject to personal jurisdiction. Computer servers, and the people responsible for them, can be located anywhere in the world, and when one user connects to a host server on the Internet, there is no telling where that server is actually located. A patentee can find itself spending enormous resources just determining *who* to sue, and where to sue. A small litigation budget could be blown before the patentee even gets close to having its day in court.

Another wrinkle with district court litigation is the possibility that the patentee can be dragged into a litigation before the patentee is ready. The Declaratory Judgment Act[100] generally allows people not to have to live under the threat of a lawsuit. If there is an actual controversy in which a potential infringer might be sued, the infringer preemptively can file its own lawsuit to have that issue resolved, without waiting for the patentee to get around to filing suit first. This can help accused infringers remove the cloud of uncertainty that arises whenever a patentee makes an accusation of infringement (e.g., by sending a cease and desist letter), but it also means that a patentee might get dragged into court earlier than planned if its target infringer winds up filing suit first.

In addition to the possibility of getting dragged into court *earlier* than planned, the Declaratory Judgment Act often also means

---

99. AMERICAN INTELLECTUAL PROPERTY LAW ASSOCIATION, 2017 REPORT OF THE ECONOMIC SURVEY (2017).

100. 28 U.S.C. § 2201(a) (2010).

that a patentee can find itself in a *different* court from what it may have planned. That target infringer will file its declaratory judgment suit in a court of its choosing, and will naturally try to find a court most favorable to the infringer. In recent years, it became standard for parties to be concerned about a "race to the courthouse" as soon as a patent dispute arose, as each party (the patentee and accused infringer) preferred to have the case litigated in a court of their choosing. Aside from the obvious "home-field advantage" concern, parties also considered the reputations of the different district courts, as some district courts have reputations for being fast and/or patent friendly. For example, the U.S. District Court for the Eastern District of Virginia has been dubbed the "Rocket Docket" for its speed (trials planned merely a year after filing of the complaint), while the U.S. District Court for the Eastern District of Texas was considered a patent-friendly court (for many years it had *never* found a patent to be invalid).

The practice of patent forum shopping, however, took a hit in 2017 with the Supreme Court decision in *TC Heartland LLC v. Kraft Foods Group Brands LLC*.[101] In that case, the Supreme Court held that the patent venue statute, 28 U.S.C. § 1400(b), when applied to domestic corporations, defines a corporation's "residence" as only its state of incorporation.[102] In the years prior to *TC Heartland*, the CAFC had adopted a more forgiving venue approach, essentially allowing large corporate patentees to be sued anywhere in the country, resulting in a disproportionate amount of patent suits being brought in patent-friendly districts like the U.S. District Court for the Eastern District of Texas (with some patent assertion companies setting up offices in that district for just that purpose). After *TC Heartland*, it will be harder for patentees to bring suit, against a corporate infringer, in a district outside the state of the infringer's incorporation.

Another factor worth considering is relative expertise in patents. U.S. district courts handle a large variety of legal disputes, and some might not be as familiar with patents and their specific issues. This can sometimes create unforeseen difficulties. For

---

101. TC Heartland LLC v. Kraft Foods Group Brands LLC, 137 S. Ct. 1514 (2017).
102. *Id.* at 1521.

example, in *KI Ventures, LLC v. Fry's Electronics Inc.*,[103] the plaintiff, KI Ventures, LLC, sought to enforce U.S. Patent No. 6,569,019, entitled "Weapon Shaped Virtual Reality Character Controller," which was directed to a video game controller in the shape of a gun, as shown in Figure 3.10.[104]

However, the district court appeared to struggle with some of the patent issues, doubting the patent's validity, and ultimately dismissed the case with prejudice. At various proceedings prior to the dismissal, the district court questioned why there were patent figures:

> THE COURT: Okay. But apparently CTA makes a sniper rifle, a submachine gun, an assault rifle and an assault rifle and sniper rifle. Well, so does the government. So does Remington and Ruger and Winchester and Colt. What's patentable about a toy gun that actually changes computer games?
>
> * * *
>
> MR. RAMEY: I'm not sure that the design on the front page of that patent is an accurate representation of the claims as they issued.
>
> THE COURT: Why is it here then?
>
> MR. RAMEY: We're not the ones that drafted the patent.
>
> THE COURT: I'm sorry, you're stuck with whatever this thing is. That's what you own.
>
> * * *
>
> THE COURT: All right. Well, tell me where in here is a picture of what's patentable. Because they all look pretty similar to that. Is there no drawing of what's patentable?[105]

---

103. KI Ventures, LLC v. Fry's Elecs. Inc., 579 Fed. Appx. 985 (Fed. Cir. 2014) (unpublished).

104. U.S. Patent No. 6,569,019 (issued May 27, 2003).

105. *Id.* at 986.

US006569019B2

(12) **United States Patent** (10) Patent No.: **US 6,569,019 B2**
Cochran (45) **Date of Patent:** **May 27, 2003**

(54) **WEAPON SHAPED VIRTUAL REALITY CHARACTER CONTROLLER**

(76) Inventor: **William Cochran**, 211 Michigan, South Houston, TX (US) 77587

(*) Notice: Subject to any disclaimer, the term of this patent is extended or adjusted under 35 U.S.C. 154(b) by 0 days.

(21) Appl. No.: **09/901,742**

(22) Filed: **Jul. 10, 2001**

(65) **Prior Publication Data**

US 2003/0013524 A1 Jan. 16, 2003

(51) **Int. Cl.**[7] **A63F 13/00**; A63F 9/24; G06F 17/00; G06F 19/00
(52) **U.S. Cl.** **463/37**; 463/47; 341/20
(58) **Field of Search** 463/36, 37, 38, 463/2, 8, 46, 47; 341/20

(56) **References Cited**

U.S. PATENT DOCUMENTS

4,395,045 A	*	7/1983	Baer	273/312
5,353,134 A	*	10/1994	Michel et al.	359/52
5,386,308 A	*	1/1995	Michel et al.	359/83
5,569,085 A	*	10/1996	Igarashi et al.	463/49

5,641,288 A	*	6/1997	Zaenglein, Jr.	434/21
5,690,492 A	*	11/1997	Herald	434/20
5,734,370 A	*	3/1998	Skodlar	345/156
5,954,507 A	*	9/1999	Rod et al.	434/19
6,005,548 A	*	12/1999	Latypov et al.	345/156
6,050,822 A	*	4/2000	Faughn	434/11
6,206,783 B1	*	3/2001	Yamamoto et al.	463/36
6,296,486 B1	*	10/2001	Cardaillac et al.	463/12
6,328,650 B1	*	12/2001	Fukawa et al.	463/36
6,328,651 B1	*	12/2001	Lebensfeld et al.	463/52
6,379,249 B1	*	4/2002	Satsukawa et al.	463/31

* cited by examiner

Primary Examiner—Denise L. Esquivel
Assistant Examiner—Marc Norman
(74) *Attorney, Agent, or Firm*—Arthur M. Dula

(57) **ABSTRACT**

The present invention is a virtual reality game controller that is shaped like a weapon such as a rifle, pistol or shotgun. The controller has at least one multiaxis controller that is actuated by movement part of the weapon, for example its forearm also has a plurality of switch controls that are positioned on the weapon to control movement and actions and attributes of a VR game character within the VR game space without interrupting the playing of the game.

4 Claims, 3 Drawing Sheets

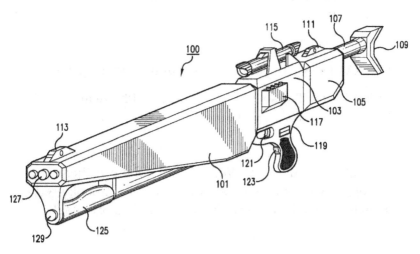

Figure 3.10 U.S. Patent No. 6,569,019

The district court focused on validity when discussing the infringe-ment contentions:

> THE COURT: Once somebody puts one control element on a firearm-looking thing, why isn't the rest of it obvious?
>
> MR. RAMEY: It is not how the patent law works, Your Honor.
>
> THE COURT: It is when what you do is obvious.
>
> MR. RAMEY: Well—
>
> THE COURT: Let me point out that there are—
>
> MR. RAMEY: We are having an invalidity argument at this point—
>
> THE COURT: I can't because you and your client won't do what they are supposed to do. I'm just asking you some questions. If you don't want to answer them, just say, I prefer not to discuss this with Your Honor and I will not discuss it with you.

* * *

> THE COURT: My question is: What makes that an invention?
>
> MR. RAMEY: Because it is useful—
>
> THE COURT: The parts are useful. You can't—in patent use a light switch.

* * *

> THE COURT: My question was: Will yours move it with the buttons as well as with the joy stick?
>
> MR. RAMEY: 100 percent.
>
> THE COURT: That's not patentable.
>
> MR. RAMEY: Your Honor, is that a statement or question?
>
> THE COURT: It's a question.
>
> MR. RAMEY: The combination of that in combination—

THE COURT: No. Answer my question.

MR. RAMEY: That is patentable. We have a patent.

We know it is patentable.

THE COURT: Counsel, having two forms of controlling the aspect is not patentable.[106]

The district court even appeared reluctant to discuss the actual language of the patent:

THE COURT: KI's patent is only on the location of the buttons on a gun-like piece of plastic.

MR. RAMEY: No, Your Honor. If you read the first—

THE COURT: Don't start quoting your patent.[107]

On appeal, the CAFC found that the district court had abused its discretion in the dismissal, and sent it back.[108] Not surprisingly, a few months later, the parties jointly agreed to dismiss the case. The patentee certainly did not expect the case to go the way that it did, and this just exemplifies some of the unforeseen difficulties that could arise in a district court litigation, and is another factor to consider when evaluating this avenue of patent enforcement.

Although difficulties can certainly arise with district court patent litigation, the district courts remain the primary avenue for the enforcement of patent rights. However, as will be discussed in the following subsections, there are alternative options to consider.

2. The U.S. International Trade Commission

As an alternative to (or in addition to) the traditional district court litigation discussed previously, a patentee may enforce its patent rights at the U.S. International Trade Commission (USITC). The USITC has the authority to bar goods from entry into the United States if it finds that importing those goods would harm the U.S.

---

106. *Id.* at 988.
107. *Id.*
108. *Id.* at 991–92.

marketplace. Since many companies manufacture their goods out-side of the United States (e.g., virtual reality computing hardware that may be configured to infringe a particular patent in use), a patentee may find that barring an infringer from importing its products would be almost as good as winning a patent infringement lawsuit.

Proceedings at the USITC are very similar to those of a district court litigation. The proceedings start with a complaint filed by the patentee (the "complainant), followed by a response filed by the accused infringer (the respondent), and then there is a period of fact discovery in which both sides may obtain information from the other. Fact discovery, and many USITC aspects, are governed by rules that closely track the Federal Rules of Civil Procedure. So one can expect the usual requests for documents, interrogatories, depositions, expert witnesses, and so on, that you normally find in a district court litigation. The proceedings culminate with a hearing before an administrative law judge (ALJ), and the hearing is conducted very much like a district court trial, with both sides presenting evidence supporting their case. After the hearing, the ALJ will issue a decision as to whether the accused products should be barred from entry into the United States, and if the ALJ's decision finds infringement, then the USITC will proceed with issuing an exclusion order instructing U.S. Customs to block the accused products from importation.

Although the USITC procedure is similar to a district court litigation, there are a few notable differences. Perhaps the biggest difference is speed. While a district court litigation could easily take several years to resolve, federal regulations require that the USITC resolve its complaints within a statutory period of 18 months. This means that everything will be compressed time-wise, putting great pressure on all parties involved. However, the patentee can take its time investigating the accused products, securing expert witnesses, and preparing strategies *before* filing the complaint, so that the time crunch is more manageable. The accused infringer, on the other hand, is often surprised by the complaint, and may end up playing catch-up all the way to the hearing. For this reason, patentees consider the USITC to be an effective way to apply pressure on the accused infringer.

Another notable difference is the fact that simply proving infringement, and defeating validity challenges, will not be enough for the patentee to get the exclusion order. The USITC's mission is not simply to prevent all infringement. Its mission is to protect the U.S. marketplace, and importation of an infringing product only hurts that marketplace if there is an existing market within the United States for goods covered by the asserted patents. To prevail, the patentee must prove the existence of this U.S. market. A patentee may do this by proving that it is selling products covered by the patent, or that the patentee has licensed others who are selling products covered by the patent. If the patentee fails to establish a U.S. market that would be harmed by the importation of the infringing product, there will be no exclusion order (even if the accused products actually infringe the asserted patent).

Another notable difference is the proverbial "third wheel." Proceedings at the USITC do not merely involve the patentee and the accused infringer. Instead, the USITC investigative staff acts as a third party to the proceedings. The staff attorneys are there to represent the interests of the American public, and the staff can participate in the proceedings like any other party—submitting discovery requests, attending depositions, questioning witnesses, filing briefs supporting/opposing motions and arguments, and so on. They are often the neutral observer whose opinion sways the ALJ on a contested issue, and their close presence can help to keep litigants from getting too carried away with litigation shenanigans.

The available remedy is also different at the USITC—the USITC does not award money damages for infringement. So while it may be possible to get a $1 billion judgment in a district court patent case,[109] the only infringement remedy for a USITC complainant is the exclusion order barring the infringer's product from entering the country. So if the infringing good is (or can be) made domestically, or if the infringer has a large supply of infringing goods

---

109. *See, e.g.*, Amended Jury Verdict at 15, Apple, Inc. v. Samsung Elecs. Co., No. 11-CV-01846 (N.D. Cal. Aug. 24, 2012); *see also* Nick Wingfield, *Jury Awards $1 Billion to Apple in Samsung Patent Case*, N.Y. Times, Aug. 24, 2012, https://www.nytimes.com/2012/08/25/technology/jury-reaches-decision-in-apple-samsung-patent-trial.html.

already in the United States, or if the patent is expiring soon, then the patentee will need to take those facts into consideration when evaluating the value of an action at the USITC.

And a final point of interest lies with the president of the United States. If the USITC were to issue an exclusion order, that order will only go into effect after a 60-day presidential review period. During that period, the president of the United States has the power to veto the exclusion order. A presidential veto is a rare occurrence, but is a possibility if, for example, diplomatic policy reasons would caution against blocking the importation of the infringing good.

3. The USPTO

The third avenue is not really an *enforcement* avenue. Rather, due to changes in U.S. patent law resulting from the AIA, the USPTO is increasingly becoming a hotbed of patent litigation activity with thousands of *inter partes* review (IPR) proceedings having been implemented since they began in 2013.[110] The only issue in an IPR is the validity of the patent; infringement is beyond the scope of the USPTO's jurisdiction, and is left for district courts (or the USITC) to decide, as discussed previously.

What is an IPR proceeding? The IPR option replaced the previously available *inter partes reexamination* option, and is basically an opportunity for an accused infringer (or anyone but the patent owner) to petition to have the validity of a patent reevaluated. That petitioner starts the IPR by filing a petition laying out the grounds of invalidity. Those grounds must be based on patents or printed publications, and must show invalidity under 35 U.S.C. § 102 (anticipation) or § 103 (obviousness). The patent owner is permitted to file a preliminary response to the petition, offering reasons why an IPR should not be instituted. Aside from simply arguing the patent's validity, the preliminary response may allege procedural defects in the petition. For example, the IPR rules place restrictions to prevent litigation gamesmanship by infringers, by giving infringers a limited time window in which to request the IPR. Rule 42.101(a)[111] requires that the IPR petition will not be granted

---

110. Monthly IPR statistics are available at USPTO, https://www.uspto.gov.
111. 37 C.F.R. § 42.101(a).

if the petitioner has previously filed a civil action to challenge the validity of the patent, and Rule 42.101(b)[112] requires that the petition will not be granted if it is filed more than one year after the petitioner has been sued for infringing the patent. The patent owner may also voluntarily disclaim one or more of the challenged claims, and no IPR will be instituted for such disclaimed claims.

From there, the petition and preliminary response will be provided to the PTAB, and if the PTAB believes that there is a reasonable likelihood that the petitioner will prevail on at least one of the challenged claims, then the PTAB will institute the IPR proceedings on some or all of the challenged claims.

After institution, the patent owner may file a response to the petition, addressing the grounds of invalidity that are at issue, and may also move to amend the claims in response to the ground of invalidity. Notably, the amendments cannot enlarge the scope of the claims of the patent or introduce new subject matter.[113]

Parties to an IPR proceeding may obtain limited discovery on issues pertaining to the grounds of invalidity. This means there can be written discovery, depositions, and experts, much like a district court litigation. Also as with district court litigation, there will be a trial to present evidence and arguments on the validity of the challenged patent claims, and the PTAB will render its decision.

The above represents the basics of IPRs, and IPR proceedings have become a significant alternative avenue to litigate patent validity issues. Through September 2017, the USPTO has received more than 7,500 IPR petitions, initiated 3,850 IPR proceedings, and reached a final written decision in 1,771 proceedings.[114] There are a number of notable considerations and distinctions for accused infringers considering an IPR. First is the fact that accused infringers' chances are better at the PTAB, and this is for several reasons:

- The PTAB will apply a "broadest reasonable interpretation" standard to claim construction, which is broader than the standard applied at the district court level, and it is easier

---

112. *Id.* § 42.101(b).
113. *Id.* § 42.121(a)(2)(ii).
114. Monthly statistics are available at USPTO, https://www.uspto.gov.

to invalidate claims given this broader interpretation than would be used at the district court level.

- A district court will presume that a patent is valid, meaning an infringer must prove invalidity by "clear and convincing" evidence. At the PTAB, there is no presumption of validity, so any evidence of invalidity will be evaluated on a level playing field.
- The PTAB is well versed in patent prosecution, so they may be more receptive to technical/complicated arguments of invalidity (as opposed to judges who query why drawings are included in patents in the first place, as in *KI Ventures*).

A second notable consideration/distinction is the speed of an IPR proceeding. The IPR rules require that an IPR proceeding take no more than one year, although that period can be extended for six months for good cause.[115] In most district court patent cases, the parties may still be mired in fact discovery issues well past the anniversary of the complaint, so with an IPR the accused infringer may be able to get a much quicker resolution on its invalidity defense.

A third notable consideration is cautionary for the petitioner. Pursuant to 35 U.S.C. § 315(e)(2), if an IPR results in a final written decision, then the petitioner is estopped from raising the same argument in a civil action or at the USITC to challenge the validity of the same patent claim. Indeed, it is even stricter than that. Not only is the petitioner estopped from raising the same argument, the petitioner is estopped from raising any ground that it "raised or *reasonably could have raised* during that *inter partes* review." This estoppel is broad, and will need to be carefully considered before an accused infringer files an IPR petition.

B. Infringement Issues

Once a patentee has decided how and where to assert its patent rights, the question of infringement naturally comes next. Patent infringement is fairly easily stated: "whoever without authority makes, uses, offers to sell, or sells any patented invention . . .

---

115. 37 C.F.R. § 42.100.

infringes the patent."[116] Resolving the allegation of infringement, however, is never that easy, and there are a number of issues that can complicate the infringement determination. First is the basic question of what the patent claims. The words used in a patent claim can often be the first thing that trips up a claim of infringement. For example, in the *Activision v. Gibson* case discussed above, the question of infringement turned on the use of the simple phrase "musical instrument," as the court ruled that the phrase required an instrument having the ability to make "musical sounds."[117] In another case involving video game controllers, the parties stipulated on the issue of infringement after the court ruled that the claim's phrase "attached to said pad" (referring to actuators in a tactile video game controller) required affixing to the *exterior* surface of the pad, and did not include being embedded *within* the pad.[118] Indeed, in most patent disputes, the details of the accused product and details of the issued patent are evident to all, and the real disagreement is in the scope to be afforded to the words in the patent claims.

However, having said that, a second infringement issue comes from some situations where the accused infringer's product details are harder to see. Some patents may cover inventions that are difficult to discern. For example, if a patent covers the manner in which a virtual world's server efficiently compresses data, it may be difficult for the patentee to actually determine whether an accused infringer is using that method in its system. In those cases, it may be only after litigation and discovery have commenced before the patentee can be certain of the infringement. Short of discovery, patentees can hire technical experts to assist with analyzing how an infringing product behaves. Messages to and from a sample product may be captured and analyzed, the power consumption at various processing phases may be measured, the components of the sample product may be disassembled and studied, and

---

116. 35 U.S.C. § 271 (2018).

117. *See* Activision Publ'g, Inc. v. Gibson Guitar Corp., No. CV 08-01653-MRP (SHx), 2009 U.S. Dist. LEXIS 21931, at *20 (C.D. Cal. Feb. 26, 2009).

118. Thorner v. Sony Computer Entm't Am. LLC, 669 F.3d 1362, 1368 (Fed. Cir. 2012) (vacating the district court's construction, and finding that "attached to said pad" could encompass either external or internal attachments).

any number of other clever technical approaches can be made to investigate a product for possible infringement.

Another primary "infringement" issue is the issue of validity.[119] There are no damages for infringement of an invalid patent, so one of the primary challenges that an infringer has is the argument that the asserted patent claim is not actually novel or nonobvious, or that the patent document otherwise fails to meet the requirements for patentability. A granted U.S. patent is *presumed* valid, but that is a rebuttable presumption.[120]

The doctrine of "unclean hands" can also present an infringement issue, since a court can equitably determine that a patent is unenforceable if the patentee comes to court with "unclean hands." In the patent context, this arises from charges that the patentee obtained the patent through deceptive practices. The patent laws place a "duty of candor" on inventors and those who are associated with the filing and prosecution of a patent application, and that duty includes a duty to disclose to the USPTO "all information known to that individual to be material to patentability."[121] If an applicant fails to abide by that duty (e.g., by failing to disclose some relevant piece of prior art), then the court can find that the patent was fraudulently obtained, and can refuse to enforce the fraudulently obtained patent. For example, in *Therasense Inc. v. Becton Dickinson & Co.*,[122] a district court deemed a patent unenforceable because the inventor failed to disclose an argument made in a European counterpart application, when the argument appeared to contradict an argument the inventor made in the U.S. application.[123] In its decision, the *Therasense* court acknowledged that the practice of alleging inequitable conduct through a breach of the "duty of candor" was so commonplace as to be "an absolute plague," and clarified the applicable standard for finding such inequitable conduct.[124]

---

119. Validity can be considered a separate question from infringement, but we have grouped it here for consideration as part of the overall infringement story.

120. 35 U.S.C. § 282 (2018) ("Presumption of validity; defenses").

121. 37 C.F.R. § 1.555 (2000).

122. Therasense Inc. v. Becton Dickinson & Co., 649 F.3d 1276 (Fed. Cir. 2011).

123. *Id.* at 1295–96.

124. *Id.* at 1289–90.

Another issue comes in the form of who is actually responsible for the infringement. Sometimes a patent may claim a method having a number of steps, but in an accused system, there may be two different entities that are responsible for performing different ones of those steps. For example, in *Akamai Technologies, Inc. v. Limelight Networks, Inc.*,[125] the patent at issue dealt with the distributed storage of large media files (e.g., movie files, web pages, etc.) in a content delivery network.[126] The asserted claim recited various steps for handling such distributed storage, and included one step of "tagging," which referred to the designation of content to be stored in servers. In the accused Limelight system, the alleged act of "tagging" was not actually done by Limelight's servers. Instead, that "tagging" was done by Limelight's end users. Liability for this type of infringement, termed "divided infringement" because the infringing acts are performed by different actors, can still be placed on one of the actors if that actor "directs or controls" the other actor's infringing actions, or if the two actors form a "joint enterprise" in working together.[127]

This is by no means an exhaustive list of the various enforcement issues that can arise in a patent litigation. Other issues such as unnamed inventors, incorrect assignees, standing for exclusive licensees, and patent exhaustion can further complicate the question of infringement.

C. Damages Issues

1. Basic Damages

A principal reason for a patentee caring about enforcement is the prospect of a damages award at the end. In late 2016, the largest patent award to date was given in a case involving Hepatitis-C treatment medication: $2.54 billion.[128] Another case, in 2015,

---

125. Akamai Techs., Inc. v. Limelight Networks, Inc., 797 F.3d 1020 (Fed. Cir. 2015).
126. *Id.* at 1024.
127. *Id.* at 1346.
128. Jury Verdict at 3, Idenix Pharm. v. Gilead Scis., Inc., C.A., No. 14-cv-00846-LPS (D. Del. Nov. 16, 2016); *see also* Barry Herman, *Lessons from the Largest Patent Damages Award in History*, Law360, Jan. 20, 2017, 10:42 a.m., https://www.law360.com/articles/882857/lessons-from-the-largest-patent-damages-award-in-history.

resulted in a $1 billion award for smartphone technologies and ornamental designs.[129] With so many dollars being awarded, damages are a huge consideration in patent cases, and there are a variety of issues to consider.

Pursuant to 35 U.S.C. § 284, "[u]pon finding for the claimant the court shall award the claimant damages adequate to compensate for the infringement, but in no event less than a reasonable royalty for the use made of the invention by the infringer, together with interest and costs as fixed by the court." There are two main options in that passage. The first, the "damages adequate to compensate for the infringement," usually comes down to a lost profits calculation. As the name implies, this calculation involves the patentee establishing the amount of profit that it lost due to the infringer's infringement. The patentee can do this, for example, by proving that it would have made the same sales that the infringer made.

The second damages option is the "reasonable royalty." The reasonable royalty is the amount of royalty payments the infringer likely would have had to pay to the patentee for a license to sell the infringing goods. A "reasonable royalty" analysis typically involves evidence of standard royalty rates in the relevant industry, with the court attempting to determine what royalty rate would have resulted from a hypothetical arms-length negotiation between the parties. By statute, the reasonable royalty is considered the floor, or minimum amount, of damages that the patentee should be permitted to recover, but sometimes it is easier to prove the reasonable royalty than the lost profits. Indeed, the $2.54 billion award mentioned above was the result of the jury's award of a 10 percent royalty on a $25 billion sales base.[130]

Note, however, that there is a time limitation on patent damages. Per 35 U.S.C. § 286, a patentee cannot recover damages for infringement occurring more than six years prior to the filing of the lawsuit. So if there is infringement, the patentee ought not sit on its rights.

129. Apple Inc. v. Samsung Elecs. Co., 786 F.3d 983 (Fed. Cir. 2015).
130. *See supra* note 128.

2. Additional Damages

While enormous damages are possible based on just the lost profits or reasonable royalty, courts are also empowered to further enhance the damages in certain situations where the infringer's actions were particularly bad. Pursuant to 35 U.S.C. § 284, "the court may increase the damages up to three times the amount found or assessed." In 2016, the U.S. Supreme Court addressed the issue of enhanced damages, confirming that enhanced damages should only be made available for "egregious cases typified by willful misconduct," but relaxed the standard previously applied by the CAFC by doing away with the CAFC's requirement for finding that the infringer's actions were "objectively reckless," and also by lowering the standard from "clear and convincing" to merely a "preponderance of the evidence."[131]

Attorney fees are another way in which damages may be enhanced. "The court in exceptional cases may award reasonable attorney fees to the prevailing party."[132] The U.S. Supreme Court has held that an "exceptional" case "is simply one that stands out from others with respect to the substantive strength of a party's litigating position (considering both the governing law and the facts of the case) or the unreasonable manner in which the case was litigated."[133] Cases brought in bad faith, or ones that are objectively baseless, are nonlimiting examples of cases that may be ripe for the award of attorney fees.

3. Design Patent Damages

The award of damages for infringement of design patents merits special discussion, because the patent laws have a special provision for them. The patent laws, at 35 U.S.C. § 289, provide for an "additional remedy for infringement of design patent," and states the following:

> Whoever during the term of a patent for a design, without license of the owner, (1) applies the patented design, or any

---

131. Halo Elecs., Inc. v. Pulse Elecs., Inc., 136 S. Ct. 1923, 1935 (2016).
132. 35 U.S.C. § 285 (2018).
133. Octane Fitness, LLC v. ICON Health & Fitness, Inc., 134 S. Ct. 1749, 1756 (2014).

colorable imitation thereof, to any article of manufacture for the purpose of sale, or (2) sells or exposes for sale any *article of manufacture* to which such design or colorable imitation has been applied shall be liable to the owner to the extent of *his total profit*, but not less than $250, recoverable in any United States district court having jurisdiction of the parties.[134]

This provision for an infringer's *total profit* came as Congress's reaction to *Dobson v. Dornan*,[135] in which a design patentee successfully proved that an infringer's carpet infringed its patented design, but was awarded only $.06 because the patentee was unable to apportion its lost profits between: (1) profits attributable to the "design" and (2) profits attributable to other aspects of the "carpet."[136]

Section 289 sought to address the problem in *Dobson*, but that provision was recently debated at the U.S. Supreme Court in *Samsung Electronics Co. v. Apple Inc.*[137] In the *Samsung* case, various products from Samsung's line of smartphone and tablets were found to infringe Apple's design patents covering several facets of their iPhone product, as illustrated in Figure 3.11.

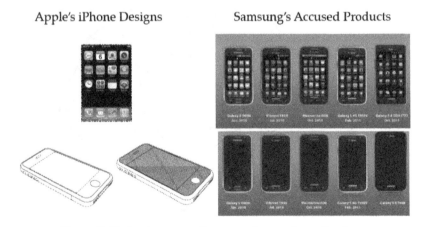

Apple's iPhone Designs   Samsung's Accused Products

Figure 3.11 Apple versus Samsung Smartphone Designs

---

134. 35 U.S.C. § 289 (2018) (emphasis added).
135. Dobson v. Dornan, 118 U.S. 10 (1886).
136. *Id.* at 17–18.
137. Samsung Elecs. Co. v. Apple Inc., 137 S. Ct. 429 (2016).

Apple was awarded $399 million—Samsung's *total profit* on the accused devices.[138]

Samsung appealed, and the key issue at the Supreme Court centered on the "article of manufacture" in § 289. Was the "article of manufacture" the entire smartphone, or just some portion of it? There was great anticipation that the Supreme Court's decision would offer guidance or a test for determining what the "article of manufacture" is, but in the end the decision merely held that the "article of manufacture" "need not be the end product sold to the consumer but may be only a component of that product."[139] Future cases will wrestle with that, and this will be an interesting damages consideration for anyone considering litigation of a design patent infringement issue.[140]

D. *Video Game Lawsuits*

As long as there is innovation and business competition in an industry, there will be patent disputes. The *Activision* and *KI Ventures* cases discussed above are just two examples highlighting the importance of claim construction and patent expertise in such cases, and the discussion that follows highlights a few additional examples in which patents were the subject of litigation.

Many will recall Atari's *Pong* as the earliest successful video game, but few may know that Atari's game was inspired by an even earlier table tennis game produced by Magnavox. Indeed, a district court even said as much in a 1977 decision in *Magnavox Co. v. Chicago Dynamic Industries*.[141] In that decision, a Chicago district court was asked to consider the validity of one of Magnavox's patents, and in doing so noted that the Magnavox table tennis game had been imitated by others:

---

138. *Id.* at 434.

139. *Id.* at 433–36.

140. For example, on remand to the district court, Apple was awarded $539 million in damages from Samsung for infringement of Apple's design patents, more than the initial award of damages, despite the narrowing guidance from the Supreme Court. Apple Inc. v. Samsung Elecs. Co., No. 11-CV-01846-LHK, 2017 WL 4776443 (N.D. Cal. Oct. 22, 2017); *see also Apple Awarded $539m in US Patent Case against Samsung*, BBC NEWS, May 25, 2018, https://www.bbc.com/news/business-44248404. Apple and Samsung ultimately settled the lawsuit in June 2018.

141. Magnavox Co. v. Chi. Dynamic Indus., 201 U.S.P.Q. 25 (N.D. Ill. 1977).

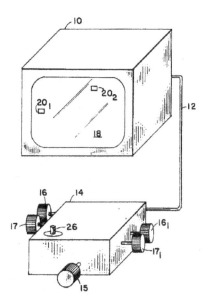

Figure 3.12 U.S. Patent No. 3,728,480

Yet there is no real evidence which I find persuasive that [Nolan Bushnell, creator of Atari's *Pong*] had conceived of anything like the Pong game prior to the time that he saw the Odyssey game. When he did see the Odyssey game, what he did basically was to copy it.[142]

In that same decision, the court recognized another one of Magnavox's patents as being "the pioneer patent in this art."[143] Suitable for a pioneering patent, consider its claim 1 and figure 1 (depicted in Figure 3.12[144]) as follows.

1. In combination with a standard television receiver, apparatus for generating "dots" upon the screen of the receiver to be manipulated by a participant, comprising:

   a control unit for generating signals representing the "dots" to be displayed, said control unit further including means for generating synchronizing signal to synchronize

---

142. *Id.*

143. *Id.*

144. U.S. Patent No. 3,728,480 (issued Apr. 17, 1973).

the television raster scan of said receiver and means for manipulating the position of the "dots" on the screen of said receiver; and

means for directly coupling the generated signals only to said television receiver whereby said "dots" are displayed only upon the screen of said receiver being viewed by the participant.

The success of *Pong* and the Odyssey led to other similarly "inspired" competitors, and that inevitably led to lawsuits that continued into the 1980s.[145] However, by the end of the decade, and into the 1990s, new players such as Atari Games Corp. (makers of the popular Atari 2600 and 5200 home consoles) and Nintendo of America (makers of the Nintendo Entertainment System (NES), aka the Famicom Home Computer System) dominated the industry, and they battled in the courts as well.[146] The issue there generally centered on software (the "10NES program") that Nintendo had placed in its console to verify that a game cartridge was licensed by Nintendo—cartridges lacking the counterpart software simply would not play. Atari tried to break the 10NES program in order to produce their own cartridges that would work with the Nintendo console, even resorting to such lengths as chemically peeling layers from the microchips in authorized NES cartridges, and requesting a copy of Nintendo's code from the U.S. Copyright Office on the (apparently false) pretense that it was needed for an ongoing lawsuit.[147] Perhaps not surprisingly in view of these unsavory actions, Atari was indeed found to have infringed Nintendo's 10NES patent.[148]

As the video game industry continued to develop and mature, innovations went beyond just making better games, and extended to the gaming devices themselves. By the late 1990s and into the

---

145. *See, e.g.*, Magnavox Co. v. Activision Inc., No. C-82-5270-CAL, 1985 WL 9496 (N.D. Cal. Dec. 27, 1985).

146. *See, e.g.*, Atari Games Corp. v. Nintendo of Am., Inc., 975 F.2d 832 (Fed. Cir. 1992); Atari Games Corp. v. Nintendo of Am., Inc., Nos. C 88-4805 FMS & C 89-0027 FMS, 1993 WL 214886 (N.D. Cal. Apr. 15, 1993).

147. *Atari Games Corp.*, 1993 WL 214886, at *1–2.

148. *Id.*

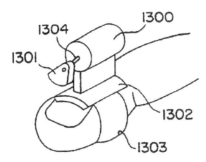

Figure 3.13 U.S. Patent No. 6,275,213

2000s, haptic feedback (e.g., vibrating controllers) was the next "big thing" in video games, and brought the next wave of video game patent lawsuits. Immersion Corp. secured an $82 million judgment against Sony Corp. on the grounds that Sony's DualShock vibrating controller infringed Immersion's haptic feedback patents.[149] Consider the figure from one of the asserted patents (Figure 3.13[150]), which shows the off-center rotating weight commonly used now in vibrating controllers.

Another vibrating controller case involved Nintendo. In *Anascape Ltd. v. Nintendo of America Inc.*,[151] the issue turned on the sufficiency of a patent's written description.[152] Anascape owned U.S. Patent No. 6,906,700[153] (the '700 Patent), entitled "3D Controller with Vibration," and asserted it against Nintendo's various controllers, including Nintendo's Wavebird and GameCube controllers.[154] Anascape was successful at trial,[155] and Nintendo was ordered to pay $21 million in damages and to stop selling the

---

149. Immersion Corp. v. Sony Computer Entm't Am. Inc., No. C 02-0710 CW, 2005 WL 680026, at *1 (N.D. Cal. Mar. 24, 2005); *see also Sony to Pay in Patent Dispute*, BLOOMBERG NEWS, Mar. 2, 2007, *available at* https://www.nytimes.com/2007/03/02/technology/02sony.html.

150. U.S. Patent No. 6,275,213 (issued Aug. 14, 2001).

151. Anascape Ltd. v. Nintendo of Am. Inc., 601 F.3d 1333 (Fed. Cir. 2010).

152. *Id.* at 1335.

153. U.S. Patent No. 6,906,700 (issued June 14, 2005).

154. *Anascape Ltd.*, 601 F.3d at 1334–35.

155. *Id.* at 1334.

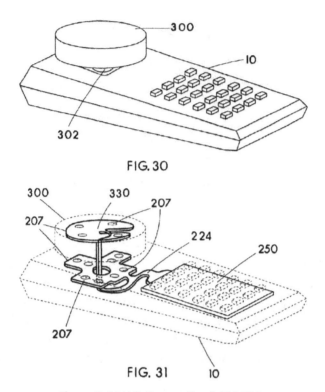

FIG. 30

FIG. 31

Figure 3.14 U.S. Patent No. 6,906,700

accused controllers.[156] However, this award was overturned on appeal.[157]

The '700 Patent claimed (in part) multiple "elements" that were each movable in two perpendicular axes, and these were allegedly infringed by the left and right thumbsticks on the accused Nintendo controllers. The '700 Patent's figures primarily showed examples having just one such element, such as a joystick, as illustrated in Figure 3.14.

The '700 Patent's specification had some textual language that suggested the use of multiple elements (e.g., saying "at least one"

---

156. Alexander Sliwinski, *Nintendo Ordered to Pay $21 Million for Patent Infringement*, ENGADGET, May 15, 2008, https://www.engadget.com/2008/05/15/nintendo-ordered-to-pay-21-million-for-patent-infringment/.

157. *Anascape Ltd.*, 601 F.3d at 1340.

when referencing the input members), but the CAFC found that this language was not present in the originally filed application, and instead was added at a later date when a continuation-in-part (CIP) application was filed in the '700 Patent's history.[158] In particular, the court noted that when the CIP application was filed, the applicant changed various passages in the original specification to de-emphasize the singular nature of the member, and to add suggestions of multiple elements.[159] One such change was the changing of the phrase "single input member" to "at least one input member" 16 times.[160]

The CAFC concluded that the claims would not be entitled to the priority date of the original filing, and instead would be entitled to the priority date of the CIP application.[161] Anascape had conceded that if its claims were not entitled to the original filing date, then its claims would be invalid as anticipated by Sony's DualShock controller, which was released after the original filing date but before the later priority date, and as a result the CAFC reversed the damages award.[162]

Turning to some more recent examples, *Nintendo of America, Inc. v. iLife Technologies, Inc.*[163] is a recent example demonstrating the use of IPR. iLife sued Nintendo for infringement of U.S. Patent No. 6,864,796[164] (the '796 Patent).[165] The '796 Patent, entitled "Systems within a Communication Device for Evaluating Movement of a Body and Methods of Operating the Same," generally describes use of an accelerometer that can sense certain kinds of movement (e.g., when an elderly person suffers a fall) and send an alert regarding the same.[166] iLife alleged that Nintendo's Wii and Wii U systems, with their motion-based controllers, infringed the '796

---

158. *Id.* at 1338 ("This is classical new matter.").
159. *Id.*
160. *Id.*
161. *Id.* at 1341.
162. *Id.* at 1335.
163. Nintendo of Am., Inc. v. iLife Techs., Inc., 717 Fed. Appx. 996 (Fed. Cir. 2017).
164. U.S. Patent No. 6,864,796 (issued Mar. 8, 2005).
165. *Nintendo of Am., Inc.*, 717 Fed. Appx. at 998.
166. *Id.*

Patent, and following a jury trial in 2017, iLife was awarded $10 million in damages.[167]

Nintendo pursued an IPR to challenge the validity of the '796 Patent.[168] The central issue in the IPR was whether a particular reference, the "Yasushi" reference,[169] could be considered prior art to the '796 Patent.[170] The '796 Patent was filed prior to the AIA, and was subject to the first-to-invent rules that existed prior to the AIA, and under those rules the PTAB found that iLife had sufficiently demonstrated that the various asserted claims were conceived and reduced to practice prior to the date of the Yasushi reference.[171] On appeal, the CAFC affirmed this finding as for some of the claims, but reversed it as to other claims, sending the case back to the PTAB to consider the validity of those other claims,[172] and this decision remains pending at the time of this writing.

There has also been an *Alice* subject-matter eligibility case in the video game realm. In *McRO, Inc. v. Bandai Namco Games America Inc.*,[173] the patentee asserted, against many of the largest video game producers, patents[174] that were directed to animation techniques for synchronizing lip and facial animations with audio in video games. The following sample claim recites a method with several steps:

> 1. A method for automatically animating lip synchronization and facial expression of three-dimensional characters comprising:

---

167. *Appeals Court Upholds iLife Patent in $10M Wii Gaming Judgment*, Rolling Stone, Dec. 28, 2017, https://www.msn.com/en-us/entertainment/gaming/appeals-court-upholds-ilife-patent-in-dollar10m-wii-gaming-judgment/ar-BBHrRro.

168. *Nintendo of Am., Inc.*, 717 Fed. Appx. at 998.

169. JP Patent Publication No. H10-295649, Yasushi.

170. *Nintendo of Am., Inc.*, 717 Fed. Appx. at 998.

171. *Id.* at 999–1000.

172. *Id.* at 1004.

173. McRO, Inc. v. Bandai Namco Games Am. Inc., 837 F.3d 1299 (Fed. Cir. 2016).

174. U.S. Patent No. 6,307,576 (issued Oct. 23, 2001); U.S. Patent No. 6,611,278 (issued Aug. 26, 2003).

obtaining a first set of rules that define output morph weight set stream as a function of phoneme sequence and time of said phoneme sequence;

obtaining a timed data file of phonemes having a plurality of sub-sequences;

generating an intermediate stream of output morph weight sets and a plurality of transition parameters between two adjacent morph weight sets by evaluating said plurality of sub-sequences against said first set of rules;

generating a final stream of output morph weight sets at a desired frame rate from said intermediate stream of output morph weight sets and said plurality of transition parameters; and

applying said final stream of output morph weight sets to a sequence of animated characters to produce lip synchronization and facial expression control of said animated characters.[175]

The district court granted judgment on the pleadings, ruling that the asserted claims were ineligible for patent protection, and the CAFC considered the issue on appeal.[176] The various defendants alleged that the claims were directed to nothing more than unpatentable algorithms and abstract ideas,[177] but the CAFC disagreed.[178] The CAFC found that the district court had oversimplified the claims in deeming them to be abstract.[179] In reversing the district court, the CAFC found that the claims recited a specific implementation of unconventional steps, with detailed and meaningful rules, that achieve an improvement over the prior art, and accordingly were eligible for protection.[180]

175. U.S. Patent No. 6,307,576 (issued Oct. 23, 2001), col. 11, ll. 27–47.
176. *McRO*, 837 F.3d at 1308–09.
177. *Id.* at 1310–11.
178. *Id.* at 1316.
179. *Id.* at 1313–14.
180. *Id.*

Conclusion

Games and immersive entertainment are in our future. If you are planning to work (or live) with these virtual worlds, be advised that careful utility and design patent planning will be necessary for success, and we hope this chapter has helped shed a little light on the patent issues and options that await.

Implications of Video Games and Immersive Entertainment in Trademark Law

4

William K. Ford
Anna L. King[1]

Takeaways

- *Probably more so than in other forms of media, incorporating trademarks into video games presents a challenge of balancing the interests of free expression with the goal of minimizing consumer confusion, and while the legal rules of this balance remain uncertain, the trend in the case law is to protect the artistic use of trademarks in video games from Lanham Act claims.*
- *Advertising and marketing efforts are increasingly integrated within entertainment media, which may create a heightened risk of consumer confusion when marks are integrated into video games.*

---

1. William K. Ford is an associate professor of law at the John Marshall Law School in Chicago. Anna King is a shareholder with the law firm Banner & Witcoff, Ltd. in its Chicago office. The first edition of this chapter was authored by Ford and Ben D. Manevitz. For complete author biographies, see the Contributors section of this book.

- *Customization options in video games and particularly virtual worlds present ill-defined risks of liability.*

Introduction

The "predominant function" of trademarks[2] is to distinguish one source of goods or services from another.[3] The Xbox, PlayStation, and Wii marks reduce consumer confusion by identifying which games are associated with Microsoft, Sony, and Nintendo, and which games will work on which consoles. Source identification, however, is not the only valuable use of a mark. Like other expressive media, video games present many opportunities to use marks for purposes other than source identification, but unlike a book or film, these opportunities are often widely available to both producers and consumers. On the producer side, game designers can use trademarks to add realism to game environments, which, depending on the type of game, may make it more appealing. Driving a Porsche or Ferrari in a racing game, for example, may be preferable to driving a fictional vehicle made up by a game designer.[4] On the consumer side, game players can use trademarks for purposes of self-expression. Some marks possess strong brand personalities

---

2. The chapter will refer to "trademarks" in the broad sense, and except where noted, the term includes related categories of marks like service marks and trade dress.

3. *See* Wal-Mart Stores, Inc. v. Samara Bros., Inc., 529 U.S. 205, 212 (2000); *see also* WILLIAM M. LANDES & RICHARD A. POSNER, THE ECONOMIC STRUCTURE OF INTELLECTUAL PROPERTY LAW 166 (2003).

4. According to the producer of *Rainbow Six Vegas*:

> We can use real cars, or we can create cars of our own . . . [b]ut we're not car designers, so they're always going to look a little bit off. It's always a plus when you can use a real product and base the modeling in the game on real stuff.

Steve Tilley, *And Now a Game from Our Sponsor*, OFFICIAL XBOX MAG., Aug. 2007, at 62, 65, *available at* https://archive.org/stream/OXM_2007_08-web#page/n27/mode/2up.

and represent "lots of information, emotion and coloration compressed into a name or symbol."[5] By associating themselves with particular marks, players can efficiently communicate information about themselves to other players.[6] A player wanting to be perceived by others as environmentally minded might prefer to drive a virtual Prius over a generic vehicle.[7] If the Prius is not included in the game by default, players may be able to add it to the game environment themselves, depending on the extent to which the game allows players to create new content.

Whenever trademarks are used without the owners' permission, whether due to the actions of designers or players or both, legal disputes are a potential result. This chapter briefly reviews some basic principles of trademark law and then provides an overview of various trademark cases involving video games and virtual worlds. As compared to other games, virtual worlds probably do not raise unique trademark issues, but some virtual worlds create broad opportunities for unauthorized trademark uses.[8] Whether augmented or virtual reality (AR/VR) games will raise any *unique* issues is not yet clear.

---

5. Charlie Hughes, *In Automotive Merger, the Brand Must Be King*, AUTOMOTIVE NEWS, May 15, 2000, at 14; *see* Jennifer L. Aaker, *Dimensions of Brand Personality*, 34 J. MARKETING RES. 347, 347 (1997).

6. *See, e.g.*, Jennifer L. Aaker, *The Malleable Self: The Role of Self-Expression in Persuasion*, 36 J. MARKETING RES. 45, 45 (1999) ("The basic argument is that attitude objects, such as brands, can be associated with personality traits that provide self-expressive or symbolic benefits for the consumer."); Aaker, *supra* note 5, at 347 ("Researchers have focused on how the personality of a brand enables a consumer to express his or her own self, an ideal self, or specific dimensions of the self through the use of a brand.") (citations omitted).

7. Although the research methodology is unclear, one marketing research firm claimed, "[w]hile just 36 percent [of buyers] cited fuel economy as a prime motivator for buying a Prius, 57 percent said their main reason was that 'it makes a statement about me.'" Vicki Haddock, *Oh, So Pious, Prius Drivers*, S.F. CHRON., July 15, 2007, at D3.

8. *See, e.g.*, Richard Acello, *Virtual Worlds, Real Battles: Trademark Holders Take on Use in Games*, A.B.A. J., Jan. 2011, at 30.

I. Overview of Trademark Protection

Trademark protection is generally acquired through the use of a mark, with protection available under both state and federal law.[9] Federal trademark claims may be litigated in both state and federal court.[10] A few marks, such as that of the Red Cross, are subject to special protection under various federal laws,[11] but the primary source of federal trademark protection is the Lanham Act, 15 U.S.C. § 1051 *et seq.* What can qualify as a trademark is broad.[12] The Lanham Act defines a trademark as "any word, name, symbol, or device, or any combination thereof" that is used to "identify and distinguish [someone's] goods, including a unique product, from those manufactured or sold by others and to indicate the source of the goods, even if that source is unknown."[13] Product packaging

---

9. 2 J. Thomas McCarthy, McCarthy on Trademarks and Unfair Competition § 16:1.50 (5th ed. 2018) ("Apart from the statutory provision of a 'constructive use,' it is not registration, but only actual use of a designation as a mark that creates rights and priority over others."). State trademark law must be consistent with federal law, or else it is invalidated by the Supremacy Clause of the U.S. Constitution. *See, e.g.,* Mariniello v. Shell Oil Co., 511 F.2d 853, 857–58 (3d Cir. 1975); Capcom Co. v. MKR Group, Inc., No. 08-0904, 2008 U.S. Dist. LEXIS 83836, at *44–45 (N.D. Cal. Oct. 10, 2008).

10. *See* 28 U.S.C. § 1338(a) (2018); 3 Anne Gilson LaLonde & Jerome Gilson, Gilson on Trademarks § 11.03[2][b][0i] (2017) ("[I]t is settled that even unregistered common law trademarks are protectable under the Lanham Act through federal question jurisdiction."); 6 J. Thomas McCarthy, McCarthy on Trademarks and Unfair Competition § 32:1 (4th ed. 2017) ("Lanham Act: concurrent jurisdiction in both federal and state courts").

11. *See* 18 U.S.C. § 706 (2018). The first part of this section criminalizes *fraudulent* uses of the Red Cross insignia. The second part criminalizes unauthorized "uses" without any reference to fraud. *Id.; see In re* Kappa Alpha Order, 2011 TTAB LEXIS 191 (T.T.A.B. June 3, 2011, re appeal of S/N 77/463,997) (reversing a trademark examining attorney's refusal to register a mark that included a Greek red cross). *See generally* Johnson & Johnson v. Am. Nat'l Red Cross, 552 F. Supp. 2d 434, 436–40 (S.D.N.Y. 2008) (discussing the history of § 706).

12. Qualitex Co. v. Jacobson Prods. Co., 514 U.S. 159, 162 (1995) ("The courts and the Patent and Trademark Office have authorized for use as a mark a particular shape (of a Coca-Cola bottle), a particular sound (of NBC's three chimes), and even a particular scent (of plumeria blossoms on sewing thread).").

13. 15 U.S.C. § 1127 (2018). The reference to a "unique product" comes from an amendment to the Lanham Act that was the result of Congress's rejection of widely criticized decisions of the Ninth Circuit Court of Appeals involving trademarks for

and design features are also protectable as trademarks or "trade dress," but like trademarks in general, packaging and design features must be nonfunctional and distinctive.[14]

To be eligible for protection, trademarks must be distinctive. More specifically, they must be capable of distinguishing one source of goods or services from another source. Marks are typically placed into one of five categories, ranging from the least to the most distinctive: (1) generic, (2) descriptive, (3) suggestive, (4) arbitrary, or (5) fanciful.[15] Although the phrase "generic trademarks" is sometimes used,[16] generic marks are not really marks at all.[17] Most of the time, generic marks cannot help consumers distinguish between different sources of goods or services. For instance, "apple" is a generic term for the fruit (but an arbitrary term for computers).[18] As all producers of apples use the term, it does not tell a consumer anything about the source of any particular apple. Occasionally, a generic term does in fact identify a single source because there is only one source of the product. Even in this

---

board games. *See* Trademark Clarification Act of 1984, Pub. L. No. 98-620, 98 Stat. 3335; Anti-Monopoly, Inc. v. General Mills Fun Group, Inc., 684 F.2d 1316 (9th Cir. 1982); Anti-Monopoly, Inc. v. General Mills Fun Group, Inc., 611 F.2d 296 (9th Cir. 1979).

14. *See* 15 U.S.C. § 1064(3) (2018) (subjecting registered marks to cancellation if they are functional); *id.* § 1125(a)(3) (providing unregistered trade dress must be shown to be nonfunctional in infringement actions); *id.* § 1125(c)(4)(A) (providing unregistered trade dress must be shown to be nonfunctional in dilution actions). A detailed discussion of functionality is beyond the scope of this chapter, but according to the Supreme Court, "'a product feature is functional,' and cannot serve as a trademark, 'if it is essential to the use or purpose of the article or if it affects the cost or quality of the article.'" TrafFix Devices, Inc. v. Mktg. Displays, Inc., 532 U.S. 23, 32 (2001) (quoting *Qualitex Co.*, 514 U.S. at 165).

15. *See* Two Pesos, Inc. v. Taco Cabana, Inc., 505 U.S. 763, 768 (1992) (citing Abercrombie & Fitch Co. v. Hunting World, Inc., 537 F.2d 4, 9 (2d Cir. 1976) (Friendly, J.)).

16. *See, e.g.,* Home Builders Ass'n v. L & L Exhibition Mgmt., Inc., 226 F.3d 944, 950 (8th Cir. 2000) ("A generic trademark or functional trade dress is not protected from copying.").

17. *See* 2 McCARTHY, *supra* note 9, § 12.1 ("The terms 'generic' and 'trademark' are mutually exclusive.").

18. *See* Boston Duck Tours, LP v. Super Duck Tours, LLC, 531 F.3d 1, 12–13 (1st Cir. 2008).

situation, trademark protection is unavailable,[19] because it would have highly anticompetitive consequences to allow one seller to monopolize a generic term in the marketplace. All sellers need to be able to refer to their apples as apples and their video games as video games. Without the freedom to do so, competitors would be forced to adopt less-efficient means of describing their goods and services, such as a lengthy and roundabout description of a video game, when simply using the term "video game" quickly communicates the same information.[20]

The other categories of marks—descriptive, suggestive, arbitrary, and fanciful marks—are either capable of becoming distinctive (descriptive marks) or are inherently distinctive (suggestive, arbitrary, and fanciful marks). These four categories of marks are therefore eligible for trademark protection.[21] Descriptive marks describe the qualities of the goods or services in some way. For frozen desserts, as one example, "the phrase 'Frosty Treats' is, at best, descriptive."[22] Descriptive marks can become distinctive by acquiring *secondary meaning*, which requires that "in the minds of the public, the primary significance of a product feature or term is to identify the source of the product rather than the product itself."[23] Secondary meaning can be acquired through things like extensive advertising and other media exposure, which can

---

19. *See, e.g.*, A.J. Canfield Co. v. Honickman, 808 F.2d 291, 299 (3d Cir. 1986) ("If chocolate fudge soda is the relevant product class, identification by the public of the term chocolate fudge soda with Canfield would prove only the obvious point that Canfield has been the sole producer of the product, and would not establish trademark status.").

20. *See, e.g.*, Custom Vehicles, Inc. v. Forest River, Inc., 476 F.3d 481, 483 (7th Cir. 2007) (Posner, J.).

21. Two types of marks that cannot be inherently distinctive are colors and product design features. *See* Wal-Mart Stores, Inc. v. Samara Bros., Inc., 529 U.S. 205, 212 (2000) ("It seems to us that design, like color, is not inherently distinctive."). Such marks must acquire secondary meaning to be protectable. *Id.*

22. Frosty Treats, Inc. v. Sony Computer Entm't Am., Inc., 426 F.3d 1001, 1005 (8th Cir. 2005).

23. Inwood Labs., Inc. v. Ives Labs., Inc., 456 U.S. 844, 851 n.11 (1982) (citing Kellogg Co. v. Nat'l Biscuit Co., 305 U.S. 111, 118 (1938)).

establish in the minds of consumers the significance of a mark as an indicator of source.[24]

As suggestive, arbitrary, and fanciful marks are inherently distinctive, they do not require proof of secondary meaning.[25] Suggestive marks involve "imagination, thought and perception to reach a conclusion as to the nature of goods."[26] "Game Power Headquarters" and "Game Power" are suggestive marks for retail video game stores.[27] "Scramble" is a suggestive mark for the classic 1981 video game involving a futuristic fighter craft.[28] Arbitrary marks involve common terms with no connection to the goods or services. "Apple" is an arbitrary mark for a computer.[29] Fanciful marks are usually novel terms invented for the product or service.[30] "SEGA," a shortened form of the earlier company name Service Games,[31] likely qualifies as a fanciful mark for video games.[32]

The Lanham Act offers two basic forms of protection for trademark owners: protection from infringement and protection from dilution. Provided a term is eligible for protection, either because it is inherently distinctive or it has acquired distinctiveness through secondary meaning, the principal question in

---

24. *See, e.g.*, Dep't of Parks & Recreation v. Bazaar del Mundo Inc., 448 F.3d 1118, 1128 (9th Cir. 2006) (quoting Carter-Wallace, Inc. v. Procter & Gamble Co., 434 F.2d 794, 802 (9th Cir. 1970)); GamerModz, LLC v. Golubev, No. 8:10-CV-1466-T-27TGW, 2011 U.S. Dist. LEXIS 116608, at *38–39 (M.D. Fla. Aug. 3, 2011).

25. *See Samara Bros., Inc.*, 529 U.S. at 210–11.

26. Abercrombie & Fitch Co. v. Hunting World, Inc., 537 F.2d 4, 11 (2d Cir. 1976) (quoting Stix Prods., Inc. v. United Merchs. & Mfrs. Inc., 295 F. Supp. 479, 488 (S.D.N.Y. 1968)).

27. Game Power Headquarters, Inc. v. Owens, No. 94-5821, 1995 U.S. Dist. LEXIS 5998, at *10 (E.D. Pa. May 4, 1995).

28. Stern Elecs., Inc. v. Kaufman, 523 F. Supp. 635, 640 (E.D.N.Y. 1981). On the game *Scramble*, see VAN BURNHAM, SUPERCADE: A VISUAL HISTORY OF THE VIDEOGAME AGE, 1971–1984, at 264 (2001).

29. Boston Duck Tours, LP v. Super Duck Tours, LLC, 531 F.3d 1, 13 n.11 (1st Cir. 2008) (dictum).

30. *See Abercrombie & Fitch Co.*, 537 F.2d at 11 n.12.

31. *See* STEVEN L. KENT, THE ULTIMATE HISTORY OF VIDEO GAMES 332–43 (2001) (discussing the origins of Sega).

32. Among SEGA Games Co., Ltd. registered trademarks is SEGA GAMES, Registration No. 5,319,260. *See also* U.S. Trademark Application Serial No. 79,219,607 (filed Feb. 1, 2017) ("SEGA").

infringement disputes is whether a junior user's use of a mark in connection with goods or services is likely to cause consumer confusion about the source or sponsorship of the goods or services.[33] Similarly, the basic test in dilution cases is whether there is a likelihood of dilution.[34]

Section 32 of the Lanham Act[35] protects registered marks from infringement, while section 43(a)[36] protects unregistered marks, including unregistered trade dress.[37] Section 43(a) defines the range of infringing activities broadly as false designations of origin, covering a likelihood of confusion as to "affiliation, connection, or association" or "origin, sponsorship, or approval."[38] In addition to protecting unregistered trademarks from confusion as to source,[39] this provision also protects against false statements of endorsement, such as a false statement that a celebrity endorses a product,[40] and, for this reason, claims under section 43(a) often

---

33. *See* 15 U.S.C. §§ 1114(1), 1125(a)(1)(A) (2018); 4 J. Thomas McCarthy, McCarthy on Trademarks and Unfair Competition § 23:1 (5th ed. 2018) ("[T]he test of likelihood of confusion is the touchstone of trademark infringement as well as unfair competition."). On the complex question of whether certain uses of a trademark do not qualify as "trademark uses" for Lanham Act purposes and cannot therefore be infringing, see *id.* § 23:11.50.

34. 15 U.S.C. § 1125(c)(1) (2018); *see* Starbucks Corp. v. Wolfe's Borough Coffee, Inc., 736 F.3d 198, 206 (2d Cir. 2013); Levi Strauss & Co. v. Abercrombie & Fitch Trading Co., 633 F.3d 1158, 1165–75 (9th Cir. 2011).

35. Lanham Act § 32, 15 U.S.C. § 1114 (2018).

36. Lanham Act § 43(a), 15 U.S.C. § 1125(a) (2018).

37. *See* Wal-Mart Stores, Inc. v. Samara Bros., Inc., 529 U.S. 205, 209–10 (2000).

38. 15 U.S.C. § 1125(a)(1)(A) (2018).

39. *See* Dastar Corp. v. Twentieth Century Fox Film Corp., 539 U.S. 23, 30 (2003) ("The Trademark Law Revision Act of 1988 made clear that § 43(a) [of the Lanham Act] covers origin of production as well as geographic origin."); Federal-Mogul-Bower Bearings, Inc. v. Azoff, 313 F.2d 405, 408 (6th Cir. 1963) ("We are further of the opinion that the word, 'origin,' in the [Lanham] Act does not merely refer to geographical origin, but also to origin of source or manufacture.").

40. *See, e.g.,* Brown v. Elec. Arts, Inc., 724 F.3d 1235, 1239 (9th Cir. 2013) ("Although claims under § 43(a) generally relate to the use of trademarks or trade dress to cause consumer confusion over affiliation or endorsement, we have held that claims can also be brought under § 43(a) relating to the use of a public figure's persona, likeness, or other uniquely distinguishing characteristic to cause such confusion."). Courts have recognized false endorsement claims related to deceased individuals as well. *See* A.V.E.L.A., Inc. v. Estate of Marilyn Monroe,

accompany claims based on the right of publicity.[41] Section 43(a) reaches much further than *explicit* misstatements about endorsements, however. As with movies, television, and other expressive media, game makers who include a reference or depiction of a trademark in their games risk a claim of infringement under section 43(a). Product placement, or the insertion of trademarks into expressive works for promotional purposes,[42] regularly occurs in video games.[43] As a result, consumers might view any use of a trademark in a game as a form of product placement. Consumers could believe such a use indicates a relationship—an "affiliation, connection, or association"—between the game maker and the trademark owner. Whether there is a likelihood of confusion in these or other situations is considered a question of fact in most circuits.[44]

In determining whether confusion is likely, each circuit relies on a similar list of non-exhaustive factors. For example, the Ninth Circuit Court of Appeals' list, usually referred to as the *Sleekcraft* factors,[45] includes: (1) strength of the plaintiff's mark, (2) proximity of the goods in the market, (3) similarity of the marks, (4) evidence of actual confusion, (5) marketing channels used, (6) degree of care exercised by consumers, (7) defendant's intent, and (8) the

---

LLC, 131 F. Supp. 3d 196, 208 (S.D.N.Y. 2015) ("Preliminarily, this Court rejects the Movants' contention that there is a blanket prohibition against false endorsement claims involving deceased celebrities.").

41. *See* William K. Ford & Raizel Liebler, *Games Are Not Coffee Mugs: Games and the Right of Publicity*, 29 SANTA CLARA COMPUTER & HIGH TECH. L.J. 1, 11 (2012) (discussing the relationship between the Lanham Act and the right of publicity). On the right of publicity generally, see Chapter 6 of this volume.

42. *See* KERRY SEGRAVE, PRODUCT PLACEMENT IN HOLLYWOOD FILMS: A HISTORY 15 (2004).

43. *See* Tilley, *supra* note 4, at 64 (noting in 2007 that "[i]n the last couple of years, in-game advertising has become serious business worth serious coin").

44. *See* 4 MCCARTHY, *supra* note 33, § 23:67 ("The clear majority of circuits follow the rule that likelihood of confusion is an issue of fact reviewed on appeal under a deferential 'clearly erroneous' standard."). For the minority view, see, for example, Oakville Hills Cellar, Inc. v. Georgallis Holdings, LLC, 826 F.3d 1376, 1379 (Fed. Cir. 2016) ("Likelihood of confusion is a question of law based on underlying findings of fact.").

45. *See* AMF, Inc. v. Sleekcraft Boats, 599 F.2d 341, 348–49 (9th Cir. 1979).

likelihood of future expansion of the product lines.[46] In some cases, not all of the factors are relevant. When a trademark is used within an artistic work, for example, courts can adapt the factors accordingly.[47]

Section 43(c) of the Lanham Act provides some limited protection where a famous mark is likely to be diluted by a junior user's use in commerce, whether or not there is a likelihood of confusion.[48] Dilution is defined in terms of "dilution by blurring" and "dilution by tarnishment."[49] Blurring is an "association arising from the similarity between a mark or trade name and a famous mark that impairs the distinctiveness of the famous mark."[50] Tarnishment is an "association arising from the similarity between a mark or trade name and a famous mark that harms the reputation of the famous mark."[51] These dilution provisions protect only famous marks, meaning marks "widely recognized by the general consuming public of the United States as a designation of source of the goods or services of the mark's owner."[52] In the interest of

---

46. *Id. See, e.g.*, Au-Tomotive Gold, Inc. v. Volkswagen of Am., Inc., 457 F.3d 1062, 1076 (9th Cir. 2006). For the Second Circuit's list, see Playtex Prods., Inc. v. Georgia-Pacific Corp., 390 F.3d 158, 162 (2d Cir. 2004); Polaroid Corp. v. Polarad Elecs. Corp., 287 F.2d 492, 495 (2d Cir. 1961). In recognition of its origin in the just-cited opinion by Judge Henry Friendly, the Second Circuit refers to its list as the *Polaroid* factors.

47. *See, e.g.*, Caterpillar Inc. v. Walt Disney Co., 287 F. Supp. 2d 913, 919 (C.D. Ill. 2003) ("This is not a case where the Court can apply the traditional likelihood of confusion factors with any degree of comfort. For example, there are no competing trademarks at issue in this case, there is only one.").

48. *Cf.* 4 McCARTHY, *supra* note 33, § 24:72 ("Some courts think that when likely confusion is found, 'dilution' follows as a matter of course. . . .").

49. Before the 2006 amendments, the Lanham Act did not refer to specific types of dilution. Now, it expressly refers to blurring and tarnishing. *See* 15 U.S.C. § 1125(c)(1) (2018).

50. *Id.* § 1125(c)(2)(B).

51. *Id.* § 1125(c)(2)(C).

52. *Id.* § 1125(c)(2)(A). Prior to the enactment of the Trademark Dilution Revision Act of 2006, Pub. L. No. 109-312, § 2, 120 Stat. 1730, 1730–31 (codified as amended at 15 U.S.C. § 1125(c)(2)(A) (2018)), some courts found that marks famous only within a market segment or niche could qualify as famous under the dilution provisions of the Lanham Act. *See, e.g.*, Thane Int'l, Inc. v. Trek Bicycle Corp., 305 F.3d 894, 908–10 (9th Cir. 2002); Times Mirror Magazines, Inc. v. Las Vegas Sports News, L.L.C., 212 F.3d 157, 164–65 (3d Cir. 2000). As a result of the 2006 amendments, courts now reject claims based on only niche fame. *See, e.g.*,

protecting free speech from an overbroad application of these definitions, this subsection of the Lanham Act lists several exclusions from the reach of the dilution provisions. These exclusions are not without complications, including some redundancies, but a somewhat simplified list of the exclusions includes the following: fair uses; comparative advertising; parody; criticism; news reporting and commentary; and noncommercial use.[53] As it implicates any use of a trademark within a game for expressive purposes, the last exclusion is of particular relevance. According to the Ninth Circuit, the exclusion for noncommercial use refers to "use that consists entirely of noncommercial, or fully constitutionally protected, speech."[54] Commercial speech is often defined as "speech that does no more than propose a commercial transaction."[55] Where the speech is noncommercial, it is entitled to more protection. In one case, the Ninth Circuit found that the use of Mattel's Barbie trademark in a song title and in the song's lyrics was indeed dilutive,[56] but because it was not purely commercial, the defendant's use of the mark was exempt from the Lanham Act's anti-dilution provisions.[57]

As in other areas of the law, parties may be found vicariously or contributorily liable for the acts of another—here the relevant

---

Luv N' Care, Ltd. v. Regent Baby Prods. Corp., 841 F. Supp. 2d 753, 757–58 (S.D.N.Y. 2012); Adidas-Am., Inc. v. Payless Shoesource, Inc., 546 F. Supp. 2d 1029, 1061 n.11 (D. Or. 2008). A 2008 case from the District of Nevada is an exception, but the court did not explain how niche fame could support a dilution claim after the 2006 amendments, nor did it even mention the amendments. *See* WEC Holdings, LLC v. Juarez, No. 07-0137, 2008 U.S. Dist. LEXIS 13841, at *13 (D. Nev. Feb. 5, 2008).

53. 15 U.S.C. § 1125 (c)(3) (2018).

54. Mattel, Inc. v. MCA Records, Inc., 296 F.3d 894, 905 (9th Cir. 2002); *see* Griffith v. Fenrick, 486 F. Supp. 2d 848, 853 (W.D. Wis. 2007) (following *Mattel*); Am. Family Life Ins. Co. v. Hagan, 266 F. Supp. 2d 682, 695–99 (N.D. Ohio 2002) (describing political speech as noncommercial).

55. Harris v. Quinn, 134 S. Ct. 2618, 2639 (2014) (quoting United States v. United Foods, Inc., 533 U.S. 405, 409 (2001)); *see Mattel*, 296 F.3d at 906. Speech that goes beyond this narrow definition of proposing a sale may still be labeled as commercial by a court. *See* Jordan v. Jewel Food Stores, Inc., 743 F.3d 509, 515–17 (7th Cir. 2014).

56. *Mattel*, 296 F.3d at 903 ("MCA's use of the mark is dilutive."). The court determined the defendant's use of the mark constituted blurring, but it did not rule on whether the use also constituted tarnishing. *Id.* at 904 n.5.

57. *Id.* at 907.

acts being ones of trademark infringement. Vicarious trademark infringement "requires 'a finding that the defendant and the infringer have an apparent or actual partnership, have authority to bind one another in transactions with third parties or exercise joint ownership or control over the infringing product.'"[58] Contributory trademark infringement requires that a defendant "(1) intentionally induces another to infringe on a trademark or (2) continues to supply a product knowing that the recipient is using the product to engage in trademark infringement."[59] Perhaps the most important question for video games and virtual worlds related to this topic is whether risks of secondary liability could hobble the ability of software providers to offer players a wide variety of customization options, because players may use these options to create new content that involves unauthorized uses of a mark, a topic raised by the *Marvel* case discussed in Section II.C.1.

II. Trademark Issues in the Video Game and Virtual World Contexts

While video games and virtual worlds can raise some difficult trademark problems, many uses of trademarks in these contexts involve conventional questions governed by well-established rules. A dispute between Mythic Entertainment and Microsoft, for example, involved Microsoft's proposed *Mythica* game and what appeared to be a relatively straightforward question: whether there was a likelihood of consumer confusion between the terms "Mythic Entertainment" and "Mythica," such that consumers might think Mythic Entertainment was associated with the *Mythica* game.[60] (The case

---

58. Perfect 10, Inc. v. Visa Int'l Serv. Ass'n, 494 F.3d 788, 807 (9th Cir. 2007) (quoting Hard Rock Cafe Licensing Corp. v. Concession Servs., Inc., 955 F.2d 1143, 1150 (7th Cir. 1992)).

59. Fonovisa, Inc. v. Cherry Auction, Inc., 76 F.3d 259, 264 (9th Cir. 1996) (citing Inwood Labs., Inc. v. Ives Labs., Inc., 456 U.S. 844, 854–55 (1982)).

60. *See Mythic Entertainment Sues Microsoft*, GAMESPOT, Dec. 23, 2003, 9:59 a.m., https://www.gamespot.com/articles/mythic-entertainment-sues-microsoft /1100-6086024/.

settled on undisclosed terms.[61]) Other trademark problems, such as the use of marks in expressive works, raise more complicated legal questions. This section briefly describes the background of several cases that illustrate common trademark problems. These examples are divided into three categories: traditional liability for the use of trademarks on physical products (like packaging), direct liability for the use of marks within a game, and secondary liability for the use of marks within a game. The issues raised by these examples will then be discussed in the substantive analysis in Section III.

A. Traditional Uses: Physical Products

1. Universal City Studios, Inc. v. Nintendo Co., Ltd.

Universal filed suit against Nintendo in April 1982, in part claiming false designation of origin under section 43(a) of the Lanham Act.[62] Universal claimed the rights to the name King Kong and claimed Nintendo's classic *Donkey Kong* game infringed these rights.[63] The district court granted summary judgment in favor of Nintendo on the trademark claims, and the Second Circuit affirmed.[64] The Second Circuit held there was no question of fact about whether there was a likelihood of consumer confusion between the marks "King Kong" and "Donkey Kong." As both marks include the word "Kong," the court emphasized that trademarks must be viewed as a whole, not as fragments.[65] The court noted that "Donkey" and "King"—one-half of each mark—sound nothing alike and then concluded that Donkey Kong does not even "evoke or suggest the

---

61. Curt Feldman, *Microsoft and Mythic Settle Lawsuit*, GAMESPOT, May 25, 2004, https://www.gamespot.com/articles/microsoft-and-mythic-settle-lawsuit/1100-6099223/.

62. Universal City Studios, Inc. v. Nintendo Co., 578 F. Supp. 911, 914 (S.D.N.Y. 1983), *aff'd*, 746 F.2d 112 (2d Cir. 1984).

63. *Universal City Studios*, 746 F.2d at 114. As Universal's trademark claim was also tied to the character and story within the game, this case was only partly about the use of the marks on the physical arcade cabinet. *Id.*

64. *Id.* at 113.

65. *Id.* at 117.

name of King Kong."[66] The court also implied it viewed the terms "Kong" and "King Kong" as generic for "apes and other objects of enormous proportions."[67]

2. Incredible Technologies, Inc. v. Virtual Technologies, Inc.

Incredible Technologies filed suit against Virtual Technologies in February 2003, in part claiming infringement under section 43(a).[68] Incredible Technologies produced *Golden Tee Fore!*, a golf arcade game, and claimed the game's cabinet and control panel, including the trackball, constituted protectable trade dress. It claimed Virtual Technologies' competing game, *PGA Tour Golf*, infringed this trade dress.[69] The Seventh Circuit affirmed the district court's denial of a preliminary injunction, agreeing that the cabinets of the two games were similar only in ways that all arcade game cabinets are similar, which suggests the court viewed these designs as generic.[70] The Seventh Circuit also agreed that the control panel and trackball system for *Golden Tee Fore!* were functional and therefore ineligible for trade dress protection.[71]

3. Square Enix Co. v. Wholesale Gallery, Inc.

Square Enix filed suit against several defendants in February 2008, in part claiming trademark infringement under section 32 of the Lanham Act and false designation of origin under section 43(a).[72] Square Enix was the producer of the *Final Fantasy* line of games and related merchandise and possessed more than a dozen regis-

---

66. *Id.* at 117–18. This finding would seem to be in tension with the court's view that Donkey Kong "obviously parodies the King Kong theme." *Id.* at 116.

67. *Id.* at 117. The court did not quite say the terms are generic in the context of the dispute, but it came close when it said, "The 'Kong' and 'King Kong' names are widely used by the general public and are associated with apes and other objects of enormous proportions." *Id.* The court rejected all of Universal's evidence of actual confusion, including survey evidence, which the court described as "badly flawed." *Id.* at 118.

68. Incredible Techs., Inc. v. Virtual Techs., Inc., 400 F.3d 1007, 1009 (7th Cir. 2005).

69. *Id.* at 1009–10.

70. *Id.* at 1015–16.

71. *Id.*

72. Complaint at 17–20, Square Enix Co. v. Wholesale Gallery, Inc., No. 08-00875 (C.D. Cal. Feb. 8, 2008).

trations related to the *Final Fantasy* mark.[73] In addition to games, Square Enix's product line included miniature replica swords based on the ones used in the *Final Fantasy* games.[74] These swords were apparently distinctive and easily identified with the *Final Fantasy* games. Many of these swords had unique names, such as "Cloud's Buster Sword" and "Sephiroth's Masamune Sword."[75] According to Square Enix, the defendants marketed unauthorized replicas of the swords, which were likely to cause confusion among consumers about their source.[76] The defendants consented to a judgment against them in January 2009. The terms included a permanent injunction barring the defendants from, among other things, infringing Square Enix's trademarks.[77] Several of the defendants further agreed to pay Square Enix a total of $600,000.[78]

B. In-Game Uses: Direct Liability

1. E.S.S. Entertainment 2000, Inc. v. Rock Star Videos, Inc.

E.S.S. Entertainment filed suit against Rockstar Games and Take-Two Interactive Software in April 2005, claiming (in part) trade dress infringement under section 43(a).[79] E.S.S. Entertainment operated the Play Pen Gentleman's Club in Los Angeles, California,

---

73. *Id.* at 8–12.

74. *Id.* at 13.

75. *Id.* at 6.

76. *Id.* at 15.

77. *See* Final Judgment upon Consent against Defendants Millennium Empire Corporation d/b/a www.Kingofswords.com and Al Tomaselli, Square Enix Co. v. Wholesale Gallery, Inc., No. 08-0875 (C.D. Cal. Jan. 16, 2009); Final Judgment upon Consent against Defendant Pacific Solution Marketing, Inc., Square Enix Co. v. Wholesale Gallery, Inc., No. 08-0875 (C.D. Cal. Jan. 16, 2009); Final Judgment upon Consent against Defendants Wholesale Gallery, Inc., Edgework Imports, Inc., Top Swords, Inc., Khalil Butt, Mohammad Shabbir, and Nadia Shabbir, Square Enix Co. v. Wholesale Gallery, Inc., No. 08-0875 (C.D. Cal. Jan. 16, 2009). *See also* Luke Plunkett, *Square Enix Settles Lawsuit with Sword Pirates*, KOTAKU, Feb. 24, 2009, https://kotaku.com/5159871/square-enix-settles-lawsuit-with-sword-pirates.

78. *See* Notice of Satisfaction of Monetary Portion of Judgment, Square Enix Co. v. Wholesale Gallery, Inc., No. 08-0875 (C.D. Cal. Feb. 12, 2009); *see also* Plunkett *supra* note 77.

79. E.S.S. Entm't 2000, Inc. v. Rock Star Videos, Inc., 444 F. Supp. 2d 1012 (C.D. Cal. 2006), *aff'd*, 547 F.3d 1095 (9th Cir. 2008). Rockstar Games, Inc. was erroneously sued as Rock Star Videos, Inc. *See id.* n.1.

and Rockstar included a "gentlemen's club" called the "Pig Pen" in its best-selling game *Grand Theft Auto: San Andreas.*[80] Although the parties disputed the *extent* of the similarities beyond the similar names, there were clearly some similarities between the Play Pen and Pig Pen marks.[81] The Ninth Circuit affirmed the district court's grant of summary judgment for the defendants, holding that Rockstar's use of the modified Play Pen marks was protected by the First Amendment.[82]

2. Electronic Arts, Inc. v. Textron, Inc.

Four years after settling similar litigation in a district court in Texas,[83] Electronic Arts (EA) filed for a declaratory judgment against the defendants in January 2012, claiming that its use of the trademarks associated with three helicopters in the *Battlefield 3* video game did not infringe the defendants' trademark rights.[84] The helicopters included the AH-1Z "Viper" or "Zulu Cobra," the UH-1Y "Venom" or "Super Huey," and the V-22 "Osprey."[85] The intellectual property rights in these helicopters were controlled by Textron Innovations Inc. and the helicopters were manufactured by Bell Helicopter Textron Inc.[86] The defendants counterclaimed, in part, for infringement of Textron Innovations' registered trademarks under section 32 of the Lanham Act, for infringement of Textron Innovations' unregistered marks and trade dress under section 43(a), and for false designation of origin under section 43(a).[87] The registered marks included the alphanumeric

---

80. *E.S.S. Entm't 2000*, 444 F. Supp. 2d at 1014–18.

81. *See id.* at 1022 ("Defendants contend that some of the letters of the Pig Pen logo are in a different font than they are in the Play Pen logo. Plaintiff disputes this, and contends that the two logos use the same font.") (footnote omitted).

82. *See E.S.S. Entm't 2000*, 547 F.3d at 1101.

83. *See* Final Judgment, Bell Helicopter Textron, Inc. v. Elec. Arts, Inc., No. 4:06-0841 (N.D. Tex. Feb. 15, 2008); Order Denying Defendant's Motion to Dismiss at 1–2, Bell Helicopter Textron, Inc. v. Elec. Arts, Inc., No. 4:06-0841 (N.D. Tex. Dec. 6, 2007).

84. *See* Complaint for Declaratory Relief, Elec. Arts, Inc. v. Textron, Inc., No. 3:12-0118 (N.D. Cal. Jan. 6, 2012).

85. *See* Defendants' Answer and Counterclaims at 9, Elec. Arts, Inc. v. Textron, Inc., No. 3:12-0118 (N.D. Cal. May 7, 2012).

86. *Id.*

87. *See id.* at 24–28.

designations for each helicopter (e.g., UH-1Y).[88] The unregistered marks included the more conventional names of the helicopters (e.g., Super Huey).[89] The trade dress included various design features of the helicopters (e.g., "the design and shape of the fuselage and chin bubble on the UH-1Y").[90] Relying on the nominative fair use doctrine (discussed in Section III.A) and the First Amendment, EA moved to dismiss the counterclaims.[91] The district court in California denied the motion in July 2012.[92] The case settled on confidential terms in 2013.[93]

3. Dillinger, LLC v. Electronic Arts, Inc.

Dillinger, LLC filed suit against EA in October 2009, claiming (in part) infringement of a federally registered trademark under section 32 of the Lanham Act, false designation of origin under section 43(a), and a violation of Indiana's right of publicity law.[94] Dillinger owned trademark rights in the name John Dillinger, "the legendary gentleman-bandit,"[95] and controlled his post-mortem right of publicity.[96] EA made reference to Dillinger in both *The Godfather* and *The Godfather II* video games, incorporating "Dillinger" into the names of two weapons, a "Dillinger Tommy Gun" and a "Modern Dillinger."[97] The district court in Indiana granted EA's motion for summary judgment in June 2011 on First Amendment grounds.[98]

4. Ultimate Creations, Inc. v. THQ, Inc.

Ultimate Creations filed suit against THQ, Inc. in April 2005, claiming infringement of a federally registered trademark under section 32

---

88. *See* Elec. Arts, Inc. v. Textron, Inc., No. 3:12-0118, 2012 U.S. Dist. LEXIS 103914, at *4 (N.D. Cal. July 25, 2012).

89. *Id.*

90. *Id.*

91. *Id.* at *4–5.

92. *Id.* at *16.

93. *See* Stipulation of Dismissal with Prejudice, Elec. Arts, Inc. v. Textron, Inc., No. 3:12-0118 (N.D. Cal. May 20, 2013).

94. *See* Complaint for Damages and Injunctive Relief at 8–11, Dillinger, LLC v. Elec. Arts, Inc., No. 1:09-1236 (S.D. Ind. Oct. 1, 2009).

95. *Id.* at 1.

96. *Id.* at 2.

97. *See* Dillinger, LLC v. Elec. Arts, Inc., 795 F. Supp. 2d 829, 831 (S.D. Ind. 2011).

98. *See id.* at 836.

of the Lanham Act, false designation of origin under section 43(a), and infringement of a common law trademark.[99] Ultimate Creations owned the trademark rights associated with the Ultimate Warrior, a former professional wrestler most closely associated with World Wrestling Entertainment (previously known as the World Wrestling Federation). THQ produced a variety of wrestling games that included a Create-A-Wrestler feature, which allowed players to create custom characters for use in the game.[100] Ultimate Creations claimed that "one playing the game can create the Ultimate Warrior character including using the costume, the Ultimate Warrior logo, face paint, marks, trade dress and moves that were used by the Ultimate Warrior and associated with the Ultimate Warrior,"[101] thereby creating a likelihood of confusion about Ultimate Creations' association with THQ's games. The district court denied THQ's motion for summary judgment in January 2008.[102] The case settled on undisclosed terms in September 2008.[103]

5. Brown v. Electronic Arts, Inc.

Retired professional football player Jim Brown filed suit against EA in March 2009, claiming (in part) unfair competition—essentially false endorsement—because of EA's unlicensed use of Brown's likeness in its *Madden NFL* football games.[104] While the games did not include Brown's name, they did incorporate other identifying features of Brown and other unnamed players, such as their

---

99. Ultimate Creations, Inc. v. THQ Inc., No. CV-05-1134-PHX-SMM, 2008 U.S. Dist. LEXIS 8224, at *5 (D. Ariz. Jan. 24, 2008).

100. *Id.* at *3.

101. Complaint at 4, Ultimate Creations, Inc. v. THQ Inc., No. 05-1134 (D. Ariz. Apr. 14, 2005).

102. *Ultimate Creations*, 2008 U.S. Dist. LEXIS 8224, at *4.

103. *See* Order, Ultimate Creations, Inc. v. THQ Inc., No. 05-1134 (D. Ariz. Sept. 29, 2008) (ordering the transcript of the settlement conference sealed); Order, Ultimate Creations, Inc. v. THQ Inc., No. 05-1134 (D. Ariz. Sept. 22, 2008) (granting stipulated dismissal).

104. *See* Brown v. Elec. Arts, Inc., 724 F.3d 1235, 1239 (9th Cir. 2013); Complaint, Brown v. Elec. Arts, Inc., No. 09-1598 (C.D. Cal. Mar. 6, 2009); First Amended Complaint, Brown v. Elec. Arts, Inc., No. 09-1598 (C.D. Cal. July 22, 2009). On the interpretation of Brown's unfair competition claim as a false endorsement claim, see *Brown*, 724 F.3d at 1239.

teams, positions, ages, heights, and weights.[105] The district court dismissed Brown's claim on the basis of the First Amendment.[106] Relying and expanding upon its previous decision in *E.S.S. Entertainment*, the Ninth Circuit affirmed the dismissal.[107]

C. In-Game Uses: Secondary Liability

1. Marvel Enterprises, Inc. v. NCsoft Corp.

Marvel sued NCsoft Corp., NC Interactive, Inc., and Cryptic Studios in January 2005 for copyright and trademark infringement because of content in the defendants' *City of Heroes* massively multiplayer online role-playing game (MMORPG), including content created both by the defendants and the players.[108] The claim for direct trademark infringement was based on the defendants' use of a character on the game packaging and within the game. Marvel claimed this character, known as the Statesman, infringed its marks associated with the Captain America character.[109] Marvel also claimed the defendants were secondarily liable for contributory and vicarious infringement.[110] Using the *City of Heroes* Creation Engine, players could create their own superhero characters for the game, and Marvel claimed some of these superheroes directly infringed its trademarks.[111] According to Marvel, the defendants were liable for aiding these acts of direct infringement by the players.[112] The defendants successfully sought the dismissal of most

---

105. *Brown*, 724 F.3d at 1240.

106. *Id.* at 1239.

107. *Id.* at 1248. The Ninth Circuit did not consider Brown's state law claims in this appeal, *id.* at 1240 n.2, but the right of publicity issues raised by this case are discussed in Chapter 6.

108. *See* Second Amended Complaint, Marvel Enters., Inc. v. NCsoft Corp., No. 04-9253 (C.D. Cal. Jan. 25, 2005). The complaint also included claims for intentional interference with actual and prospective economic advantage and for declaratory relief.

109. *Id.* at 19–20, 24–25.

110. *See id.* at 21.

111. *Id.* at 2.

112. *Id.* at 21. Some of the *City of Heroes* characters Marvel presented as evidence of infringement were created by Marvel (rather than by players of the game) and were stricken from the complaint. *See* Marvel Enters., Inc. v. NCsoft Corp., No. 04-9253, 2005 U.S. Dist. LEXIS 8448, at *4–6 (C.D. Cal. Mar. 9, 2005).

of the trademark claims on the grounds that the players' uses of Marvel's marks were not acts of direct infringement because the players did not use the marks in commerce. Without acts of direct infringement, there could be no secondary liability on the part of the defendants. The case settled in December 2005.[113]

III. Analysis of Trademark Issues in Video Games and Virtual Worlds

Although it is quite possible that courts treat video games differently than traditional forms of media without explicitly acknowledging that they do so,[114] most applications of trademark law to video games and virtual worlds probably raise conventional trademark problems. The most difficult issues are probably ones that have always been difficult, such as balancing the goal of minimizing consumer confusion with the goal of facilitating free speech. This section analyzes several of the problems that commonly arise in the video game context with an emphasis on some of these more difficult issues.[115]

While the use of marks on physical goods can involve a relatively straightforward analysis of the likelihood of confusion between two marks on competing goods, such as the possibility of confusion between the two marks in *Universal City Studios* ("King Kong" and "Donkey Kong") or between the two arcade cabinet designs in *Incredible Technologies*, other questions remain more challenging. Many game worlds are populated with images that can be successfully merchandised as products. The Master Chief's

---

113. *See* Stipulation of Voluntary Dismissal with Prejudice, Marvel Enters., Inc. v. NCsoft Corp., No. 04-9253 (C.D. Cal. Dec. 16, 2005); *see also* Press Release, NCsoft Corp., Marvel Entertainment, Inc., NCsoft Corporation, NC Interactive, Inc., Cryptic Studios, Inc. Settle All Litigation (Dec. 15, 2005), http://kr.ncsoft.com/global/board /view.aspx?BID=mc_press&BC=&SYear=&SType=&SWord=&PNo=1&BNo=58.

114. *See generally* Ford & Liebler, *supra* note 41 (discussing the treatment of games for purposes of the right of publicity as compared to other forms of media).

115. Many of the issues discussed in this section are also discussed in Candidus Dougherty & Greg Lastowka, *Virtual Trademarks*, 24 Santa Clara Computer & High Tech. L.J. 749 (2008).

helmet from *Halo* is one example.[116] Some of these images are distinctive and arguably subject to trademark protection. The swords from *Final Fantasy*, the subject matter of the *Square Enix* case, are examples. That case involved the difficult question of how to treat the marketing of unauthorized goods, such as distinctive swords, where the trademarks are the goods.[117] In these situations, consumers may be indifferent to whether the product comes from the trademark owner or from some other source because the mark serves an aesthetic purpose rather than a source identification purpose.[118] It may even be feasible to avoid all pre-sale confusion by clearly indicating the product is unlicensed, but *post-sale* confusion, which is actionable under the Lanham Act,[119] may be more difficult to eliminate. Once the packaging is gone, so too may be the disclaimer.[120]

As compared to uses on physical products for purposes of source identification, the use of marks in expressive works raises significant implications for free speech. Although several courts found early video games undeserving of First Amendment protection,[121] the U.S. Supreme Court confirmed in 2011 that

---

116. The Legendary Edition of *Halo 3* included a replica of the Master Chief's helmet. *See* Tom Ham, *Halo 3: The Master Chief at Peak Performance*, WASH. POST, Oct. 5, 2007, at WE53.

117. *Compare* Au-Tomotive Gold, Inc. v. Volkswagen of Am., Inc., 457 F.3d 1062 (9th Cir. 2006), *with* Int'l Order of Job's Daughters v. Lindeburg & Co., 633 F.2d 912 (9th Cir. 1980). *See generally* Stacey L. Dogan & Mark A. Lemley, *The Merchandising Right: Fragile Theory or* Fait Accompli?, 54 EMORY L.J. 461 (2005).

118. *See Au-Tomotive Gold*, 457 F.3d at 1072–74. *See generally* Graeme B. Dinwoodie, *The Death of Ontology: A Teleological Approach to Trademark Law*, 84 IOWA L. REV. 611, 689–701 (1999) (discussing aesthetic functionality).

119. *See, e.g.*, Gen. Motors Corp. v. Urban Gorilla, LLC, 500 F.3d 1222, 1227 (10th Cir. 2007) ("Recognizing that the Lanham Act was intended to protect the market as a whole from confusion as to the source of a product, we, like our sister circuits, hold that the likelihood of post-sale confusion is relevant to the trade dress infringement inquiry."); *Au-Tomotive Gold*, 457 F.3d at 1077–78; Ferrari S.P.A. Esercizio Fabriche Automobili E Corse v. Roberts, 944 F.2d 1235, 1244–45 (6th Cir. 1991); Lois Sportswear, U.S.A., Inc. v. Levi Strauss & Co., 799 F.2d 867, 872–73 (2d Cir. 1986).

120. *See Au-Tomotive Gold*, 457 F.3d at 1077–78.

121. Malden Amusement Co. v. City of Malden, 582 F. Supp. 297, 299 (D. Mass. 1983) ("I hold on the merits of the present case that video games are not protected speech within the First Amendment. . . ."); Am.'s Best Family Showplace Corp. v.

video games are entitled to First Amendment protection.[122] The Court said:

> Like the protected books, plays, and movies that preceded them, video games communicate ideas—and even social messages—through many familiar literary devices (such as characters, dialogue, plot, and music) and through features distinctive to the medium (such as the player's interaction with the virtual world). That suffices to confer First Amendment protection.[123]

Games have become much more complex over time and many contain more than the simple "plot" of an arcade game like *Space Invaders* or *Pac-Man*.[124] While hardly the norm, some of the best known modern games contain political commentary, which is "at the core of what the First Amendment is designed to protect."[125] An entire book is devoted to the cultural and political significance

---

City of New York, 536 F. Supp. 170, 174 (E.D.N.Y. 1982) ("[A]lthough video game programs may be copyrighted, they 'contain so little in the way of particularized form of expression' that video games cannot be fairly characterized as a form of speech protected by the First Amendment.") (quoting Stern Elecs., Inc. v. Kaufman, 669 F.2d 852, 857 (2d Cir. 1982)); Tommy & Tina, Inc. v. Dep't of Consumer Affairs of the City of New York, 117 Misc. 2d 415, 424 (N.Y. Sup. Ct. 1983) ("[T]his court . . . finds that the video games are not a form of speech protected by the First Amendment."), *aff'd*, 464 N.Y.S.2d 132 (N.Y. App. Div. 1983), *aff'd*, 464 N.E.2d 988 (N.Y. 1984).

122. *See* Brown v. Entm't Merchs. Ass'n, 564 U.S. 786, 790 (2011). *Brown* was the end result of years of litigation in the lower courts about various attempts at the state and local levels to restrict minors' access to violent video games. *See generally* William K. Ford, *The Law and Science of Video Game Violence: Who Lost More in Translation?*, in TRANSLATING THE SOCIAL WORLD FOR LAW: LINGUISTIC TOOLS FOR A NEW LEGAL REALISM (Elizabeth E. Mertz et al. eds., 2016); William K. Ford, *The Law and Science of Video Game Violence: What Was Lost in Translation?*, 31 CARDOZO ARTS & ENT. L.J. 297 (2013).

123. *Brown*, 564 U.S. at 790.

124. Early home computer adventure games contained some sort of plot (or at least more text than games like *Space Invaders*), but the courts probably were not thinking about these types of games because the focus of early regulations was on arcades and arcade games. On the history of adventure games, see MATT BARTON, DUNGEONS & DESKTOPS: THE HISTORY OF COMPUTER ROLE-PLAYING GAMES (2008); Mark J.P. Wolf, *Genre Profile: Adventure Games*, in THE VIDEO GAME EXPLOSION: A HISTORY FROM PONG TO PLAYSTATION® AND BEYOND 81–90 (Mark J. P. Wolf ed., 2008).

125. Virginia v. Black, 538 U.S. 343, 365 (2003).

of the *Grand Theft Auto* series, for example.[126] *BioShock* lets the player explore an underwater libertarian paradise gone mad in a city built by a character who is part Ayn Rand and part Howard Hughes.[127] *The Simpsons Game* mocks those who would regulate video games.[128] Games do not, of course, need political content to be protected by the First Amendment. Even speech that seeks to do no more than entertain is protected by the First Amendment.[129] Strong trademark law protection has the potential to chill or burden socially valuable speech by preventing authors from using trademarks in their works.

On the other hand, weak trademark protection risks confusion among consumers. Many uses of trademarks in expressive works, such as films, television programs, and video games, are in fact advertisements. Product placement in the game industry dates back to at least 1994, if not earlier.[130] It was in that year that EA included sponsored billboard advertisements for Panasonic and Adidas in *FIFA International Soccer*.[131] The use of product placements in video games and virtual worlds has been increasing over

---

126. *See* THE MEANING AND CULTURAL SIGNIFICANCE OF GRAND THEFT AUTO: CRITICAL ESSAYS (Nate Garrelts ed., 2006).

127. *See* BIOSHOCK (2K Games 2007); *see also* Paul Restuccia, *It's a BioShock from Quincy!*, BOSTON HERALD, Sept. 16, 2007, at 28. According to one review, Ayn Rand's philosophy is "a frame of reference that informs absolutely everything about *BioShock*." KATE BERENS & GEOFF HOWARD, THE ROUGH GUIDE TO VIDEOGAMES 62 (2008). Alas, *BioShock* still may not qualify as art. *See* Mike Musgrove, *Monster Fun. But Is It Art?*, WASH. POST, Sept. 15, 2007, at F1.

128. In the game, Marge Simpson leads a mob incited by a parody of *Grand Theft Auto* entitled *Grand Theft Scratchy*, an "M" rated game purchased by her underage son, Bart Simpson. *See* THE SIMPSONS GAME (EA 2007).

129. Winters v. New York, 333 U.S. 507, 510 (1948) ("We do not accede to appellee's suggestion that the constitutional protection for a free press applies only to the exposition of ideas. The line between the informing and the entertaining is too elusive for the protection of that basic right. Everyone is familiar with instances of propaganda through fiction. What is one man's amusement, teaches another's doctrine.").

130. Some earlier games, such as *Chase the Chuck Wagon* for the Atari 2600 or the *Kool-Aid Man* games for the Atari 2600 and Intellivision, do not quite fit the usual definition of product placement because the whole game is about the product.

131. Tilley, *supra* note 4, at 1.

time.[132] Widespread knowledge of product placement and licensing practices increases the likelihood of confusion when marks are used without permission. Weak protection also allows forms of free riding that some courts consider unfair, even if no confusion results.[133]

As a practical matter, many recent judicial decisions have found in favor of defendants who have incorporated a mark into an expressive work without permission, regardless of the procedural posture.[134] The *Textron* and *Ultimate Creations* cases were exceptions to this trend.[135] Assuming the plaintiffs' marks were valid in these or similar cases, the critical and recurring question is whether the defendants needed permission to use the marks. Analogous situations occur in fictional works in film, television, music, and books. Nonfictional works, such as newspapers, are less of a

---

132. *See* SCOTT DONATON, MADISON & VINE: WHY THE ENTERTAINMENT AND ADVERTISING INDUSTRIES MUST CONVERGE TO SURVIVE 13–23 (2004).

133. *See, e.g.*, Dogan & Lemley, *supra* note 117, at 478–95; David J. Franklyn, *Debunking Dilution Doctrine: Toward a Coherent Theory of the Anti-Free-Rider Principle in American Trademark Law*, 56 HASTINGS L.J. 117, 118 (2004) ("[P]laintiffs often win on their dilution claims. Why is this so? This Article argues that the plaintiff success rate is due largely to the fact that judges and juries seek to vindicate an interest that is considerably different than the interest which dilution law purports to protect. The hidden interest is a desire to punish free-riding. There is a basic conviction that one should not reap where one has not sown.").

134. *See, e.g.*, Twentieth Century Fox Television v. Empire Distribution Inc., 875 F.3d 1192, 1195 (9th Cir. 2017) (affirming a grant of summary judgment); VIRAG, S.R.L. v. Sony Computer Entm't Am. LLC, 699 Fed. Appx. 667, 668 (9th Cir. 2017) (unpublished) (affirming a grant of a motion to dismiss); Caterpillar Inc. v. Walt Disney Co., 287 F. Supp. 2d 913 (C.D. Ill. 2003) (denying a motion for a temporary restraining order); *see also* William K. Ford, *Restoring* Rogers*: Video Games, False Association Claims, and the "Explicitly Misleading" Use of Trademarks*, 16 J. MARSHALL REV. INTELL. PROP. L. 306, 324–28 (2017) (collecting cases).

135. *See* Elec. Arts, Inc. v. Textron Inc., No. 3:12-0118, 2012 U.S. Dist. LEXIS 103914 (N.D. Cal. July 25, 2012) (denying EA's motion to dismiss); Ultimate Creations, Inc. v. THQ Inc., No. CV-05-1134-PHX-SMM, 2008 U.S. Dist. LEXIS 8224 (D. Ariz. Jan. 24, 2008) (denying defendant's motion for summary judgment). For examples not involving video games, see, for example, Anheuser-Busch, Inc. v. Balducci Publ'ns, 28 F.3d 769 (8th Cir. 1994) (instructing the district court to enter judgment for the plaintiff); Am. Dairy Queen Corp. v. New Line Prods., Inc., 35 F. Supp. 2d 727 (D. Minn. 1998) (granting plaintiff's motion for a preliminary injunction).

problem. Virtual worlds can have newspapers,[136] but a trademark reference in a straight news story, whether in a physical or virtual newspaper, is less likely to generate litigation as compared to uses on vehicles or buildings in a fictional video game or virtual world. The law is quite protective of news reporting and commentary,[137] so litigation trying to prevent such uses, even in a virtual context, is much less likely to succeed.

In general, the video game industry probably relies on licensing more than industries based on traditional media like film. Absent a license, a mark is less likely to appear in a game than in a film, though there will always be exceptions, such as the cases discussed in this chapter. Determining the licensing practices of any industry from publicly available sources is difficult, but several examples suggest game makers are often unwilling to risk litigation by using marks without permission. The licensing information found on game packaging, inside instruction manuals (now a less common feature of games), and elsewhere demonstrates an extensive reliance on licensing. A specific example is the conspicuously missing mark in Microsoft's *Project Gotham Racing 3*. In this game, the races take place on city streets, including the Las Vegas Strip. The map includes many casino buildings with real-world counterparts. Many of these buildings include the real-world names. The Wynn building, however, is labeled only with the generic name "Casino."[138] Presumably, Microsoft lacked permission to use the Wynn name and decided to be cautious. An unauthorized use might have provoked a claim based on section 43(a). Another example comes from an article covering in-game advertising. In an interview, the producer of *Rainbow Six Vegas* implied that

---

136. *See, e.g.*, Mark Glaser, *Reuters Closes Second Life Bureau, but (Virtual) Life Goes On*, MEDIASHIFT, Feb. 19, 2009, http://mediashift.org/2009/02/reuters-closes -second-life-bureau-but-virtual-life-goes-on050 (discussing media coverage and participation in *Second Life*).

137. *See* U.S. CONST. amend. I; 15 U.S.C. § 1125(c)(3)(B) (2018) (defining "[a]ll forms of news reporting and news commentary" as not actionable as trademark dilution); *see also* 17 U.S.C. § 107 (2018) ("[T]he fair use of a copyrighted work, . . . for purposes such as *criticism, comment, news reporting*, teaching . . . , scholarship, or research, is not an infringement of copyright.") (emphasis added).

138. *See* PROJECT GOTHAM RACING 3 OFFICIAL GAME GUIDE 19 (2005) (including screenshot of the "Casino").

automobile trademarks, including automobile trade dress, would not be used in a game without permission.[139] The implication is that *unlicensed* vehicles that look just like the real things will not be used. This caution is understandable: vehicle designs, or parts of a vehicle's design, may be protectable as trade dress.[140]

Industry practices likely affect consumer perceptions, making a practice of licensing self-reinforcing. As J. Thomas McCarthy describes the circularity phenomenon of trademark law: "In trademark law, it is consumer perception that creates a likelihood of confusion. And it is likelihood of confusion that creates 'the law' that requires permission for a given use of a mark. Thus, if a significant number of consumers think that permission is needed, then permission is needed. "[141]

Where it is standard to license marks for games, consumers will come to learn the industry's norm. They are then more likely to be confused when marks are used in games without licenses. Industry practices could, of course, lead to the opposite result too. For example, consumer confusion over the unlicensed use of vehicle design trade dress may be unlikely, even if the modifications to the vehicle are slight.

Despite the implication to the contrary in the *Rainbow Six Vegas* article, unlicensed vehicles in many games have obvious real-world counterparts. One article describes the changes made in several games as removing the logos and making only slight

---

139. Tilley, *supra* note 4, at 2.

140. *See, e.g.,* Gen. Motors Corp. v. Lanard Toys, Inc., 468 F.3d 405, 416 (6th Cir. 2006) ("Both the military Humvee and the civilian Hummer share common appearance elements which constitute a trade dress (specifically, the grille, slanted and raised hood, split windshield, rectangular doors, and squared edges)."); Ferrari S.P.A. Esercizio Fabriche Automobili E Corse v. Roberts, 944 F.2d 1235, 1237 (6th Cir. 1991) (holding that Ferrari was entitled to trade dress protection in the "exterior shape and appearance of two of its automobiles"); Liquid Glass Enters., Inc. v. Dr. Ing. h.c.F. Porsche AG, 8 F. Supp. 2d 398, 402 (D.N.J. 1998) ("Liquid Glass does not dispute that Porsche has a registered trademark in its crest and the stylized word PORSCHE, as well as a protectable trade dress in the Porsche 911.").

141. 4 MCCARTHY, *supra* note 33, § 24:9.

changes to the vehicle designs.[142] The deletion of word marks and logos on the vehicles may be a widely recognized signal to consumers that the use of a vehicle design is unlicensed. As a result, where it is standard to use vehicle trade dress without a license (so long as the logos are removed), consumers will come to learn the industry's norm and then are not likely to be confused when vehicle trade dress is used in games without licenses.

As already noted, licensing practices appear to be much different in the film industry, regardless of consumer perceptions. Unfortunately, there is a lack of systematic documentation of the practices in either industry, but the district court record in *Wham-O, Inc. v. Paramount Pictures* provides some evidence of the film industry's practices.[143] *Wham-O* involved the unauthorized use of Wham-O's Slip 'N Slide product in the film *Dickie Roberts: Former Child Star*.[144] The court determined that consumers were not likely to be confused by the use of the product in the movie and therefore think Wham-O was associated with the movie.[145] The court also noted, "As a matter of custom, defendants do not seek the permission of manufacturers of name-brand products to use those products in [their] films."[146] In support of this statement, the court referred to a declaration of Scott Martin, Paramount's senior vice president of intellectual property and associate general counsel. According to Martin:

---

142. *See* Nick Walkland, *Thrill of the Chase*, ELECTRONIC GAMING MONTHLY, Mar. 2003, at 103, 104 ("*Driver 3*'s vehicles aren't the shiny, licensed real McCoys seen in *The Getaway* or *Gran Turismo*. . . . In the end Reflections [i.e., the developer of *Driver 3*] relied on the same tactic used in *Driver*, *Driver 2*, and *Stuntman*: They made the vehicles look similar to recognizable cars but then removed logos and changed the models slightly to the point where 'the legal people are happy[.]'"); *see also* Kevin Gifford, *DRIV3R'S Ed*, ELECTRONIC GAMING MONTHLY, July 2004, at 84, 88 ("You won't find any licensed cars in *DRIV3R*, but you will find more than 70 machines to drive, running the gamut from sensible Volkswagen Passat clones to Ferrari-ish sports cars.").

143. Wham-O, Inc. v. Paramount Pictures Corp., 286 F. Supp. 2d 1254 (N.D. Cal. 2003).

144. *Id.* at 1256.

145. *Id.* at 1262.

146. *Id.* at 1258.

Paramount did not seek permission from Wham-O for the use of the Slip 'N Slide in the Film, nor did Paramount seek permission from any other trademark owner for the use of any other trademarked products in the Film (including Wesson Oil, Dickie's Volkswagen which explodes, the child's stroller in which Dickie rides, the bicycle which he rides and crashes, the Ford Taurus with which he collides, items of set dressing, etc.). I am not aware of any legal requirement that permission be obtained from trademark owners before a trademarked product can be used or referred to in a motion picture. It is not Paramount's practice to seek such permission.[147]

Martin continued with a description of industry practices generally:

I am familiar with the production clearance practices at the other motion picture studios and it is my understanding that no motion picture studios seeks [sic] permission from trademark owners before using or referring to a trademarked product in a motion picture. In my twelve years with Paramount I am not aware of any claims of trademark infringement being asserted against Paramount based on the use of a trademarked product in a motion picture. I am also not aware of any such infringement claim being made against any other motion picture studio based on an on-screen use of a trademarked product.[148]

A leading treatise on clearance practices in the film industry supports the conclusion that absent special circumstances (such as

---

147. Declaration of Scott M. Martin in Support of Defendant Paramount Pictures Corporation and Happy Madison Productions, Inc.'s Opposition to Plaintiff's Motion for a Temporary Restraining Order at 2–3, Wham-O, Inc. v. Paramount Pictures Corp., 286 F. Supp. 2d 1254 (N.D. Cal. 2003) (No. 03-04071).

148. *Id.* It is not clear from Martin's declaration how to determine when studios, including Paramount, will deviate from their standard practices and ask permission to include a mark in a film. Even Paramount sometimes obtains permission. According to Ohio State University's student newspaper, Paramount received permission from Ohio State University to use the university's trademarks in its 1999 remake of *The Out-of-Towners. See* Rick Jun Li, *OSU Logo in Demand as Entertainment Prop*, LANTERN, Apr. 5, 1999, http://thelantern.com/1999/04/osu-logo-in-demand-as-entertainment-prop/.

an unusually litigious trademark owner), film studios need not seek permission for using a trademark in a film.[149]

Why there would be a significant difference between the licensing practices of the film and video game industries is not clear, especially if consumers are aware of the use of product placement in both industries. As a practical matter, and one not clearly tied to whether consumer confusion is likely, the cost to avoid licensing problems should be lower in the video game industry. Filming in a city may result in dozens or hundreds of marks appearing in the background,[150] making it costly to secure licensing arrangements with every trademark owner whose marks appear somewhere in a scene. Filmmakers must make an effort to avoid or remove marks, and prior to computerized editing, removing marks from a particular scene was likely more difficult. Game makers, by contrast, do not usually point a camera at a cityscape and appropriate the imagery *en masse*. Instead, game makers "build" even their real-world locations,[151] suggesting that the appearance of a mark in a game is a choice and one that can be easily avoided. These differences in costs and methods could partially explain the difference in industry licensing practices. Additionally, the video game industry is much younger than the film industry and developed during a

---

149. *See* Michael C. Donaldson & Lisa A. Callif, Clearance & Copyright 312 (4th ed. 2014) ("A filmmaker's right to include trademarks within a film is clear.").

150. Even the design of a building without any visible logos may be the basis for an assertion of trademark rights. For example, *Driver: Parallel Lines* includes a depiction of the Empire State Building on the packaging artwork. On the back of the game's box is the following: "The Empire State Building Design is a trademark of Empire State Building Company LLC is used with permission." *See* Driver: Parallel Lines (Atari 2006) (PlayStation 2 version). A similar claim can be found on the Empire State Building website. *See* Empire State Building, *Terms and Conditions*, http://www.esbnyc.com/terms-conditions (last visited July 25, 2018) (*See* the "Copyrights, Trademarks, and Other Intellectual Property" section: "All trademarks, service marks and trade names, including but not limited to the mark EMPIRE STATE BUILDING and the visual equivalent of the Empire State Building, are trademarks of ESRT Observatory TRS, L.L.C. and/or its affiliates and are proprietary to us.").

151. Watch Dogs (Ubisoft 2014) provides a useful example of how video game producers deal with real-world locations. For a discussion of how the game's producers researched and then "built" a version of Chicago as the game's primary setting, see Christopher Borrelli, *"Watch Dogs" Makes Chicago a Digitized Surveillance State*, Chi. Trib., May 9, 2014, at A+E1.

time when trademark licensing became more common. Trademark licensing began to flourish in the 1970s, probably due in part to several judicial decisions favoring trademark owners.[152] The 1970s is the decade in which the video game industry began.[153] Thus, it would not be surprising if game makers were more reluctant to use marks without authorization. Unlike in the film industry, there was never a long-standing custom of doing otherwise. But even in an industry where substantial efforts are made to use marks only with authorization, trademark disputes are inevitable. When marks work their way into video games or virtual worlds, either intentionally or otherwise, several defenses are available to game makers. The following subsections consider two defenses, the nominative fair use "defense" and the First Amendment defense. The discussion then turns to two other issues: the place of secondary liability in games with user-generated content and the applicability of the misappropriation doctrine in trademark disputes.

A. Nominative Fair Use

The nominative fair use defense may protect an unauthorized use of a mark, including the unauthorized use of a mark in an expressive work like a video game, but there is significant uncertainty associated with this doctrine. It is not even clear that the nominative fair use "defense" qualifies as a defense in the usual sense of the term.[154] Depending on the circuit, it may be an affirmative defense

---

152. *See* Dogan & Lemley, *supra* note 117, at 472–73 ("What explains the explosive growth of the licensing market for trademark merchandise? The answer appears to lie in a handful of judicial decisions from the 1970s and 1980s that emboldened trademark holders to demand payment for merchandise bearing their marks.").

153. *See* William K. Ford, *Copy Game for High Score: The First Video Game Lawsuit*, 20 J. INTELL. PROP. L. 1, 2 (2012) ("Commentators and industry historians generally agree that the multi-billion dollar video game industry began forty years ago in November 1972 with Atari's release of *Pong*."). The first commercial, coin-operated video game, *Computer Space*, debuted in 1971. *See* BURNHAM, *supra* note 28, at 71. The first home video game console, the Magnavox Odyssey, debuted in 1972. *Id.* at 79.

154. *See* Toyota Motor Sales, U.S.A., Inc. v. Tabari, 610 F.3d 1171, 1182 (9th Cir. 2010) ("The district court treated nominative fair use as an affirmative defense to be established by the Tabaris only after Toyota showed a likelihood of confusion

or it may be a modification to the usual approach for assessing the likelihood of confusion.[155] The statutory or classic fair use defense applies when a defendant uses a word or other symbol to describe its own products, not the plaintiff's products.[156] The nominative fair use defense, by contrast, is "designed to protect the ability of others to use a mark 'to describe [their own] product.'"[157] The defense originated with Judge Alex Kozinski's opinion for the Ninth Circuit in *New Kids on the Block v. News America Publishing, Inc.*[158] The case involved two newspapers conducting a telephone poll about the New Kids on the Block musical group.[159] For 95 cents per minute, callers could vote for their favorite member of the group.[160] The New Kids, who did not authorize the poll, filed a "shotgun complaint" with ten claims, including claims under section 43(a).[161] Because the statutory fair use defense involves using a mark to describe one's own products, it did not cover using the New Kids' mark to describe the New Kids. The Ninth Circuit recognized nominative fair use as an alternative defense.[162] Despite its ubiquity in discussions of trademark law, the nominative fair use defense has been adopted only by a minority of circuits and even

---

under *Sleekcraft*. This was error; nominative fair use 'replaces' *Sleekcraft* as the proper test for likely consumer confusion whenever defendant asserts to have referred to the trademarked good itself."); Diller v. Barry Driller, Inc., No. 12-7200, 2012 U.S. Dist. LEXIS 133515, at *10 n.3 (C.D. Cal. Sept. 10, 2012) ("Although raised by Defendants, nominative fair use is not a defense, but an adapted application of the likelihood of confusion test.").

    155. *See* Tiffany (NJ) Inc. v. eBay Inc., 600 F.3d 93, 102 n.7 (2d Cir. 2010) ("The Third Circuit treats the doctrine as an affirmative defense, while the Ninth Circuit views the doctrine as a modification to the likelihood-of-confusion analysis of the plaintiff's underlying infringement claim.") (citations omitted).

    156. *See* 15 U.S.C. § 1115(b)(4) (2018); *see, e.g.*, New Kids on the Block v. News Am. Publ'g, Inc., 971 F.2d 302, 308 (9th Cir. 1992).

    157. Universal Commc'n Sys., Inc. v. Lycos, Inc., 478 F.3d 413, 424 (1st Cir. 2007) (quoting *New Kids on the Block*, 971 F.2d at 308).

    158. *New Kids on the Block*, 971 F.2d 302.

    159. *Id.* at 304.

    160. *Id.*

    161. *Id.* at 304–05.

    162. *Id.* at 308.

then only with modifications from the original version adopted by the Ninth Circuit.[163]

The Ninth Circuit summarized the nominative fair use analysis as follows (and explicitly referred to it as a defense): "In cases where a nominative fair use defense is raised, we ask whether (1) the product was 'readily identifiable' without use of the mark; (2) defendant used more of the mark than necessary; or (3) defendant falsely suggested he was sponsored or endorsed by the trademark holder. "[164] The third prong of the nominative fair use defense essentially calls for an analysis of the likelihood of confusion, but without the established list of *Sleekcraft* factors to consider.[165] As

---

163. *See, e.g.,* Int'l Info. Sys. Sec. Certification Consortium, Inc. v. Sec. Univ., LLC, 823 F.3d 153, 168 (2d Cir. 2016) ("[W]e hold that, in nominative use cases, district courts are to consider the Ninth Circuit and Third Circuit's nominative fair use factors, in addition to the *Polaroid* factors."); Swarovski Aktiengesellschaft v. Bldg. #19, Inc., 704 F.3d 44, 50 (1st Cir. 2013) ("In the First Circuit, we have recognized the 'underlying principle' of nominative fair use, but like several other circuits, we have never endorsed any particular version of the doctrine."); Rosetta Stone Ltd. v. Google, Inc., 676 F.3d 144, 155 (4th Cir. 2012) ("We hasten to add that we are not adopting a position about the viability of the nominative fair-use doctrine as a defense to trademark infringement or whether this doctrine should formally alter our likelihood-of-confusion test in some way."); Century 21 Real Estate Corp. v. Lendingtree, Inc., 425 F.3d 211, 228 (3d Cir. 2005) (concluding that the Ninth Circuit's nominative fair use defense "suffers from a lack of clarity" and then endorsing an alternative version of the defense); PACCAR Inc. v. TeleScan Techs., L.L.C., 319 F.3d 243, 256 (6th Cir. 2003) ("This circuit has never followed the nominative fair use analysis. . . . We are not inclined to adopt the Ninth Circuit's analysis here."). *But see* State Farm Mut. Auto. Ins. Co. v. Sharon Woods Collision Ctr., Inc., No. 07-457, 2007 U.S. Dist. LEXIS 86651, at *25–27 (S.D. Ohio Nov. 26, 2007) (stating the status of the nominative fair use test under the Sixth Circuit's *PACCAR* decision is unclear); *see also* Mark P. McKenna & Shelby Niemann, *2016 Trademark Year in Review*, 92 Notre Dame L. Rev. Online 112, 133 (2017) ("Though no circuit has affirmatively rejected the [nominative fair use] doctrine, most circuits have not expressly accepted it either.").

164. Toyota Motor Sales, U.S.A., Inc. v. Tabari, 610 F.3d 1171, 1175–76 (9th Cir. 2010) (quoting Playboy Enters., Inc. v. Welles, 279 F.3d 796, 801 (9th Cir. 2002)); *see also New Kids on the Block*, 971 F.2d at 308.

165. *See* Brother Records, Inc. v. Jardine, 318 F.3d 900, 908 n.5 (9th Cir. 2003) ("[W]e note that the third requirement of the nominative fair use defense—the lack of anything that suggests sponsorship or endorsement—is merely the other side of the likelihood-of-confusion coin."); McKenna & Niemann, *supra* note 163, at 133 ("Though it seems clear that the *New Kids* court meant the third factor to refer to additional conduct beyond mere use of the mark that would suggest

confusion must not be likely for a nominative use to be fair,[166] the doctrine lacks the ordinary qualities of a defense. Classic fair use is a defense to the plaintiff's showing of a likelihood of confusion.[167] Nominative fair use, by contrast, is *not* a defense to a showing that there is a likelihood of confusion. Instead, it is a different list of factors for determining whether confusion is likely. After *New Kids*, the Ninth Circuit further held that the nominative fair use defense shifts the burden to the defendant to show a *lack* of confusion, but the Ninth Circuit later concluded that this holding is inconsistent with the Supreme Court's case law.[168] The burden of showing a likelihood of confusion therefore remains with the plaintiff.[169] But once the plaintiff satisfies this burden, nominative fair use is of no help to the defendant in the Ninth Circuit.

Two cases illustrate the limited benefit of nominative fair use to defendants in the Ninth Circuit (and any other court that follows its lead). *E.S.S. Entertainment 2000, Inc. v. Rock Star Videos,*

---

sponsorship or affiliation, courts applying *New Kids* often reduced the third factor to a confusion inquiry. Indeed, the Ninth Circuit held that the *New Kids* factors replaced the likelihood of confusion factors. . . ."). Under the Second Circuit's approach, it appears a court must consider the likelihood of confusion twice, once using the usual *Polaroid* list of factors and then again using the Ninth Circuit's unstructured third nominative fair use factor. *See Int'l Info. Sys. Sec. Certification Consortium*, 823 F.3d at 169 ("[W]hen considering the third nominative fair use factor, courts must not, as the district court did here, consider only source confusion, but rather must consider confusion regarding affiliation, sponsorship, or endorsement by the mark holder.").

166. *Toyota Motor Sales*, 610 F.3d at 1182 ("A finding of nominative fair use is a finding that the plaintiff has failed to show a likelihood of confusion as to sponsorship or endorsement.").

167. *See* KP Permanent Make-Up, Inc. v. Lasting Impressions I, Inc., 543 U.S. 111, 121–22 (2004) ("Since the burden of proving likelihood of confusion rests with the plaintiff, and the fair use defendant has no free-standing need to show confusion unlikely, it follows (contrary to the [Ninth Circuit's] view) that some possibility of consumer confusion must be compatible with fair use, and so it is.").

168. *See* Fortune Dynamic, Inc. v. Victoria's Secret Stores Brand Mgmt., Inc., 618 F.3d 1025, 1031 (9th Cir. 2010) ("We have recognized a nominative fair use *defense* and a classic fair use defense.") (emphasis added); *Toyota Motor Sales*, 610 F.3d at 1175 ("In cases where a nominative fair use *defense* is raised. . . .") (emphasis added).

169. *See Toyota Motor Sales*, 610 F.3d at 1182–83.

Inc. is one example.[170] In creating a strip club for *Grand Theft Auto: San Andreas*, Rockstar Games, the defendant in *E.S.S. Entertainment*, drew inspiration from the trademark and building of an actual Los Angles strip club called the Play Pen, but it modified these elements in creating its own strip club for *Grand Theft Auto: San Andreas*, which Rockstar called the Pig Pen.[171] As the logo of Rockstar's fictional strip club was not identical to the plaintiff's mark and Rockstar was not commenting on the Play Pen *"per se,"* the Ninth Circuit held that the nominative fair use defense was inapplicable.[172] In the Ninth Circuit's view, the nominative fair use defense applies only when a mark is used without modification by the defendant or when the defendant intends some comment on the plaintiff's product or service.[173]

Unlike the *E.S.S. Entertainment* case, *Electronic Arts, Inc. v. Textron Inc.*[174] is an example where the court applied the defense, but it was of limited value to EA, the declaratory judgment plaintiff. EA claimed its use of Textron's helicopters in *Battlefield 3* was a nominative fair use and asked the U.S. District Court for the Northern District of California to dismiss the defendants' counterclaims against it.[175] The parties disagreed about "whether the helicopters are readily identifiable without use of the trademark."[176] The parties also disagreed about "whether EA used more of the marks than necessary to identify the helicopters."[177] And this disagreement, by itself, sufficed to negate the first two elements of the nominative fair use defense, at least on a motion to dismiss.[178] As to whether there was a likelihood of confusion about sponsorship or endorsement, the court noted that the defendants' helicopters are

---

170. E.S.S. Entm't 2000, Inc. v. Rock Star Videos, Inc., 547 F.3d 1095 (9th Cir. 2008).

171. *Id.* at 1097–98.

172. *Id.* at 1099.

173. *Id.*

174. Elec. Arts, Inc. v. Textron Inc., No. C 12-0118 WHA, 2012 U.S. Dist. LEXIS 103914 (N.D. Cal. July 25, 2012).

175. *See id.* at *13–16.

176. *Id.* at *15.

177. *Id.*

178. *Id.* at *14–15.

prominently used in the game and that consumers could plausibly think Textron licensed the trademarks to EA or even provided technical assistance for the game.[179] The prevalence of licensing in the industry makes this confusion even more likely.[180] While the back of the game's box included a disclaimer, the court thought "teenage users . . . anxious to rip open the package and play in the game" might not see it.[181] The district court might have given more consideration to the defense had it been brought in the context of a motion for summary judgment, rather than a motion to dismiss, but the court's opinion suggested EA would fare no better in that situation.[182] The court said there were "questions of disputed fact as to all three elements" of the nominative fair use defense.[183] Based on Ninth Circuit precedent, the court also said that the likelihood of confusion is a jury question when industry licensing customs are well known to consumers.[184] Absent an obvious parody of a mark, it may be particularly difficult for a defendant using a mark within a video game to prevail with a nominative fair

---

179. *Id.* at *11, 15.
180. *Id.* at *15.
181. *Id.* at *12–13, 15.
182. *See id.* at *14–16.
183. *Id.* at *15.
184. *Id.* (quoting Abdul-Jabbar v. Gen. Motors Corp., 85 F.3d 407, 413 (9th Cir. 1996)). In *Abdul-Jabbar*, Kareem Abdul-Jabbar objected to the use of his birth name, Lew Alcindor, in an Oldsmobile commercial, claiming in part a violation of section 43(a) of the Lanham Act. 85 F.3d at 409–10. The Ninth Circuit's holding in this case would ordinarily deny a defendant summary judgment in such situations and would send these cases to a jury. The court said:

> [The] use of celebrity endorsements in television commercials is so well established by commercial custom that a jury might find an implied endorsement in General Motors' use of the celebrity's name in a commercial, which would not inhere in a newspaper poll. Newspapers and magazines commonly use celebrities' names and photographs without making endorsement contracts, so the public does not infer an endorsement agreement from the use. Many people may assume that when a celebrity's name is used in a television commercial, the celebrity endorses the product advertised. Likelihood of confusion as to endorsement is therefore a question for the jury.

Id. at 413.

use defense, given that product placement and licensing practices in video games are likely well known to consumers.[185] The First Amendment, however, provides another avenue to defendants.

B. The First Amendment

Courts traditionally avoid resorting to constitutional doctrines to resolve cases when nonconstitutional grounds are available.[186] In keeping with this tradition, Judge Pierre Leval of the Second Circuit argues that courts can and should avoid resolving trademark disputes on First Amendment grounds, in part to avoid constitutional rulings that are difficult to undo.[187] To avoid unnecessary recourse to the Constitution, he argues that courts need to apply the Lanham Act with a view towards accommodating free speech values.[188] Despite Judge Leval's view to the contrary, courts do sometimes rely on the First Amendment in trademark cases, including Judge Leval's own court.

The dominant test for protecting First Amendment interests in the trademark context comes from the Second Circuit's decision in *Rogers v. Grimaldi*.[189] In *Rogers*, the defendant distributed a film entitled *Ginger and Fred*, for which Ginger Rogers sued, claiming a violation of section 43(a) of the Lanham Act.[190] The Second Circuit determined that the titles of artistic works deserve heightened protection from infringement claims in order to protect the First Amendment interests of authors and consumers.[191] The Second Circuit said the balancing of free speech interests with the interest

---

185. *See* Elizabeth L. Rosenblatt, *Rethinking the Parameters of Trademark Use in Entertainment*, 61 FLA. L. REV. 1011, 1032 (2009) ("Also notable is the degree to which the consuming public has become aware of the practice of product placement.").

186. *See, e.g.*, Lyng v. Nw. Indian Cemetery Protective Ass'n, 485 U.S. 439, 445 (1988) ("A fundamental and longstanding principle of judicial restraint requires that courts avoid reaching constitutional questions in advance of the necessity of deciding them."); United States v. Sandoval-Lopez, 122 F.3d 797, 802 n.9 (9th Cir. 1997) ("We avoid constitutional questions when an alternative basis for disposing of [a] case presents itself.").

187. Pierre N. Leval, *Trademark: Champion of Free Speech*, 27 COLUM. J.L. & ARTS 187, 207–10 (2004).

188. *Id.*

189. Rogers v. Grimaldi, 875 F.2d 994 (2d Cir. 1989).

190. *Id.* at 996–97.

191. *Id.* at 997–1002.

of avoiding consumer confusion "will normally not support application of the [Lanham] Act unless [1] the title has no artistic relevance to the underlying work whatsoever, or, [2] if it has some artistic relevance, unless the title explicitly misleads as to the source or the content of the work."[192] The *Rogers* test therefore tolerates some consumer confusion in the interest of protecting speech. Other circuits have adopted this test.[193] After the decision in *Rogers v. Grimaldi*, the Second Circuit and other courts expanded *Rogers* application beyond just titles to other uses of trademarks within artistic works.[194] In *E.S.S. Entertainment*, for example, the Ninth Circuit relied on *Rogers* in affirming the district court's grant of summary judgment to Rockstar Games where the use of the plaintiff's mark was within *Grand Theft Auto: San Andreas*.[195] As with nominative fair use, however, significant uncertainty remains about when video game creators can use trademarks without permission from the owner.

Although it is the dominant test, courts have applied *Rogers* inconsistently.[196] The inconsistency is not so much tied to the first

---

192. *Id.* at 999. An exception is when one literary title is confusingly similar to another literary title. *Id.* n.5 ("This limiting construction would not apply to misleading titles that are confusingly similar to other titles. The public interest in sparing consumers this type of confusion outweighs the slight public interest in permitting authors to use such titles.").

193. *See, e.g.*, Parks v. LaFace Records, 329 F.3d 437, 451–52 (6th Cir. 2003) ("We thus apply the *Rogers* test to the facts before us."); Mattel, Inc. v. MCA Records, Inc., 296 F.3d 894, 902 (9th Cir. 2002) ("We agree with the Second Circuit's analysis and adopt the *Rogers* standard as our own."); Westchester Media v. PRL USA Holdings, Inc., 214 F.3d 658, 665 (5th Cir. 2000) ("This Circuit has adopted the Second Circuit's approach. . . .").

194. *See, e.g.*, Cliffs Notes, Inc. v. Bantam Doubleday Dell Publ'g Group, Inc., 886 F.2d 490, 494–95 (2d Cir. 1989) (applying *Rogers* to the question of "whether the appearance of a work's cover is confusingly similar to the trademark elements of an earlier cover"); E.S.S. Entm't 2000, Inc. v. Rock Star Videos, Inc., 547 F.3d 1095, 1099 (9th Cir. 2008) ("Although [the *Rogers*] test traditionally applies to uses of a trademark in the title of an artistic work, there is no principled reason why it ought not also apply to the use of a trademark in the body of the work."); E.S.S. Entm't 2000, Inc. v. Rock Star Videos, Inc., 444 F. Supp. 2d 1012, 1038 (C.D. Cal. 2006) (collecting cases), *aff'd*, 547 F.3d 1095 (9th Cir. 2008).

195. *E.S.S. Entm't 2000*, 547 F.3d at 1099–101.

196. *See* Thomas M. Byron, *Spelling Confusion: Implications of the Ninth Circuit's View of the "Explicitly Misleading" Prong of the* Rogers *Test*, 19 J. INTELL. PROP. L. 1 (2011); Rosenblatt, *supra* note 185, at 1071–72.

prong of the *Rogers* test (i.e., whether the use of the mark is artistically relevant to the work), but to the second prong of the test (i.e., whether a use of a mark is explicitly misleading). *E.S.S. Entertainment* arguably represents a very narrow view of *Rogers'* scope. The court explained the second prong of *Rogers* in the following way:

> ESS also argues that Rockstar's use of the Pig Pen "'explicitly misleads as to the source or the content of the work.'" This prong of the test points directly at the purpose of trademark law, namely to "avoid confusion in the marketplace by allowing a trademark owner to prevent others from duping consumers into buying a product they mistakenly believe is sponsored by the trademark owner." *The relevant question, therefore, is whether the Game would confuse its players into thinking that the Play Pen is somehow behind the Pig Pen or that it sponsors Rockstar's product.*[197]

The Ninth Circuit's framing of the "relevant question" suggests that, much like a nominative use that is fair, a use that is protected by the *Rogers* test is one that does not create a likelihood of confusion. In applying the test, the court explained that confusion was not likely in *E.S.S. Entertainment* because the Pig Pen strip club was an incidental part of *Grand Theft Auto: San Andreas* and because no one would think that the owner of the real-world Play Pen strip club produced the game (though the usual framing of this latter issue is whether consumers would think the owner of the strip club was associated with the game by virtue of granting Rockstar a license).[198] Under *E.S.S. Entertainment*, it is not clear what is left of the *balance* between avoiding consumer confusion and protecting speech in artistic works.[199] While it is not clear that the Ninth Circuit meant to reduce the *Rogers* test to just the usual question of whether there is a likelihood of confusion, the resolution of the

---

197. *E.S.S. Entm't 2000*, 547 F.3d at 1100 (citations omitted and emphasis added).

198. *Id.* at 1100–01.

199. This issue appears to have been clarified by Brown v. Elec. Arts, Inc., 724 F.3d 1235 (9th Cir. 2013), and subsequent decisions. *See infra* notes 214–230 and accompanying text.

motion to dismiss in *Electronic Arts v. Textron, Inc.* suggests that this is a plausible reading of *E.S.S. Entertainment*.

The litigation between EA and Bell Helicopter and Textron Innovations illustrates the potential interest in free expression in these cases and also supports the narrow reading of *Rogers* under *E.S.S. Entertainment*. In the earlier litigation between the parties, Bell Helicopter and Textron filed a trademark infringement suit in the U.S. District Court for the Northern District of Texas.[200] The suit involved three EA games: *Battlefield Vietnam, Battlefield Vietnam: Redux,* and *Battlefield 2.* In part, the suit implicated the use of the UH-1 Huey helicopter in the Vietnam-era games.[201] Bell Helicopter and Textron claimed they received "substantial revenues from licensing the use of Bell's Helicopters . . . in connection with products such as motion pictures, aircraft models, video games and computer software."[202] As the Huey is among the standard imagery included in Vietnam movies, television shows, and games,[203] Bell Helicopter and Textron were asserting a right to control an essential element for the creation of expressive works about the Vietnam War—an element that is not even an ordinary consumer product.[204]

---

200. Plaintiffs' Second Amended Original Complaint, Bell Helicopter Textron, Inc. v. Elec. Arts, Inc., No. 06-841 (N.D. Tex. May 1, 2007).

201. *Id.* at 5.

202. *Id.* at 4.

203. As a few examples, Hueys commonly appear on the cover of Vietnam-era works, including video games, such as *Vietcong: Purple Haze* (Illusion Softworks a.s. 2004) (Xbox edition); board games, such as *Vietnam 1965–1973* (Victory Games 1984); and role-playing games, such as *The Revised Recon* (Palladium Books 1986). Perhaps the most famous scene in *Apocalypse Now* is the one featuring a fleet of Huey helicopters. APOCALYPSE NOW (Omni Zoetrope 1979).

204. The specific Huey model mentioned in the complaint might occasionally be purchased for nonmilitary uses. *See* Al Vinikour, *Vicar of Volo Wins the Game*, CHI. SUN-TIMES, Nov. 6, 2007, at A2, *available at* http://www.pressreader.com/usa /chicago-sun-times/20071106/284580238447135 ("[Greg] Grams [the owner of the Volo Auto Museum in Illinois] also has the only two privately-owned Military UH-1 (Huey) helicopters in the world. To be allowed to purchase them he had to swear that he would never allow the choppers to fly."). Other Huey models are purchased by nonmilitary personnel more often. *See, e.g.,* Gregory Alan Gross, *San Diego Fire-Rescue Helicopter Makes Debut*, SAN DIEGO UNION-TRIB., July 7, 2005, at B-3, B-8, *available at* http://legacy.sandiegouniontribune.com/uniontrib/20050707 /news_1m7copter.html ("The copter is a twin-engine version of the familiar Huey

Nevertheless, the Texas district court denied EA's motion to dismiss (without writing an opinion).[205]

The approach of the Northern District of California in the more recent litigation between EA and Bell Helicopter and Textron Innovations also supports the narrow reading of *Rogers* under *E.S.S. Entertainment*. While no particular piece of military equipment used in the more modern *Battlefield 3* game may be as iconic as the Huey in the Vietnam War, Bell Helicopter and Textron Innovations referred to EA's desire to portray combat realistically, noting "EA's obsession with combat realism."[206] The district court did not consider whether EA's use of the helicopter trademarks was artistically relevant to the work, but the court said EA could not satisfy the second prong of the *Rogers* test.[207] The district court explained that in evaluating the second prong of the *Rogers* test, the Ninth Circuit considered whether players of *Grand Theft Auto: San Andreas* would be confused, but concluded confusion was unlikely based on the facts of the case.[208] Like the Ninth Circuit, the district court did not engage in any balancing. Instead, it provided reasons why consumers might think Textron was affiliated in some way with *Battlefield 3* and therefore denied EA's motion to dismiss.[209] After *Textron*, it was not clear what was left of the *Rogers* test under *E.S.S. Entertainment* beyond asking whether consumer confusion is likely and, as with the third prong of the nominative fair use analysis, answering this question based on whatever facts the court considers relevant.

The decision of the Southern District of Indiana on a motion for summary judgment in the *Dillinger* case stands in sharp contrast to *E.S.S. Entertainment* and *Textron*. After concluding that the use of Dillinger's name for the guns in *The Godfather* games was

---

helicopter. With the Sheriff's Department's recent purchase of two single-engine Hueys, three medium-lift firefighting helicopters are now permanently stationed in San Diego County.").

205. Order Denying Defendant's Motion to Dismiss, *supra* note 83, at 1–2.

206. Defendants' Answer and Counterclaims at 13, Elec. Arts Inc. v. Textron Inc., No. 3:12-0118 (N.D. Cal. May 7, 2012).

207. *See* Elec. Arts, Inc. v. Textron Inc., No. 3:12-0118, 2012 U.S. Dist. LEXIS 103914, at *8–9 (N.D. Cal. July 25, 2012).

208. *See id.* at *11–12.

209. *See id.* at *15–16.

artistically relevant, the court turned to whether EA did anything explicitly misleading.[210] The district court said that "some affirmative statement of the plaintiff's sponsorship or endorsement" would be required for EA to fail this prong of the *Rogers* test.[211] And while it considered consumer confusion unlikely based on the plaintiff's lack of evidence, the court made clear that if it had thought confusion was likely, the extent of the confusion would still be balanced against the First Amendment interests.[212]

The Ninth Circuit, in a more recent opinion issued after both *E.S.S. Entertainment* and *Textron*, seems to have reversed course and suggests that the application of the *Rogers* test in *Dillinger* is correct. Thus, at least in the Ninth Circuit, the original version of the *Rogers* test appears once again to be controlling.[213] In *Brown v. Electronic Arts, Inc.*,[214] Brown claimed that EA violated the Lanham Act when it used his likeness in the *Madden NFL* football games without his permission. Brown asserted a claim under section 43(a).[215] The Ninth Circuit affirmed the district court's dismissal of Brown's Lanham Act claim.[216] The Ninth Circuit decided that the use of Brown's likeness had some artistic relevance to the game since one of EA's expressive goals was realism.[217] In applying the second prong of *Rogers*, the court emphasized that EA did nothing

---

210. *See* Dillinger, LLC v. Elec. Arts Inc., No. 1:09-cv-1236-JMS-DKL, 2011 U.S. Dist. LEXIS 64006, at *11–18 (S.D. Ind. June 16, 2011).

211. *Id.* at *18.

212. *Id.* at *22 ("The Court cannot simply infer that the Dillinger name confuses the public, let alone that such confusion outweighs First Amendment concerns.").

213. For a detailed discussion of various applications of the *Rogers* test, see Ford, *supra* note 134. The article argues that courts have developed three versions of the *Rogers* test. *Rogers* I is the original version and provides strong First Amendment protection. *Rogers* II provides moderate First Amendment protection and results in unpredictable outcomes. *Rogers* III equates the second prong of the original test—whether a use is explicitly misleading—with an analysis of whether a use is likely to cause confusion. Thus, *Rogers* III provides weak First Amendment protection, if any at all. *See id.* at 315–16.

214. Brown v. Elec. Arts, Inc., 724 F.3d 1235 (9th Cir. 2013).

215. *Id.* at 1238–39.

216. *Id.* at 1239.

217. *Id.* at 1243 ("Given the acknowledged centrality of realism to EA's expressive goal, and the importance of including Brown's likeness to realistically recreate one of the teams in the game, it is obvious that Brown's likeness has at least some artistic relevance to EA's work.").

to *explicitly* mislead consumers about Brown's involvement with the game.[218] Brown did not provide sufficient evidence to show that EA had made an "explicit indication," "overt claim," or "explicit misstatement" that caused consumer confusion.[219]

Important in the Ninth Circuit's decision in *Brown* is its emphasis on the nature of statements that suffice to meet the second prong of *Rogers*. The court repeatedly emphasized that misleading statements or other evidence of a defendant's attempt to mislead must be explicit; any evidence of consumer confusion not tied to explicit misstatements is irrelevant.[220] The reasoning given by the *Brown* court clearly resembles the original test set forth by the Second Circuit in *Rogers*.

Two subsequent video game decisions suggest that the original version of *Brown* is now the controlling approach in the Ninth Circuit. Both cases were decided by the Northern District of California. In *Mil-Spec Monkey, Inc. v. Activision Blizzard, Inc.*,[221] the district court granted the defendant's motion for partial summary judgment on the plaintiff's Lanham Act and related state law claims.[222] Activision included a digital version of Mil-Spec Monkey's "angry monkey" morale patch in *Call of Duty: Ghosts*.[223] Mil-Spec Monkey asserted several claims that amounted to false association claims. After finding that the video game at issue was speech entitled to First Amendment protection, the district court proceeded to apply the *Rogers* test.[224] The court found the patch to be artistically relevant to the game.[225] It also relied on *Brown* and *Dillinger* and found that Activision did nothing to explicitly mislead consumers

---

218. *Id.* at 1245–47.

219. *Id.* (quoting Rogers v. Grimaldi, 875 F.2d 994, 1001 (2d Cir. 1989)).

220. *See id.*; *see also* Ford, *supra* note 134, at 320–21 (noting that the Ninth Circuit in *Brown* "italicized the word 'explicitly' for emphasis more than once" and "dismissed the relevance of any evidence of consumer confusion not tied to some explicit misstatement by Electronic Arts").

221. Mil-Spec Monkey, Inc. v. Activision Blizzard, Inc., 74 F. Supp. 3d 1134 (N.D. Cal. 2014).

222. *Id.* at 1144.

223. *Id.* at 1136–37.

224. *Id.* at 1140–42.

225. *Id.* at 1142–43.

with its use of the mark in the game.[226] Therefore, partial summary judgment in favor of Activision on the plaintiff's trademark claims was warranted.

In *VIRAG S.R.L. v. Sony Computer Entertainment America LLC,*[227] the plaintiffs asserted Lanham Act violations based on Sony's use of a trademark in two of its games, *Gran Turismo 5* and *Gran Turismo 6*. The mark appeared on a bridge located on a racetrack in the games. The district court dismissed the plaintiffs' Lanham Act claims.[228] The court applied the *Rogers* test, finding that the logo had artistic relevance and that there was no evidence that Sony used the mark to "explicitly" mislead, therefore coming to the same result as it did in *Mil-Spec Monkey.*[229] In an unpublished opinion, the Ninth Circuit affirmed the district court's decision.[230]

In sum, there is significant variation associated with the two doctrines most often thought to balance the competing interests of preventing consumer confusion and protecting free expression, but the trend in recent cases is to protect expressive uses of marks from Lanham Act claims. A recent decision of the Ninth Circuit involving a television program explicitly rejects any conflation of the likelihood of confusion test with the second prong of the *Rogers* test.[231] Thus, *Brown*'s approach to the *Rogers* test may now be firmly entrenched in the Ninth Circuit. How other circuits will respond to these issues is much less uncertain, but the Second Circuit may soon have an opportunity to weigh in. In the fall of 2017, AM General filed suit in the Southern District of New York against Activision Blizzard, claiming assorted Lanham Action violations due to Activision Blizzard's unlicensed use of AM General's iconic

---

226. *Id.* at 1143.

227. VIRAG S.R.L. v. Sony Computer Entm't Am. LLC, No. 3:15-cv-01729-LB, 2015 U.S. Dist. LEXIS 111211 (N.D. Cal. Aug. 21, 2015), *aff'd*, VIRAG, S.R.L. v. Sony Computer Entm't Am. LLC, 699 Fed. Appx. 667, 668 (9th Cir. 2017) (unpublished).

228. *Id.* at *40–41.

229. *Id.* at *27–39.

230. *See VIRAG*, 699 Fed Appx. at 668.

231. *See* Twentieth Century Fox Television v. Empire Distribution Inc., 875 F.3d 1192, 1199 (9th Cir. 2017).

Humvee marks in the *Call of Duty* video game series.[232] The case is analogous to the *Textron* cases, and the 2012 *Textron* decision is a very favorable (nonbinding) authority for AM General, but the bulk of the Ninth Circuit case law weighs in favor of Activision Blizzard. This case may be the one in which the Second Circuit clarifies how it will apply the *Rogers* test to video games and to expressive works generally. If the two leading courts of appeals for entertainment-related litigation embrace the strong form of First Amendment protection represented by the Ninth Circuit's *Brown* decision, it will go a long way towards enhancing the creative freedom of the video game industry.

IV. Secondary Liability

As compared to the previous issues, questions about secondary liability may involve greater novelty in the application of trademark law to video games. Game producers provide players with pen and paper, so to speak, but unlike real-world pen and paper producers, game publishers typically have the ability to supervise and regulate players' artistic activities. In *Marvel Enterprises, Inc. v. NCsoft Corp.*,[233] Marvel claimed the defendants were liable both for vicarious and contributory infringement because *City of Heroes'* players were creating characters that allegedly infringed Marvel's registered and common law trademarks.[234] The district court dismissed all of the claims premised on secondary liability, finding that Marvel failed to allege direct infringement on the part of the players.[235] More specifically, the district court held that Marvel failed to allege that the players were using Marvel's marks "in commerce in connection with any sale or advertising of goods and services."[236] Without acts of direct infringement, there can be no

---

232. *See* Complaint, AM Gen. LLC v. Activision Blizzard, Inc., No. 2:17-08644 (S.D.N.Y. Nov. 7, 2017).
233. Marvel Enters., Inc. v. NCsoft Corp., No. 04-9253, 2005 U.S. Dist. LEXIS 8448 (C.D. Cal. Mar. 9, 2005).
234. *Id.* at *12–18.
235. *Id.* at *19–20.
236. *Id.* at *13.

secondary liability.[237] Additionally, it would seem there was little basis for a claim of vicarious liability, as the players and the defendant did not have a partnership, real or apparent.[238] The interesting question must therefore center on contributory infringement. But unlike the district court in the *Ultimate Creations* case, the district court in *Marvel* dismissed the infringement claims.[239] One difference between the two cases is that Ultimate Creations did not claim that THQ was contributorily liable for the actions of the players. Other courts might not dismiss a claim of contributory infringement when players create unlicensed characters, but Ultimate Creations did not even raise the question.

Although the implications of customization options would seem to raise issues primarily of secondary liability, Ultimate Creations instead claimed THQ was *directly* liable because it provided the tools that facilitated the creation of unlicensed characters.[240] Ultimate Creations claimed the mere fact that players knew they could create a wrestler similar to the Ultimate Warrior was evidence of actual confusion.[241] Of course, whether it was evidence of actual confusion depended on whether players thought THQ obtained permission to provide these tools. Knowledge that an Ultimate Warrior character can be created in various THQ games alone is not evidence of confusion. Ultimate Creations argued that "the purpose of trademark law is to prevent the producers from free riding on their rivals mark. . . ."[242] Free riding, however, may or may not involve confusion.[243] Providing protection beyond

---

237. *See id.* at *11–14.

238. *Id.*

239. *Id.* at *19–20.

240. *See* Ultimate Creations, Inc. v. THQ Inc., No. CV-05-1134-PHX-SMM, 2008 U.S. Dist. LEXIS 8224, at *5 (D. Ariz. Jan. 24, 2008).

241. Response in Opposition to Defendant THQ's Motion for Summary Judgment or in the Alternative Partial Summary Judgment at 7–8, Ultimate Creations, Inc. v. THQ, Inc., 2008 U.S. Dist. LEXIS 8224 (D. Ariz. May 9, 2007) (No. 05-1134), 2007 U.S. Dist. Ct. Motions LEXIS 62526, at *13–14.

242. *Id.* at *15 (citing New Kids on the Block v. News Am. Publ'g, Inc., 971 F.2d 302, 305 (9th Cir. 1992)).

243. *See* WCVB-TV v. Boston Athletic Ass'n, 926 F.2d 42, 45 (1st Cir. 1991) (opinion by Breyer, C.J.) ("As a general matter, the law *sometimes* protects investors from the 'free riding' of others; and *sometimes* it does not. . . . Just how, when and where the law should protect investments in 'intangible' benefits

preventing a likelihood of confusion (or dilution) expands the boundaries of trademark protection beyond its traditional scope, but some judicial decisions do suggest that at least some free riding is actionable under the Lanham Act, even without a showing of confusion.[244]

Customization in video games and virtual worlds is a powerful feature with the potential to enhance their expressive and entertainment value. The potential for liability, however, remains ill defined. Typical features available in many online games, such as the ability of players to sell in-game assets, could change the result of a case like *Marvel* because the use of the marks would more clearly constitute a use in commerce. Maybe more so than the other trademark issues discussed in this chapter, issues of controlling player customization options, especially through doctrines of secondary liability, raise questions whose real-world analogues are not very analogous.

---

or goods is a matter that legislators typically debate, embodying the results in specific statutes, or that common law courts, carefully weighing relevant competing interests, gradually work out over time. The trademark statute does not give the appellants any 'property right' in their mark *except* 'the right to prevent confusion.'").

244. Boston Athletic Ass'n v. Sullivan, 867 F.2d 22, 33 (1st Cir. 1989) ("Defendants' shirts are clearly designed to take advantage of the Boston Marathon and to benefit from the good will associated with its promotion by plaintiffs. Defendants thus obtain a 'free ride' at plaintiffs' expense. In the oft quoted words of the Supreme Court in *International News Service v. Associated Press*, . . . because the Boston Marathon has achieved its renown as a result of BAA's 'expenditure of labor, skill, and money,' such unlicensed use of BAA's mark would permit defendants to 'reap where [they have] not sown.' Like Rosie Ruiz, a notorious imposter in the 1980 Boston Marathon, defendants would be given a medal without having run the course. Under these facts, the plaintiffs have to prove, of course, that the defendants are trading on plaintiffs' mark and good will. We do not think, however, that plaintiffs also have to prove that members of the public will actually conclude that defendants' product was *officially* sponsored by the Marathon's sponsor (whoever that sponsor may be).") (citations omitted) (quoting Int'l News Serv. v. Associated Press, 248 U.S. 215, 239 (1918)). *But see WCVB-TV*, 926 F.2d at 45 ("[T]he *Sullivan* opinion, taken as a whole, makes clear that the court, in using the language appellants cite, referring to a 'free ride,' and taking 'advantage' of another's good will, did not intend to depart from ordinary principles of federal trademark law that make a finding of a 'likelihood of confusion' essential to a conclusion of 'violation.'").

V. Unfair Competition: Trademark Infringement and Misappropriation

Unfair competition refers to a broad range of unlawful activities, of which trademark infringement is the most prominent example.[245] Misappropriation is another example.[246] Misappropriation is often defined with reference to the Supreme Court's decision in *International News Service v. Associated Press*.[247] In that case, the Associated Press (AP) claimed the International News Service (INS), a rival wire service, was "pirating" news from the AP.[248] INS copied news from AP sources on the East Coast and then wired these news items to the West Coast for use in INS newspapers.[249] By doing so, INS was sometimes able to scoop the AP newspapers on the West Coast.[250] In affirming an injunction against INS, the Court recognized, as a matter of federal common law, a property right in "hot news," a right independent of any copyright protection.[251]

Unfortunately, the Supreme Court described the misappropriation doctrine with an "abstract pronouncement of a grand principle [with] no obvious boundaries."[252] Interpreted broadly, the misappropriation doctrine poses at least two risks. First, the doctrine's vagueness adds to the difficulties of predicting what acts of copying may result in litigation and liability. Second, a broad approach

---

245. For a list of acts falling under the general heading of unfair competition, see 1 J. Thomas McCarthy, McCarthy on Trademarks and Unfair Competition § 1:10 (4th ed. 2017). The longest chapter in the *Restatement (Third) of Unfair Competition* is devoted to trademarks. *See* Restatement (Third) of Unfair Competition §§ 9–35 (1995).

246. *See* Restatement (Third) of Unfair Competition § 38 & cmt. a (1995) ("This Section states the general rule governing the protection of [information and other intangible] trade values.").

247. Int'l News Serv. v. Associated Press, 248 U.S. 215 (1918). The background of the case is covered in Douglas G. Baird, *The Story of* INS v. AP: *Property, Natural Monopoly, and the Uneasy Legacy of a Concocted Controversy, in* Intellectual Property Stories 9 (Jane C. Ginsburg & Rochelle Cooper Dreyfuss eds., 2006).

248. *Int'l News Serv.*, 248 U.S. at 231.

249. Baird, *supra* note 247, at 9.

250. *Id.*

251. *See Int'l News Serv.*, 248 U.S. at 240–41.

252. Baird, *supra* note 247, at 32.

to misappropriation conflicts with federal copyright and patent law. It increases the scope of what may *not* be copied above and beyond the balance struck by federal intellectual property laws.[253] While *International News Service* is no longer binding as federal common law—the Supreme Court later held there is no such thing as "federal general common law"[254]—lower courts have relied on *International News Service* in applying state unfair competition laws. The Second and Seventh Circuits have limited misappropriation claims, however, to "hot news" situations directly analogous to *International News Service* itself, meaning situations where one party collects information of a highly time-sensitive nature and another party, in competition with the first, copies the information in such a way as to undermine the incentives to collect the information in the first place.[255]

Although the case had nothing to do with "hot news," the district court in *Ultimate Creations* relied on the misappropriation doctrine in denying THQ's motion for summary judgment.[256] In so doing, the district court blurred the line between trademark infringement and the misappropriation doctrine.[257] Ultimate Creations asserted that THQ committed trademark infringement and unfair competition under both the Lanham Act and the common

---

253. *See, e.g.*, Summit Mach. Tool Mfg. Corp. v. Victor CNC Sys., Inc., 7 F.3d 1434, 1441–42 (9th Cir. 1993).

254. Erie R.R. v. Tompkins, 304 U.S. 64, 78 (1938); *see* Confold Pac., Inc. v. Polaris Indus., Inc., 433 F.3d 952, 960 (7th Cir. 2006) (noting *International News Service* is "no longer authoritative because it was based on the federal courts' subsequently abandoned authority to formulate common law principles in suits arising under state law though litigated in federal court").

255. *See Confold*, 433 F.3d at 960; Nat'l Basketball Ass'n v. Motorola, Inc., 105 F.3d 841, 852 (2d Cir. 1997). The First Circuit has suggested it agrees with the Second Circuit. *See* EKCO Group, Inc. v. Travelers Indem. Co. of Ill., 273 F.3d 409, 412 n.1 (1st Cir. 2001). The *Restatement (Third) of Unfair Competition* similarly limits the reach of *International News Service*. *See* RESTATEMENT (THIRD) OF UNFAIR COMPETITION § 38 cmt. c (1995).

256. *See* Ultimate Creations, Inc. v. THQ, Inc., No. CV-05-1134-PHX-SMM, 2008 U.S. Dist. LEXIS 8224, at *17–18 (D. Ariz. Jan. 24, 2008).

257. *See generally* DAVID L. LANGE & H. JEFFERSON POWELL, NO LAW: INTELLECTUAL PROPERTY IN THE IMAGE OF AN ABSOLUTE FIRST AMENDMENT 28–33, 155 (2009) (discussing how the misappropriation doctrine in *International News Service* and trademark infringement have come to overlap through a concern that one party will "reap where it has not sown").

law.[258] In making out its common law unfair competition claim, Ultimate Creations relied on the elements of a *misappropriation* claim as summarized in *McCarthy on Trademarks and Unfair Competition*:

(1) Plaintiff made a substantial investment of time, effort and money into creating the thing misappropriated such that the court can characterize that "thing" as a kind of property right.
(2) Defendant appropriated the "thing" at little or no cost, such that the court can characterize defendant's actions as "reaping where it has not sown."
(3) Defendant has injured plaintiff by the misappropriation.[259]

Creating a likelihood of confusion is not among the elements.

The district court's analysis of the misappropriation doctrine is difficult to follow. In a section of the court's opinion labeled "Common Law Trademark Infringement," the court said, "Unfair competition is determined with reference to the character and circumstance of the business."[260] At this point, the court cited *International News Service* and added:

[C]ourts are given wide discretion in deciding whether the conduct is unfair due to the flexible nature of the [unfair competition] tort. . . . [T]he tort of unfair competition may involve several equitable considerations. For example, a defendant may not misappropriate something from the plaintiff for the purpose of using it for defendant's own profit and to the disadvantage of the plaintiff.[261]

---

258. Response in Opposition to Defendant THQ's Motion for Summary Judgment or in the Alternative Partial Summary Judgment, *supra* note 241, at *30–32 ("THQ Has Infringed UCI's Common Law Trademarks and Has Committed Common Law Unfair Competition").

259. 2 McCarthy, *supra* note 9, § 10:49 (citation omitted); *see* Response in Opposition to Defendant THQ's Motion for Summary Judgment or in the Alternative Partial Summary Judgment, *supra* note 241, at *32 (listing elements).

260. *Ultimate Creations*, 2008 U.S. Dist. LEXIS 8224, at *17–18.

261. *Id.*; *cf.* Balt. Bedding Corp. v. Moses, 34 A.2d 338, 342 (Md. 1943) ("What constitutes unfair competition in a given case is governed by its own particular facts and circumstances. Each case is a law unto itself, subject, only, to the general principle that all dealings must be done on the basis of common honesty

Despite the reference to "wide discretion," the court then said, without explanation, that Ultimate Creations "must demonstrate the existence of customer confusion."[262] Why was not clear. The court's discussion at least suggests that misappropriation provides a viable alternative to demonstrating a likelihood of confusion.

A broad reading of *International News Service* conflicts with the prevailing view among the courts. The Ninth Circuit, which binds the district court in the *Ultimate Creations* case, has restricted the scope of the misappropriation doctrine by requiring an extra element beyond those listed by McCarthy. According to the Ninth Circuit, this extra element could be a likelihood of confusion,[263] which then makes the misappropriation claim little different from a trademark infringement claim. The district court's decision potentially departed from this approach. Given the amorphous nature of the misappropriation doctrine, departing from the prevailing view of *International News Service* makes it more difficult for parties to predict what actions will expose them to liability—or at least to prolonged litigation.

Conclusion

Commercial video games have changed radically since the days of *Pong*, but many of the trademark problems remain the same. While issues of secondary liability may be somewhat novel, issues involving the use of marks on physical goods, including arcade cabinets and software packages, present similar questions as before. Even the use of marks within expressive works, including video games and virtual worlds, is hardly novel. Nevertheless, advertising and marketing are becoming more and more integrated within entertainment generally. A consequence of this integration could be changed consumer expectations and changes in the

---

and fairness, without taint of fraud or deception. Wherever, in any case, these elements of fair trade are found to be lacking equity will grant protection against the offending party.").

262. *Ultimate Creations*, 2008 U.S. Dist. LEXIS 8224, at *18.

263. Summit Mach. Tool Mfg. Corp. v. Victor CNC Sys., Inc., 7 F.3d 1434, 1439–42 (9th Cir. 1993).

risk of consumer confusion when marks are integrated into video games and virtual worlds. At the same time, efforts to prevent consumer confusion must be balanced with reasonable principles of fair use and with First Amendment interests in free expression. Unfortunately, the nature of this balance remains uncertain in the courts, and will likely remain uncertain until the U.S. Supreme Court addresses this issue. In the meantime, the decisions in the courts of the Ninth Circuit, the most popular circuit for this type of litigation, are now more clearly on the side of free expression. And should the *AM General* case reach the Second Circuit, it will be a key case for industry professionals to monitor.

Implications of Video Games and Immersive Entertainment and the Law of Trade Secrets

5

Thomas J. Mihill[1]
Steven M. Kushner
Adam C. Losey

Takeaways

- *Trade secrets are controlled by both federal and state law; specific applications may vary by jurisdiction.*
- *Only "secrets" that provide an economic benefit as a result of the secrecy are protected.*
- *Reasonable efforts under the circumstances are required to protect the secrecy of the information, but game developers can protect information in their source code as long as only the object code is publicly distributed.*
- *Trade secret protection for software can coexist with copyright registration of the software.*

---

1. Thomas J. (T.J.) Mihill is a partner with Owen, Gleaton, Egan, Jones & Sweeney, LLP. Steven M. Kushner is a partner of the firm Fellows LaBriola LLP. Adam C. Losey is a partner of the firm Losey PLLC. For complete author biographies, see the Contributors section of this book.

Introduction

Trade secret protection applies to the information that a company keeps confidential and from which it derives an economic advantage because of such confidentiality. Most other forms of intellectual property (IP) protection, such as copyrights, patents, and trademarks, are governed exclusively or largely by federal law. By contrast, trade secret law derives from both state and federal law.

The basic elements of trade secret protection were laid down in the middle of the 19th century, and have not changed substantially since then.[2] Further, there is no reason to believe that the nature of trade secret law will change appreciably in the foreseeable future, because the law in its current form is adequate to handle most, if not all, new developments in business and technology.

I. Trade Secrets Generally

A. What Is a Trade Secret and What Can Be Protected?

Trade secret law was formerly controlled entirely by state law; this changed with the Defend Trade Secrets Act of 2016 (DTSA), 18 U.S.C. § 1836 *et seq*. The DTSA allows an owner of a trade secret to sue in federal court where trade secrets have been misappropriated. While the DTSA provides federal trade secret protections, it does not preempt state law trade secret protections. The DTSA provides a federally uniform definition of a trade secret standard for misappropriation. It further allows nationwide service of process and execution of judgments.

Under the DTSA:

[T]he term "trade secret" means all forms and types of financial, business, scientific, technical, economic, or engineering information, including patterns, plans, compilations, program devices, formulas, designs, prototypes, methods, techniques, processes, procedures, programs,

---

2. RESTATEMENT (THIRD) OF UNFAIR COMPETITION, § 39 cmt. (a) (1995).

or codes, whether tangible or intangible, and whether or how stored, compiled, or memorialized physically, electronically, graphically, photographically, or in writing if— (A) the owner thereof has taken reasonable measures to keep such information secret; and (B) the information derives independent economic value, actual or potential, from not being generally known to, and not being readily ascertainable through proper means by, another person who can obtain economic value from the disclosure or use of the information.[3]

This federal definition of a trade secret is largely consistent with the laws of the states. Laws of the individual states are generally based on three common sources: the Uniform Trade Secrets Act (UTSA), the *Restatement of Unfair Competition*, and the *Restatement of Torts*. Given the multijurisdictional reach of the Internet, it remains unclear which jurisdiction's laws would govern much of new media, including video games and virtual worlds.[4] A practitioner therefore would be wise to be familiar with all three resources.

1. The UTSA

In the United States, the UTSA is the most common source of trade secret law, with 47 states plus the District of Columbia adopting the act.[5] States have not adopted the UTSA uniformly, however. Some states have adopted the 1979 version of the act; some have adopted the 1985 version; and some have modified the language of the act in their statutes. It is therefore critical to consult the laws of whichever jurisdiction might apply to your video game or virtual

---

3. 18 U.S.C. § 1839(3) (2016).

4. The end-user license agreement or the terms of service may specify a choice of law and venue, in an attempt to avoid jurisdictional issues. Whether such a choice of law will be respected probably depends on the issue in question. For example, some states' courts have held that the law of an individual's residence overrides any choice-of-law clause relating to matters such as the enforceability of a covenant not to compete. *See, e.g.*, United Rentals, Inc. v. Pruett, 296 F. Supp. 2d 220 (D. Conn. 2003).

5. Graham M. Liccardi, Comment, *The Computer Fraud and Abuse Act: A Vehicle for Litigating Trade Secrets in Federal Court*, 8 J. Marshall Rev. Intell. Prop. L. 155, 158 (2008). Only New York, New Jersey, and Massachusetts have not passed any version of the UTSA.

worlds issue.[6] The UTSA defines a "trade secret" as information that: (1) derives actual or potential economic value from not being generally known to, and not being readily ascertainable by proper means to other persons who can obtain economic value from its disclosure or use, and (2) is the subject of efforts that are reasonable under the circumstances to maintain its secrecy.[7]

Under the UTSA, "proper means" for ascertaining information include discovery by independent invention, reverse engineering, observing an item in public use or on public display (e.g., in a video game), and reviewing published literature.[8] Of course, it is also proper to obtain the information by license from the owner of the trade secret.[9]

2. Restatement (Third) of Unfair Competition

The *Restatement (Third) of Unfair Competition* is intended to apply to actions under the UTSA as well as common law and replaces the material in section 757 of the *Restatement of Torts*, discussed in the next section.[10] The *Restatement (Third) of Unfair Competition* states that "[a] trade secret is any information that can be used in the operation of a business or other enterprise and that is sufficiently valuable and secret to afford an actual or potential economic advantage over others."[11] Like the UTSA, the information must be valuable enough, and secret enough, to provide a competitive economic advantage. In software-based environments like video games and virtual worlds, the software source code and commentary would typically meet this standard.

---

6. Determining which jurisdiction may apply is, in itself, a challenge in the context of virtual worlds.

7. UTSA § 1(4) (1985).

8. UTSA § 1 cmt.; *see also* Nucar Consulting, Inc. v. Doyle, No. Civ.A 19756-NC, 2005 WL 820706, at *6 (Del. Ch. Apr. 5, 2005); Miles Inc. v. Cookson Am., Inc., No. Civ. A. 12,310, 1994 WL 676761, at *12 (Del. Ch. Nov. 15, 1994) (citing UTSA § 1 cmt. (1979)).

9. UTSA § 1 cmt. (1985); *see also Nucar Consulting, Inc.*, 2005 WL 820706, at *6; *Miles Inc.*, 1994 WL 676761, at *12 (citing UTSA § 1 cmt. (1979)).

10. RESTATEMENT (THIRD) OF UNFAIR COMPETITION § 39 cmt. (b) (1995).

11. *Id.* § 39.

3. Restatement of Torts

Later editions of the *Restatement of Torts* do not include trade secrets or the misappropriation thereof. Therefore, courts still use the original *Restatement of Torts* to interpret and apply state trade secret laws. Under the *Restatement of Torts*:

> A trade secret may consist of any formula, pattern, device, or compilation of information which is used in one's business. . . . It may be a formula for a chemical compound, a process of manufacturing, treating or preserving materials, a pattern for a machine or other device, or a list of customers.[12]

While the *Restatement of Torts* requires information to be in "continuous use in the operation of the business" to qualify as a trade secret,[13] under the *Restatement (Third) of Unfair Competition* or the UTSA there is no need for the trade secret to be "continuously used in one's business."[14]

The *Restatement of Torts* further lists six factors to assist in determining if information is a trade secret:

> (1) the extent to which the information is known outside [the] business; (2) the extent to which it is known by employees and others involved in [the] business; (3) the extent of the measures taken . . . to guard the secrecy of the information; (4) the value of the information to [the business] and to [its] competitors; (5) the amount of effort or money expended . . . in developing the information; [and] (6) the ease or difficulty with which the information could be properly acquired or duplicated by others.[15]

Again, as with the other two sources of trade secret law, the *Restatement of Torts* sets forth the basic requirements that the information be valuable, not generally known, and subject to secrecy efforts. Further, factor six relates to the difficulty in

---

12. RESTATEMENT OF TORTS § 757 cmt. b (1939).
13. *Id.*
14. RESTATEMENT (THIRD) OF UNFAIR COMPETITION § 39; UTSA § 1 cmt. (1985).
15. RESTATEMENT OF TORTS § 757 cmt. b (1939).

acquiring or duplicating the materials, a requirement echoed in the UTSA, which states that the information "not [be] readily ascertainable by proper means by, other persons. . . ."[16] In the case of video games and virtual worlds, this "not readily ascertainable" standard would typically include source code and might also include customer data, future product plans, and the like.

B. The Competitive Advantage Requirement

Information is only considered a trade secret if it has some sort of economic value, or confers some economic advantage over competitors by being secret. In juridical proceedings, the holder of the information must prove this. "A trade secret must be of sufficient value in the operation of a business or other enterprise to provide an actual or potential economic advantage over others who do not possess the information. The advantage, however, need not be great."[17]

The real question for application of trade secret laws to virtual worlds, however, is to whom the secret gives an advantage. Certain virtual worlds will allow users to develop trade secrets that will be to their economic advantage. The question of whether the economic advantage must be to the user in the real world or to the avatar in the virtual world or to both has not yet been addressed. The answer will likely dictate the extent to which users may benefit from trade secret laws.

While a novel product or business practice would likely convey a competitive advantage, novelty is not itself a requirement for trade secret protection. Several courts have held that the information must be novel to the extent that it is not a matter of public knowledge, but novelty of the type required for patent protection[18] is not required for trade secret protection.[19]

---

16. *Id.*; UTSA § 1(4)(i).

17. RESTATEMENT (THIRD) OF UNFAIR COMPETITION § 39 cmt. e (1995).

18. The novelty requirement in patent law is discussed in more detail in Chapter 3.

19. Kewanee Oil Co. v. Bicron Corp., 416 U.S. 470, 476 (1974) ("some novelty will be required if merely because that which does not possess novelty is usually known; secrecy, in the context of trade secrets, thus implies at least minimal

Similarly, the investment, both in terms of money and effort, made by the holder of a trade secret in developing and protecting the secret can be evidence of its competitive value.[20] Generally, the more time and effort that is exerted in developing the information, the more likely a court is to find that the information is a trade secret. As the court noted in *Metalurgical Industries, Inc. v. Fourtek, Inc.*:[21]

> It seems only fair that one should be able to keep and enjoy the fruits of his labor. If a businessman has worked hard, has used his imagination, and has taken bold steps to gain an advantage over his competitors, he should be able to profit from his efforts. Because a commercial advantage can vanish once the competition learns of it, the law should protect the businessman's efforts to keep his achievements secret.[22]

The basic test for competitive advantage is whether the owner can use some technique or method to enhance his business opportunities, as compared with his competitors. The value of information claimed as a trade secret may be established by direct evidence relating to the content of the secret and its impact on business operations, or circumstantial evidence, including the amount of resources invested by the plaintiff in the production of the information, the precautions taken by the plaintiff to protect the secrecy of the information, and the willingness of others to pay for access to the information.[23]

---

novelty"); Softel, Inc. v. Dragon Med. & Sci. Commc'n, Inc., 118 F.3d 955, 968 (2d Cir. 1997) ("novelty—at least as that term is used in patent law—is not required in a trade secret"); SI Handling Sys., Inc. v. Heisley, 753 F.2d 1244, 1255 (3d Cir. 1985); Rice Researchers, Inc. v. Hiter, 512 So. 2d 1259, 1268 (Miss. 1987).

20. *See* Cargill, Inc. v. Sears Petroleum & Transp. Corp., 388 F. Supp. 2d 37 (N.D.N.Y. 2005); Winston Research Corp. v. Minn. Mining & Mfg. Co., 350 F.2d 134 (9th Cir. 1965); Valco Cincinnati, Inc. v. N & D Machining Serv., Inc., 492 N.E.2d 814 (Ohio 1986); Tabs Ass'n, Inc. v. Brohawn, 475 A.2d 1203 (Md. Ct. Spec. App. 1984).

21. Metalurgical Indus., Inc. v. Fourtek, 790 F.2d 1195 (5th Cir. 1986).

22. *Id.* at 1201.

23. Restatement (Third) of Unfair Competition § 39 cmt. e (1995).

C. *The Secrecy Requirement*

As the moniker suggests, a trade secret must be a secret[24]—it must not be generally known or ascertainable without resorting to wrongful means.[25] Independent invention, reverse engineering, or observing an item in public use or on public display are not "wrongful means."[26]

While secrecy is required for trade secret protection, absolute secrecy is not.[27] The test for secrecy focuses as much on the efforts made to keep the information secret as on the actual results. If reasonable efforts under the circumstances are made to keep the information, process, or method a secret, then some necessary disclosure will not be viewed as forfeiting the required secrecy.[28] What exactly constitutes "reasonable efforts" to protect the secrecy will of course be very fact-specific to each company and each trade secret, but some examples of potentially reasonable methods to maintain secrecy are requiring confidentiality or nondisclosure agreements, limiting access by employees or others to those with a "need to know," keeping the secret in a locked location or under password protection, and other means to limit access or disclosure. Even with reasonable efforts, accidental disclosure may occur; however, inadvertent or accidental disclosure of a trade secret also will not necessarily cause the information to cease being a trade secret. For example, if documents containing trade secrets accidentally were placed in the trash despite

---

24. Information is not a trade secret if it is not a secret. It is not a secret if it is generally known within the industry; if it is published in trade journals, reference books, or similar materials; or if it is readily copyable from products on the market. UTSA § 1 cmt. (1985); RESTATEMENT (THIRD) OF UNFAIR COMPETITION § 39 cmt. f (1995).

25. UTSA § 1(4); RESTATEMENT (THIRD) OF UNFAIR COMPETITION § 39 cmt. f (1995). Wrongful means would include the theft or misappropriation of the trade secret, or use of the secret in violation of a license or nondisclosure agreement (NDA). UTSA § 1(1); RESTATEMENT (THIRD) OF UNFAIR COMPETITION § 43 (1995).

26. UTSA § 1 cmt.; *see also* Nucar Consulting, Inc. v. Doyle, No. Civ.A 19756-NC, 2005 WL 820706, at *6 (Del. Ch. Apr. 5, 2005); Miles Inc. v. Cookson Am., Inc., No. Civ. A. 12,310, 1994 WL 676761, at *12 (Del. Ch. Nov. 15, 1994) (citing UTSA § 1 cmt. (1979)).

27. RESTATEMENT (THIRD) OF UNFAIR COMPETITION § 39 cmt. f (1995).

28. *See* 205 Corp. v. Brandow, 517 N.W.2d 548, 551 (Iowa 1994) (holding the fact that all kitchen employees had to know crust recipe in order to prepare it daily did not destroy trade secret status).

company procedures designed to prevent such disclosure, courts have held the information can retain its trade secret status.[29]

This gives rise to one of the biggest issues for trade secret protection in virtual worlds. In most, if not all, common virtual worlds, whatever you type in the chat or say over a microphone is broadcast to all avatars within a certain distance of your avatar.[30] Because of this, "confidentiality of communication is largely illusory in many virtual worlds."[31]

> Although information could theoretically be communicated through a virtual world using third-party encryption software with a reasonable assurance that it would only be available to the sender and recipient, it rarely is. Nearly all communication in current virtual worlds is vulnerable to eavesdropping from other users and is stored on the servers of the provider for an indefinite period (theoretically available to any employee of the provider with sufficient security rights and interest). Moreover, it is protected only by a generic privacy policy, not a specific nondisclosure agreement.[32]

Some worlds do offer a way to "whisper," or communicate only with one other person, but this option would not solve the concerns of the chat records being kept and monitored. Further, it is easy to forget to select the whisper option, which may need to be selected repeatedly for each chat message in some worlds. Forgetting to set this option results in the normal broadcast of the message to all within "listening" range. Finally, many games only allow you to converse generally, or to converse with one person at a time—technological options to talk privately among a small group

---

29. *See* B.C. Ziegler & Co. v. Ehren, 414 N.W.2d 48 (Wis. Ct. App. 1987); Drill Parts & Serv. Co. v. Joy Mfg. Co., 439 So. 2d 43 (Ala. 1983). There may also be a distinction between disclosure to competitors and disclosure to customers— while disclosing a secret to customers does not erode a supplier's competitive advantage, disclosure to a competitor obviously does. UTSA § 1 cmt (1985); RESTATEMENT (THIRD) OF UNFAIR COMPETITION § 39 cmt. f (1995).

30. BENJAMIN TYSON DURANSKE, VIRTUAL LAW: NAVIGATING THE LEGAL LANDSCAPE OF VIRTUAL WORLDS 9 (2008).

31. *Id.* at 9.

32. *Id.* at 158.

are rare. There is a real possibility of inadvertent "public" disclosure if trade secrets are being discussed amongst avatars. Whether that inadvertent or accidental disclosure violates trade secrets will be fact-specific and vary according to the applicable laws.

Typically, any general disclosure destroys the required secrecy, even if the disclosure was wrongful: "[o]nce trade secrets have been exposed to the public, they cannot later be recalled."[33] In *Religious Technology Center v. Netcom On-Line Communication Services, Inc.*,[34] the Northern District of California dealt with an early case of public disclosure of wrongfully obtained information over the Internet.[35]

The plaintiff's trade secrets were posted in public Usenet groups, where they could have been viewed by anyone, including the plaintiff's competitors.[36] The court expressed concern over the fact "that any Internet user, including those using 'anonymous remailers' to protect their identity, can destroy valuable intellectual property rights by posting them over the Internet," and further noted that "[t]he anonymous (or judgment proof) defendant can permanently destroy valuable trade secrets, leaving no one to hold liable for the misappropriation."[37] Nonetheless, "[w]hile the court [was] persuaded by the . . . evidence that those who made the original [Internet] postings likely gained the information through improper means . . . this does not negate the finding that, once posted, the works lost their secrecy."[38]

A more recent case reiterates this point. In *Xfire, Inc. v. IGN Entertainment, Inc.*, a judge refused to grant a temporary restraining order to a plaintiff seeking to stop a competitor from accessing its "buddy list" because it could not show that the list was a secret.[39] One of the main issues before the court was the viability of Xfire's

33. Religious Tech. Ctr. v. Netcom On-Line Commc'n Servs., Inc., 923 F. Supp. 1231, 1254 (N.D. Cal. 1995).
34. *Religious Tech. Ctr.*, 923 F. Supp. 1231.
35. *Id.* at 1238.
36. *Id.* at 1239.
37. *Id.* at 1256.
38. *Id.*
39. Xfire, Inc. v. IGN Entm't, Inc., No. C 06-6475 SI, 2006 WL 2990203 (N.D. Cal. Oct. 19, 2006).

trade secret. Xfire provided a software tool that allowed users to keep track of where and when other gamers were online.[40] IGN created a competing product called "Comrade" that allowed users to create a "buddy list" of gamers to see who was playing online.[41]

Comrade users created the buddy list by using the "buddy sync tool," which extracted a user's buddy list information from the Xfire service and copied some portions into Comrade.[42] Xfire contended this misappropriated its trade secrets, infringed its copyrights, and violated the Electronic Communications Privacy Act.[43]

The court noted that there were issues as to whether Xfire had any trade secret protection over the buddy list information, as there was conflicting evidence as to whether the information was kept secret.[44] Xfire contended that IGN's Comrade product copied private information from Xfire's website, while IGN stated that Comrade only accessed information publicly available on Xfire's website.[45] The court noted that there were "serious questions as to whether . . . the buddy lists are 'generally known [to] the public' by virtue of being accessible on Xfire's website, as well as whether plaintiff has taken steps to maintain secrecy of those lists."[46]

It is critical, therefore, that the trade secret remain secret, and equally critical that the person claiming trade secret protection show that he or she took reasonable steps to protect the secrecy. In *Religious Technology Center v. Netcom On-Line Communication Services, Inc.*, the court noted that there were

> elaborate means taken to ensure the confidentiality . . . including use of locked cabinets, safes, logging and identification of the materials, availability of the materials at only a handful of sites worldwide, electronic sensors attached to documents, locked briefcases for transporting works, alarms, photo identifications, security personnel, and

---

40. *Id.* at *1.
41. *Id.*
42. *Id.*
43. *Id.*
44. *Id.* at *2.
45. *Id.* at *1 n.1.
46. *Id.* at *2.

confidentiality agreements for all of those given access to the materials.[47]

The court found these to be sufficiently reasonable under the circumstances.[48] By contrast, a company that sought to stop the publication of its alleged trade secrets but had no written or oral confidentiality agreements, did not mark documents confidential, engaged in widespread dissemination of the materials, had no internal or external controls, had no system of document retrieval, and gave no warnings to third parties of the confidential nature of its materials was found not to be taking any reasonable steps to protect its alleged trade secret.[49]

A common element in all these analyses is the confidentiality or nondisclosure agreement, which is a basic precaution for protecting secrecy. While confidentiality agreements with employees are not strictly necessary, courts will consider whether such agreements are in place, as these agreements evidence efforts to maintain secrecy.[50] When a trade secret is shared with a customer or supplier, however, confidentiality agreements are generally necessary, as there is otherwise no duty requiring secrecy.[51]

D. Trade Secret Information Protected by Other IP Laws

Trade secret protection varies from other forms of IP protection, but in some cases can coexist with other protections for the same information. Trade secret statutes offer protection that is in some

---

47. Religious Tech. Ctr. v. Netcom On-Line Commc'n Servs., Inc., 923 F. Supp. 1231, 1254 (N.D. Cal. 1995).

48. *Id.*

49. Hoffman-LaRoche, Inc. v. Yoder, 950 F. Supp. 1348, 1362–64 (S.D. Ohio 1997).

50. *See* Water Servs., Inc. v. Tesco Chems., Inc., 410 F.2d 163 (5th Cir. 1969) (finding confidentiality agreement with employees strong evidence of trade secret status); Sanford v. RDA Consultants, Ltd., 535 S.E.2d 321 (Ga. Ct. App. 2000) (finding trade secret protection whether or not confidentiality agreement was valid); Lee v. Cercoa, Inc., 433 So. 2d 1 (Fla. Dist. Ct. App. 1983) (finding trade secret protection even though employee did not sign a confidentiality agreement).

51. "FrieNDAs," or NDAs executed by informal means (e.g., verbal agreements), are unlikely to carry much weight or authority in the event of a legal dispute. Trusting another is not criminal, but under the law and in the absence of fine print, it seldom offers adequate protection with respect to trade secrets.

ways far more broad, and in some ways far more restrictive, than other forms of IP protection.

1. Copyright

In comparison to copyright law, trade secret law may provide broader protections because many states do not require that the material be fixed in a tangible medium in order to qualify for trade secret protection.[52] Federal law explicitly includes "intangible" information in the DTSA's definition of trade secret.[53] Also, facts may be eligible for trade secret protection, but are not eligible for copyright protection. Another benefit to trade secret protection is that it can last indefinitely, as long as the information remains secret, while copyright protection is for a limited (though lengthy) term. Notably, copyright protection does not require that the work protected provide any competitive advantage, and of course there is no requirement to keep the work secret.

Information protected by trade secret law may also be protected by copyright if it meets the requirements for copyright protection (an original work of authorship fixed in any tangible medium of expression).[54] Generally, a copyrightable work is protected by copyright from the moment it is affixed in a tangible medium.[55] Therefore, if the information subject to trade secret protection is also protectable by copyright, it is legally protected by copyright from the moment the secret is written down. As a practical matter, however, copyright protection cannot be enforced in a court without the copyright being registered.[56] If a copyright owner wishes to sue an infringer, the copyright registration is the key to

---

52. *See* Union Carbide Corp. v. Tarancon Corp., 742 F. Supp. 1565 (N.D. Ga. 1990) (finding the process was a trade secret despite never being set out in a tangible form prior to litigation); Johns-Manville Corp. v. Guardian Indus. Corp., 586 F. Supp. 1034 (E.D. Mich. 1983) (finding that trade secret had merely to be *capable* of being embodied in a tangible form). *But see In re* Hercules Auto. Prods., Inc., 245 B.R. 903 (Bankr. M.D. Ga. 1999) (holding that a customer list not set out in tangible form was not entitled to trade secret protection).

53. 18 U.S.C. § 1839(3) (2016).

54. 17 U.S.C. § 102(a) (2018). For more detail on what is and is not subject to copyright protection, see Chapter 2.

55. *Id.*

56. *Id.* § 411(a).

the courthouse door—no suit can be brought without the work first being registered with the U.S. Copyright Office.

Copyright registration generally requires the deposit of a copy of the work,[57] which could destroy the secrecy required for trade secret protection. However, of particular interest to video games and virtual worlds is the fact that a trade secret and copyright registration can coexist in the realm of computer software. This is possible because there are special deposit provisions for computer programs that contain trade secrets. Where the program contains trade secrets, the U.S. Copyright Office allows several options for certain limited portions of the program to be deposited rather that the entire program, and allows trade secret information to be redacted (i.e., blocked out) in the portions that would possibly contain trade secret information.[58] Therefore, the game designer who wishes to keep certain information a trade secret does not have to forego copyright registration of the work.

2. Patent

As mentioned previously, many things may be eligible for protection as a trade secret but would not be patentable due to the novelty requirement.[59] Patents are also protected for only a limited term, where a trade secret may be protected forever. Like copyrights, there is no requirement that a patent be kept secret. To the contrary, details of an invention must be disclosed in order to qualify for patent protection.

Patents by their nature disclose the process of the patent. Therefore, patented subject matter cannot also constitute a trade secret because the disclosures required for issuance of a patent destroy trade-secret status. That said, the subject matter of patent applications can constitute trade secrets as long as they remain

---

57. *Id.* § 408.

58. 37 C.F.R. § 202.20(c)(2)(vii)(A)(2) (1984); U.S. COPYRIGHT OFFICE, CIRCULAR 61: COPYRIGHT REGISTRATION FOR COMPUTER PROGRAMS (2017), http://www.copyright.gov /circs/circ61.pdf.

59. Softel, Inc. v. Dragon Med. & Sci. Commc'n, Inc., 118 F.3d 955, 968 (2d Cir. 1997) ("novelty—at least as that term is used in patent law—is not required in a trade secret"). A more detailed description of the novelty requirement, as well as the other requirements for patentability, is included in Chapter 3.

confidential until public disclosure is required. Thus, information can be kept a trade secret up to the actual publication of the patent application or grant of a patent,[60] and can retain trade secret status if the patent application is abandoned or rejected prior to publication.

This was highlighted by a recent U.S. circuit court opinion (authored by then-Judge Gorsuch before his Supreme Court appointment) that held that patent law does not preempt trade secret protection.[61] The plaintiff alleged that its trade secrets were misappropriated and used in a patent, and he brought a trade secret claim against the patent holder.[62] Although the patent holder's disclosure almost certainly removed the possibility of future trade secret protection, it did not destroy the trade secret claim itself.[63] Thus, inventors who develop something that can be protected by either trade secret or patent are faced with a choice— "[t]hey may keep their ideas secret with the protection of state law but run the risk of potential independent discovery by others. Or they may disclose their ideas and enjoy the ensuing legal monopoly afforded by federal patent law."[64] Of course, the legal monopoly comes at significant cost and effort and only lasts for a limited time, so inventors may prefer state trade secret protection.

II. Trade Secrets in Video Games and Virtual Worlds

A. Gameplay: What Players/Users See

Based on the fact that trade secrets must be secret, any element in the game that can be publicly viewed by the players (once the game is launched publicly) could not be considered a trade secret.

---

60. Patent applications in the United States are published after 18 months, unless steps are taken within one year of filing the patent application to prevent publication per 37 C.F.R. § 1.211 (2016).
61. Russo v. Ballard Med. Prods., 550 F.3d 1004, 1011–14 (10th Cir. 2008).
62. *Id.* at 1006.
63. *Id.* at 1008.
64. *Id.* at 1013.

All trade secrets for game companies and game designers must therefore be "behind the scenes." This does not mean that there can be no trade secret issues in gameplay. Two areas where these issues may potentially arise are in the revealing of real-world trade secrets by a player in a game, and the development of trade secrets within the game by a player or group of players.

1. Real-World Trade Secrets Revealed In-Game

Trade secret protection could be violated through misappropriation and probably defeated through disclosure by a player in a virtual world unlawfully revealing trade secret information to another player or to the world as a whole.[65] An employee or officer of company A who wishes to pass along a trade secret to an employee or officer of company B may arrange to do so in a virtual world, such as *EVE Online* or *Second Life*, or through a console game with an online multiplayer aspect. The game or virtual world can increase the actual or perceived anonymity of the parties.

For one thing, players are acting through avatars, making it difficult to know who is behind the computer screen. In addition, while the information passed through chat might not be guaranteed to be secret due to the keeping of chat logs, it would be particularly difficult for a company whose secrets were exposed to be able to find the specific chat log, if the log still existed, and identify the avatar revealing the information. The company would then have to determine the owner of the avatar, which many virtual world providers will not easily provide.[66] These extra levels of anonymity, real or perceived, may give people additional incentive or ability to sell, trade, or otherwise misappropriate and distribute trade secrets online.

---

65. Of course, as discussed elsewhere in this chapter, the use of many virtual world or video game chat functions can also result in the inadvertent disclosure of trade secrets even if there is a lawful and legitimate attempt to share a trade secret with another avatar with a legitimate need to know the secret.

66. *See* Eros, LLC, v. Leatherwood, No. 8:07-cv-1158-T-24TGW (M.D. Fla. filed July 3, 2007); *see generally* Harris Weems Henderson, Note, *Through the Looking Glass: Copyright Protection in the Virtual Reality of Second Life*, 16 J. INTELL. PROP. 165, 174 (2008).

Many companies have a presence in *Second Life* through property or "islands."[67] This and other online worlds will continue to attract real-world business. This commercialization does not always sit well with players,[68] who sometimes grief[69] and harass these companies in the game.[70] A griefer with access to a company's trade secret might retaliate by distributing or publicizing that trade secret on a company's virtual site. Of course, a person intent on harming a company by revealing a trade secret would not have to do so in a game where the company has a virtual presence. However, virtual worlds offer the opportunity for millions of people to be exposed to the trade secret. A griefer who can display or distribute a trade secret to even a small percentage of those players in the virtual world can cause harm to a company in the real world.

It is important to note that, in addition to the violation of trade secret laws, actions taken by players to improperly share, reveal, or distribute trade secrets will likely be a violation of the virtual world's or online game's end-user license agreement (EULA), discussed in Chapter 1. Most EULAs expressly forbid the posting or transfer of content that infringes or violates IP rights.[71] They sometimes expressly forbid the sharing of inside, proprietary, or confidential information learned or disclosed as part of an employment or nondisclosure agreement, which certainly applies to trade

---

67. David Kirkpatrick, *Coldwell Banker's Second Life*, Fortune, Mar. 23, 2007, http://money.cnn.com/2007/03/22/technology/fastforward_secondlife.fortune/index.htm; Urizenus Sklar, *Nissan Retools*, Aplhaville Herald, Apr. 26, 2007, 12:43 a.m., http://alphavilleherald.com/2007/04/nissan_retools.html.

68. Kristina Dell, *Second Life's Real-World Problems*, Time, Aug. 9, 2007, http://www.time.com/time/magazine/article/0,9171,1651500,00.html.

69. "Griefing" is abusing the game or playing in a way intended to cause grief, harm, or embarrassment to other players.

70. Dell, *supra* note 68; *see also* Mitch Wagner, *Toyota Under Attack by Second Life Griefers*, InformationWeek, Apr. 9, 2007, 3:56 a.m., https://www.informationweek.com/desktop/toyota-under-attack-by-second-life-griefers/d/d-id/1053823?.

71. *See, e.g.*, CCP hf, *EVE Online—End User License Agreement* § 10(C)(ii), https://community.eveonline.com/support/policies/eve-eula-en/ (last updated May 24, 2018).

secrets.[72] Most EULAs also generally forbid posting any content or taking any actions that violate state, federal, or international law.[73]

2. In-Game Trade Secrets Developed by Players

As online games and virtual worlds continue to develop and allow for user-created or user-run businesses, the potential for a player to develop trade secrets within a game itself grows. These trade secrets could provide real-world benefits, or they could be strictly in-game.

In the real world, there are several ways in which a player could benefit from an in-game trade secret. In *Second Life*, for example, many players run in-game businesses that generate real-world income.[74] In fact, these in-game companies have created real-world millionaires.[75] These businesses would have the same potential for trade secrets as any real-world, brick-and-mortar business. Additionally, there is a real-world market for the purchase and sale of game characters, game items, and game currency.[76] This means the very act of playing the game, advancing in levels, and acquiring in-game items, tools, and wealth may constitute a business.

Perhaps the most obvious example of this type of business would be "gold farming." Gold farming is the practice of employing multiple people to play a game around the clock, earning in-game

---

72. Linden Lab, *Second Life Terms and Conditions* § 1.6, http://secondlife.com /corporate/tos.php (last visited July 25, 2018).

73. CCP hf, *supra* note 71, § 10(C)(i); Linden Lab, *supra* note 72, § 1.6; Blizzard Entertainment, Inc., *Terms of Use for Blizzard's Websites*, https://www .blizzard.com/en-us/legal/511dbf9e-2b2d-4047-8243-4c5c65e0ebf1/terms-of-use -for-blizzards-websites (last visited July 25, 2018).

74. Second Life, *Business*, https://secondlife.com/destinations/business (last visited July 25, 2018).

75. Roger Parloff, *Anshe Chung: First Virtual Millionaire*, CNN MONEY, Nov. 27, 2006, 11:25 a.m., http://money.cnn.com/blogs/legalpad/2006/11/anshe-chung-first -virtual-millionaire.html.

76. *See* Chris Yarbrough, *How to Purchase a World of Warcraft Account on eBay, and Not Get Ripped Off*, EZINE ARTICLES, July 10, 2006, http://ezinearticles .com/?How-to-Purchase-a-World-of-Warcraft-Account-on-eBay,-and-Not-Get -Ripped-Off&id=240398; *see also* GameWar—The World's Largest MMO Accounts Store, *Homepage*, http://www.gamewar.com (last visited July 25, 2018).

goods later sold to other players in the real world for profit.[77] Gold farming can also be undertaken through an automated process, installing a game account and a macro on one or more computers that run constantly, following the same steps and gathering wealth.[78] If a person were to develop a particularly effective macro for generating wealth or were to discover an activity that generated far more value for time spent, and thereby made more real-world profit per hour spent in-game, the macro or activity could easily fall under the definition of trade secrets. It should also be noted at this time that gold farming or any use of macros or cheats, as well as the selling of in-game goods or accounts, is prohibited by the EULAs of most current games, despite being widely practiced.[79]

It is also possible that trade secrets could exist strictly in-game, benefiting only the player's character or avatar. Take for example *EVE Online*. Corporations lie at the very core of this game, where every player starts as an employee of one of the corporate or military powers.[80] *EVE Online* encourages the players in these corporations to amass power through strategic multiplayer gameplay.[81] It is certainly possible that a group of players engaged in gaining power for their characters' corporation could develop techniques or discover information that benefits the group and provides an advantage over other *EVE Online* corporations and characters. Properly protected, these could be trade secrets. The question will be, do they have economic value? In other words, do they provide actual or potential economic advantage, as required by the UTSA or the *Restatement (Third) of Unfair Competition*?[82] Can

---

77. Julian Dibbell, *Owned! Intellectual Property in the Age of eBayers, Gold Farmers, and Other Enemies of the Virtual State or, How I Learned to Stop Worrying and Love the End-User License Agreement, in* THE STATE OF PLAY: LAW, GAMES, AND VIRTUAL WORLDS 140 (Jack M. Balkin & Beth Simone Noveck eds., 2006).

78. *Id.* at 141.

79. *See generally* CCP hf, *supra* note 71, Linden Lab, *supra* note 72; Blizzard Entertainment, Inc., *supra* note 73.

80. EVE Wiki, *Corporation*, http://eve.wikia.com/wiki/Corporation (last visited July 25, 2018).

81. *Id.*

82. *See* UTSA § 1(4) (1985); RESTATEMENT (THIRD) OF UNFAIR COMPETITION § 39 (1995).

that advantage be solely to one's character in the game? Further, if the trade secret is valuable in the virtual world, but all trade secret law is state-specific, what law will apply—the state of the player, the state of the game developer, or some other jurisdiction? And what will be the proper venue—where the tort was committed, where the tortious injury was felt, or the choice of venue provided by the EULA?

If trade secrets can exist solely to provide value in-game, the real-world business aspects discussed previously could also be in-game trade secrets. If a player were to discover a particularly effective technique for earning wealth or gaining levels, that knowledge would be valuable to his or her character and would provide an advantage over others. Arguably, the concept of trade secrets could even be applied in the context of multiplayer console games, if one player knows a technique others do not. For example, a character in a war-themed console game, playing online against others, may know of a particularly advantageous position from which to snipe at other players. In console-based player versus player games, such as sports games or fighting games, knowing the specific button combinations that allow for special moves certainly provides an advantage over others who do not know those combinations. Properly protected, this knowledge could conceivably fall under a broad definition of trade secrets, especially if the information is used in the context of real-world video game competitions for cash or prizes (though the duration of its status as a trade secret may be short-lived as others strive to replicate the technique).

As noted previously, the number of games with the potential for player-generated trade secrets continues to grow. However, the current state of affairs actually limits the likelihood that they would belong to the players. This is because the vast majority of online games and virtual worlds have EULAs that state that all IP created in the game belongs to the game company.[83] This clause in the EULA would mean that even if a player develops or discovers a trade secret, the trade secret may actually belong to

---

83. CCP hf, *supra* note 71, § 10(A); Blizzard Entertainment, Inc., *supra* note 73, § 2.

the game company. However, other game models exist where the player retains ownership rights to at least some player-created IP.[84] Indeed, some EULAs and terms of service have specific provisions permitting such user-generated content, which is often created by fans and users. Under these agreements and model, the player may retain his or her trade secret, which would likely encourage the development and protection of such information. The authors believe it is likely that this split will continue, with social and business-based virtual worlds allowing more individual ownership and creation, while game-based virtual worlds keep more control over player creation, and thus control the play and content of their games.

The anonymity of the player also presents difficulty in the enforcement of in-game trade secrets. Take the preceding *EVE Online* example: the owner of the trade secret is unlikely to know the true identity of others in his or her corporation. Even if a player knows or discovers the game identity of the person misappropriating the secret, that does not provide a real-world identity upon which to serve process for a trade secret action. The plaintiff would likely have to file an action against a John Doe and subpoena the game company for the personal information.[85] Further, the cost of bringing a lawsuit to protect one's in-game trade secret would almost certainly vastly outweigh the value of the injunction and any damages (to the extent any could be quantified and proven).

B. Game Design: Behind the Scenes

While there has been a great deal of interest in and attention to the issues of law in virtual worlds, little has been said about the issues of trade secrets for game developers and gaming companies. This is largely because the types of knowledge and information that a game developer or game company may want to protect as a trade secret is substantially the same as the information protected by a company manufacturing a more conventional product.

---

84. Linden Lab, *supra* note 72, § 1.1.

85. Which is the technique used by the plaintiff in Eros, LLC, v. Leatherwood, No. 8:07-cv-1158-T-24TGW (M.D. Fla. filed July 3, 2007).

Customer lists and customer information are commonly subject to trade secret protection. A game company would also have information regarding its customers, clients, and players, and could protect that information as a trade secret.[86] Companies in various markets also commonly protect product design as a trade secret. A game company could protect its product design in the sense that it keeps certain game elements, such as deep backstory or actual game mechanics, trade secrets.[87] A game company could also protect its product design by keeping its development tools and other software a trade secret.

In fact, any aspect of a business that provides an advantage, if properly protected, can be a trade secret in any business, including game companies. Information on management techniques, marketing strategies, financial plans, growth strategies, customer and employee contracts, pricing, and suppliers are all potentially protectable as trade secrets and all apply to companies focused on game development and design.

One area of specific importance to game developers and game companies is the trade secret protection of computer programs and software. Many state statutes, including Alabama, Georgia, Idaho, Montana, and Ohio, specifically identify programs or computer software to be protectable as a trade secret.[88] Federal law explicitly includes "program devices . . . programs, or codes" in the federal definition of a trade secret.[89] Even if the statute does not specifically include software, courts often have held that source code is protectable as a trade secret.[90]

---

86. *See* Weseley Software Dev. Corp. v. Burdette, 977 F. Supp. 137 (D. Conn. 1997).

87. Shannon Appelcline, *Trials, Triumphs & Trivialities #148: Online Games & the Law, Part Three: Patents, Trade Secrets & Licenses*, Skotos Articles, May 14, 2004, http://www.skotos.net/articles/TTnT_/TTnT_148.phtml.

88. Ala. Code § 8-27-2(1)(b) (1975); Ga. Code Ann. § 10-1-761(4) (1996); Idaho Code § 48-801(4) (2015); Mont. Code § 30-14-402(4) (2017); Ohio Rev. Code § 1333.61(D) (2017).

89. 18 U.S.C. § 1839(3) (2016).

90. *See, e.g.,* United States v. Cox, 73 F. Supp. 2d 751 (S.D. Tex. 1999); Synopsys, Inc. v. Nassda Corp., No. C 01-2519 SI, 2002 WL 32749138 (N.D. Cal. Sept. 16, 2002); Oracle Am., Inc. v. Google, Inc., 750 F.3d 1339 (Fed. Cir. 2014).

One interesting aspect of computer programs as trade secrets is that the general rule of disclosure does not apply. Generally, when information is itself the output or product of a business, disclosure of the information through the sale of the product destroys the secrecy and thereby removes trade secret protections. Computer programs, on the other hand, can be sold, downloaded, or otherwise distributed and used without necessarily disclosing the trade secrets contained therein, especially if only object code is provided.[91] A game company may therefore choose to maintain trade secret protection on its algorithms for graphic rendering, multiplayer communication, memory allocation and conservation, and the like, even when the game company distributes or provides its object code to others.

One recent case dealing with the protectability of trade secrets in video game source code is *Lilith Games (Shanghai) Co. Ltd. v. UCool, Ltd.*,[92] in which the defendant UCool obtained a copy of the plaintiff Lilith Games' software code and allegedly used it to create the defendant's game.[93] Lilith Games brought claims for copyright infringement and theft of trade secrets, and asked for a preliminary injunction.[94] In looking at the trade secret, the district court determined that "it cannot be questioned that Lilith derives independent economic value from [the game] and by extension its protected source code" and further determined that "Lilith's efforts to maintain the confidentiality of its source code . . . were sufficiently reasonable to maintain the code as a trade secret."[95] While the district court ultimately denied the preliminary injunction on the basis that Lilith Games did not show a likelihood of irreparable harm, the court did specifically state that Lilith Games

---

91. *See* Gates Rubber Co. v. Bando Chem. Indus., Ltd., 9 F.3d 823 (10th Cir. 1993); Dickerman Assocs., Inc. v. Tiverton Bottled Gas Co., 594 F. Supp. 30 (D. Mass. 1984); Telex Corp. v. IBM Corp., 510 F.2d 894 (10th Cir. 1975).

92. Lilith Games (Shanghai) Co. Ltd. v. UCool, Ltd., No. 15-CV-01267-SC, 2015 WL 5591612 (N.D. Cal. Sept. 23, 2015).

93. *Id.* at *1.

94. *Id.* at *2.

95. *Id.* at *9.

had demonstrated a strong likelihood of success on the merits of both the copyright and trade secrets claims.[96] The case later settled.

Hardware development can also give rise to trade secrets issues, as it did in *ZeniMax Media, Inc. v. Oculus VR, LLC*[97] (relating to the software and hardware used to develop virtual reality headsets). This case, again, was the subject of motions to dismiss by multiple defendants, but the court found that plaintiffs had sufficiently pled a cause of action for misappropriation of trade secrets.[98] The case went through several years of vigorous litigation and ultimately resulted in a jury trial. The jury found that there was no theft of trade secrets in this instance, although they did award $500,000,000 in damages for copyright violations and breach of nondisclosure agreements.[99] Therefore, while the jury found that there was a theft of confidential information, there was some issue that prevented the jury from finding that the information rose to the level of trade secret. Nonetheless, the trade secret argument was good enough to survive years of motions and get to a jury.

In the realm of console gaming, not only the hardware and software, but also the manner in which a game company controls the game programs that can be used with its console can be a trade secret. In *Atari Games Corp. v. Nintendo of America, Inc.*,[100] the court addressed Nintendo's claims of copyright infringement and trade secret violations relating to this issue.[101] Nintendo had created a program that would allow its console, equipped with a "master chip" or "lock," to accept and play only games that contained a "slave chip" or "key."[102] Using reverse engineering processes and

---

96. *Id.* at *13.

97. ZeniMax Media, Inc. v. Oculus VR, LLC, 166 F. Supp. 3d 697 (N.D. Tex. 2015).

98. *Id.* at 704.

99. Jeff Grubb, *ZeniMax v. Oculus: Jury Orders Facebook's VR Company to Pay $500 Million Because Paler Luckey Broke His NDA*, VENTUREBEAT, Feb. 1, 2017, 12:59 p.m., https://venturebeat.com/2017/02/01/zenimax-v-oculus-jury-orders-facebooks-vr-company-to-pay-500-million-because-palmer-luckey-broke-his-nda/.

100. Atari Games Corp. v. Nintendo of Am., Inc., 975 F.2d 832 (Fed. Cir. 1992).

101. *Id.* at 836.

102. *Id.*

a reproduction of the program from the U.S. Copyright Office,[103] Atari was able to manufacture its own chip to unlock the Nintendo console and allow the console to play an Atari game.[104] While the court focused almost exclusively on the copyright claims and held that Atari likely infringed Nintendo's copyright through the obtaining and reverse engineering of the code obtained from the U.S. Copyright office,[105] it does show another game element that can be protected as a trade secret. Atari did not, however, run afoul of trade secret laws because reverse engineering a trade secret is not an "improper means" of obtaining it.[106]

III. Applying the Traditional Analysis to Video Game and Virtual World Issues

The types of trade secrets held by game companies do not differ in any meaningful respect from those of any other companies. Thus, statutes and case law in many jurisdictions specifically authorize trade secret protection for software.

In the area of trade secrets held by players, however, there are several unanswered questions. In the hypothetical case of the disgruntled employee who shares trade secrets online, or of the griefer who disseminates trade secrets throughout the virtual world, the issue of the player's anonymity is a key concern. It may be impossible for a company to identify the person violating their trade secrets solely from a character name or appearance, unless that person were so careless as to use all or part of his or her real name in creating his or her character. While some online games and virtual worlds try to collect personal information and obtain accurate real-world identities, people creating avatars may use false information, thereby frustrating the search for wrongdoers.

---

103. Interestingly, the ability to file redacted code with the U.S. Copyright Office may eliminate the ability to access those secrets in the deposit copy.

104. *Atari Games Corp.*, 975 F.2d at 836–37.

105. *Id.* at 847.

106. *See* UTSA § 1 cmt. (1985).

Even if the personal information provided by the user is real, how does one actually obtain it? Online game and virtual world operators tend to keep their player information confidential (and that information, as a customer list, may be a trade secret of the game company itself).[107] How does one convince Linden Lab, or Blizzard, or CCP that trade secrets have been misappropriated and that he or she needs a player's identity? Merely stating that it is so cannot be sufficient, as anyone could write to the game administrator, claim that a certain avatar has misappropriated trade secrets, and demand the player's personal information. It would seem risky for a game company to comply with such a request.

The person who is claiming that trade secrets were misappropriated could bring a suit or bill of discovery against John Doe, identified as the owner/player of the character, and use the subpoena power of the court to force the game company to produce Doe's identity. Filing such a suit, however, is an expensive proposition. Typically, this type of litigation would involve obtaining the Internet protocol address of Doe, at which point the litigant would then need to subpoena the applicable Internet service provider to determine the router associated with Internet access by Doe—a process that may well lead to a foreign or public Wi-Fi connection and no way to specifically identify Doe.

Finally, the question of whether purely in-game benefits can even qualify for trade secret protection is not clear and will need to be addressed. Do purely in-game benefits "provid[e] an economic benefit or advantage," as required by trade secret statutes? While it is easy to see how player activities that generate income or other economic benefit in the real world, particularly in the sense of *Second Life* goods and services, can be trade secrets, it is not so clear that purely in-game benefits would qualify. Does knowledge that makes your character more competitive as compared to other characters provide value, even if there is a secondary market through which you could sell your character to someone else? Is the information and strategy that makes your *EVE Online* corporation more powerful than others a competitive

107. *See, e.g.,* Eros, LLC, v. Leatherwood, No. 8:07-cv-1158-T-24TGW (M.D. Fla. filed July 3, 2007).

advantage? To what extent any such advantage must provide economic benefit to the player as opposed to the character is not clear under current case law.

IV. What Remedies Are Available for Trade Secret Misappropriation?

Trade secret misappropriation under state or federal law is normally governed by a three-year statute of limitations.[108] However, where a defendant has kept a misappropriated trade secret confidential but has continued to use it for commercial advantage, the continuing tort theory may extend that limitations period for longer than three years from the very first act of misappropriation.[109] There are various remedies, both legal and equitable, available to trade secret holders.

A. Injunctive Relief

An injunction is an important remedy in trade secret cases because it is the most effective way to prevent the initial or continued use or disclosure of a trade secret, which would destroy the trade secret and its value. Given the relatively short life cycle of products in the video games and virtual worlds area, injunctive relief to stop the disclosure or use of a misappropriated trade secret may be the only meaningful remedy.

Trade secret cases present burden of proof challenges in that a plaintiff cannot reveal the trade secrets in pleadings or in open court during the judicial proceeding, or the trade secret is lost. Obviously, it would be highly undesirable for a video game company, for example, to have to present its source code in court and in front of a competitor. Thus, a plaintiff is limited to prosecuting its case without placing the trade secret into evidence, or must petition to have the case proceed under seal.[110] If the trade secret

---

108. Andrew Greenberg, Inc. v. Svane, Inc., 36 A.D.3d 1094, 1098 (N.Y. App. Div. 2007).
109. *Id.*
110. UTSA § 5.

is revealed not under seal, its confidential nature is lost and it may no longer qualify as a trade secret.

To show that the plaintiff will suffer irreparable injury, as is required to obtain an injunction, can be tricky in a trade secret case if the economic nature of the harm is obvious and money damages may adequately compensate for the economic harm. However, even if the injury is compensable in damages, some courts have held that the irreparable harm element is satisfied if the following circumstances exist: (1) there is difficulty in proving damages with reasonable certainty; (2) there is difficulty in procuring suitable substitute performance by means of money awarded as damages; and (3) there is a likelihood that an award could not be collected.[111] Further, courts often find irreparable harm in trade secret cases based on the likelihood that the party accused of misappropriation would attempt to license the secret to others outside the jurisdiction of the court, or on the difficulty in quantifying in monetary terms the impact of present or future lost sales and diminished customer relationships.[112] The destruction of the value of secret customer lists[113] or the inability to compete fairly may also cause irreparable injury.[114]

State trade secret statutes also generally allow preliminary injunctions where misappropriation of trade secrets is threatened.[115] Federal law under the DTSA also allows preliminary injunctive relief. In the video game and virtual worlds industries where employee turnover is high, the "inevitable disclosure" doctrine may come into play. Specifically, this doctrine deals with circumstances where a former employee (such as a chief technology officer) hired away by a competitor would have to inevitably use or disclose trade secrets in order to carry out his or her duties for his new

---

111. Apollo Techs. Corp. v. Centrosphere Indus. Corp., 805 F. Supp. 1157, 1210 (D.N.J. 1992).

112. *See, e.g.*, Imi-Tech Corp. v. Gagliani, 691 F. Supp. 214, 231 (S.D. Cal. 1986).

113. Preferred Elec. & Wire Corp. v. Katz, 462 F. Supp. 1178, 1189 (E.D.N.Y. 1978).

114. Alexander & Alexander Benefit Servs., Inc. v. Benefit Brokers & Consultants, Inc., 756 F. Supp. 1408, 1415 (D. Or. 1991).

115. UTSA § 2(a) (1985); Lemmon v. Hendrickson, 559 N.W.2d 278, 279 (Iowa 1997).

employer.[116] There is no uniform test for when the inevitable disclosure doctrine applies, but generally courts have relied upon the following factors in determining whether disclosure is inevitable: (1) is the new employer a competitor? (2) what is the new job? (3) has the former employee been less than candid about his or her new position? (4) has the plaintiff clearly identified the trade secrets that are at risk? (5) has actual trade secret misappropriation already occurred? (6) did the former employee sign a nondisclosure and/or noncompetition agreement? (7) does the new employer have an express policy against use of others' trade secrets? (8) is it possible to "sanitize" the former employee's new position?[117]

In limited instances and in states that recognize the theory, the inevitable disclosure doctrine can be used to enjoin a former employee from working in his or her specialty or from working for the competitor at all, even in the absence of a noncompetition agreement.[118]

B. Damages

Damages may be recovered in a trade secret case when the wrongful use of trade secrets has generated an economically measurable effect. A variety of categories of damages are available in trade secret cases, depending on the jurisdiction in which the harm occurred. These types include compensatory damages, restitution, royalties, punitive damages, and attorneys' fees and costs.

C. Criminal Actions

Similar to copyright law, in addition to injunctions and money damages, those who misappropriate trade secrets may face criminal charges for their actions. The Economic Espionage Act of 1996 provides a maximum fine of $500,000 for individuals and $5 million for organizations, and a maximum prison term of ten years, for the

---

116. *See, e.g.*, PepsiCo v. Redmond, 54 F.3d 1262 (7th Cir. 1995); Essex Group v. Southwire Co., 501 S.E.2d 501 (Ga. 1998).

117. *See, e.g.*, Maxxim Med., Inc. v. Michelson, 51 F. Supp. 2d 773 (S.D. Tex. 1999).

118. *See, e.g.*, *PepsiCo*, 54 F.3d 1262; *Essex Group*, 501 S.E.2d 501; *see also* Elizabeth A. Rowe, *When Trade Secrets Become Shackles: Fairness and the Inevitable Disclosure Doctrine*, 7 Tul. J. Tech. & Intell. Prop. 167 (2005).

theft of trade secrets.[119] Many states have also adopted statutes that make the misappropriation of trade secrets a criminal offense.

Additionally, there are statutes at both the federal and state levels that prohibit hacking and other computer crimes, arising from the unauthorized access, use, or copying of computers and computer files (and the resulting potential for access to trade secrets). At the federal level, the Electronic Communications Privacy Act prohibits the unauthorized access to electronic communications and storage.[120] At the state level, every state has enacted a computer crimes law that prohibits the unauthorized use of or access to a computer or computer data.[121] Most, if not all, of these statutes also provide for a private cause of action for a violation. Therefore, to the extent the trade secret information was stored on a computer or in another electronic format, such as voicemail or e-mail, the person accessing and misappropriating the trade secret may have violated these statutes as well.

Conclusion

While trade secrets have not garnered the same attention as patents and copyrights in the context of online games and virtual worlds, they are valuable to game designers, publishers, and players. Trade secret laws allow companies to protect information that may not be patentable or copyrightable, and add further protective elements to some copyrighted works, especially computer software. Trade secret protection can also last indefinitely, so long as the information provides value and remains secret. Trade secrets used inside the game environments raise interesting and innovative questions as to whether they are the kind of property interest to which the laws may apply. It remains to be seen how courts will resolve trade secret issues in online games and virtual worlds.

---

119. 18 U.S.C. §§ 1831–1832 (2006).

120. *Id.* § 2701 (2006).

121. FindLaw, *State Computer Crime Laws*, https://statelaws.findlaw.com /criminal-laws/computer-crimes.html (last visited July 25, 2018) (listing computer crime statutes by statute number on a state-by-state basis).

Rights of Publicity

6

Lynne Boisineau
Ben Manevitz[1]

Takeaways

- *The right of publicity is an individual's right to prevent others from commercially exploiting his or her identity, such as voice, name, likeness, image, and so on, without permission. This right is given to everyone, not just to celebrities, but it does not apply to nonhumans (e.g., entities, groups, institutions, or animals).*
- *If you violate someone's right of publicity, you can be forced to edit, remove, or take down the content in question and/or pay monetary damages to the individual based on the commercial value of that person's identity.*
- *In the United States, the right of publicity is unevenly protected, with many states having no protection at all or only common law protection. In contrast, other states not only have statutes in place, but some of those statutes offer post-mortem protection lasting decades after the deceased individual has passed.*
- *The right of publicity is typically owned by the person whose name, likeness, image, or voice is being used, but it can be owned by that person's heirs, assigned away, or licensed to a third party.*

---

1. Lynne Boisineau is the founding partner of Boisineau Law. Ben Manevitz is principal of the Manevitz Law Firm. For complete author biographies, see the Contributors section of this book.

- *Virtual reality and augmented reality present unique challenges to the protection and enforcement of the right of publicity, not just with respect to avatars, but also humans who may be visible in augmented reality environments.*
- *The First Amendment is a defense to a right of publicity claim, but limits apply. For example, video games are entitled to First Amendment protection, and courts struggle to balance right of publicity claims against the First Amendment defenses.*

Introduction

In the United States, the right of publicity protects a person's identity in the form of persona, name, likeness, image, and/or voice from unauthorized commercial use by another. The right of publicity has its origins in privacy law. Specifically, the misappropriation of the name or likeness of another is one of the four privacy claims listed in the *Restatement (Second) of Torts*.[2] However, New York led the charge in 1903, enacting the first statute designed specifically to protect an individual's right of publicity.[3]

To date, the right of publicity suffers from uneven protection, ranging from very narrow to broad. In some states, only military personnel are protected. In others, the right of publicity applies to all individuals and even encompasses a post-mortem period.[4] The lack of uniform duration and requirements for bringing a right of publicity claim in a particular state raises challenges for plaintiffs and defendants alike in assessing what is at stake, how to analyze the claim, and what the risks are in pursuing or defending such a claim. The right of publicity is currently only recognized in roughly 38 states via common law protection, and only 22 states have codified protection of the right of publicity.[5] These state laws vary greatly in terms of the duration of protection during a person's lifetime, whether the particular law protects the person's image or

---

2. RESTATEMENT (SECOND) OF TORTS § 652 (1977).

3. Rothman's Roadmap to the Right of Publicity, *New York*, http://www .rightofpublicityroadmap.com/law/new-york (last updated Jan. 11, 2016).

4. Right of Publicity, *Statutes & Interactive Map*, http://rightofpublicity.com /statutes (last visited July 26, 2018).

5. *Id.*

persona after death, and whether registration or use of the right of publicity during that person's lifetime is a prerequisite to accessing that protection.

The advent of various forms of technology such as virtual reality and augmented reality has made this area of law even harder to predict. Although it is possible to borrow concepts from case law relating to video games and right of publicity, virtual and augmented reality uses of a person's likeness, image, voice, persona, and so on add an extra layer of complexity. Virtual reality contains only avatars in a fully simulated, digital environment, but augmented reality incorporates real-world items, buildings, and humans into a partially digital environment. To the extent that avatars and digital characters are based on actual humans, right of publicity issues arise in the same manner as they do in video games with some exceptions. In a video game, characters may be secondary to a main purpose, such as dancers in the background of a bar that is only a fleeting scene in the game, or zombies that you shoot to get from one place to another on a particular quest. On the other hand, video game characters may take center stage, as is the case in sports video games.

Virtual reality, in contrast, can be used in an unlimited number of ways, not just gaming. It can be used by students to dissect virtual frogs in a classroom, by chief executive officers for honing their public speaking skills, by history buffs to explore ancient Greece, and the like. Given that there are ways that virtual reality diverges from video games, new problems and issues could arise that do not fit nicely into the existing video game right of publicity concepts that have been defined by the courts. Augmented reality is even more troublesome, since it combines virtual reality with the real world and will be used in a multitude of ways once the technology is perfected. In an augmented reality environment, for example, the viewer sees virtual images and real humans, buildings, surroundings, and so on as well. In one recently popular example, gamers hunting Pokémon in the smartphone game Pokémon GO were able to see and take photos of surrounding areas with virtual characters shown in those scenes, and then post them on the Internet. While most of these uses were noncommercial, some were related to advertising or marketing campaigns by local business offering discounts for posting online photos or checking in at those establishments with photos containing Pokémon characters. To the extent that these images contained the likeness of third parties who did not consent to the use of their right of publicity to drive traffic to a particular business or to show up on that business's website, right of publicity issues might arise.

I. The Development of Right of Publicity Protection in the United States

The right of publicity began as a "right to privacy" tort that was concerned with protecting an individual's right to keep his or her dignity and be free of the disclosure of private facts that might be embarrassing or cause mental anguish by being publicly revealed.[6] At the beginning of the 20th century, that legal right expanded to include the right of a person to control the commercial use of his or her image in an unauthorized advertisement, an implied endorsement that was never given, or any other type of misappropriation causing damage to that person. It was at this time that some states began codifying the "right to privacy" laws into laws designed to specifically protect the right of publicity of an individual where his or her persona was misused for unauthorized commercial purposes. Building on that, some states even incorporated post-mortem protections, the ability to transfer the right of publicity via contract, and other expansions of the original doctrine. The seminal case on the right of publicity is *Haelan Laboratories, Inc. v. Topps Chewing Gum, Inc.*[7] There, the Second Circuit held that a company that had paid for the exclusive right to use the image of a certain major league baseball player had been damaged by the use of an image of that same player on a competing company's baseball cards.[8] Specifically, the court agreed with Haelan that a common law right of publicity did exist; it was assignable; and that this right was not the same as the statutory right of privacy that

---

6. William L. Prosser, *Privacy*, 48 Cal. L. Rev. 383 (1960).
7. Haelan Labs., Inc. v. Topps Chewing Gum, Inc., 202 F.2d 866 (2d Cir. 1953).
8. *Id.* at 868.

already existed at the time.[9] In other words, since the ballplayer in question had a property right in his own image, he had the ability to control its use in commerce via contracts with third parties. Thus, the right of publicity was born.

A. Elements

The elements of a right of publicity infringement claim according to *The Rights of Publicity and Privacy* by J. Thomas McCarthy are as follows: (1) the "Plaintiff owns an enforceable right in the identity or persona of a human being"; and (2)(A) "Defendant, without permission, has used some aspect of identity or persona in such a way that plaintiff is identifiable from defendant's use"; and (2)(B) "Defendant's use is likely to cause damage to the commercial value of that persona."[10] However, recovery of such a claim is much more difficult for noncelebrity plaintiffs, as showing the commercial value of the person's identity or persona is much more challenging (although not impossible).[11]

1. What Is Protected

a. Name

The right of publicity protects not just a person's given name, but any name that identifies the individual, including nicknames. For example, Muhammad Ali won a right of publicity case against a magazine publisher for a cartoon of an African American man in a boxing ring with the caption "The Greatest"—a nickname that Ali constantly used to refer to himself.[12] In another case that settled, Lindsay Lohan sued E*Trade for a commercial wherein one baby accuses another baby, named Lindsay, of becoming a "milkoholic."[13]

---

9. *Id.*
10. 1 J. Thomas McCarthy, The Rights of Publicity and Privacy § 3:2 (2d ed. 2018) (listing the elements of a prima facie case).
11. *Id.* § 4:20 ("The better view is that previous commercial 'exploitation' is not a condition precedent for possession of a right of publicity for a living plaintiff.").
12. Ali v. Playgirl, Inc., 447 F. Supp. 723 (S.D.N.Y. 1978).
13. Lohan v. E*Trade Sec. LLC, No. 601016/2010 (N.Y. Sup. Ct. Apr. 20, 2010); *see also* Jonathan Stempel, *Lindsay Lohan Sues over "Milkaholic" E*Trade Ad*, Reuters, Mar. 10, 2010, 8:31 a.m., https://www.reuters.com/article/us-lohan-etrade-lawsuit/lindsay-lohan-sues-over-milkaholic-etrade-ad-idUSTRE6283HD20100310.

And, interestingly enough, if a celebrity legally or informally changes his or her given name to adopt a stage name, that does not mean the person's real name is up for grabs. Unauthorized commercial use of the person's prior name is also a violation of the right of publicity, whether or not the person still uses that name.[14] In other words, there is no concept of a right of publicity defense of abandonment for failure to use the prior name in interstate commerce, as there is for federal trademark infringement cause of action.

b. Likeness/Image/Picture

An unauthorized commercial use of a person's likeness, via an artist's rendering, a photograph or digital image, a look-alike model, or even a stylized facsimile of that person can be actionable. In one recent pending case, Olivia de Havilland, the 101-year-old legendary Hollywood actress, filed suit against the use of her name, likeness, and identity in the television series "Feud: Bette and Joan" by FX Networks and Ryan Murphy Productions.[15] In that production, actress Catherine Zeta-Jones plays the part of Olivia de Havilland so accurately that every aspect of Olivia de Havilland's real-life appearance at the 1978 Academy Awards was "replicated to precision," from the clothes to the jewelry, to the hair and makeup.[16] Ms. de Havilland initially won against FX's anti-strategic lawsuit against public participation (SLAPP) motion, even though FX won on the issues of right of publicity and false light.[17] Ms. de Havilland filed a petition for review requesting reversal of the ruling by the Los Angeles County Superior Court, but the California Supreme Court refused to revive Ms. de Havilland's case.[18]

In one similar case that settled a few years back, Old Navy was sued by Kim Kardashian for a commercial in which a look-alike

---

14. Abdul-Jabbar v. Gen. Motors Corp., 85 F.3d 407, 415–16 (9th Cir. 1996).

15. de Havilland v. FX Networks, LLC, 21 Cal. App. 5th 845 (Cal. Ct. App. 2018); *see also* David Canfield, *7 Things Olivia de Havilland Wants Ryan Murphy to Know about Her in the New Lawsuit against Him*, VULTURE, July 1, 2017, http://www.vulture .com/2017/07/olivia-de-havilland-lawsuit-against-ryan-murphy-details.html.

16. *de Havilland*, 21 Cal. App. 5th at 851.

17. *Id.* at 870–71.

18. de Havilland v. FX Networks LLC, No. S248614 (Cal. May 4, 2018).

model, Melissa Molinaro, was featured.[19] Kardashian's claim was that Old Navy deliberately tried to make viewers think that they were watching *her*, and not Molinaro.[20] Kardashian claimed that Old Navy caused her damage, as Kardashian had her own clothing line for sale at that same time with Old Navy's rival, Sears.[21] Apparently not learning from their older sister's lawsuit, Kardashian's younger sisters, Kylie and Kendall Jenner, battled right of publicity claims in 2017 for superimposing their own images and initials over photographs of famous musical artists such as Ozzy Osbourne, The Doors, Tupac Shakur, and Notorious B.I.G.[22]

Sometimes, however, these cases fail, as in the case in which the heirs of Rosa Parks sued Target over a series of six books, a movie, and a plaque, all featuring images and discussions of Rosa Parks and her life, including her contributions to the civil rights movement.[23] There, the Eleventh Circuit held that a qualified privilege applied to such items, since the subject of Parks, a figure of great historical significance, was a matter of public concern and interest, and she played a major role in the civil rights movement—a topic that remains of great concern to the public today.[24]

In some jurisdictions, an individual claiming a violated right of publicity must prove that the right existed before the alleged violation. For instance, in *Pesina v. Midway Manufacturing Co.*,[25] the

---

19. Eriq Gardner, *Kim Kardashian Settles Lawsuit over Look-Alike in Old Navy Ad*, HOLLYWOOD REP., Aug. 29, 2012, 8:30 a.m., https://www.hollywoodreporter.com /thr-esq/kim-kardashian-settles-lawsuit-look-alike-old-navy-gap-366522.

20. *Kim Kardashian Settles Lawsuit with Old Navy After Label Used a Lookalike in Ad*, DAILY MAIL, Aug. 29, 2012, 3:59 p.m., http://www.dailymail.co.uk/tvshowbiz /article-2195455/Kim-Kardashian-settles-lawsuit-Old-Navy-label-used-lookalike -Melissa-Molinaro-ad.html.

21. Christie D'Zurilla, *Kim Kardashian, Old Navy Settle over Commercial Starring Lookalike*, L.A. TIMES, Aug. 29, 2012, http://articles.latimes.com/2012/aug/29 /entertainment/la-et-mg-kim-kardashian-old-navy-settle-lawsuit-melissa-molinaro.

22. Adam White, *Kendall and Kylie Jenner to Be Sued by The Doors for Appropriating Image for Fashion Line*, TELEGRAPH, July 4, 2017, http://www.telegraph .co.uk/music/news/kendall-kylie-jenner-sued-doors-appropriating-image-fashion/.

23. Rosa & Raymond Parks Inst. for Self Dev. v. Target Corp., 812 F.3d 824 (11th Cir. 2016) (Rosenbaum, J.).

24. *Id.* at 831–32.

25. Pesina v. Midway Mfg. Co., 948 F. Supp. 40 (N.D. Ill. 1996).

martial artist Pesina was hired by the makers of the *Mortal Kombat* game series to model for some of the games' characters, and in particular for the motion capture of his moves for the character Johnny Cage.[26] Pesina's contract contemplated the coin-operated version of the games.[27] When those same games were licensed for home versions, Pesina claimed, *inter alia*, that the game designers had infringed his right of publicity, insofar as the Johnny Cage character was based on him.[28] Pesina's claims were made under both the common law right of publicity and the Lanham Act's false endorsement provisions (i.e., unfair competition).[29] The Northern District of Illinois stated that a plaintiff claiming the infringement of the right of publicity "must show that, prior to the defendant's use, the plaintiff's name, likeness, or persona had commercial value," and that to make a claim under the Lanham Act, the plaintiff must make a showing that he has some "celebrity status or public recognition" such that the plaintiff's identity would have the commercial value protectable under that act.[30]

c. Voice

The right of publicity is also designed to protect the voice of a specific individual—although such cases typically involve a singer or actor with a particularly distinctive voice, such as Tom Waits[31] or Bette Midler,[32] both of whom filed right of publicity claims after sound-alike vocals appeared in commercials without their permission. In the case of Tom Waits, the singer has such a unique voice that the court described it as follows: "Like how you'd sound if you drank a quart of bourbon, smoked a pack of cigarettes and swallowed a pack of razor blades. . . . Late at night. After not sleeping for three days."[33] There, Waits had once allowed a song of his to be used in a commercial—and had regretted the decision. He

---

26. *Id.* at 41–42.
27. *Id.* at 42.
28. *Id.*
29. *Id.*
30. *Id.* at 42–43.
31. Waits v. Frito-Lay, Inc., 978 F.2d 1093 (9th Cir. 1992).
32. Midler v. Ford Motor Co., 849 F.2d 460 (9th Cir. 1988).
33. *Waits*, 978 F.2d at 1097 (quoting a Tom Waits fan).

was very vociferous in his displeasure and disapproval of such endorsements.[34] The ad agency hired to create the campaign for Frito-Lay was inspired by one of Waits's songs, and auditioned several singers, one of whom sounded so much like Waits that the creative team did a "double take"—as did Waits himself upon hearing the jingle.[35] In an instance where there is evidence that the commercial entity has acted with malice or "conscious disregard" of the person's right of publicity, the court will uphold punitive damages, as was the case with Waits's victory.[36]

It should be noted that the inclusion of one's voice as a part of the right of publicity is not universally accepted;[37] the exact contours of right of publicity protection are very much subject to each individual state's statutes and precedent.

d. Persona/Identity

A person's identity or persona can also be infringed. This description pertains to the sum total of the person's features or a character played by that person. For example, Vanna White famously sued Samsung for a commercial featuring a robot in an evening gown, necklace, and blonde wig who was turning over letters on a board of the same type used by White in her job as the hostess of the game show "Wheel of Fortune."[38] Although the robot was not human, and obviously was not a look-alike human model, White argued that her persona was infringed by the commercial, as it was apparent that Samsung was alluding to a future world where White's job would be taken over by a robot.[39] Although White lost on her *statutory* claim of right of publicity infringement, the Ninth Circuit found that White raised issues of material fact about her common law claim of right of publicity infringement, as well as her

---

34. *Id.*
35. *Id.*
36. *Id.* at 1106–06; *see also* DONALD E. BIEDERMAN, LAW AND BUSINESS OF THE ENTERTAINMENT INDUSTRIES 246–47 (5th ed. 2006).
37. *See* Romantics v. Activision, 574 F. Supp. 2d 758 (E.D. Mich. 2008) (finding that the right of publicity does not protect the sound of a voice or combination of voices, and publicity claim directed to voice/music is preempted by the Copyright Act).
38. White v. Samsung Elecs. Am., Inc., 971 F.2d 1395, 1396 (9th Cir. 1992).
39. *Id.* at 1396–97.

Lanham Act claims.[40] However, there was a strong dissent in the case by Judge Alex Kozinski criticizing this decision as being an improper enlargement of the right of publicity to the point that it impinges upon free speech—an opinion that many right of publicity practitioners share.[41]

B. Types of Potential Claims Overlapping with the Right of Publicity

1. Breach of Contract

Ideally, any use of a person's image in a commercial sense would begin with arms' length negotiations between a company and a professional model and would entail a written contract setting forth the scope and nature of the use of that person's right of publicity. However, even if best practices are followed at all times, problems can still arise. For example, if a model's contract is for a specific time period, and products are distributed after that time period in packaging bearing the person's image outside the scope of the agreement, or if the model approved a specific pose/image that is contracted for but other images from the photo shoot are used years later from an internal photo archive that the marketing department thinks is pre-cleared and allowable material, it can lead to liability. Furthermore, recordkeeping or changes in technology can introduce issues that were not foreseeable at the time the right of publicity release was executed. Specifically, most companies keep records only for a specific time frame and, under the ordinary course of business, purge records older than five, seven, or ten years. However, if the right of publicity contract is for a longer time period and cannot be produced if there is a conflict, it could lead to a "he said/she said" battle that is more expensive than the profits made by the product featuring the model. Companies must also be careful of data migration on servers in terms of producing evidence of the exact date or year that photos were taken and when permission was granted, especially in the event

---

40. *Id.* at 1399.

41. White v. Samsung Elecs. Am., Inc., 989 F.2d 1512 (9th Cir. 1993) (mem.) (Kozinski, J., dissenting).

that the contract cannot be located or there is a need to prove the date of a particular photo used. It could affect the statute of limitations, damages, or other aspects of the case.

In addition, even if records are meticulously kept for a long time, if a right of publicity release is granted for 20–30 years, it can affect the scope of rights that the individual intended and envisioned upon signing the agreement. For example, an endorsement contract signed in the 1970s would not have contemplated the Internet, social media, smartphone apps, virtual reality, augmented reality, and the like. Even though computers and video games existed at the time, they in no way reflected today's realities and the ability to copy and publish images available to billions of people around the world in a matter of seconds.

In terms of contracts involving the right of publicity and release language, a best practices approach would be to include a provision along the lines of "technology now known or hereafter developed throughout the universe" in an attempt to curtail future litigation if a new medium opens the door to a different way to utilize a person's right of publicity in a commercial way. However, such language may or may not hold up in court. Specifically, courts are hesitant to close all avenues of redress for the person who has licensed or otherwise contracted use of his or her right of publicity, if it appears that the scope of consent may have been exceeded. Further, even though the language is clear, there may be issues of contract law that would apply to address such scope issues, such as unconscionability and adhesion contracts. Chapter 1 discusses contracts related to video games in greater detail.

Another problematic area is unlockables, customization, Easter eggs, and other special features in electronic entertainment. All of these can lead to exceeding the scope of consent in video games, virtual reality, and augmented reality. For example, even if a video game developer secures a right of publicity release from an actor, model, or singer, it is critical to ensure that the document is properly drafted, as exceeding the scope of what is contracted for can lead to expensive consequences. For example, if the right of publicity release is for use in a game at a particular level or in connection with specific songs or actions, but special features such as unlockables make other variations possible that were not considered by the person and contracted for, liability could arise. In one case, discussed more fully in Section I.D.3.c, No Doubt's lead singer, Gwen Stefani, was not made aware that her avatar could be unlocked and made to sing songs from other bands, songs that were originally vocalized by males and/or contained content she felt was disparaging to women.[42]

2. Fraudulent Inducement

Fraudulent inducement is a contract law term that technically is not a "right of publicity" cause of action but can be used in some instances that involve the right of publicity. It typically accompanies a breach of contract claim. The elements of a claim for fraudulent inducement are the "representation of a material fact, falsity, scienter, deception, and injury."[43] This crossover cause of action is typically used when a defendant has evidence that a photographer, video game developer, or other person contracting with the model or musical artist has promised to only use the defendant's right of publicity in connection with a particular medium (such as print ads), in a specific portion of a video game (a particular level or in story mode only), or in a narrow geographic region, and so forth, and the contract is silent as to scope of use or the limitations discussed between the parties prior to the execution of the contract. Although there is an express writing showing consent of the use of the defendant's right of publicity, it can be shown that material information was misrepresented or withheld, while the scope of the consent was knowingly exceeded by means of deception. In the case of a famous model or musical artist—the type of defendant who would typically be in this position—the injury likely will be easier to prove since prior contracts may detail the value of the defendant's right of publicity or social media commentary might clearly demonstrate the injury and negative consequences suffered by the defendant.

---

42. No Doubt v. Activision Publ'g, Inc., 192 Cal. App. 4th 1018, 1023–25 (Cal. Ct. App. 2011).

43. Dalessio v. Kressler, 6 A.D.3d 57, 61 (N.Y. App. Div. 2004) (quoting Channel Master Corp. v. Aluminium Ltd. Sales, 4 N.Y.2d 403, 407 (N.Y. 1958)).

3. Trademark Infringement under the Lanham Act

At times, the right of publicity crosses over with the Lanham Act and raises issues of trademark law and/or misappropriation. For example, a defendant that is not likely to win a right of publicity claim, or wishes to avoid a state court action for some reason, may consider filing a federal claim for violation of the Lanham Act in relation to trademark infringement (in a case where there is a federal trademark registration for the person's name or nickname or common law use of that name in interstate commerce), or for the misappropriation of his or her likeness and/or false endorsement. In one famous case, Paris Hilton sued a company that produced a card that showed Hilton's face and featured her trademark expression "That's hot!" along with the caption "Paris's First Day as a Waitress."[44] Hallmark claimed the use of Hilton's name and catchphrase was a parody and protected under the First Amendment.[45] After taking the case up to the Ninth Circuit, the case settled when the court disagreed that Hallmark's use of Hilton's identity was protected speech, and it became clear that Hallmark might have a difficult time showing transformative use.[46]

In another case, Shaquille O'Neal, affectionately known to fans as "Shaq," filed a lawsuit for trademark infringement and unfair competition (among other things) via his company, Mine O'Mine, the owner of the registered trademarks for his name and nickname.[47] The complaint alleged infringement of those trademarks by an online retailer called Shaqtus Orange Clothing Co. that sold clothing and miscellaneous collectable items.[48] The goods at issue there contained a caricature of a cactus named "Shaqtus" bearing features belonging to O'Neal, his jersey number, and/or basketball indicia, allegedly designed to harken to Shaq's persona, as O'Neal's nickname became "The Big Shaqtus" after he moved teams to play for the Phoenix Suns.[49] In that case,

---

44. Hilton v. Hallmark Cards, 599 F.3d 894, 899 (9th Cir. 2010).
45. *Id.* at 899–900.
46. *Id.* at 909–12.
47. Mine O'Mine, Inc. v. Calmese, No. 2:10-CV-0043-KJD-PAL, 2011 WL 2728390 (D. Nev. July 12, 2011), *aff'd*, 489 Fed. Appx. 175 (9th Cir. 2012).
48. *Id.* at *1.
49. *Id.*

the plaintiff claimed that there was a high likelihood of confusion based on the similarities of the marks (a mash-up of O'Neal's name and the term "cactus"), the strength of the mark (which here was strong), the proximity of the goods, marketing channels used, type of goods, and the degree of care likely to be exercised by the relevant consuming public.[50] The court agreed with the plaintiff and cited defendants' intent to cause confusion in selecting the mark in the first place, as well as the likelihood of expansion of the product lines, as additional support for the decision.[51] Additional trademark case law is discussed in Chapter 4.

4. False Endorsement/False Designation of Origin under the Lanham Act

In the Vanna White case discussed earlier, the court noted that "[a] celebrity is entitled to vindicate property rights in his or her identity under this section of the Lanham Act, because he has an economic interest in his identity akin to that of a traditional trademark holder."[52]

With respect to Lanham Act cases based on a theory of false endorsement, a musical artist named Robert Burck who performs under the stage name "The Naked Cowboy" sued Mars, Inc. over a commercial involving an M&M's character wearing Burck's standard performance costume of an all-white ensemble consisting of cowboy boots, underwear, and a cowboy hat, while playing a white guitar.[53] In a case like this, unlike an instance where the person's name is mentioned[54] or a look-alike *human* model has been used,[55] a plaintiff may have difficulty showing that there was misappropriation of his "picture" or "of a portrait" of a "living person" under right of publicity law. This is especially true if the courts of that state literally interpret the statute and there is no common law recourse for the acts of the defendant, such as was the case for

---

50. *Id.* at *2.

51. *Id.* at *8.

52. Facenda v. N.F.L. Films, Inc., 488 F. Supp. 2d 491, 503–04 (E.D. Pa. 2007) (citing White v. Samsung Elecs. Am., Inc., 971 F.2d 1395 (9th Cir. 1992)).

53. Burck v. Mars, Inc., 571 F. Supp. 2d 446 (S.D.N.Y. 2008).

54. *See, e.g., Mine O'Mine, Inc.*, 2011 WL 2728390.

55. *See, e.g.*, White v. Samsung Elecs. Am., Inc., 971 F.2d 1395 (9th Cir. 1992).

Burck, who was unable to meet the stringent parameters of New York's right of publicity statute.[56]

However, in an instance such as a cartoon character dressed as a recognizable musical artist, actor, model, or the like, another option is filing an action for false endorsement under section 43(a) of the Lanham Act, which applies in instances where:

> [a]ny living person who, on or in connection with any goods or services, . . . uses in commerce . . . false or misleading representation of fact, which—
>
> . . .
>
> is likely to cause confusion . . . or to deceive as to the affiliation, connection, or association of such person with another person, or as to the origin, sponsorship, or approval of his or her goods, services, or commercial activities by another person.[57]

Burck was able to avail himself of the Lanham Act and the court allowed his case to proceed on the false endorsement claim even though his right of publicity claim failed.[58]

Similarly, in the case between the owner of Marilyn Monroe's rights and A.V.E.L.A., the right of publicity claims had been dismissed, but when A.V.E.L.A. sued the estate of Marilyn Monroe for a declaratory judgment of noninfringement, the estate counterclaimed with the Lanham Act—citing damages on the grounds of false endorsement.[59] In that case, the court articulated the additional burden that a plaintiff in a Lanham Act case bears that is not present in a right of publicity case—a likelihood of consumer confusion must be shown.[60] The A.V.E.L.A. dispute that began years ago between the parties is ongoing. And in 2017, a judge in the Southern District of New York issued a ruling allowing A.V.E.L.A.'s counterclaim to proceed on the question of whether

---

56. *Burck*, 571 F. Supp. 2d at 450–51.

57. Lanham Act § 43(a)(1)(A), 15 U.S.C. § 1125(a)(1)(A) (2012).

58. *Burck*, 571 F. Supp. 2d 446.

59. A.V.E.L.A., Inc. v. Estate of Marilyn Monroe, LLC, 131 F. Supp. 3d 196 (S.D.N.Y. 2015).

60. *Id.* at 205.

the trademarks owned by the estate of Marilyn Monroe are subject to cancellation on the grounds that the marks lack distinctiveness or have become generic.[61] In another declaratory judgment action, Virtual Marilyn, LLC filed a similar suit against the estate of Marilyn Monroe regarding its copyrighted computer-generated character "VM2-Virtual Marilyn," a fictional character "adopting the persona of Marilyn Monroe" and featured in an audiovisual work that Virtual Marilyn, LLC had registered with the U.S. Copyright Office.[62] That suit was terminated because proof of service of the complaint was never filed, but it likely would have tracked the outcome of the A.V.E.L.A. case if it had proceeded.[63]

5. Copyright

The right of publicity in a work of art is a distinct right that is not identical to the copyright in that same work. In some cases though, copyright preemption may apply. Preemption is discussed in Section I.D.3, but there are times when a plaintiff might assert only the copyright claim in a work, rather than attempting to bring a right of publicity claim. This is especially true in an instance where an artist owns both the copyright in the work as well as being featured in the work. For example, if a famous artist were to take a selfie or to paint a self-portrait that a commercial entity used in a commercial or advertisement, the artist would likely have better success with a copyright lawsuit, provided that the work was registered with the U.S. Copyright Office *before* the infringement occurred. This is because copyright protection comes with statutory damages and attorneys' fees in some cases.[64] It also has a far more predictable outcome due to the fact that it enjoys federal protection granted in the U.S. Constitution.[65] A copyright suit gives the plaintiff a more powerful enforcement tool, as the artist (or the artist's heirs)

---

61. A.V.E.L.A., Inc. v. Estate of Marilyn Monroe, LLC, 241 F. Supp. 3d 461 (S.D.N.Y. 2017).

62. Virtual Marilyn, LLC v. Estate of Marilyn Monroe, LLC, No. 1:14-cv-07938-SAS (S.D.N.Y. 2014).

63. *Id.*

64. 17 U.S.C. § 504 (2018).

65. U.S. CONST. art. 1, § 8, cl. 8.

would have an easier time proving damages and it would not matter where the infringement took place in terms of the protection afforded. In the real world, a plaintiff would typically assert both types of claims, as well as any Lanham Act claims available, as an "insurance policy" in case one or more of the other claims were dismissed for some reason. Information on copyright cases in relation to video games generally can be found in Chapter 2.

C. Variations in State Law

One of the most difficult aspects of right of publicity law is the vast disparity between the right of publicity laws of each state. Since most businesses advertise on the Internet, which can be viewed from almost anywhere, and most larger companies ship into several states, regions, or offer nationwide service, this creates a thorny issue of liability. For example, from the plaintiff's side, each case must be analyzed in terms of the number of years of protection, whether there is post-mortem protection, and whether those rights must have been registered or used by the individual prior to the alleged right of publicity violation. Take the duration of protection—it can last from ten to 100 years beyond a person's lifetime or, in some states, indefinitely (so long as it is being used).[66] There are also instances where a statutory claim in a particular state can fail, but the elements of a common law claim can be met. And since the majority of right of publicity cases settle due to the difficulty in predicting outcomes, there is a lack of case law providing solid guidance in any given state. On top of that, circuit splits are more common and the appellate courts are often unwilling to entertain any right of publicity cases unless they contain a constitutional law crossover such as the First Amendment or copyright issues. In fact, to date, there has been only one Supreme Court right of publicity case decided![67]

---

66. Right of Publicity, *supra* note 4.
67. Zacchini v. Scripps-Howard Broad. Co., 433 U.S. 562 (1977).

D. Defenses

1. First Amendment

There has always been tension between freedom of speech and right of publicity in the United States.[68] The United States was founded on the principle that its citizens should be free to speak their minds and share those opinions with others, either privately or via a free press; exercise religious freedom; create artwork that expresses the artist's viewpoint—even if that is critical of another person, an entity, or the government; and the like. Because of America's tendency to fiercely guard such freedoms, there are many ways in which a person's name, likeness, persona, and voice can be used without that person's authorization, even for a commercial purpose, if such use falls within the protective ambit of the First Amendment.[69] However, this does not mean that the First Amendment trumps any and all uses of a person's right of publicity. All U.S. courts have advocated a balance between the First Amendment and the right of publicity, but the specific process for such balancing has proven difficult to articulate and has led to disparate balancing tests, numerous dissents, and apparently conflicting outcomes in certain circuits.

a. Newsworthy Exception

Although there is a broad swath of First Amendment protection surrounding most stories found in the news that feature a person's identity or persona, there are exceptions to the newsworthy exception that are important to understand, as they offer some guidance as to the metes and bounds of the First Amendment's ability to provide a full defense to a right of publicity claim. For example, it must be a *current* matter of public interest—publishing old photographs

---

68. *See, e.g.,* ETW Corp. v. Jireh Publ'g, Inc., 332 F.3d 915 (6th Cir. 2003); Cardtoons, L.C. v. Major League Baseball Players Ass'n, 95 F.3d 959 (10th Cir. 1996); *but see* White v. Samsung Elecs. Am., Inc., 989 F.2d 1512 (9th Cir. 1993) (mem.) (Kozinski, J., dissenting).

69. *See, e.g.,* Ross v. Roberts, 222 Cal. App. 4th 677 (Cal. Ct. App. 2013) (finding a rap song's use of a former drug dealer's name protected by the First Amendment); *ETW Corp.,* 332 F.3d 915 (finding an artist's use of Tiger Wood's likeness in a painting protected by the First Amendment); *Cardtoons, L.C.,* 95 F.3d 959 (finding parody trading cards of baseball players protected by the First Amendment).

of a person unrelated to the newsworthy event are not afforded First Amendment protection. Neither are actions protected by the First Amendment when a reporting piece becomes more of a commercial use of a person's likeness by the news entity, rather than an informational one that pertains to a subject of public interest.

The most famous case, and the only U.S. Supreme Court case touching on the right of publicity, is *Zacchini v. Scripps-Howard Broadcasting.*[70] Hugo Zacchini performed a "human cannonball" act perfected by his father for decades at carnivals, fairs, and circuses around the world.[71] As an entertainer, his act consisted of a drawn-out build up to the 15 second climax of him being shot out of a cannon (sometimes over a carousel) into a net approximately 200 feet away.[72] In the Zacchini case, a local television station filmed all 15 seconds of the act's climax at an Ohio county fair, and aired the entirety of it without Zacchini's permission.[73]

The trial court granted summary judgment for Zacchini, which was reversed by the appellate court.[74] The Ohio Supreme Court held that the television station had a constitutional privilege "to include in its newscasts matters of public interest that would otherwise be protected by the right of publicity, absent an intent to injure or to appropriate for some nonprivileged purpose."[75] The U.S. Supreme Court disagreed—balancing the First Amendment with the state's valid interest in protecting its citizens' right of publicity.[76] In other words, the U.S. Supreme Court made it clear that the First Amendment does not automatically trump a state right of publicity claim.[77]

---

70. *Zacchini*, 433 U.S. 562.

71. *Id.* at 564–65; *see also* Paul Guzzo, *Hugo Zacchini, Who Wowed Crowds as Human Cannonball, Dead at 88*, TAMPA BAY TIMES, Nov. 14, 2016, http://www.tampabay.com/news/obituaries/hugo-zacchini-who-wowed-crowds-as-human-cannonball-dead-at-88/2302266.

72. *Zacchini*, 433 U.S. at 564–65; *see also* Video: Human Cannonball—Zacchini the Modern Münchhausen (Weird Reels 2014), https://www.youtube.com/watch?v=EuTzWPJ73vY.

73. *Zacchini*, 433 U.S. at 565.

74. *Id.* at 564–65.

75. *Id.* at 565.

76. *Id.* at 578.

77. *Id.* at 577.

The U.S. Supreme Court held that the news media did not have blanket immunization under the First Amendment to record and broadcast Zacchini's *entire act* without his permission.[78] Such a holding would deprive a performer of the right to control his or her commercial image—and diminish or negate the value of that performance.[79] The thrust of the U.S. Supreme Court's argument was that if the public were to see the act in its entirety for free on the news, there would be less of an incentive to purchase a ticket to see it live at the fair.[80] In addition, the actions of the television station went to "the heart of petitioner's ability to earn a living as an entertainer."[81]

Another exception to the newsworthy defense is triggered when a person's name, likeness, or image is used to "boost" a current story with facts from that person's past. An example of this is *Toffoloni v. LFP Publishing Group, LLC.*[82] In that case, the mother of Nancy Benoit, a murder victim who had made her living as a model and professional wrestler, brought suit against LFP for publishing nude photos of her deceased daughter in *Hustler Magazine* near the time of her death.[83] The Court of Appeals for the Eleventh Circuit found that the newsworthiness exception under the First Amendment did *not* apply to the photographs because there was no nexus to the current matter of public concern (i.e., her murder).[84] Specifically, if *Hustler* had used the photographs alone, the newsworthy exception could never apply, and even though *Hustler* included a biographical article adjacent the photographs, the article "was incidental to the photographs."[85] After analyzing the magazine cover, the table of contents, and the title of the article, all of which mentioned Benoit's name and the words "nude" or "au natural,"

---

78. *Id.* at 574–75.
79. *Id.* at 576.
80. *Id.*
81. *Id.*
82. Toffoloni v. LFP Publ'g Group, LLC, 572 F.3d 1201, 1213 (11th Cir. 2009).
83. *Id.* at 1204–05.
84. *Id.* at 1209–10.
85. *Id.* at 1209.

the court stated that "[t]he heart of this article was the publication of nude photographs—not the corresponding biography."[86]

b. Satire and Parody

In the November 1983 issue of *Hustler Magazine*, an advertisement that was deemed to be a parody appeared that depicted then-popular fundamentalist minister Jerry Falwell in a negative light.[87] Specifically, the mock interview and advertisement intimated that Falwell had engaged in incestuous activities with his mother in an outhouse while drunk.[88] Falwell had founded the Moral Majority, a "patriarchal protest movement," in 1979 and was still involved in politics at the time of the *Hustler Magazine* ad. Not surprisingly, Falwell's suit contained invasion of privacy claims, intentional infliction of emotional distress, as well as others.[89] The Supreme Court ruled that although the statements were highly offensive, such speech could not reasonably be construed to state actual facts about Falwell—a public figure—as U.S. citizens have a right to criticize or satirize public figures and officials.[90] The exception to this rule is if the defendant implies that the patently offensive statements are true with "actual malice"[91]—something that did not occur in the *Hustler* case where the magazine included notifications in the table of contents and at the bottom of the page indicating that the account was fictional.

c. Art and Drama

With respect to art and drama, the tension is readily apparent between the right of publicity and the First Amendment. In the case *ETW Corp. v. Jireh Publishing, Inc.*,[92] the Sixth Circuit looked at a work of art by the artist Rick Rush that depicted Tiger Woods in various standing and crouching positions in a single creative work

---

86. *Id.*
87. Hustler Magazine, Inc. v. Falwell, 485 U.S. 46 (1988).
88. *Id.* at 48.
89. *Id.*
90. *Id.* at 57.
91. *Id.* at 56.
92. ETW Corp. v. Jireh Publ'g, Inc., 332 F.3d 915 (6th Cir. 2003).

entitled "The Masters of Augusta."[93] Rush is an artist known for depicting numerous sports figures in various scenes that capture the "style" of the particular athlete's performance (e.g., Walter Payton, Michael Jordan, Nolan Ryan, Jack Nicklaus, and Martina Navratilova, to name a few).[94] In this case, the court examined the various transformative elements of the limited edition Tiger Woods lithograph under the "transformative test."[95] Because the artist's vision included not only the clubhouse located at the Augusta National grounds, but also included several well-known golfers from past ages looking on at Woods and seemingly encouraging his performance at the competition, the court found that the work was "entitled to the full protection of the First Amendment."[96] In particular, the work employed creative elements and did not depict literal elements of Tiger Woods' actual performance during the competition. Instead, it contained artistic elements that outweighed "any adverse effect" on the market for other authorized Tiger Woods merchandise—Woods would "still be able to reap substantial financial rewards from authorized appearances and endorsements."[97]

2. Fair Use

There are several different tests that the various courts use for determining whether fair use applies in a right of publicity case, the most popular of which are the predominant use test,[98] the *Rogers* test,[99] and the transformative use test[100] (based largely on copyright principles).

a. The Predominant Use Test

The predominant use test looks at the purpose of the allegedly infringing work. For example, does it stand on its own merit as

93. *Id.* at 918.

94. *Id.* at n.1.

95. *Id.* at 938.

96. *Id.* at 937.

97. *Id.* at 938.

98. Doe v. TCI Cablevision, 110 S.W.3d 363 (Mo. 2003) (en banc).

99. Rogers v. Grimaldi, 875 F.2d 994, 1003–04 (2d Cir. 1989).

100. Comedy III Prods., Inc. v. Gary Saderup, Inc., 25 Cal. 4th 387 (Cal. 2001).

an artistic work, is it a piece meant to criticize a public individual and/or his or her actions, or is it an expressive object designed to ignite comment or controversy? These types of uses likely will be protected by the First Amendment and will be deemed a fair use of a person's name, image, or likeness. In contrast, if the item at issue is clearly designed to draw customers in based on the popularity or notoriety of the person's right of publicity, and the use is overtly commercial in nature—implying an endorsement or sponsorship of the third-party product or service—such use likely will be deemed infringing. In other words, if the purpose behind the use of a person's name, persona, or photograph is to exploit that person's right of publicity to create new customers or boost sales of the item being sold, then the person can usually recover on a right of publicity claim.

The predominant use test was articulated in *Doe v. TCI Cablevision*,[101] in which hockey player Tony Twist sued comic book creator Todd McFarlane for unauthorized use of his image in the form of the comic book character Antonio "Tony Twist" Twistelli in the comic book series *Spawn*.[102] The Missouri court, rejecting both the *Rogers* test and the transformative use test, opted to create its own test, which looked to the "predominant use" of the contested work:

> If a product is being sold that predominantly exploits the commercial value of an individual's identity, that product should be held to violate the right of publicity and not be protected by the First Amendment, even if there is some "expressive" content in it that might qualify as "speech" in other circumstances. If, on the other hand, the predominant purpose of the product is to make an expressive comment on or about a celebrity, the expressive values could be given greater weight.[103]

---

101. *Doe*, 110 S.W.3d 363 (en banc).
102. *Id.* at 365.
103. *Id.* at 374 (quoting Mark S. Lee, *Agents of Chaos: Judicial Confusion in Defining the Right of Publicity—Free Speech Interface*, 23 Loy. L.A. Ent. L. Rev. 471, 500 (2003)).

b. The Rogers Test

The *Rogers* test is the result of a lawsuit filed by Ginger Rogers regarding a Federico Fellini film entitled *Ginger and Fred* featuring a couple that performs a music hall act imitating Fred Astaire and Ginger Rogers.[104] The *Rogers* test requires that the court first look to whether or not the use of the person's name, likeness, or persona is "wholly unrelated" to the content of the work or "explicitly misleads" the end user into believing that the person whose right of publicity was used endorsed the item.[105] In the case of the movie *Ginger and Fred*, such use was clearly related to the storyline of two aging performers who reunite to do their act years after their heyday.[106] More importantly, the work was not a thinly veiled advertisement that capitalized on the fame of Ginger Rogers to lure customers and fans of hers into buying third-party goods/services.[107]

c. The Transformative Use Test

The transformative use test was formulated by the California Supreme Court in *Comedy III Productions, Inc. v. Gary Saderup, Inc.*,[108] a 2001 case involving depictions of the comedy group the Three Stooges on lithographic prints and screen images.[109] In that case, the court adapted and applied the transformative test from the fair use defense previously used in copyright law, employing "a balancing test between the First Amendment and the right of publicity based on whether the work in question adds significant creative elements so as to be transformed into something more than a mere celebrity likeness or imitation."[110] The court further detailed that "when a work contains significant transformative elements, it is not only especially worthy of First Amendment protection, but it is also less likely to interfere with the economic interest protected

---

104. *Rogers*, 875 F.2d at 996.

105. *Id.* at 1005.

106. *Id.* at 996–97.

107. *Id.* at 1004–05.

108. Comedy III Prods., Inc. v. Gary Saderup, Inc., 25 Cal. 4th 387 (Cal. 2001).

109. *Id.* at 393.

110. *Id.* at 391.

by the right of publicity."[111] However, the court did not just bring the defense over from copyright law intact, but rather recognized that some aspects of that defense are "particularly pertinent" to the right of publicity defense.[112]

The transformative use test formulated in *Comedy III* uses five factors to determine whether a work is sufficiently transformative to obtain First Amendment protection.[113] The first factor is if "the celebrity likeness is one of the 'raw materials' from which the original work is synthesized," then that work is more likely to be found to be transformative if "the depiction or imitation of the celebrity is the very sum and substance of the work in question."[114] The second factor indicates that the work is more likely to be found to be protected if the work is "primarily the defendant's own expression," provided that the expression is "something other than the likeness of the celebrity."[115] The third factor provides that the court's inquiry should be "more quantitative than qualitative," and should inquire as to "whether the literal and imitative or the creative elements predominate in the work."[116] In the fourth factor, the court set out a "subsidiary inquiry" for use in close cases, which examines whether "the marketability and economic value of the challenged work derive primarily from the fame of the celebrity depicted."[117] Finally, the fifth factor of the transformative use test finds a work not to be transformative "when an artist's skill and talent is manifestly subordinated to the overall goal of creating a conventional portrait of a celebrity so as to commercially exploit his or her fame."[118]

Applying this test to the case at hand, the California Supreme Court found that the lithographs and t-shirts featuring the images of the Three Stooges were not transformative, as the court could

---

111. *Id.* at 405.
112. *Id.* at 404.
113. *Id.* at 405–08.
114. *Id.* at 406.
115. *Id.*
116. *Id.* at 407.
117. *Id.*
118. *Id.* at 408.

"discern no significant transformative or creative contribution"[119] that was made in using the actors' images. Rather, while the court recognized the "undeniable skill" of the artist, it found that this "skill is manifestly subordinated to the overall goal of creating literal, conventional depictions of The Three Stooges so as to exploit their fame."[120] Finally, the court noted that "were we to decide that [the artist's] depictions were protected by the First Amendment, we cannot perceive how the right of publicity would remain a viable right other than in cases of falsified celebrity endorsements."[121]

3. Copyright Preemption

Copyright preemption is an idea that is fairly recent in our country's history, and was only enacted by Congress by way of the Copyright Act of 1978. Specifically, 17 U.S.C.A. § 301(a)–(b) sets forth the "boundary line between federal and state power."[122] Unfortunately for intellectual property lawyers and their clients, some ambiguity about Congress's full intention on preemption is built into the act. An "illustrative list" of preemption exceptions in the September 3, 1976, House Report specifically carving out the right of publicity as not equivalent to the exclusive rights within the general scope of copyright was stricken at the 11th hour, leaving us with inconsistent notions about whether or not there is copyright preemption of right of publicity claims.[123] The majority of courts say that there is no preemption.[124] The rationale for this is that the right of publicity is a personal right that protects "human identity," which does not fall within the ambit of copyrightable subject matter.[125] On the other hand, the minority view is that some preemption occurs in specific, narrow types of fact patterns, such as where the "unauthorized use of plaintiff's composition—is the same as that of copyright and is therefore

---

119. *Id.* at 409.
120. *Id.*
121. *Id.*
122. 2 J. THOMAS MCCARTHY, THE RIGHTS OF PUBLICITY AND PRIVACY § 11:47 (2d ed. 2018).
123. H.R. REP. NO. 94-1476, at 132 (1976).
124. 2 MCCARTHY, *supra* note 122, § 11:50.
125. *Id.*

preempted."[126] An example of the minority view is a performance of a person, group, or athlete that is being recorded for purposes of simultaneous broadcast—the right of publicity and the copyrighted work are one and the same in such a case.[127]

The copyright preemption test involves the "two doors" of § 301(a), namely: (1) the right of publicity claim is not equivalent to the copyright, and (2) the subject matter of the claim falls outside the scope of copyrightable subject matter.[128]

a. The Right of Publicity after Death

One way in which right of publicity laws vary from state to state is when such laws protect the rights of celebrities, during life alone or after death as well. Right of publicity protection after death is only available in the following states: Arizona, California, Florida, Georgia, Hawaii, Illinois, Indiana, Kentucky, Michigan, Nebraska, Nevada, New Jersey, Ohio, Oklahoma, Pennsylvania, South Carolina, Tennessee, Texas, Virginia, and Washington.[129] Whether a celebrity's image is protected after his or her death in a particular state can depend on whether the famous celebrity was domiciled in that state and whose estate is diligent in protecting and licensing those rights.

b. Development of the Post-Mortem Right of Publicity Law

The litigation over the post-mortem rights of beloved actress Marilyn Monroe has led to an evolution in this area of the law. The post-mortem right of publicity in California was amended in 2007 after the ruling in federal district courts in both California and New York held that a property right that did not exist at the time of a person's death could not be devised by will.[130] These decisions

---

126. Motown Record Corp. v. George A. Hormel & Co., 657 F. Supp. 1236, 1240–41 (C.D. Cal. 1987).

127. 2 McCarthy, *supra* note 122, § 11:54.

128. *Id.* § 11:47.

129. Rothman's Roadmap to the Right of Publicity, *The Law*, http://www.rightofpublicityroadmap.com/law/ (last visited July 26, 2018).

130. *See* Cal. Civ. Code § 3344.1 (2012) (amending the statute to clarify the boundaries of post-mortem right of publicity protection in California in response to the rulings in Milton H. Greene Archives, Inc. v. CMG Worldwide, Inc., 568 F. Supp. 2d 1152 (C.D. Cal. 2008), and Shaw Family Archives, Ltd. v. CMG Worldwide, Inc., 589 F. Supp. 2d 331 (S.D.N.Y. 2008)).

were made in the litigation that transpired in regard to the estate of Marilyn Monroe, and in both instances the court held that the post-mortem right of publicity of the actress was not inheritable through her will due to the fact that she died in 1962, before the right of publicity existed in the state of California.[131] The Marilyn Monroe litigation spans more than ten years, involves multiple plaintiffs and defendants (as some of the cases were filed on a declaratory judgment basis), and has been tried in California, Indiana, and New York courts.[132]

Over the years, Marilyn Monroe's estate has fought vigorously, attempting to shut down the use of her image by photographers in an attempt to maintain control over all merchandise displaying Monroe's image—a licensing business that brings in tens of millions of dollars per year to her estate. More than 50 years after her death, the public is still obsessed with Marilyn Monroe, and clamoring for more items with her image on them. The difficulty in having so many disparate laws in the states that have right of publicity protection, and the fact that many states have none, is that it can lead to forum shopping. For example, many movie stars and famous folk have homes in Los Angeles, New York City, and other regions, some of which are outside the United States. When a celebrity dies, it can often be argued that the person was "domiciled" in multiple jurisdictions. But the heirs of that person's estate need to choose a single domicile for various legal purposes. In the case of Marilyn Monroe, those managing her estate chose New York as her "domicile" for tax purposes—a choice that made enforcing her right of publicity difficult, as can be seen by the numerous lawsuits.[133] However, the courts have been firm on the

131. *See* Milton H. Greene Archives, Inc. v. CMG Worldwide, Inc., 568 F. Supp. 2d 1152, 1156 (C.D. Cal. 2008); Shaw Family Archives, Ltd. v. CMG Worldwide, Inc., 589 F. Supp. 2d 331, 333–34 (S.D.N.Y. 2008).

132. *See generally Shaw Family Archives*, 589 F. Supp. 2d 331; *Milton H. Greene Archives*, 568 F. Supp. 2d 1152, *aff'd sub nom.* Milton H. Greene Archives, Inc. v. Marilyn Monroe, LLC, 692 F.3d 983 (9th Cir. 2012) (Milton II); A.V.E.L.A., Inc. v. Estate of Marilyn Monroe, LLC, 34 F. Supp. 3d 311 (S.D.N.Y. 2015); A.V.E.L.A., Inc. v. Estate of Marilyn Monroe, LLC, 131 F. Supp. 3d 196 (S.D.N.Y. 2015).

133. *Milton H. Greene Archives*, 568 F. Supp. 2d at 1196–97.

stance that you cannot pick and choose domiciles to take the most advantage of various types of laws.[134] In other words, to give the estate of Marilyn Monroe the option to choose New York domicile to maximize tax savings, and then turn around and claim California domicile for the best enforcement of her right of publicity would be unfair, as a potential defendant would never be able to analyze any situation if all that was required by the estate of a deceased celebrity would be to change the official domicile when it suited the plaintiff.

Faced with rejections of its right of publicity claims, the estate of Marilyn Monroe has tried instead to enforce her image via trademark law. In 2015, a judge in the Southern District of New York allowed a trademark infringement case to proceed, rejecting A.V.E.L.A., Inc.'s claim that the trademark suit was "a thinly veiled attempt to assert a right that does not exist—a right of publicity in Marilyn Monroe."[135] Judge Katherine Polk Failla carefully distinguished the two causes of action in her ruling, and held that "[t]he key distinction between a right of publicity and a false endorsement claim is that the latter requires a showing of consumer confusion."[136] However, two years later, that same judge also denied the estate of Marilyn Monroe's motion to dismiss A.V.E.L.A.'s declaratory judgment complaint and permitted a counterclaim to cancel the trademarks owned by the estate of Marilyn Monroe on the grounds that they have become generic.[137] Clearly, unless some uniform right of publicity guidance is achieved, both plaintiffs and defendants will have a very incomplete map of how to move forward in any right of publicity dispute, and it appears that even trademark law may not be enough to save the day unless there is very clear evidence of likelihood of confusion or actual confusion.

---

134. *Id.; see also Milton II*, 692 F.3d at 999–1000.

135. *A.V.E.L.A., Inc.*, 131 F. Supp. 3d at 204–05.

136. *Id.* at 205.

137. A.V.E.L.A., Inc. v. Estate of Marilyn Monroe, LLC, 241 F. Supp. 3d 461 (S.D.N.Y. 2017).

c. Variations in State Law and Call for Federal Law

In California, the post-mortem right of publicity was recognized
in *Lugosi v. Universal Pictures*.[138] However, the holding of this 1979
case was very narrow, and the court noted that this post-mortem
right existed rarely, if ever.[139] In response to this ruling, the California Legislature opted to create a statutory post-mortem right
of publicity in 1985, and changed the numbering of the statute to
California Civil Code section 3344.1 in a 1999 amendment.[140] These
amendments also extended the term from the life of the author
plus 50 years to the life of the author plus 70 years, repealed
the previous exemptions and replaced them with those found in
section 3344.1(a)(2) and (3), and added section 3344.1(n), which
states that the act applies to the finding of liability when the
circumstances leading to a claim "occur directly in this state."[141]
Claims of such rights can be registered with the California secretary of state, and potential licensees can check with the secretary's registry to find the contact information to obtain consent to
use that person's name or likeness.[142] Unlike in some states, the
deceased person's rights are protected in California whether or
not that person exploited the right of publicity during his or her
lifetime.[143] The damages for infringing the state law are set at $750
and actual damages, as well as any profits from the unauthorized
use that are attributable to the use and that are not taken into
account when computing the actual damages.[144] Punitive damages,
as well as attorneys' fees and costs for the prevailing party, are
also available under the statute.[145] The statute also includes burden shifting between the injured party and the alleged violator, in
that the injured party only has to provide proof of gross revenue

---

138. Lugosi v. Universal Pictures, 25 Cal. 3d 813 (Cal. 1979).
139. *Id.* at 823 (holding, by majority, that post-mortem right of publicity only
exists if the right of publicity was exercised during the person's life); *see also* 2
MCCARTHY, *supra* note 122, § 9:22.
140. 2 MCCARTHY, *supra* note 122.
141. CAL. CIV. CODE § 3344.1(1)(n) (2012); *see also* 2 MCCARTHY, *supra* note 122.
142. CAL. CIV. CODE § 3344.1(f)(2).
143. *Id.* § 3344.1(h).
144. *Id.* § 3344.1(a).
145. *Id.*

attributable to the use, the burden then shifts to the violator, who is required to prove his or her deductible damages.[146]

Another difficulty is that even in jurisdictions where the test to be used is set in stone, courts within the same circuit can wind up with seemingly inconsistent outcomes, especially where the First Amendment is involved. And when those tests are applied in the video game context, the picture is less clear, as the concepts do not always translate neatly from traditional media to newer platforms and formats. In that regard, it is even more difficult when analyzing such issues in relation to virtual reality and augmented reality, as they are newer technologies with less guidance from the courts.

As noted previously, one early case addressing the tension between the right of publicity and the First Amendment was the Second Circuit case *Rogers v. Grimaldi*.[147] The *Rogers* test, briefly, protects the title of a work against a famous person's Lanham Act claims if the work in question: (1) has some "artistic relevance" to the underlying work and (2) does not "explicitly mislead[] as to the source or the content of the work."[148]

The *Rogers* test has also been applied in other cases. For instance, in *Parks v. LaFace Records*,[149] Atlanta-based musical group OutKast released a song entitled "Rosa Parks."[150] Parks brought suit against OutKast and LaFace Records on various grounds, including the right of publicity.[151] The only connection between the song and Parks was one fairly tangential reference in the hook, to wit, "Ah ha, hush that fuss/Everybody move to the back of the bus. . . ."[152]

The district court in *Parks* granted summary judgment to defendants, applying the *Rogers* test.[153] The Sixth Circuit, while reversing, nonetheless adopted the *Rogers* test as the proper test

---

146. *Id.*
147. Rogers v. Grimaldi, 875 F.2d 994 (2d Cir. 1989); discussed more fully *supra* notes 105–107.
148. *Id.* at 1000.
149. Parks v. LaFace Records, 329 F.3d 437 (6th Cir. 2003).
150. *Id.* at 442.
151. *Id.* at 442–44.
152. *Id.* at 442.
153. *Id.* at 444.

in that circumstance.[154] The case was remanded because it was not clear as a matter of law that the OutKast song would satisfy the *Rogers* test.[155]

There is authority for the proposition that the bar for "artistic relevance" is very low. In *ESS Entertainment 2000 v. Rock Star Videos, Inc.*,[156] Rock Star Videos produced and sold *Grand Theft Auto: San Andreas*, which included the fictional city of Los Santos (based on Los Angeles), which in turn included the fictional/virtual strip club Pig Pen, based on plaintiff's real-life strip club Play Pen.[157] While this case appears to be more about trademark than publicity rights, the Ninth Circuit's analysis of the *Rogers* rule is important here. The Ninth Circuit set the bar for the "artistic relevance" prong of the test at "merely . . . above zero."[158] The case is often cited for that proposition alone.[159] However, other cases, such as the Sixth Circuit's decision in *Parks*, speak to a possible higher standard for "artistic relevance."[160]

Another effort to balance the First Amendment and the right of publicity is the "predominant use" test.[161] As discussed previously, the predominant use test looks to what the main purpose of the product or work is to determine the extent of its protection as free expression.

---

154. *Id.* at 451–52.

155. *Id.* at 459.

156. ESS Entm't 2000 v. Rock Star Videos, Inc., 547 F.3d 1095 (9th Cir. 2008).

157. *Id.* at 1096–98.

158. *Id.* at 1100.

159. *See, e.g.*, Brown v. Elec. Arts, Inc., 724 F.3d 1235, 1243 (9th Cir. 2013); Univ. of Ala. Bd. of Trs. v. New Life Art, Inc., 683 F.3d 1266, 1278 (11th Cir. 2012); Fighters Inc. v. Elec. Arts, Inc., No. CV 09-06389 SJO (VBKx), 2009 WL 10699504, at *8 (C.D. Cal. Oct. 30, 2009). The authors' opinion is that more carefully read, the court was looking to the Play Pen recreation as a facet of a broader "artistically relevant" goal, where recreating something evocative of the Play Pen was a necessary part of the overall artistic goal of creating a faux-Los Angeles. That is, the Play Pen alone may not be particularly artistically relevant, but that prong of the test is satisfied because the Play Pen is an element in a broader aggregate, which aggregate has the requisite artistic relevance.

160. *Parks*, 329 F.3d at 448–49.

161. Doe v. TCI Cablevision, 110 S.W.3d 363 (Mo. 2003) (en banc); discussed more fully *supra* notes 101 and 103.

Both the *Rogers* test and the predominant use test were developed from trademark law; the *Rogers* test in particular was useful with regard to the use of famous persons in the *titles* of various works. In addressing the tension between rights of publicity and the First Amendment with regard to the *content* of the contested works, jurisprudence turned to copyright law to strike the balance.

The "transformative use" test, which finds its roots in copyright law, is more appropriate in determining the First Amendment balance with respect to the *content* of an expressive work than the other tests, because copyright law is similarly concerned with the content of whatever expressive work is in dispute.

There is a fair amount of case law guiding an understanding of the transformative use test in action. A California court applied the same transformative use test in *Winter v. D.C. Comics*.[162] In *Winter*, musicians Johnny and Edgar Winter sued over the alleged infringement of their likenesses in the form of comic book characters Johnny and Edgar Autumn.[163] Notably, the Winter brothers are albino, as were the Autumn brothers, although the comic book depicted the Autumn brothers as "villainous half-worm, half-human[s]."[164]

There is little debate that comic books in general are entitled to First Amendment protection, and the California Supreme Court applied the transformative use test, holding that "the comic books are transformative and entitled to First Amendment protection."[165] A driving factor in the court's decision was the reasoning that the characters were "but cartoon characters . . . in a larger story, which is itself quite expressive."[166] The court held that the comic books "are not just conventional depictions of plaintiffs but contain significant expressive content other than plaintiffs' mere likenesses" and "[t]o the extent the drawings of the Autumn brothers resemble plaintiffs at all, they are distorted for purposes of lampoon, parody or caricature."[167]

---

162. Winter v. D.C. Comics, 30 Cal. 4th 881 (Cal. 2003).
163. *Id.* at 886.
164. *Id.*
165. *Id.* at 890.
166. *Id.*
167. *Id.*

In 2006, the California courts addressed the question in the context of video games. In the case *Kirby v. Sega*,[168] singer, fashion designer, artist, and choreographer Kierin Kirby—known as Lady Miss Kier—made claims of personality appropriation against the game manufacturer Sega claiming that Sega had appropriated her distinctive retro 1960s look and "ooh la la" expression when creating the character Ulala, a space-age news reporter in the game *Space Channel 5*.[169]

Sega presented evidence from the game's creator that the character Ulala was originally created as a male character, but was later changed to a female character to appeal to the female audience.[170] It also presented evidence that the character's dance moves were created by a Japanese choreographer who had never heard of the plaintiff when doing so, and that the game featured no references to any music by the plaintiff.[171] The court evaluated the similarities between Lady Miss Kier and the Ulala character, such as that both were thin, had similarly shaped eyes, red lips, red or pink hair, wore brightly colored retro clothing, and "used phrases such as 'groove,' 'meow,' 'delish,' and 'I won't give up.'"[172] However, the court ultimately held in favor of Sega, finding that there were material issues of fact relevant to whether the defendants had misappropriated Kirby's likeness in the character in the game.[173] Among the features the court noted were the differences between Lady Miss Kier's image and those of the character Ulala, most notably that the game was set in outer space, while the plaintiff's image was 1960s retro style.[174] The court ultimately determined that while there were similarities between Ulala and Lady Miss Kier, the various differences were transformative enough to warrant First Amendment protection, barring Kirby's claim.[175]

---

168. Kirby v. Sega, 144 Cal. App. 4th 47 (Cal. Ct. App. 2006).
169. *Id.* at 50–52.
170. *Id.* at 51.
171. *Id.*
172. *Id.* at 55–56.
173. *Id.* at 59.
174. *Id.*
175. *Id.* at 61–62.

Where *Kirby* dealt with a significantly "transformed" depiction of a famous personality, on the opposite end of that spectrum of transformation are cases where the court examines precise depictions in video games. In *No Doubt v. Activision*,[176] for instance, the band No Doubt brought a breach of contract and misappropriation claim against game publisher Activision over the use of the band members' images and voices in the game *Band Hero*, a game that allows players to simulate musical performances using the avatars and music of famous musicians.[177] No Doubt had licensed the use of their names and likenesses—as well as three songs—for use in the game, even participating in the production of the game so as to achieve more accurate and realistic appearances.[178] The game, however, allowed players to "unlock" the No Doubt avatars at a certain point, and have the avatars then play other musicians' songs.[179] The band complained of the in-game ability of players to "unlock" the No Doubt avatars and show them in various contexts to which No Doubt objected, to wit: playing other musicians' songs, performing individually, or singing with voices not their own.[180] No Doubt argued that the game's display of their avatars in that context violated No Doubt's rights of publicity.[181]

Activision attempted to defeat No Doubt's claims on motion, claiming that the publicity claim must fall to the First Amendment.[182] The trial court, applying the transformative use test, rejected that defense,[183] and the California Court of Appeals upheld

176. No Doubt v. Activision Publ'g, Inc., 192 Cal. App. 4th 1018 (Cal. Ct. App. 2011).
177. *Id.* at 1022.
178. *Id.* at 1023–24.
179. *Id.* at 1024.
180. *Id.*
181. *Id.* It is worthwhile to point out that Activision's defense in this case included an argument that the features complained of were widely known and that the band (or its management) should have been aware of the features. The opinion does not address that point directly, but even so it is a caution to attorneys counseling such clients that they should make best efforts to fully understand the various features and possibilities of emerging technologies such as video games and make sure that the clients are aware of and approve such features and possibilities.
182. *Id.* at 1025.
183. *Id.*

that decision, engaging in its own "transformative use" analysis.[184] The court found that the avatars in the game were nontransformative imitations of the real-life musicians. "Nothing in the creative elements of *Band Hero* elevates the depictions of No Doubt to something more than 'conventional, more or less fungible, images' of its members that No Doubt should have the right to control and exploit."[185] The creative elements of the game did not transform the images of the band members to an extent that would bar the band's right of publicity claims.[186]

There is a lot of room on the spectrum between *Kirby* and *No Doubt.* For instance, in *Washington v. Take-Two,*[187] Michael "Shagg" Washington—backup singer and model for the group Cypress Hill—alleged that the game publisher had made an unauthorized use of his likeness in the game *Grand Theft Auto: San Andreas*, using details of Shagg's life and his physical appearance as the basis of the game's character CJ.[188] Despite evidence that Washington had given his photo to the game developers, which later ended up in the defendant's files, as well as the fact that his name appears in the game's credits as a model,[189] the court found that his claim was not likely to survive the transformative use test that would be part of Take-Two's First Amendment defense.[190] The determination came down to whether Washington could prove that the CJ character indeed infringed on Washington's likeness, which the judge indicated would have taken the form of tattoos, birthmarks, or physical features, or somehow connected the character's backstory to his own.[191] Instead, the judge noted in an unpublished opinion that the "Plaintiff is relying entirely on CJ's physical appearance in the game, but that appearance is so generic that it necessarily includes

---

184. *Id.* at 1022.

185. *Id.* at 1035 (quoting Comedy III Prods., Inc. v. Gary Saderup, Inc., 25 Cal. 4th 387, 408 (Cal. 2001)).

186. *Id.*

187. Washington v. Take-Two Interactive Software, Inc., No. B232929, 2012 WL 5358709 (Cal. Ct. App. Oct. 31, 2012) (unpublished table decision).

188. *Id.* at *1.

189. *Id.* at *3.

190. *Id.* at *11–12.

191. *Id.* at *5, 11.

hundreds of other black males."[192] The judge also found that the CJ character's physical appearance changed during the game depending on how much the character ate or exercised, as did his clothing or accessories.[193] The court further found that the *No Doubt* case did not control in this case—but *Kirby* did, as

> "the No Doubt avatars . . . perform rock songs, the same activity by which the band achieved and maintains its fame. . . . [Nothing in the video game] transform(s) the avatars into anything other than exact depictions of No Doubt's members doing exactly what they do as celebrities." Here, however, Washington has presented no evidence demonstrating that the plot or characters of GTA: San Andreas have any relevance to his life or his purported fame.[194]

In some instances, the relevant statute will essentially incorporate some version of the "transformative use" analysis. In a pair of New York cases, Lindsay Lohan (a former child actor who in later years was famous primarily for being famous) and Karen Gravano (a "mob wife") made complaints very similar to those presented in *Washington*. The cases survived motions to dismiss at the trial level, but the appellate division reversed, finding that the relevant characters in the *Grand Theft Auto* game had been sufficiently transformed from their ostensible models such that the use complained of was not use of the complaining party's "name, portrait or picture" as required by statute.[195] That case was recently affirmed with the court holding that the character alleged

---

192. *Id.* at *5.

193. *Id.*

194. *Id.* at *12 (quoting No Doubt v. Activision Publ'g, Inc., 192 Cal. App. 4th 1018, 1036 (Cal. Ct. App. 2011)).

195. Gravano v. Take-Two Interactive Software, Inc., 142 A.D.3d 776 (N.Y. App. Div. 2016) (Gravano and Lohan's cases were decided together), *aff'd sub nom.* Lohan v. Take-Two Interactive Software, Inc., 31 N.Y.3d 111 (N.Y. 2018). In addition, the relevant statutes were inapplicable because the game was deemed a "work of fiction and satire" deserving First Amendment protection rather than a piece of "advertising or trade" addressed in the relevant statute. *See also* Pesina v. Midway Mfg. Co., 948 F. Supp. 40, 42 (N.D. Ill. 1996) ("[T]he plaintiff alleging unauthorized use of his likeness must show that the likeness was recognizable. . . . The video images of Mr. Pesina's movements were extensively altered prior

to be based on Lohan had a generic "style, look, and persona of a modern, beach-going young woman . . ." (in reference to Lohan), and that *Grand Theft Auto* character Andrea Bottino was similarly unrecognizable as Gravano.[196]

The right of publicity litigation has been particularly prolific in the sports video game context. Much as a singer's voice is an important aspect of his or her image that a celebrity would want to protect, so too are the distinguishing characteristics of a high-profile college or professional athlete. Be it the player's jersey number, size, race, hometown, statistics, tattoos, or other recognizable features, these attributes are an important part of what sets the athlete apart, and are hence part of that athlete's right of publicity. It is the use of these attributes in sports video games such as *NCAA Football* and *Madden NFL* that have come to a head in recent years in the form of litigation against the National Collegiate Athletic Association (NCAA), the National Football League (NFL), and game publisher Electronic Arts (EA).[197] Perhaps more so than music video games, realism is crucial to sports video games. Consequently, the virtual depiction of the real game is more important than ever. This realism also means that multiple levels of clearance are involved in depicting the game, from licensing team and league logos to licensing venues and commentators. While game publishers have paid handsomely to license the images and logos of colleges, professional sports teams, and leagues, coaches, stadiums, facilities, commentators, and announcers, for much of the history of sports games, the publishers have not spent nearly as much, if anything, on the use of the players' likenesses. This is what has been alleged in a series of cases brought by former NCAA players alleging that their likenesses were used in college football video

---

to being incorporated into the games. Thus, after comparing Mr. Pesina and the game character, Johnny Cage, who allegedly resembles the plaintiff, only 6% of 306 Mortal Kombat users identified Mr. Pesina as the model.").

196. *Lohan*, 31 N.Y.3d at 121; Gravano v. Take-Two Interactive Software, Inc., 31 N.Y.3d 988, 990 (N.Y. 2018).

197. *See, e.g.*, Davis v. Elec. Arts, Inc., 775 F.3d 1172 (9th Cir. 2015); Brown v. Elec. Arts, Inc., 724 F.3d 1235 (9th Cir. 2013); Hart v. Elec. Arts, Inc., 717 F.3d 141 (3d Cir. 2013); *In re* NCAA Student-Athlete Name & Likeness Licensing Litig., 724 F.3d 1268 (9th Cir. 2013).

games that earned many millions of dollars without the players' respective authorization.

Where the depiction of professional sports can mean rather complex licensing for a game publisher, college sports presents an even greater quandary for a game maker. The NCAA licenses most of the names and logos of the Division I schools through the Collegiate Licensing Company.[198] NCAA bylaws, however, prohibit student athletes from authorizing the use of their names or likenesses for financial gain.[199] These rules are intended to maintain the amateur nature of college sports and curb abuses that could be made by college boosters, agents, or other parties trying to influence the outcome of college sporting events. While the rules prohibit the use of player names in the game, they do permit other details of a player's identity to be used, such as statistics, details relating to that player's dress or style of play, height, and weight. So while the average person may not be able to pick out the dominant players featured in such a game, a college football fan may be able to pick out particular players, and hardcore fans would certainly be able to recognize most players on the basis of these identifying features.

A set of related cases involving EA sports video games have explored the contours of the right of publicity as applied to athletes depicted in video games. The primary case, out of the Third Circuit, is *Hart v. Electronic Arts.*[200] In *Hart*, plaintiff Ryan Hart,

---

198. *See* NCAA, *NCAA Licensing Program FAQS,* http://www.ncaa.org /championships/marketing/ncaa-licensing-program-faqs (last visited July 26, 2018).

199. NCAA, 2017–18 NCAA DIVISION I MANUAL Rule 12.5.2.1(a) (2017), http://www .ncaapublications.com/productdownloads/D118.pdf. Until 2014, the prohibition was more explicitly included in certain forms NCAA players were required to sign, but that form provision was removed by the NCAA, almost certainly in response to the 2014 antitrust decision in O'Bannon v. Nat'l Collegiate Athletic Ass'n, 7 F. Supp. 3d 955 (N.D. Cal. 2014), *aff'd in relevant part*, 802 F.3d 1049 (9th Cir. 2015), *cert. denied*, ___ U.S. ___ (2016). *See* also Marc Edelman, *Removing the NCAA Name-and-Likeness Release Is Just "Smoke and Mirrors" in the Fight for College Athlete Rights*, FORBES, July 25, 2014, 9:51 a.m., https://www.forbes.com /sites/marcedelman/2014/07/25/ncaa-name-and-likeness-release-is-just-smoke-and -mirrors/. The *O'Bannon* decision would seem to make the rule illegal under federal antitrust laws, but the prohibition remains nonetheless.

200. *Hart*, 717 F.3d 141.

who was a quarterback for Rutgers University from 2002 to 2005, sued EA on the basis that the EA game *NCAA Football* included an avatar that while not named "Ryan Hart," had included all of his characteristics.[201] Exacerbating the similarity, the in-game avatar played quarterback for the in-game Rutgers team, and the game was released while Hart was still enrolled at Rutgers.[202] Hart argued (unsurprisingly) that the avatar was an improper exploitation of his likeness so as to constitute a violation of his right of publicity.[203] In 2011, the district court ruled that EA's use was protected by the First Amendment,[204] but the Third Circuit, applying the transformative use test, overturned that decision:

> The digital Ryan Hart does what the actual Ryan Hart did while at Rutgers: he plays college football, in digital recreations of college football stadiums, filled with all the trappings of a college football game. This is not transformative; the various digitized sights and sounds in the video game do not alter or transform [Hart]'s identity in a significant way.[205]

In *Keller v. Electronic Arts* and some consolidated cases, the Ninth Circuit was presented with facts substantively identical to those in *Hart*.[206] Applying the transformative use test, the court there engaged in an analysis similar to that in *Hart*, and came to the same conclusion.[207]

A useful comparison can be drawn with the case *Brown v. Electronic Arts*.[208] In *Brown*, the underlying facts were substantially similar, to wit: EA was using a closely modeled avatar of plaintiff Jim Brown—widely regarded as one of the best professional

---

201. *Id.* at 145–47.

202. *Id.*

203. *Id.*

204. *Id.* at 147.

205. *Id.* at 166.

206. *In re* NCAA Student-Athlete Name & Likeness Licensing Litig., 724 F.3d 1268 (9th Cir. 2013). The Ninth Circuit opinion addressed essentially identical claims made by some nine plaintiffs with respect to EA's football and basketball games. *Id.* at 1272 n.2.

207. *Id.* at 1273–78 (citing *Hart*, 717 F.3d 141).

208. Brown v. Elec. Arts, Inc., 724 F.3d 1235 (9th Cir. 2013).

football players of all time—in its *Madden NFL* series of football video games.[209] For procedural reasons,[210] the decision in *Brown* focuses narrowly on Brown's claims of false endorsement under the Lanham Act, and explicitly did not analyze any claims he might have brought under non-Lanham right of publicity statutes.[211] The lower court dismissed the claims, accepting EA's First Amendment defense and applying the *Rogers* test. The Ninth Circuit upheld the district court's determination.[212]

In the *Keller* case, the Ninth Circuit acknowledged the *Brown* decision, but rejected extending the *Rogers* test to the *Keller* facts.[213] The Ninth Circuit distinguished between Lanham Act false endorsement claims and claims directed to the right of publicity, and refused to apply the *Rogers* test to the latter claims:

> Although we acknowledge that there is some overlap between the transformative use test formulated by the California Supreme Court and the *Rogers* test, we disagree that the *Rogers* test should be imported wholesale for right-of-publicity claims. . . . As the history and development of the *Rogers* test makes clear, it was designed to protect consumers from the risk of consumer confusion—the hallmark element of a Lanham Act claim. . . . The right of publicity, on the other hand, does not primarily seek to prevent consumer confusion. . . . Rather, it primarily "protects a form of intellectual property [in one's person] that society deems to have some social utility." . . . The right of publicity protects the *celebrity*, not the *consumer*.[214]

---

209. *Id.* at 1239–40.

210. The district court had dismissed the federal claims on a 12(b)(6) motion and then declined to exercise supplemental jurisdiction over the invasion of privacy and unfair and unlawful business practices state law claims. The appeal was taken from the Lanham Act dismissal. *Id.* at 1240.

211. *Id.* at n.2 ("We emphasize that this appeal relates only to Brown's Lanham Act claim. Were the state causes of action before us, our analysis may be different and a different outcome may obtain.").

212. *Id.* at 1248.

213. *In re* NCAA Student-Athlete Name & Likeness Licensing Litig., 724 F.3d 1268, 1279–82 (9th Cir. 2013).

214. *Id.* at 1280–81 (citations omitted).

The *Brown* and *Keller* decisions were filed by the Ninth Circuit on the same day. Taking the two together, it seems that where the analysis narrowly considers trademark or Lanham Act claims, the *Rogers* test still has some value, but for right of publicity claims in the more general sense, the transformative use test is coming to the fore.

Conclusion

The right of publicity has developed as an area of the law having significant potential impact on the video game industry. Although governed by a patchwork of differing state and related federal laws, the basic framework for determining appropriate use seems to be emerging. The most important considerations in determining whether or not a famous person will have a viable right of publicity claim are: (1) how closely the in-game use hews to the likeness of the famous person and (2) how similar the in-game context is to the real life context of the famous person's exploitation of his or her own fame. The less similar the likeness or context, the more "transformative" the use will considered, and the stronger the game maker's defense will be. At the same time, any endorsement or misleading use of a famous person—especially with respect to the title of a creative work—will be judged according to the overlapping but dissimilar *Rogers* test.

The exact contours of the intersection between publicity rights and video games are still not fully developed. New cases are still being brought testing the edges of the doctrine. In January 2017, Lenwood Hamilton, erstwhile football player and professional wrestler, filed suit in Pennsylvania against the makers of the video game *Gears of War*. Hamilton claims, *inter alia*, that the game misappropriates his voice and physical attributes as the basis for the in-game character Cole Train.[215] One distinguishing element of the Hamilton claims in comparison to those made in *Hart* and *Keller* et al. is that the actual appropriation is more in question. Defendants

---

215. Second Amended Complaint, Hamilton v. Speight, No. 2:17-cv-00169-AB (E.D. Pa. Apr. 14, 2017).

have explicitly denied same,[216] although Hamilton points to a number of similarities between himself and the Cole Train character, including

> that both are black (and 'Cole Train' is the only black avatar in the Gears of War series), they both played professional football (although in Gears of War the game is called 'thrashball'), Cole Train's number is 83 (same year that Hamilton played for the Philadelphia Eagles—1983), the derby hat, wristbands, a front gold tooth, and a striking resemblance of both physiognomy and body build.[217]

In addition, Hamilton claims that, based on the opinion and report of a forensic voice examiner, the Cole Train voiceover is identifiably Hamilton's.[218] The defendants in *Hamilton* have moved for dismissal on various grounds including the assertion that any such appropriation is sufficiently transformative under *Hart* such that the claim is defeated by the First Amendment.[219] As of this writing, the motion has been fully briefed, but no decision has issued.

Further, it takes only some imagination to anticipate the debates that might be just around the corner in this field. For instance, although the various EA games all allowed for some modification of the various player avatars by the end-user/player, both the Third and Ninth Circuits dismissed that ability as having little bearing on the determination whether or not EA's use of the likenesses was sufficiently transformative.[220] The *Hart* court noted further that where a player could make "larger potential changes, such as a different body type, skin tone, or face, Appellant's likeness is not transformed; it simply ceases to be."[221]

---

216. Defendant's Motion to Dismiss, Hamilton v. Speight, No. 2:17-cv-00169-AB (E.D. Pa. Apr. 28, 2017).

217. Second Amended Complaint, *supra* note 215, ¶ 63.

218. *Id.* ¶¶ 75–77.

219. Defendant's Motion to Dismiss, *supra* note 216, at 9–16.

220. *See* Hart v. Elec. Arts, 717 F.3d 141, 168 (3d Cir. 2013) ("Given that [Hart]'s unaltered likeness is central to the core of the game experience, we are disinclined to credit users' ability to alter the digital avatars in our application of the Transformative Use Test to this case.").

221. *Id.* at 168–69.

It is an open question as to what liability might attach to the game manufacturer producing a game that does not, initially, make use of a famous person's likeness, but allows modifications to the various avatars allowing end-users/players to closely resemble famous individuals. Such modifications are simple data sets, and it is not difficult to imagine a third party providing the information sufficient to modify the avatars. If there is harm to a famous person's right of publicity, if that harm is amenable to redress, and who might bear that liability are all questions that have not squarely been addressed by the courts, but which it seems fair to anticipate will be in the future.

International Considerations of Video Games and Immersive Entertainment

7

Ken Cheney[1]

Takeaways

- *When residents of different jurisdictions interact or transact business within or via an online game or other virtual reality system, intellectual property laws of multiple jurisdictions can be simultaneously implicated, and the choice of whose venue and law to use is not always clear.*
- *U.S. intellectual property law is generally not applied extraterritorially; however, various treaties attempt to harmonize international law.*
- *Enforcement of some intellectual property rights involving conduct occurring within or via virtual reality systems may be analogized to a body of law that has developed around Internet websites.*

---

1. Ken Cheney is a partner at Morgan, Lewis & Bockius LLP. For complete author biographies, see the Contributors section of this book.

- *Arbitration or choice-of-law provisions in end-user license agreements may be used to circumvent some issues. However, these private agreements are not likely to resolve the myriad of complex international issues presented by virtual transactions.*

Introduction

Among the many difficult issues facing the online community today, perhaps the one that increases in importance as virtual reality systems grow is the international scope of law applicable to interactions between users, and between the users and the owners or hosts (providers), of such systems. While international legal issues can be extremely thorny in the real world, they can be exponentially trickier in online virtual environments, in which international interaction—and commensurately, international trade and piracy—is limited only by bandwidth.

By their very nature, online game environments and virtual reality-based systems (or "online virtual environments," generally), including virtual worlds created for social interaction, are configured for international scope. There are countless online games and social platforms springing up around the globe, many with more than 100 million active members.[2] As of 2017, the global massively multiplayer online (MMO) gaming market reached US $26.9 billion yearly, and is estimated to reach US $44.6 billion by 2022.[3] At the same time, the virtual world-based game *Minecraft* has reached 100 million registered users, with approximately 74

---

2. Wikipedia, *List of Virtual Communities with More Than 100 Million Active Users*, https://en.wikipedia.org/wiki/List_of_virtual_communities_with_more_than _100_million_active_users (last edited July 26, 2018); Henry Fong, 5 *Things You Need to Know about Chinese Social Media*, FORBES, Oct. 25, 2012, http://www.forbes .com/sites/ciocentral/2012/10/25/5-things-you-need-to-know-about-chinese-social -media.

3. Press Release, Research and Markets, Global Massively Multiplayer Online (MMO) Gaming Market—Forecast to Reach $44.6 Billion by 2022 (Nov. 15, 2017), https://www.businesswire.com/news/home/20171115005641/en/Global-Massively -Multiplayer-Online-MMO-Gaming-Market.

million active users.[4] Facebook boasts a membership of more than two billion monthly users around the world.[5]

Virtual reality- and augmented reality-based environments in general are expanding. Facebook acquired virtual reality headset maker Oculus Rift to expand portions of its social network platform into the realm of online virtual environments.[6] As of 2018, 170 million people have become users of virtual reality, and it is estimated that more than one billion people will regularly access virtual reality and augmented reality content by 2020,[7] with a predicted yearly revenue from virtual reality devices at US $30 billion.[8]

Today, e-sports—professional organized multiplayer video game competitions, often within virtual environments—is the thing. E-sports includes all types of games, from established professional sports to strategy and first-person shooters. Traditional global media companies such as ESPN are broadcasting these virtual sports competitions, and advertisers are quickly buying in.[9] More people watched the 2017 *League of Legends* Mid-Season Invitational than the Super Bowl and National Basketball Association championship combined![10] As of 2018, e-sports generates roughly $620 million in yearly branding-related review, split between

---

4. Craig Smith, *17 Amazing Minecraft Facts and Stats*, DMR, July 24, 2018, https://expandedramblings.com/index.php/minecraft-statistics.

5. Josh Constine, *Facebook Now Has 2 Billion Monthly Users . . . and Responsibility*, TECHCRUNCH, June 27, 2017, https://techcrunch.com/2017/06/27/facebook-2-billion-users/.

6. Chris Welch, *Facebook Buying Oculus VR for $2 Billion*, VERGE, Mar. 25, 2014, http://www.theverge.com/2014/3/25/5547456/facebook-buying-oculus-for-2-billion/in/3631187.

7. Robert Kendal, *VR Stats Every Business Leader Should See*, BOSS MAG., https://thebossmagazine.com/virtual-reality-statistics-infographic (last visited July 26, 2018).

8. *Augmented/Virtual Reality to Hit $150 Billion Disrupting Mobile by 2020*, DIGI-CAPITAL, Apr. 6, 2015, http://www.digi-capital.com/news/2015/04/augmentedvirtual-reality-to-hit-150-billion-disrupting-mobile-by-2020/#.VXjT5vlgd2J.

9. Robert Elder, *The eSports Competitive Video Gaming Market Continues to Grow Revenues & Attract Investors*, BUS. INSIDER, Mar. 21, 2018, http://www.business insider.com/esports-market-growth-ready-for-mainstream-2018-3-21.

10. Bradmore & Magus, *2017 Mid-Season Invitational by the Numbers*, LEAGUE OF LEGENDS, July 10, 2017, https://www.lolesports.com/en_US/articles/2017-mid-season-invitational-numbers.

advertising and sponsoring, which is expected to increase to US $800 million by 2019.[11]

Indeed, online virtual environments are now an integral part of computer-based gaming, enabling participants from all over the world to participate in a seamless virtual experience, occupying a single online space (or collection of spaces). Within this context, it may be impossible (subject to language barriers) to distinguish the national origin of one user from another. With such a large number of users, whether a virtual world or other similar virtual environment (including those based on social networks) should be considered the legal equivalent of a virtual "nation," with its own set of laws or moral codes, may one day become a fascinating debate.

Despite providing the "feeling" of a single nation of members, online virtual reality-based games and other virtual environments are inherently limited by the real world. Not only are the members of these online virtual environments acting within the borders of the countries in which they are located, but the online virtual environment itself exists only as embodied within computer servers or networks—which themselves are located in a specific, albeit sometimes transitory,[12] geographical location. Moreover, online virtual environments are largely closed networks, accessible only to those with user accounts. As a result, the online virtual environment, and generally everything stored on that network, necessarily is under the control of its host, service provider, or system administrator. Much like websites, online virtual environments would not exist without their respective hosts. The hosts implement the code, sell the service, and have complete control over all aspects of the virtual environment at all times—and have a fixed presence. In this context, an online virtual environment, by itself, is not really international at all.

The average (nonprofessional) gamer spends nearly six hours a week playing online games, and more than an hour and a half

---

11. *See* Elder, *supra* note 9.

12. With current computer technology, such as cloud computing, the server location for a social network may shift physical locations with world load requirements.

watching others play.[13] The amount of time that the international community of social network members spends within social networks is even more—on average nearly two hours daily, or five years and four months over a lifetime.[14] In 2015, it was estimated that a member of a virtual world spends roughly 18 hours a week inside the world.[15] It is thus not surprising how many cross-border transactions routinely take place within or via these environments. As of 2016, the trading of virtual goods for online gaming accounted for more than $15 billion in yearly revenue.[16] Virtual currencies are on the rise, with analysts estimating that the global market value of the top 100 convertible virtual currencies has reached a staggering US $121 billion.[17] These figures, of course, do not account for the incalculable *informal* transactions that take place each day within the virtual environments themselves, or the advertising within and around virtual environments.

In an economic context, an online virtual environment is not unlike a global e-commerce web page that allows individuals around the world to promote and sell their products to individuals in other countries. Arguably, certain international conflicts can be avoided when an e-commerce web page offers different ecosystems to different countries, for example, by virtue of using

---

13. LIMELIGHT NETWORKS, THE STATE OF ONLINE GAMING—2018 (2018), http://img03 .en25.com/Web/LLNW/%7B6be6d024-012c-4d8b-b230-9c0c9c98e597%7D_SOOG .pdf; Mike Milligan, *Gaming Goes Mainstream for Both Playing and Watching*, LIMELIGHT NETWORKS, Mar. 28, 2018, https://www.limelight.com/blog/state-of-online -gaming-2018.

14. Evan Asano, *How Much Time Do People Spend on Social Media? [Infographic]*, SOCIALMEDIATODAY, Jan. 4, 2017, https://www.socialmediatoday.com/marketing /how-much-time-do-people-spend-social-media-infographic.

15. CELIA PEARCE ET AL., VIRTUAL WORLDS SURVEY REPORT: A TRANS-WORLD STUDY OF NON-GAME VIRTUAL WORLDS—DEMOGRAPHICS, ATTITUDES, AND PREFERENCES 48 (Mar. 2015), http://cpandfriends.com/wp-content/uploads/2015/03/vwsurveyreport_final _publicationedition1.pdf.

16. Alon Bonder, *5 Lessons from the $15 Billion Virtual Goods Economy*, VENTUREBEAT, Dec. 25, 2016, 8:02 a.m., https://www.venturebeat.com/2016/12/25/5 -lessons-from-the-15-billion-virtual-goods-economy.

17. OFFICE OF THE DIRECTOR OF NATIONAL INTELLIGENCE, RISKS AND VULNERABILITIES OF VIRTUAL CURRENCY—CRYPTOCURRENCY AS A PAYMENT METHOD (2017 Public-Private Analytic Exchange Program), https://www.dni.gov/files/PE/Documents/9—2017 -AEP_Risks-and-Vulnerabilities-of-Virtual-Currency.pdf.

country-specific domain extensions. However, most online virtual environments are fluid universes that provide their members the appearance of being in a single world that encompasses activity from all nations of the world at once.

As is the case with any international community or the Internet as a whole, the international nature of online virtual environments and its economy raises a number of difficult issues in the area of intellectual property, including choice-of-law and personal and subject-matter jurisdiction, or protection rights in general. These issues are made especially complex by the fact that, from the vantage point of the intellectual property author, owner, or litigant, there is no true overarching "international" intellectual property law. While international treaties and conventions do exist, there is no single set of laws or rules that govern conduct affecting the "virtual" exploitation of intellectual property across national borders.

This chapter provides an overview of some issues that are likely to be faced in applying copyright, trademark, and patent law to transactions or events that may take place both within the boundaries of online virtual environments (as "virtual worlds") and simultaneously across international borders. The chapter briefly discusses how U.S. law may apply to online game and other online virtual environment-related legal issues that involve foreign entities and jurisdictions, and considers some of the subtle differences between U.S. law and its foreign equivalents, with particular focus on Europe and China.

I. International Copyright Issues in Online Games and Virtual Environments

The Internet's role in allowing rapid unauthorized dissemination of an author's work is already a subject of discussion, and the creation and exploitation of copyrighted or original works of authorship within an online game or virtual environment by the host of the virtual environment or by member users only raises more issues under copyright law. In some cases, determinations of copyright ownership and the right to sue, as well as forum selection, may be governed by an end-user license agreement (EULA), which itself may be the subject of international conflict issues outside the scope of this book.

EULA issues aside, it is conceivable that a player who creates a "virtual" work, for example in *Minecraft* or the virtual world *Second Life*, would want some attribution or protection so that others cannot monetize or plagiarize his or her work—particularly given that the monetization of user-created items is a growing driving force for membership and interactions within the online virtual environment in the first instance. However, whether these player-created *visual* creations within the online virtual environment are actually protectable may vary depending on what nation's laws apply. The host of a foreign-based online virtual environment may seek to avoid liability for its inclusion of content protected in the United States. The current body of international law may provide some guidance in unraveling these and what seems to be an endless number of other increasingly complex legal scenarios.

A. Choice of Law and Conflict of Laws

Notwithstanding attempts to harmonize international copyright law, there are many differences in copyright laws between countries around the world. These differences pertain to issues such as the criteria and subject matter of protection, the nature of rights accorded, the identity of the author and copyright owner, and the existence of "moral rights."

Choice-of-law or conflict-of-law issues may arise in a situation in which, for example, two or more co-authors, each located in a different jurisdiction, pool their efforts to create a work of authorship. For example, a company responsible for the creation of an online game may employ developers in a different country to contribute to the development of the game. Two players within a virtual environment—each in a different country—may jointly construct a work based on tools and resources available within the virtual environment. Alternatively, an author in one locale may modify (within the virtual environment) a preexisting work created by a resident of another jurisdiction to create a new, derivative work. Issues may also arise when a copyrighted work (e.g., a sound recording, photograph, or motion picture) is uploaded to a server located in one jurisdiction where it can be simultaneously viewed or downloaded by residents of numerous other jurisdictions.

The major international copyright treaty, known as the Berne Convention for the Protection of Literary and Artistic Works, makes some effort to resolve copyright issues in the real world. Under the Berne Convention, authors are provided the same protections in each member country that nationals enjoy under the laws of that country.[18] The choice-of-law rule under the Universal Copyright Convention similarly provides national treatment.[19] Thus, under either convention, an author who is a national of a member state or who first publishes his or her work in a member state should be entitled to the same copyright protection in each other member state as that member state provides its own nationals.[20]

1. Conflicts in Copyright Ownership

Neither the U.S. Copyright Act nor the Berne Convention contains any substantive provisions governing international copyright disputes surrounding the *ownership* of a copyrighted work (e.g., between competing co-owners or assignees).[21] Those issues still

---

18. Berne Convention for the Protection of Literary and Artistic Works, Sept. 9, 1886, art. 5, § (1), S. Treaty Doc. No. 99-27 (1986), 828 U.N.T.S. 221 [hereinafter Berne Convention] ("Authors shall enjoy, in respect of works for which they are protected under this Convention, in countries of the Union other than the country of origin, the rights which their respective laws do now or may hereafter grant to their nationals, as well as the rights specially granted by the convention."). Enacted into U.S. copyright law at section 104 of the Copyright Act, which provides that unpublished works "are subject to protection under this title without regard to the nationality or domicile of the author" and "works . . . when published, are subject to protection under this title. . . ." 17 U.S.C. § 104(a), (b)(1)–(6) (2009).

19. Universal Copyright Convention, Sept. 6, 1952, art. II, 25 U.S.T. 1341, 943 U.N.T.S. 178, http://portal.unesco.org/en/ev.php-URL_ID=15381&URL_DO=DO_TOPIC&URL_SECTION=201.html.

20. *Id.*

21. *See* Itar-Tass Russian News Agency v. Russian Kurier, Inc., 153 F.3d 82, 90 (2d Cir. 1998) (citing Restatement (Second) of Conflict of Laws § 222); Maxwell Comm'n Corp. v. Societe Generale, 93 F.3d 1036, 1047 (2d Cir. 1996) ("international law . . . questions arising under what is usually called private international law, or the conflict of laws, and concerning the rights of persons within the territory and dominion of one nation, by reason of acts, private or public, done within the dominions of another nation—is part of our law." (quoting Hilton v. Guyot, 159 U.S. 113, 163 (1985))).

must be resolved with reference to a particular jurisdiction's copyright law, but which? U.S. courts have looked to common law principles of private international law.[22]

In the landmark case *Itar-Tass Russian News Agency v. Russian Kurier, Inc.*,[23] the U.S. Court of Appeals for the Second Circuit held that an ownership dispute involving works created by Russian nationals and first published in Russia should be adjudicated under Russian law.[24] Reasoning that copyright is a form of property—wherein "the interests of the parties in the property are determined by the law of the state with the 'most significant relationship' to the property and the parties"—the court found that the law of the "country of origin" as defined by the Berne Convention determines the ownership of a copyright.[25] Other circuits have followed *Itar-Tass* to similar conclusions.[26] The Southern District of New York later followed *Itar-Tass* to apply the law of the United Kingdom to works first published in the United Kingdom whose copyrights or exclusive rights were owned by a U.K.-based company.[27]

In defining "country of origin," the Berne Convention gives preference to the member state in which the work is first published, but favors the public when a work is published simultaneously in several member countries (by limiting copyright duration to that of the country granting the shortest term of protection).[28] For works published simultaneously in member and nonmember

---

22. *Itar-Tass*, 153 F.3d at 90–91 n.11.

23. *Itar-Tass*, 153 F.3d 82.

24. *Id.* at 90–91 (noting "one procedural qualification. Under United States law, an owner (including one determined according to foreign law) may sue for infringement in a United States court only if it meets the standing test of 17 U.S.C. § 501(b), which accords standing only to the legal or beneficial owner of an "exclusive right."). *Accord* RCTV Int'l Corp. v. Rosenfeld, No. 13-23611-CIV-SIMONTON, 2016 WL 6818955, at *7 (S.D. Fla. Sept. 30, 2016).

25. *Itar-Tass*, 153 F.3d at 90–91.

26. *See, e.g.*, Bridgeman Art Library, Ltd. v. Corel Corp., 25 F. Supp. 2d 421, 425 (S.D.N.Y. 1998) (citing *Itar-Tass*, 153 F.3d at 90); Lahiri v. Universal Music & Video Distrib., Inc., 513 F. Supp. 2d 1172, 1176 n.4 (C.D. Cal. 2007) ("Initial ownership of a copyrighted work is determined by the laws in the work's country of origin"); Saregama India Ltd. v. Mosley, 635 F.3d 1284 (11th Cir. 2011).

27. *Bridgeman*, 25 F. Supp. at 425 (citing *Itar-Tass*, 153 F.3d at 90).

28. Berne Convention, *supra* note 18, art. 5, § (4)(a)–(c).

countries, the Berne signatory country prevails.[29] For unpublished works or works first published in a nonmember country only, the member country of which the author is a national prevails.[30]

However, online virtual environments (or online exchanges generally) quickly challenge the traditional concept of "first publication." For a work first made available or distributed *within* an online virtual environment, publication could simultaneously occur where it is uploaded, from the server upon which it is stored, where it is predominantly downloaded or accessed, and where the virtual world is run and managed.

In *Kernal Records Oy v. Mosley*,[31] a foreign record company brought a copyright action against U.S. defendants for alleged infringement of a sound recording in the United States.[32] The plaintiff had not registered the copyright in the United States, and the court was required to determine whether the plaintiff was required to register the work prior to suing for infringement as required by the U.S. Copyright Act, or was exempt from requirement due to the United States' participation in the Berne Convention.[33] The district court found that, because the work was "first published" on the Internet, it was *simultaneously* published in the United States and other nations, and thus was a "United States work" requiring the copyright holder to register the work prior to suing for infringement.[34]

The Eleventh Circuit affirmed *Kernal Records Oy*, but not without criticizing the district court's assumption that *all* "online" or "Internet" publications result in simultaneous worldwide publications.[35] The Eleventh Circuit explained that, although simultaneous publication may be presumed based on availability of a work on a *public* website, "such a presumption could not apply to restricted

29. *Id.* § (4)(b).
30. *Id.* § (4)(b)–(c).
31. Kernal Records Oy v. Mosley, 794 F. Supp. 2d 1355 (S.D. Fla. 2011), *aff'd*, 694 F.3d 1294 (11th Cir. 2012).
32. *Id.* at 1358.
33. *Id.* at 1358–59.
34. *Id.* at 1362–68.
35. *Kernal Records Oy*, 694 F.3d at 1306.

websites, peer-to-peer networks, and e-mail."³⁶ In what countries a work was published via these other distribution methods "require[s] additional evidence, such as the country of residence of the users . . . or the recipient of a certain e-mail."³⁷ Assessing both temporal and geographic evidence, the court found that the evidence was inconclusive as to the extent of publication, including whether the work at issue was first published on an "online" system limited to Australia or on a public website available worldwide, but nevertheless affirmed the district court, reasoning that the plaintiff failed to provide evidence that the work was indeed a foreign work exempt from registration.³⁸ While the trend currently appears to favor finding works posted on the Internet as "published," some courts have indicated that a public display (via the Internet) alone may not be sufficient to reach that conclusion,³⁹ and that further inquiry into the "purpose" for which the work was posted is also relevant to the analysis.⁴⁰

Publication within an online virtual environment may conceivably be analogized to publication on an Internet website, or perhaps a restricted website since online games and virtual reality-based environments are generally closed systems that require specific access requirements. Thus, it remains unclear and fact-specific as to whether a foreign work first displayed or otherwise fist published therein would be considered by a court following *Kernal Records Oy* as being a "United States work"—or whether the work could be considered simultaneously published in any particular country for the purpose of determining the "country of origin" under the Berne Convention.⁴¹ Examinations of the online

---

36. *Id.* at 1305–06.

37. *Id.* at 1306.

38. *Id.* at 1311–12.

39. *See* Elliot v. Gouverneur Tribune Press, Inc., No. 7:13-CV-00055(MAD/TWD), 2014 WL 12598275, at *3 (N.D.N.Y. Sept. 29, 2014) (noting criticism of a 2002 decision in which source code was deemed published when it "went live" and could be freely copied) (citing Rogers v. Better Bus. Bureau v. Metro. Houston, Inc., 887 F. Supp. 2d 722, 730–31 (S.D. Tex. 2012)).

40. *See* Palmer/Kane LLC v. Gareth Stevens Publ'g, No. 1:15-cv-7404-GHW, 2017 WL 3973957, at *12 (S.D.N.Y. Sept. 7, 2017).

41. *See* Berne Convention, *supra* note 18, art. 5.

virtual environment itself, and the geographic locations of its participants, are likely to play a role in the determination.

Itar-Tass did not address choice-of-law issues concerning assignments of rights;[42] however, some courts have been willing to extend *Itar-Tass* principles to assignments.[43] Other courts have looked to other authorities to address copyright assignments.[44] *Itar-Tass* also does not specifically address reversion of rights in which some or all of an author's assigned rights in a work are recaptured by the author when certain conditions are met.

Before *Itar-Tass*, the Second Circuit, in *Corcovado Music Corp. v. Hollis Music, Inc.*,[45] found that the United States was the proper forum to resolve a copyright action (for renewal rights) involving works authored in Brazil despite a forum selection clause (in the original Brazilian conveyance) requiring that any disputes be resolved in Brazil, because the copyright action "arises" under the Copyright Act and not out of the contract.[46] Since *Itar-Tass*, at least one court has distinguished *Corcovado* as being applicable to copyrights that predate the United States joining the Berne Convention.[47] Despite this timing, several courts have continued to follow *Corcovado* in evaluating copyright-related forum selection clauses.[48]

---

42. Itar-Tass Russian News Agency v. Russian Kurier, Inc., 153 F.3d 82, 91 n.11 (2d Cir. 1998).

43. *See* Fahmy v. Jay-Z, 788 F. Supp. 2d 1072 (C.D. Cal. 2011) (adopting plaintiff's application of Egyptian law due to the Egyptian national composer and song's first publication in Egypt, in analyzing whether rights to derivative works could be transferred under Egyptian law, and licenses at issue effectively transferred the right).

44. Fed. Treasury Enter. Sojuzplodoimport v. SPI Spirits Ltd., 726 F.3d 62, 71–72 (2d Cir. 2013) (declining to consider *Itar-Tass* for validity of an assignment, and applying the "standing test" of the Copyright Act).

45. Corcovado Music Corp. v. Hollis Music, Inc., 981 F.2d 679 (2d Cir. 1993).

46. *Id.* at 685.

47. *See* RCTV Int'l Corp. v. Rosenfeld, No. 13-23611-CIV-SIMONTON, 2016 WL 6818955, at *9 (S.D. Fla. Sept. 30, 2016).

48. *See* Phillips v. Audio Active, Ltd., 494 F.3d 378, 381, 391–92 (2d Cir. 2007); Arma v. Buyseasons, Inc., 591 F. Supp. 2d 637, 645 (S.D.N.Y. 2008) ("Where, as in the present action, the rights being asserted do not originate from the contract containing the forum selection clause, the clause does not apply").

2. Works for Hire

Many computer programs—such as those that make up an online game or virtual reality system—are often created under work-for-hire situations in which the entity commissioning the work becomes the recognized or de jure author. However, some countries do not allow for a complete transfer of a work, even when commissioned by a traditional contractor under a work-for-hire agreement. For example, in Germany, German copyrights can never be fully assigned except by inheritance,[49] and the commissioning entity may only obtain "exploitation rights" similar to an exclusive license, which may not be further granted on a nonexclusive basis without consent of the original author.[50] Accordingly, in multinational game development, the laws of multiple different countries may impact the ownership of the work.

Determining up front which law applies may help to resolve future copyright ownership issues. Under *Itar-Tass*, the law applicable to work for hire generally falls under the law applied to ownership issues.[51] In the United Kingdom, like the United States, computer programs are protected as literary works,[52] with those created during the course of employment being owned by the employer.[53] In this regard, courts in both nations have generally distinguished between works created by an employee (under a "contract of service") or by an independent contractor (as

---

49. Urheberrechtsgesetz [UrhG] [Act on Copyright and Related Rights], v. 9.9.1965 (BGBl. I S. 1273), last amended by Gesetzes v. 1.9.2017 (BGBl I S. 3346), art. 29 (F.R.G.), https://www.gesetze-im-internet.de/englisch_urhg/index.html.

50. *Id.* arts. 34–35.

51. *See* Itar-Tass Russian News Agency v. Russian Kurier, Inc., 153 F.3d 82, 93 (2d Cir. 1998) (determining Russian law applied to ownership issues, Russian version of the work-for-hire doctrine applied).

52. Copyright, Designs, and Patents Act 1988, c. 48, pt., §3 [hereinafter UK Copyright, Designs, and Patents Act] (U.K. National Archives), https://www.legislation.gov.uk/ukpga/1988/48/section/3; *see also* Apple Computer, Inc. v. Franklin Computer Corp., 714 F.2d 1240 (3d Cir. 1983) (finding that computer code is considered a literary work under U.S. copyright law).

53. UK Copyright, Designs, and Patents Act, *supra* note 52, § 9, http://www.legislation.gov.uk/ukpga/1988/48/section/9/enacted.

"contract for services"), where a contractor retains the copyright unless there is an agreement to the contrary.[54]

In China, however, works created in the course of employment generally vest in the author, while providing the employer the right to exploit the work.[55] The Regulations on Computers Software Protection carve out software specifically, such that software created in China using the resources of a Chinese company belongs to the company *ab initio*.[56] In *Splitfish AG v. Bannco Corp.*,[57] the court, in following *Itar-Tass*, turned to Chinese copyright law to resolve whether software was owned by the plaintiff company even though it was unclear whether the authors of the software were actual employees of the company when it was created.[58] The court found that the ownership of the software vested originally in the company "because the Chinese Copyright Law defines works created in the course of employment broadly to include any 'work created by a citizen in the fulfillment of tasks assigned to him by a legal entity or other organization.'"[59]

It is also notable that the Berne Convention recognizes moral rights that exist independently of an author's economic rights, even after those economic rights have been transferred.[60] This is why those who contributed to developing a computer program are often credited (e.g., in the credits) even though the company publishing the computer program may be listed as the legal "author" of the computer program. The United Kingdom has codified moral

---

54. *See* Cmty. for Creative Non-Violence v. Reid, 490 U.S. 730 (1989); *Ownership of Copyright Works*, U.K. INTELL. PROP. OFF., Aug. 19, 2014, https://www.gov.uk /guidance/ownership-of-copyright-works.

55. *Compare* Copyright Law of the People's Republic of China (promulgated by the Standing Committee of the National People's Congress, Sept. 7, 1990, revised Feb. 26, 2010, effective Apr. 1, 2010), § 2, art. 14, 2010 P.R.C. Laws (P.R.C.), http:// www.wipo.int/wipolex/en/text.jsp?file_id=466268, *with* Splitfish AG v. Bannco Corp., 727 F. Supp. 2d 461, 466 (E.D. Va. 2010).

56. *See* Regulations on Computers Software Protection, Decree of the State Council of the People's Republic of China No. 339, Jan. 1, 2002, art. 13, http://www .wipo.int/edocs/lexdocs/laws/en/cn/cn002en.pdf.

57. *Splitfish* , 727 F. Supp. 2d 461.

58. *Id.* at 465–66.

59. *Id.* at 466.

60. Berne Convention, *supra* note 18, art. 6bis.

rights and, specifically, the right to be identified as the author of a work.[61]

3. Fixation as a Requirement for Copyright

Many countries, including the United States and Canada, require that a work be "fixed in a tangible medium of expression" to obtain copyright protection.[62] However, the Berne Convention leaves it up to its member states to decide whether to implement this requirement.[63] Spain, France, and Australia do not have this requirement.[64]

Arguably, the visual (and virtual) works rendered by an online game or other virtual reality-based environment are embodied by the computer program that performs the rendering, and thus the visual expression of a virtual environment itself would be protectable (according to the relevant nation's laws) as fixed in whatever tangible medium of expression the computer program is in. However, most online virtual environments allow participants to create items, structures, and even landscapes that can also be seen as visual works produced by the participant authors. It is debatable whether copyright extends to virtual items, given that works are generally required to be fixed in a tangible medium of expression. Does storage of a digital item on a server or drive (which inevitably has physical, tangible hardware parts) sufficiently fix a digital item, or must the work be printed or otherwise produced onto a more traditional medium, such as paper, to be copyright-protectable?

The Tenth Circuit held that three-dimensional digital models can be sufficiently original to warrant copyright protection and, citing section 102(a) of the Copyright Act, suggested that digital models displayed on a computer and electronically transmitted could be "original works of authorship fixed in any tangible

---

61. UK Copyright, Designs, and Patents Act, *supra* note 52, pt. IV, § 77, http://www.legislation.gov.uk/ukpga/1988/48/section/77/enacted.

62. *See* 17 U.S.C. § 102(a) (1990) ("Copyright protection subsists . . . in original works of authorship fixed in any tangible medium of expression. . . ."); *see also* Berkman Klein Center for Internet & Society at Harvard University, *Module 3: The Scope of Copyright Law* [hereinafter Berkman], http://cyber.harvard.edu/copyrightforlibrarians/Module_3:_The_Scope_ of_Copyright_Law (last visited July 30, 2018).

63. Berne Convention, *supra* note 18, art. 2, § 2; *see also* Berkman, *supra* note 62.

64. *See* Berkman, *supra* note 62.

medium of expression, *now known or later developed.*"[65] The Ninth Circuit, however, has found that, while a game itself is copyrightable, activity generated by the players (i.e., "gameplay") within the game would not be fixed in a tangible medium of expression.[66] Thus, while it remains uncertain as to whether a player-created structure in *Minecraft* or other virtual reality-based environment could receive protection *ab initio* based solely on its visual creation within the virtual environment, at least in the United States, it is even more uncertain whether a U.S. court (e.g., applying *Itar-Tass*) could find a protectable copyright in a player-created structure based on another nation's laws that have not implemented a strict fixation requirement.

It is notable that a separate treaty—the Agreement on Trade-Related Aspects of Intellectual Property Rights (TRIPS)[67]—requires its member states to extend copyright protection to live musical performances, irrespective of whether the performance is fixed.[68] While online virtual environments have yet to become harbors for vast audiences of live music, musicians can likely rest assured that their virtual performances will likely be protected by copyright in most nations, even though any visual accompaniment may not.

B. Territoriality of Copyright Infringement

A different set of conflict-of-law rules applies to international or cross-border claims for copyright infringement. The overarching concept in copyright infringement claims, as applied by *Itar-Tass* and others, is that of "territoriality," with claims localized in relation to *where* specific acts of infringement occurred.[69] In this

---

65. Meshwerks, Inc. v. Toyota Motor Sales U.S.A., Inc., 528 F.3d 1258, 1269 (10th Cir. 2008) (citing 17 U.S.C. § 102(a) (1990)).

66. Order Denying Motion to Dismiss at 3–4, Davis v. Elec. Arts, Inc., No. 10-cv-03328-RS (N.D. Cal. Dec. 11, 2017) (contrasting football game recordings as satisfying the copyright requirement as works "fixed" in tangible medium).

67. Agreement on Trade-Related Aspects of Intellectual Property Rights, Apr. 15, 1994, 108 Stat. 4809, 1869 U.N.T.S. 299 [hereinafter TRIPS]. TRIPS was originally a part of the General Agreements on Tariffs and Trade (GATT), and was negotiated towards the end of the Uruguay Round in 1994.

68. Berkman, *supra* note 62.

69. Itar-Tass Russian News Agency v. Russian Kurier, Inc., 153 F.3d 82, 91 (2d Cir. 1998).

regard, U.S. copyright law notably protects works "published in the United States *or elsewhere*,"[70] when the work is registered in the United States.[71] And, U.S. courts have enforced U.S. copyright registrations of works even when the works were not subject to protection in their country of creation and first publication.[72] It is thus possible that software or other digital work published in a foreign nation could conceivably obtain protection in the United States, irrespective of whether official copyright protection was obtained in the foreign nation.[73]

Building upon the "undisputed axiom that U.S. copyright law has no extraterritorial application,"[74] U.S. copyright law does not generally apply to acts occurring *outside* U.S. territories, regardless of whether the same acts would infringe had they occurred within a U.S. territory. A primary infringing activity outside the United States "cannot serve as the basis for holding liable under the Copyright Act one who is merely related to that activity within the United States."[75]

1. The "Place" of Infringement in an Online Virtual Environment

Copyright disputes arising entirely under foreign law will often fall outside the subject-matter jurisdiction of U.S. courts.[76] If, however, a specific act of infringement occurs within the United States, a

---

70. Copyright Act of 1976 § 401(a), 17 U.S.C. § 401(a) (1988).

71. *See also* 17 U.S.C. § 411(a) (2018) (requiring a work to be registered in the United States prior to suit).

72. *See, e.g.*, Hasbro Bradley, Inc. v. Sparkle Toys, Inc., 780 F.2d 189, 192–93 (2d Cir. 1985) (holding toys created by a Japanese national and first published in Japan received copyright protection under U.S. law despite not warranting copyright protection under Japanese law). *See also* 17 U.S.C. § 411(a) (2018) (requiring a work to be registered in the United States prior to suit).

73. *See, e.g.*, *Hasbro Bradley, Inc.*, 780 F.2d at 192–93.

74. 3 DAVID NIMMER & MELVILLE B. NIMMER, NIMMER ON COPYRIGHT § 12.04[A][3][b] (2018); *see also* Subafilms, Ltd. v. MGM-Pathe Commc'ns Co., 24 F.3d 1088, 1093–94, 1096 (9th Cir. 1994) (quoting 3 NIMMER & NIMMER, *supra*, § 12.04[A][3][b]).

75. *Subafilms, Ltd.*, 24 F.3d at 1093 (citing 3 NIMMER & NIMMER, *supra* note 74, § 12.04[A][3][b]).

76. *See, e.g.*, Bridgeman Art Library, Ltd. v. Corel Corp., 25 F. Supp. 2d 421, 430–31 (S.D.N.Y. 1998).

claim can arise under U.S. law, regardless of whether the act is part of a continuing course of infringement that takes place abroad.[77]

The territoriality rule can be employed with reasonable certainty when analyzing the importation of tangible goods and evaluating international infringement cases arising from the transmission or distribution of *digital copies* of works by entities from a single foreign jurisdiction. For example, a website distributing pirated video games would be liable for violating the "distribution right" (or its local equivalent) in each country to which the infringing file was transmitted.

However, when an act of copyright infringement allegedly takes place entirely in an online virtual environment, whether a "distribution" occurred in any particular territory becomes less certain, and territoriality principles are harder to apply. For example, where does the alleged infringement take place if a Canadian national copies and distributes a U.S. resident's protected work entirely within an online virtual environment hosted on a Korean server, to residents of other countries outside the United States, and the distributed work is viewable on U.S. computers? Or, if a U.S. resident makes available copyrighted photographs for viewing and download, and a French national downloads and reposts the photographs in various locations throughout an online virtual environment? What about a foreign (outside the United States) musician who plays (or streams) copyrighted music live from a virtual nightclub?

Such scenarios present several possibilities as to whether or where infringement took place. Courts have found that a public musical performance takes place at each and every place streamed audio or video is received and output (i.e., wherever the receiving computer or playback media device of each recipient is located).[78]

---

77. *See, e.g.,* Eng'g & Distribution, LLC v. Shandong Linglong Rubber Co., 682 F.3d 292, 306–09 (4th Cir. 2012) (citing Update Art, Inc. v. Modiin, 843 F.2d 67 (2d Cir. 1988)).

78. *See, e.g.,* ITSI T.V. Prods., Inc. v. Cal. Auth. of Racing Fairs, 785 F. Supp. 854 (E.D. Cal. 1992) (finding transmissions originating in the United States and received in Mexico were subject to Mexican, not U.S., copyright law); Twentieth Century Fox Film Corp. v. iCraveTV, No. Civ. A. 00-121, 2000 WL 255989, at *7 (W.D. Pa. Feb. 8, 2000) (finding plaintiffs were likely to succeed in showing that defendants

Courts have also found that *uploading* or *downloading* copyrighted content can constitute a reproduction or distribution, if not both, and thus infringement takes place wherever and whenever material is uploaded (or downloaded) to a server by a user.[79] Accordingly, uploading or downloading protected content to or from a U.S. computer could be seen as infringement within the United States, regardless of where the server hosting the online environment is located. But what if the content is merely displayed via the local computer and not "downloaded" to be stored locally?

The Ninth Circuit has adopted the "server test,"[80] in which a copyright holder's exclusive "display right" is violated if a computer owner "stores an image as electronic information *and* serves that electronic information directly to the user. . . ."[81] In *Perfect 10, Inc. v. Amazon.com, Inc.*,[82] a search engine operator was found to have violated the display right of an owner of digital images by storing and displaying thumbnails of those images, but not by in-line *linking* to the full-size images.[83] In a later case, the storage of full-size images on servers in Russia was held not to constitute direct copyright infringement in the United States, even though "the image[s] could be downloaded from a server abroad by

---

are unlawfully publicly performing plaintiffs' copyrighted works in the United States, by "transmitting (through use of 'streaming' technology) performances of the works to the public by means of the telephone lines and computers that make up the Internet"); Video Pipeline, Inc. v. Buena Vista Home Entm't, 342 F.3d 191, 197 (3d Cir. 2003) (streaming movie previews likely to violate rights of public performance and display).

79. *See, e.g.*, A&M Records, Inc. v. Napster, Inc., 239 F.3d 1004, 1014–15 (9th Cir. 2001) (finding "Napster users who upload file names to the search index for others to copy violate plaintiffs' distribution rights"); BMG Music v. Gonzalez, 430 F.3d 888, 889 (7th Cir. 2005) (noting "[t]he foundation of [Grokster] is a belief that people who post or download music files are primary infringers").

80. Not every jurisdiction has adopted the "server test." In a recent opinion, the Southern District of New York declined to apply the "server test" in case involving photos embedded into online news articles. *See* Goldman v. Breitbart News Network, LLC, 302 F. Supp. 3d 585, 590–93 (S.D.N.Y. 2018).

81. Perfect 10, Inc. v. Amazon.com, Inc., 508 F.3d 1146, 1159–60 (9th Cir. 2007) (emphasis added).

82. *Perfect 10, Inc.*, 508 F.3d 1146.

83. *Id.* at 1159–60.

someone in the United States."[84] Accordingly, the location where an allegedly infringing copy of the work is actually *stored* and from where it is transmitted are likely to be factors in an infringement analysis by a U.S. court, with direct infringement unlikely without something more than a potential for incidental downloads or display in the United States. The analysis becomes somewhat murky in augmented or mixed realities, where the work may not be stored but may be visualized as if it is actually within a U.S. resident's living room.

On the other hand, the streaming of audio or video (e.g., the transmission of sound recordings from content within the online virtual environment) to U.S. customers of a website has been found to be within the subject-matter jurisdiction of U.S. courts.[85] However, subject-matter jurisdiction was not found where a foreign defendant obtained and then rebroadcast a U.S. protected work outside the United States.[86] On this basis, a court may struggle to find subject-matter jurisdiction in the situation where a foreign party copies a work protected in the United States and distributes the work, via an online virtual environment, from one foreign jurisdiction to another without any transmission to the United States. One possible analogy may include the sale of copyright-protected works as objects (files) between the inventories of two foreign users' avatars, without any display of those objects other than on computers outside of the United States.

2. Secondary Liability for Foreign Actions

Secondary liability for copyright infringement, whether contributory or vicarious, raises many complex issues. The majority of U.S. courts hold that a claim for infringement cannot be brought under

---

84. Perfect 10, Inc. v. Yandex N.V., No. C 12-01521 WHA, 2013 WL 4777189, at * 4 (N.D. Cal. Sept. 6, 2013).

85. *See* cases cited *supra* note 78.

86. *See, e.g.*, ITSI T.V. Prods., Inc. v. Cal. Auth. of Racing Fairs, 785 F. Supp. 854, 866–67 (E.D. Cal. 1992) (dismissing infringement claims for lack of subject-matter jurisdiction after finding U.S.-originated transmissions received in Mexico were subject to Mexican, not U.S., copyright law).

the U.S. Copyright Act solely on authorization within the United States of acts that entirely occur abroad.[87]

The Ninth Circuit recognized in *Subafilms, Ltd. v. MGM-Pathe Communications Co.*[88] that secondary liability for copyright infringement requires a predicate act of primary (or direct) infringement within the United States, and thus no action for infringement would lie for claims that were "solely [due to] authorization within the territorial boundaries of the United States of acts that occur entirely abroad."[89] Subafilms sued Warner Home Video, Inc. and others for causing the videocassette distribution (through foreign parties) of the Beatles animated motion picture *Yellow Submarine* around the world.[90] In reversing the district court's finding of contributory infringement, the *Subafilms* court held explicitly that "the mere authorization of acts of infringement that are not cognizable under the United States copyright laws because they occur entirely outside of the United States does not state a claim for infringement under the Copyright Act."[91] In other words, without direct infringement in the United States, there can be no liability for contributory infringement for authorizing the foreign infringing acts.

Conversely, if a person or entity located abroad engages in conduct that facilitates infringement in the United States, then that person or entity may be held liable under U.S. law.[92]

Some courts have either distinguished or declined to follow *Subafilms*.[93] *Curb v. MCA Records, Inc.*[94] questioned *Subafilms'* tying of the authorization right to contributory infringement, but nevertheless found that the unauthorized creation of duplicate master tapes for release into foreign countries appeared to amount to

---

87. *See, e.g.*, Subafilms, Ltd. v. MGM-Pathe Commc'ns Co., 24 F.3d 1088, 1089 (9th Cir. 1994).

88. *Subafilms, Ltd.*, 24 F.3d 1088.

89. *Id.* at 1089.

90. *Id.* at 1089–90.

91. *Id.* at 1099.

92. *See* Armstrong v. Virgin Records, Ltd., 91 F. Supp. 2d 628, 635 (S.D.N.Y. 2000).

93. *See, e.g.*, Expediters Int'l of Wash., Inc. v. Direct Line Cargo Mgmt. Serv., Inc., 995 F. Supp. 468, 476 (D.N.J. 1998); Nat'l Football League v. PrimeTime 24 Joint Venture, No. 98 CIV. 3778(LMM), 1999 WL 163181 (S.D.N.Y. Mar. 24, 1999).

94. Curb v. MCA Records, Inc., 898 F. Supp. 586 (M.D. Tenn. 1995).

an infringement of the plaintiff's reproduction right in the United States, a right that *Subafilms* avoided.[95] The court cited 17 U.S.C. § 106, which provides "the owner of a copyright . . . the exclusive rights to do and to *authorize*" the reproduction and distribution of copyrighted materials.[96] Another court adopted *Curb*'s reasoning to reject a U.S. defendant's territorial argument that it was not liable for directing and authorizing Asian affiliates to use infringing copies of software, noting that *Curb* was "more closely adapted to our modern age of telefaxes, Internet communication, and electronic mail systems," and finding that "the mere authorization of infringing acts abroad constitutes direct infringement and is actionable under United States Copyright Law."[97] Still, many courts continue to follow *Subafilms*, and repudiate the treatment of authorization as an actionable predicate act.[98]

In an online virtual environment, authorization that would lead to contributory infringement may occur in real time based on communications between avatars. The ability to direct infringing acts through the uses of instant chat appears much more nefarious, and some could argue for revisiting whether such an authorization, without direct infringement in the United States, should be actionable, or at least be seen as a predicate act.

3. Minimizing Infringement Exposure through Takedown Procedures

In many cases, online hosts and/or service providers associated with an online game or other virtual reality-based environment have some protection if they act promptly on knowledge of allegedly infringing content. As in U.S. law,[99] Chinese and European laws mandate notice and takedown by "online hosts" or "network service providers," who must expeditiously remove or disable access

---

95. *Id.* at 594.

96. *Id.* at 595–96.

97. *Expediters*, 995 F. Supp. at 476–77.

98. *See, e.g.*, Geophysical Serv. v. TGS-NOPEC Geophysical Co., 850 F.3d 785, 799 (5th Cir. 2017); Levitin v. Sony Music Entm't, 101 F. Supp. 3d 376, 385 (S.D.N.Y. 2015); Illustro Sys. Int'l, LLC v. Int'l Bus. Machs. Corp., No. 3:06-CV-1969-L, 2007 WL 1321825, at *13 (N.D. Tex. May 4, 2007).

99. *See* Digital Millennium Copyright Act § 512(c), 17 U.S.C. § 512(c) (2010).

to hosted content upon (written) notification of alleged copyright infringement/illegality in order to maintain limited liability against potential infringement.[100] Chinese law includes similar provisions, including a provision that the host/provider must promptly reinstate the material if an explanatory statement is made.[101]

Article 14 of the European Union (EU) Electronic Commerce Directive applies to content hosts in relation to all "illegal activity or information," and provides safe harbor from liability for online hosts who do not have "actual knowledge" of the activity or information, so long as the online host acts expeditiously to remove or disable access to the information.[102] Unlike its detailed U.S. counterpart,[103] the directive does not set out notice-and-takedown procedures, instead suggesting member states encourage voluntary agreements between trade bodies and consumer associations to specify notice-and-takedown processes.[104] As most EU countries do not have explicit national rules regarding notice of infringement, takedown, counter notice, and put back, some notice requirement aspects can be derived from common principles of law.

C. Proposed Copyright Reform in Europe and China

The European Commission (EC) recognizes a need for a modernization of its copyright rules to fit the digital age.[105] In 2015, the EC adopted the Digital Single Market Strategy, which promises, among other things, legislation to enhance cross-border access

---

100. Regulations for the Protection of the Right of Communication through Information Network art. 2 (2006) (P.R.C.), http://www.cpahkltd.com /UploadFiles/20100315165559735.pdf; Directive 2000/31/EC, art. 14, 2000 O.J. (L 178) 13 (EC).

101. *See* Matthew Alderson & Grace Yang, *Copyright Takedowns in China*, China L. Blog, Nov. 16, 2015, https://www.chinalawblog.com/2015/11/copyright -takedowns-in-china.html.

102. Directive 2000/31/EC, art. 14, 2000 O.J. (L 178) 13 (EC); *see also* Organization for Economic Cooperation and Development, The Role of Internet Intermediaries in Advancing Public Policy Objectives 146 (2011).

103. *See, e.g.*, 17 U.S.C. §§ 512(c)(1)(C), 512(c)(3)(A)(i)–(vi), 512(f), 512(g)(2) (A),(C), 512(g)(3)(A)–(D) (2018).

104. Laura Lee Stapleton, E-Copyright Law Handbook 13–53 (2002).

105. *See* European Commission, *Modernisation of the EU Copyright Rules*, https://ec.europa.eu/digital-single-market/en/modernisation-eu-copyright-rules (last updated July 4, 2018).

to copyright-protected content services, adopt modern rules for online and digital cross-border purchases, and provide a more harmonized copyright system.[106] Proposed legislation in each one of these areas, when enacted, could impact and/or facilitate transactions within online virtual environments, at least within the EU. The United Kingdom's access to the Digital Single Market will ultimately be affected by Brexit, but as of publication of this book there is a lack of clarity as to how specific issues will be affected.[107]

Some digital world and open source advocates object to a proposed requirement that Internet platforms hosting "large amounts" of user-uploaded content monitor user behavior to identify and prevent copyright infringement.[108] Arguments against such requirements include the creation of barriers to the development of source code by imposing liability on platforms used by developers (a fundamental sector for the Digital Single Market),[109] and harm to community projects like Wikipedia, scientific repositories, and code-hosting platforms, who only accept freely licensed uploads, but would likely be forced to implement content upload filters required by one of the proposals.[110]

---

106. European Commission, COM(15)192 final, https://eur-lex.europa.eu/legal-content/EN/TXT/PDF/?uri=CELEX:52015DC0192&from=EN.

107. *Clarity Needed on UK Access to Digital Single Market Post-Brexit, Commons Select Committee*, U.K. PARLIAMENT, Mar. 28, 2017, https://www.parliament.uk/business/committees/committees-a-z/commons-select/european-scrutiny-committee/news-parliament-20151/digital-market-access-report-published-16-17/.

108. *See, e.g.*, Save Code Share, *Homepage*, https://savecodeshare.eu/ (last visited July 30, 2018); Polina Malaja, *EU Copyright Review: Tell Legislators to Save Code Share*, FREE SOFTWARE FOUND. EUR., May 10, 2017, https://fsfe.org/news/2017/news-20171005-01.en.html.

109. *See* PCBOFE, *Release of OFE & FSFE White Paper: European Copyright Reform—Impact on Free and Open Source Software and Developer Communities*, OPENFORUM EUR., Sept. 8, 2017, http://www.openforumeurope.org/release-ofe-fsfe-paper-european-copyright-reform-impact-free-open-source-software-developer-communities/.

110. Julia Reda, *Censorship Machines (Article 13)*, JULIA REDA, Dec. 13, 2017, https://juliareda.eu/eu-copyright-reform/censorship-machines/; Julia Reda, *EU Copyright Reform/Expansion*, JULIA REDA, https://juliareda.eu/eu-copyright-reform/ (last updated July 10, 2018).

In China, the National Copyright Administration issued the 13th Five-Year Plan on Copyright in 2017,[111] which focuses on copyright public enforcement and supervision mechanisms,[112] and considers single system of copyright registration and search. Indeed, Chinese copyrights are on the rise[113] and, with increased attention and resources from specialized courts[114] and foreign companies winning verdicts,[115] long-held sentiment that China's intellectual property laws were unbalanced with respect to other nation's intellectual property laws may be dissipating. Open source software is also arguably doing well in China, with increased appreciation of altruistic and strategic gains, despite innate tension between investing in development and developers to differentiate products and giving code away for free.[116] Nevertheless, reaction to China's plan for reform has been mixed.[117] Some suggest other

---

111. *The 3rd Revision of China's Copyright Law Is in Sight*, IPR IN CHINA, Feb. 27, 2017, 10:52:51, http://www.chinaipr.gov.cn/article/iplaw/201702/1902106.html.

112. NATIONAL COPYRIGHT ADMINISTRATION, 13TH FIVE-YEAR PLAN ON COPYRIGHT (2017), https://chinaipr2.files.wordpress.com/2017/02/fiveyearplan.docx (scroll down for English version of the plan) (including copyright legal system improvements; "at all levels persist[ing] in combining routine supervision and special operations, [to] crack down on piracy"; a push for legitimate software; and increasing copyright society service levels, promoting continuous copyright industry development, strengthening copyright awareness training, and deepening copyright international exchange and cooperation).

113. *Country's Copyright Registrations Soar*, CHINA DAILY, Nov. 10, 2017, 14:17:30, http://www.chinaipr.gov.cn/article/copyright/201711/1913123.html.

114. *China Strengthens Judicial Protection of Intellectual Property through Specialized IPR Courts*, CIP NEWS, Sept. 5, 2017, 12:23:21, http://www.chinaipr.gov .cn/article/iplaw/201709/1910563.html.

115. *The Lego Group Wins Case against Manufacturers of Bela Products in China*, LEGO, Dec. 7, 2017, 8:57, https://www.lego.com/en-us/aboutus/news-room/2017 /december/lego-group-wins-case-against-bela.

116. Steve Moore, *Is Open Source Alive in China?*, INSIDE MACHINE LEARNING, Sept. 5, 2017, https://medium.com/inside-machine-learning/is-open-source-alive -in-china-3f606aafbd3b.

117. *See* Mark Cohen, *China's Plan for Copyright Creativity*, CHINA IPR, Feb. 16, 2017, https://chinaipr.com/2017/02/16/chinas-plan-for-copyright-creativity/ (Mark Cohen is a senior counsel on China at the U.S. Patent and Trademark Office (USPTO) and a professor at University of California at Berkeley Law School); *see also* Shruti Rana, *The Global Battle over Copyright Reform: Developing the Rule of Law in the Chinese Business Context*, 53 STAN. J. INT'L L. 89 (2017) (comparing copyright regimes in proposing how China may effectively reform its copyright system and enhance public awareness of copyright norms and functions).

aspects (e.g., criminal copyright reform) should match any bolstered copyright protection.[118]

II. International Trademark Issues

Trademark rights, in general, are limited geographically and actual ownership of a mark within a region is not typically complicated by international borders. Brand recognition within an online virtual environment, however, is capable of reaching multiple geographical regions and international boundaries at once, and modern online virtual environments provide numerous ways to monetize the content. This instantaneous access to a rapidly increasing global community is a key factor in the enormous amount of money being spent on brand recognition within the realm of e-sports.[119] Additionally, many online virtual environments enable the members themselves to build virtual businesses and to create custom advertisements promoting their businesses or targeting a specific demographic of the virtual environment, broadcasting those advertisements (or those of third parties) within the environment upon payment of a surcharge.

Accordingly, a user logging in to an online virtual environment in the United States may browse (in 3D) for and purchase products originating in foreign countries and view product advertising created by foreign merchants. Moreover, the advertising may include use of a mark protected in the United States, and, but for its unprotected status abroad, the foreign user would be enjoined from using the mark in the advertisement. This is only one example of the many problems that could likely arise as the commercialization of online virtual environments becomes more significant.

---

118. Mark Cohen, *Should the NPC Also Consider Criminal Copyright Reform When It Considers Copyright Reform?*, CHINA IPR, Mar. 11, 2017, https://chinaipr .com/2017/03/11/should-the-npc-also-consider-criminal-copyright-reform-when-it -considers-copyright-reform/.

119. *See* Elder, *supra* note 9.

A. Ownership and Territoriality

Unlike copyrights, registration of a nongeneric or nondescriptive trademark or service mark is generally accomplished by prosecution before each nation's trademark office. A foreign merchant should be able to obtain a U.S. registration for his or her virtual store services, so long as the mark is used to identify and distinguish the services and their source apart from other aspects of the online virtual environment.[120] Goods sold under the mark via the virtual store may be registrable provided a mechanism for U.S. customers to order the goods is provided.[121]

The Paris Convention for the Protection of Industrial Property is premised on the idea that each nation's law shall have only territorial application.[122] Thus, the laws of a foreign country will generally not prohibit the foreign use of a locally protected mark, and the same mark can be owned be a different entity in multiple countries.[123] In an online virtual environment, it is easy to imagine run-ins between virtual store owners with confusingly similar names, and each selling similar products.

Most countries follow a first-to-file system, wherein the first person to register a mark is entitled to the exclusive use of the mark regardless of any previous use within that country. If the mark is ultimately determined to be allowable (e.g., by having distinctive character) under a nation's laws, then registration is granted in that nation. The failure to use the mark in commerce, however, may make the mark vulnerable to cancellation. Some countries adhere to a common law system in which registration is not required to establish ownership rights in a mark, as long as the mark has been in continuous commercial use within the

---

120. *See* USPTO, U.S. DEPARTMENT OF COMMERCE, TRADEMARK MANUAL OF EXAMINING PROCEDURE § 1301.04(h)(iv)(C) (Oct. 2017 ed.) [hereinafter TMEP]; *In re* Florists' Transworld Delivery, Inc., 119 U.S.P.Q.2d 1056, 1057, 1062 (T.T.A.B. 2016).

121. *See* TMEP, *supra* note 120, § 904.03(i).

122. Vanity Fair Mills, Inc. v. T. Eaton Co., 234 F.2d 633, 638–40 (2d Cir. 1956).

123. 5 J. THOMAS MCCARTHY, MCCARTHY ON TRADEMARKS AND UNFAIR COMPETITION § 29:1 (5th ed. 2017).

geographical area in which the rights are to be enforced.[124] For example, in the United States, the first party to use a mark in interstate commerce in connection with the sale of particular goods or services is deemed the "senior user" of the mark and gains certain common law rights to the mark in the particular geographic area in which the mark is used.[125]

One exception to the rule that a mark must be used in commerce before it is recognized as protectable in that nation is the "well-known" marks doctrine.[126] Under the Paris Convention,[127] member nations are required to provide protection to well-known marks not yet registered,[128] for example by providing a mechanism to oppose applications or cancel registrations of confusingly similar marks filed after the mark became well known.[129] Accordingly, an unregistered famous mark could be found to be senior to a mark registered in the United States, and a court could find a likelihood of confusion between the marks among U.S. consumers.[130]

There is some disagreement among U.S. courts in how well-known marks should be treated. The Second Circuit found that

---

124. Australia and the United Kingdom protect unregistered trademarks under the common law doctrine of passing off. *See* IP Australia, *Benefits of Registering a Trade Mark*, https://www.ipaustralia.gov.au/trade-marks/understanding-trade -marks/benefits-trade-marks (last updated Mar. 17, 2016); UK Intellectual Property Office, *Apply to Register a Trade Mark*, https://www.gov.uk/how-to-register-a-trade -mark/unregistered-trade-marks (last visited July 30, 2018).

125. *See* Allard Enters. v. Advanced Programming Res., Inc., 249 F.3d 564, 571–72 (6th Cir. 2001). This is provided that another user who has not yet used the mark has not filed an intent-to-use application under 15 U.S.C. § 1051(b). *See also* USPTO, *Trademark Applications—Intent-to-Use (ITU) Basis*, https://www.uspto .gov/trademarks-application-process/filing-online/intent-use-itu-applications (last modified Oct. 3, 2017); TMEP, *supra* note 120, § 201.01.

126. 5 McCarthy, *supra* note 123, § 29:4.

127. Paris Convention for the Protection of Industrial Property, as last revised at the Stockholm Revision Conference, July 14, 1967, 21 U.S.T. 1583, 828 U.N.T.S. 305 [hereinafter Paris Convention], http://www.wipo.int/treaties/en/text.jsp?file _id=288514.

128. World Intellectual Property Organization (WIPO), *Well-Known Marks*, http://www.wipo.int/sme/en/ip_business/marks/well_known_marks.htm (last visited July 30, 2018).

129. Joint Recommendation concerning Provisions on the Protection of Well-Known Marks (WIPO 2000), http://www.wipo.int/edocs/pubdocs/en/marks/833 /pub833.pdf.

130. *See* 5 McCarthy, *supra* note 123, § 29:4.

the well-known marks doctrine has not been incorporated in U.S. law,[131] a finding that some legal scholars disagree with.[132] The Ninth Circuit, however, held that a "well-known" mark had to have more than just a "secondary meaning"—it had to be known to a "substantial percentage" of persons in the relevant American market.[133]

B. Difficulty in Protecting Marks Subject to Global Exposure

A mark used in an online virtual environment could conceivably be viewable to multiple participating members, each in a different nation, at the same time. Given the territorial application of trademark law and each nation's specific registration requirements, showing actual use in commerce or obtaining registration in *each* nation may seem an almost impossible undertaking.

Numerous treaties attempt to harmonize international law, at least with regard to ownership and registration. Under the Paris Convention, an applicant in one contracting state who later seeks to register a mark in any other contracting state is entitled to the filing date of the original application if the later foreign application is filed within six months of the original application.[134] The Madrid System for the International Registration of Marks[135] provides an owner of a mark protection in several countries by filing one application directly with his or her own national or regional trademark

---

131. *See* ITC Ltd. v. Punchgini, Inc., 482 F.3d 135, 163 (2d Cir. 2007) ("[W]e do not ourselves discern in the plain language of sections 44(b) and (h) a clear congressional intent to incorporate a famous marks exception into federal unfair competition law.").

132. *See* 5 McCARTHY, *supra* note 123, § 29:4 ("In the author's view, the well known or famous marks doctrine . . . is incorporated into United States domestic law through the operation of Lanham Act § 43(a), § 44(b) and § 44(h).").

133. Grupo Gigante SA de CV v. Dallo & Co., Inc., 391 F.3d 1088, 1095–98 (9th Cir. 2004).

134. 15 U.S.C. § 1126(d)(1) (2002); *see also* Vanity Fair Mills, Inc. v. T. Eaton Co., 234 F.2d 633, 644 (2d Cir. 1956) (discussing the benefits of section 44 of the Lanham Act, codified in 15 U.S.C. § 1126).

135. The Madrid System is governed by two treaties, the Madrid Agreement (1891) and the Madrid Protocol (1989). *See* Madrid Agreement concerning the International Registration of Marks, 1891, effective July 15, 1892 (Stockholm Act, 1967 and amended in 1979); Protocol Relating to the Madrid Agreement concerning the International Registration of Marks, adopted at Madrid on June 27, 1989.

office.[136] Even so, international applications filed via the Madrid System are subject to the filing procedures of each nation state.[137] TRIPS[138] extends protections to services,[139] allows registrability on distinctiveness acquired through use,[140] and grants an owner the exclusive right to prevent others from using similar marks where such use would result in a likelihood of confusion.[141]

Despite the numerous treaties between nations, no current law—international or domestic—specifically addresses the global reach of a mark within an online virtual environment that spans multiple nations, and granting rights in a mark is still seen as a matter of national sovereignty. The implementation of these agreements is left to the subsequent enactment under domestic law of each member state. Even with the protections of international registration (Madrid System) or foreign priority (Paris Convention), an applicant attempting to protect a mark that is reachable through an online virtual environment may still be faced with the overwhelming task and costs of quickly resolving in which countries it is feasible to prosecute the mark within the priority period, while at the same time preparing for the possibility of being forced to protect the mark through litigation under the domestic law of each country.

It therefore becomes apparent that until some form of universal registration system is taken up by yet another international convention, registration of marks to be used in online virtual environments will continue under the practices of each country and its regional trademark offices, and courts will be left to decide matters of registration and competing trademark use based upon domestic law as part of, but not exclusive of, each nation's obligation under existing international treaties.

---

136. WIPO, *Madrid—The International Trademark System*, http://www.wipo.int/madrid/en/ (last visited July 30, 2018).

137. *See* Siegrun D. Kane, Kane on Trademark Law: A Practitioner's Guide §§ 6:7.4–.5 (5th ed. 2007) (applications received in the United States from WIPO are still reviewed post registration for conformance to U.S. practice).

138. TRIPS, *supra* note 67.

139. *Id.* art. 15(1).

140. *Id.* art. 15.

141. *Id.* art. 16.

C. Enforcement and the Special Case of Foreign Defendants

A plaintiff seeking to remove an infringing mark from within an online game or virtual environment may first seek to contact the game's host for assistance, wherein the host's EULA may provide some guidance. However, whether the matter is quickly resolved may depend on factors outside the scope of the EULA, and thus subject to the willingness of the host to assist.

Subject-matter jurisdiction is of particular concern when applying the Lanham Act to foreign defendants not residing or operating in the United States. It could be perceived that some may seek to use online virtual environments to circumvent trademark rights for profit, and perhaps cause problems for owners of marks who enjoy protection through registration in their own country. Even if extraterritorial application of the Lanham Act could be applied, and a basis for personal jurisdiction exists, one question still remains—how can domestic law deal with a foreign defendant who is using a protected mark "in commerce" within an online virtual environment?

In the seminal case *Steele v. Bulova Watch Co.*,[142] the U.S. Supreme Court held that a U.S. district court had subject-matter jurisdiction to award relief against acts of trademark infringement by a U.S. citizen in a foreign country.[143] The Court articulated that jurisdiction was proper where the defendant's conduct had a substantial effect on commerce in the United States, the defendant was a U.S. citizen, and there was no conflict with trademark rights established under the foreign law.[144] As expected, there is some disagreement as to how *Bulova Watch* should be applied. The Second Circuit interpreted *Bulova Watch* as requiring the defendant to be a U.S. citizen,[145] and that the Lanham Act "should not be given an extraterritorial application against foreign citizens acting under

---

142. Steele v. Bulova Watch Co., 344 U.S. 280 (1952).

143. *Id.* at 289.

144. *Id.* at 285–86; *see also* Vanity Fair Mills, Inc. v. T. Eaton Co., 234 F.2d 633, 642 (2d Cir. 1956).

145. *Vanity Fair Mills*, 234 F.2d at 642–43; *see also* Calvin Klein Indus., Inc. v. BFK Hong Kong, Ltd., 714 F. Supp. 78, 79–80 (S.D.N.Y. 1989).

presumably valid trade-marks in a foreign country."[146] In *McBee v. Delica Co.*,[147] the First Circuit refused to apply the Lanham Act to a Japanese website, even though the website was reachable in the United States.[148] While the court did not specifically reach the issue, the court indicated that "the Lanham Act can be applied against foreign corporations or individuals in appropriate cases," suggesting that the threshold effect on commerce might be different for U.S. citizens than foreign entities.[149]

Arguably, the case for jurisdiction could be stronger where the foreign defendant uses a mark protected in the United States in connection with advertising distributed through an online virtual environment to directly solicit and sell to U.S. customers.[150] However, the simple placement of the protected mark within advertising on the online virtual environment by the foreign defendant may not meet the substantial effects test of *Bulova Watch*, without further proof that sales are being diverted from U.S. commerce. In this regard, where there is minimal impact on U.S. commerce, the plaintiff may consider whether the nature of the advertisement and related facts are better suited for a copyright claim.[151]

III. Comparative Patent Law Issues

Patent protection is achieved only by the application for, and grant of, a patent in the country in which patent protection is

---

146. *Vanity Fair Mills*, 234 F.2d at 643.

147. McBee v. Delica Co., 417 F.3d 107 (1st Cir. 2005).

148. *See id.* at 120.

149. *Id.* at 118–19.

150. *Id.* at 112–14, 124 (holding no subject-matter jurisdiction where the allegedly infringing website was not directed at the United States, was created and hosted in Japan, was written primarily in Japanese characters, does not allow online purchases, the retailer only shipped domestically in Japan although some retail stores arranged shipping to the United States, and the retailer generally had a policy to decline orders from the United States).

151. *See* Sadhu Singh Hamdad Tr. v. Ajit Newspaper Adver., Mktg. & Commc'ns, Inc., 503 F. Supp. 2d 577, 581–82 n.6 (E.D.N.Y. 2007) (plaintiff brought copyright claim for deliberate copying of trade name and logo).

sought, in accordance with the laws of that country.[152] The details of each nation's patent laws are extensive and dreadfully complex. However, TRIPS sets certain minimum standards for protection,[153] requiring member states to make patents "available for any inventions, whether products or processes, in all fields of technology, provided that they are new, involve an inventive step and are capable of industrial application."[154]

Accordingly, most countries have implemented examination procedures by which patent applications are rejected if the subject matter of the proposed invention is not new (anticipated—i.e., all the claimed features are in the prior art) or lacks an inventive step (made obvious by the prior art). These principles are synonymous with the principles of anticipation and obviousness as set forth in sections 102 and 103 of the U.S. patent laws.[155] Certain jurisdictions also require that an invention be capable of "industrial application"[156] (limited by a few specific statutory exclusions), which is similar to the U.S. requirement that an invention have a "useful purpose."[157] Each jurisdiction also imposes certain limits on what "subject matter" is eligible for patentability, with computer-related inventions receiving heightened scrutiny and recently being the topic of much literary discussion and judicial debate.

---

152. WIPO IP Services, *Frequently Asked Questions*, http://www.wipo.int/tk/en /resources/faqs.html (last visited July 30, 2018).

153. World Trade Organization, *Frequently Asked Questions about TRIPS [Trade-Related Aspects of Intellectual Property Rights] in the WTO*, http://www.wto.org /english/tratop_e/TRIPS_e/tripfq_e.htm (last visited July 30, 2018).

154. TRIPS, *supra* note 67, art. 27.1.

155. Codified at 35 U.S.C. § 101 *et seq.* (2012).

156. *See, e.g.*, European Patent Convention, Oct. 5, 1973, art. 52, 1065 U.N.T.S. 199 [hereinafter EPC]; Protocol on Patents and Industrial Designs within the Framework of the African Regional Intellectual Property Organization (ARIPO) § 3(9) (adopted Dec. 10, 1982, amended Aug. 13, 2004); Japanese Patent Act art. 29(1); Korean Patent Act art. 29 (Military Act No. 950, promulgated Dec. 31, 1961, amended by Act No. 8462, May 17, 2007).

157. TRIPS, *supra* note 67, art. 27 n.5; 35 U.S.C. § 101 (2012).

A. Eligibility of Inventions Directed to Online Virtual Environments and Computer-Related Subject Matter

There is no universal definition of the boundaries on what subject matter is eligible for patentability. While the U.S. courts and U.S. Patent and Trademark Office (USPTO) continue to struggle to develop a succinct, usable test to determine whether claims are ineligible under U.S. law because they encompass an abstract idea,[158] patent offices and courts around the world continue to struggle to define whether business methods and computer software in general—including gaming—should be patentable at all. For example, methods directed to rules for playing games are expressly excluded from patentability in Europe[159] and Japan[160] but merely subject to other eligibility requirements in China, Singapore, and the United States. China prohibits methods directed to "gambling" unless examining the subject matter for registration in Macau.[161]

Virtual game environments are graphics intensive and, as such, patent applications directed to them are likely to include some form of computer software and/or method claims. While each jurisdiction imposes different requirements on subject-matter eligibility, international examiners have generally required that claims include some form of technical innovation relating to a physical characteristic to overcome obstacles to patentability.

China has recently relaxed examination barriers to business methods and software patents, and the country is now considered to be more open to granting of such applications than, for example,

---

158. *See* Amdocs (Isr.) Ltd. v. Openet Telecom, Inc., 841 F.3d 1288, 1293 (Fed. Cir. 2016).

159. The EPC explicitly excludes from patentability, subject matter directed to "schemes, rules and methods for performing mental acts, playing games or doing business, and programs for computers." EPC, *supra* note 156, art. 52(2)(c).

160. EXAMINATION GUIDELINES FOR PATENT AND UTILITY MODEL IN JAPAN pt. III, ch. 1, §§ 2.1.4, 2.2, https://www.jpo.go.jp/tetuzuki_e/t_tokkyo_e/files_guidelines_e/03_0100_e.pdf.

161. *See* STATE INTELLECTUAL PROPERTY OFFICE OF THE PEOPLE'S REPUBLIC OF CHINA, GUIDELINES FOR EXAMINATION 118 (2006), http://www.sipo.gov.cn/zhfwpt/zlsqzn/guidelines2006(EN).pdf; *see also Bruno Nunes of BN IP Explains How Patent Prosecution and Licensing Works in Macau, a Market Dominated by Gaming and Pharma*, IPPRO PATS., Feb. 22, 2017, http://www.ippropatents.com/countryfocus/country.php?country_id=133.

U.S. practice where stricter criteria are used to determine patent eligibility under 35 U.S.C. § 101 after *Alice Corp. v. CLS Bank International*.[162] On the other hand, European examination is notorious for being especially challenging—particularly when it comes to claims directed to computer programs—and where subject-matter eligibility is generally viewed through the lens of an inventive step.

In Europe, the framework for evaluating the inventive step of claims directed to computer programs (i.e., computer-implemented methods) was defined in a 2002 decision of a Technical Board of Appeal of the European Patent Office (EPO).[163] According to the decision, the inventive step should be evaluated by taking account of all claimed features that contribute to the technical character of the invention. Features making no technical contribution cannot support the presence of the inventive step. The decision noted that the boards of appeal apply a problem-and-solution approach, in which a technical problem "must actually be solved by the solution claimed, [and] all the features in the claim should contribute to the solution."[164] In some aspects, similar reasoning has been applied by the USPTO, which looks to whether patent claims directed to computer-related features actually implement an improvement to the function of the computer.[165] Even so, features that provide a technical effect cannot save a claim that overall lacks novelty or is obvious.

In another early decision, an EPO Technical Board of Appeal found a method for modeling a physical system in a computer to lack an inventive step.[166] The board analogized features directed to defining objects and their instances, and the relationships between

---

162. Alice Corp. v. CLS Bank Int'l, 134 S. Ct. 2347 (2014); *see also* Siyue Zhang, *Revised Patent Examination Guidelines (II): China Relaxing Barriers to Business Method and Software Patents*, LUNG TIN IP ATT'YS NEWSL., Mar. 2017, http://www .lungtin.com/UploadFile/Files/2017/12/7/1513151155e603d07-6.pdf.

163. EPO Boards of Appeal Decision T 0049/99 (2002); EPO Boards of Appeal Decision T 0641/00 (2002).

164. *Id.*

165. Memorandum from Robert W. Bahr, Deputy Commissioner for Patent Examination Policy, USPTO, to Patent Examining Corps (May 19, 2016) at 2 (citing Enfish, LLC v. Microsoft Corp., 822 F.3d 1327 (Fed. Cir. 2016)), https://www.uspto .gov/sites/default/files/documents/ieg-may-2016_enfish_memo.pdf.

166. EPO Boards of Appeal Decision T 0049/99 (2002).

the objects (i.e., information modeling), to human activity, and found the claimed features to lack technical character. The board then dismissed the remaining claimed features directed to storing the relationships between the objects in a database and collapsing the objects and their attributes into an object table as lacking an inventive step in view of prior art database literature. Recent EPO decisions continue to follow this line of reasoning.[167]

Accordingly, European patents directed to online virtual environments are often expected to contain subject matter directed to improvements that reflect consideration of the technical hardware processes behind the online virtual environments rather than to the relationships within the online virtual environments or what is seen in online virtual environments. It could also be possible to obtain European patents related to online virtual environments when they are directed to a novel way of interacting with a user interface that produces a credible technical effect. This appears to be consistent with TRIPS's directive that patentability be available to new and inventive "technology."[168]

Patents are indeed being issued in Europe that are directed to online virtual environments, and claims that have not been rejected based on ineligible subject matter in the EPO include transferring an avatar between (two) virtual world systems,[169] providing position information for avatars in a virtual world,[170] generating terrain in a virtual world in accordance with procedural rules,[171] and creating an equivalent representation of a virtual world object for a physical object, including sensing characteristics and structure data of a physical object using a set of intelligent sensors.[172]

---

167. *See* EPO Boards of Appeal Decision T 1370/11 (2016).

168. TRIPS, *supra* note 67, art. 27(1).

169. *See* European Application No. 20120823557 (filed Aug. 17, 2012), Search Opinion (dated Apr. 20, 2015).

170. *See* European Application No. 20100720955 (filed Mar. 29, 2010).

171. *See* European Application No. 20050779613 (filed May 4, 2005).

172. *See* European Application No. 20090252782 (filed Dec. 29, 2008).

B. Filing Issues for Online Virtual Environments and Internet-Related Inventions

Most countries follow a first-to-file system, wherein the first person to file a patent application is entitled to priority over all others regarding the invention. In this regard, any publication of the invention prior to a filing will generally render the invention ineligible for patent protection.

In many cases, public disclosure of an invention includes the mere "public use" of the invention. Since online virtual environments are generally made available to anyone on the Internet, it is conceivable that use of the invention in one country has the potential to preclude patentability in all countries.

U.S. courts have long ago determined that an electronic publication on a foreign website, including an online database or Internet publication, constitutes a "printed publication" in the United States as long as it is accessible to persons concerned with the art to which the document relates.[173] There is no bright line rule as to whether a court would consider an online virtual environment the equivalent of a website. Determining whether "public use" within the online virtual environment occurs in the United States or a foreign country also becomes an interesting dilemma. For instance, does disclosure of prior art in a foreign user's virtual "residence" in a foreign-based virtual world bar patentability in the United States?

Some countries provide a limited grace period (e.g., six or 12 months) after a disclosure in which an application for the invention may be filed. For example, U.S. patent law allows an applicant one year to file a patent application for an invention that the *applicant* previously disclosed.[174] Other countries, such as Canada, China, Japan, and Korea have similar provisions. On the other hand, the EU follows an "absolute novelty" requirement in which any form of public use or publication prior to application bars patentability.[175]

---

173. USPTO, U.S. Department of Commerce, Manual of Patent Examining Procedure § 2128 (9th ed. 2018) [hereinafter MPEP]; *see also In re* Wyer, 655 F.2d 221, 227 (C.C.P.A. 1981).

174. 35 U.S.C. § 102(b)(1) (2015) (as amended by the Leahy-Smith America Invents Act).

175. *See* EPC, *supra* note 156, art. 54(2).

One strategy commonly used for Internet-related applications is to file an application under the Patent Cooperation Treaty (PCT), which makes it possible for an applicant to reserve the right to seek protection in several countries simultaneously by filing one application directly with his or her own regional patent office or the International Bureau of the World Intellectual Property Organization (WIPO) in Geneva.[176] Under the Paris Convention,[177] this filing may be based on an earlier-filed national application, if filed within 12 months of the earlier-filed application (or within six months for a design patent), and provides the applicant a mechanism to file the application and pay the required fees in each of the designated countries within 30 months from the earliest priority date.[178] During this time, the applicant of the PCT application is also provided a search and written opinion by the designated international search authority and afforded the opportunity to request preliminary examination.[179] Additionally, a favorable report regarding novelty, inventive step, and industrial applicability may provide an applicant the opportunity to request accelerated examination when the application is nationalized in one or more of the designated countries.[180]

---

176. WIPO, PCT FAQs: Protecting Your Inventions Abroad: Frequently Asked Questions about the Patent Cooperation Treaty (PCT) 4–5 (2006), *available at* http://www.wipo.int/pct/en/basic_facts/faqs_about_the_pct.pdf. Similar to the PCT and Madrid System, an applicant can deposit a single international application with WIPO or the national office of a country that is a party to the treaty to secure protection in as many member countries as the applicant wishes. *See* WIPO, *Industrial Designs*, http://www.wipo.int/designs/en/ (last visited July 30, 2018). As with other priority systems, each country makes an individual determination of whether protection is available.

177. Paris Convention, *supra* note 127, art. 4, § C.

178. WIPO, *Time Limits for Entering National/Regional Phase under PCT Chapters I and II*, http://www.wipo.int/pct/en/texts/time_limits.html (last visited July 30, 2018) (note that some countries allow applications to be filed within 31 months of their priority date).

179. *See* MPEP, *supra* note 173, §§ 1864, 1878.

180. WIPO, *PCT-Patent Prosecution Highway Pilot (PCT-PPH and Global PPH)*, http://www.wipo.int/pct/en/filing/pct_pph.html (last visited July 30, 2018); *see also* USPTO, *Patent Prosecution Highway (PPH)—Fast Track Examination of Applications*, https://www.uspto.gov/patents-getting-started/international-protection/patent-prosecution-highway-pph-fast-track (last modified July 2, 2018).

Thus, an applicant wishing to seek international protection for an online virtual reality-based invention may use PCT filings to obtain instant worldwide priority of the application, thereby preventing disclosure issues associated with implementing the invention in any particular jurisdiction. The applicant may then use the preliminary examination process to get an idea of the novelty and inventiveness of his or her application before deciding whether to nationalize the application in any particular country.

C. Some Issues Involving International Inventorship

Many countries, including the United States, have procedures in place that protect the transfer of sensitive innovations to other countries without approval from the relevant patent office.[181] Inventions involving online virtual environments and other Internet-related technologies are often implemented globally, and companies that implement them are increasingly employing foreign inventors as part of their critical workforce. However, some countries require that their inventor residents first obtain government approval prior to the export of inventive subject matter, irrespective of whether a domestic application is first filed.[182] Violations may include, in some cases, fines or imprisonment.[183] Accordingly, when an application implicates sensitive subject matter or foreign inventors, the applicant may consider first obtaining a foreign filing license and/or filing the first application within the foreign jurisdiction as a PCT application to prevent or minimize such issues.

---

181. *See* Sealectro Corp. v. L.V.C. Indus., Inc., 271 F. Supp. 835, 837 (E.D.N.Y. 1967) (discussing provisions enacted "to prevent disclosure of information which through premature publication might adversely affect the welfare of the country"); *see* also 35 U.S.C. § 184 (protecting "sensitive" inventions"); USPTO, *Patent FAQs— Getting Started—Other*, https://www.uspto.gov/help/patent-help#type-getting -started (last modified Dec. 5, 2016).

182. *See, e.g.*, Patent Law of the People's Republic of China (promulgated by the Standing Committee of the National People's Congress, Mar. 12, 1984, revised Dec. 27, 2008, effective Oct. 1, 2009), art. 20, 2009 P.R.C. Laws (P.R.C.) [hereinafter China's Patent Law]; L614-18, L614-20 du 17 mars 2017 de Code de la propriété intellectuelle [Law No. 614-18, Law No. 614-20 of Mar. 17, 2017 on the Intellectual Property Code], J.O., Mar. 24, 2017 [hereinafter France's Intellectual Property Code].

183. *See, e.g.*, China's Patent Law, *supra* note 182, art. 20; France's Intellectual Property Code, *supra* note 182, Law No. 615-15.

D. Enforceability against Foreign Defendants

While the geographical scope within an online virtual environment may bring foreign defendants closer in virtual proximity, or, in some cases, contribute to the minimum contacts needed to assert personal jurisdiction, it does not *ipso facto* resolve territorial sovereignty or conflict-of-law issues. The U.S. Patent Act provides liability for uses, sales, or offers for sale "within the United States Courts."[184] However, U.S. patent laws are generally not applied extraterritorially, and thus no infringement can occur when a patented product is made or sold in another country.[185]

One exception to this rule is when a defendant "supplies or causes to be supplied . . . from the United States all or a substantial portion of the components of a patented invention" to create the infringing activity.[186] Thus, software generated in the United States and then used to create an infringing product overseas may create liability for infringement within the United States. However, this exception has been limited to "the very components supplied from the United States, and not copies thereof."[187] Specifically, in *Microsoft Corp. v. AT&T Corp.*,[188] the Supreme Court held that shipping a master disk from the United States to a foreign jurisdiction in which infringing copies were made by the inclusion of further software modifications by a foreign entity was not actionable under U.S. law.[189]

In assessing whether a system or computer medium claim is infringed "within the United States," courts also look to how that device is used or controlled by U.S. users. Specifically, courts have found that where U.S. users control and derive a beneficial use from a device located overseas that infringes a claimed system, those users use the infringing device in the United States.[190] Courts need not focus on the "situs of use of each claimed element within the claimed invention" (i.e., individual elements of the claim), but,

---

184. 35 U.S.C. § 271(a) (2018).
185. Microsoft Corp. v. AT&T Corp., 550 U.S. 437, 442–45 (2007).
186. 35 U.S.C. § 271(f) (2018).
187. *Microsoft Corp.*, 550 U.S. at 453.
188. *Microsoft Corp.*, 550 U.S. 437.
189. *Id.* at 453–54.
190. Renhcol Inc. v. Don Best Sports, 548 F. Supp. 2d 356, 365 (E.D. Tex. 2008).

rather, analyze the claimed "invention as a whole to determine where the 'claimed system as a whole . . . is put into service.'"[191]

In *Renhcol Inc. v. Don Best Sports*,[192] the court determined that it was U.S. users of a foreign website that controlled execution of code on the website and benefited from the code's execution, and thus the situs of use of the allegedly infringing storage medium was the United States.[193] For example, the users controlled the execution of "code for receiving" when they accessed the website and entered their information.[194] The court distinguished this type of control from the control a website owner has over requests managed by the website.[195]

While the foregoing analysis may apply in determining whether a device with components used collectively infringed an apparatus claim,[196] it is generally not applicable to method claims.[197] Contrary to an apparatus or system in which the components are used collectively, "use of a method requires performance of each of the recited steps."[198] As such, there can be no infringement in the United States if at least one step of the claimed method is found to be performed outside the United States.[199] This is true even if there is a solid case for personal jurisdiction, or if the defendant is a U.S. citizen.[200]

---

191. *Id.* at 361 (citing NTP, Inc. v. Research in Motion, Ltd., 418 F.3d 1282, 1317 (Fed. Cir. 2005) (abrogated on other grounds)).

192. *Renhcol*, 548 F. Supp. 2d 356.

193. *Id.* at 365.

194. *Id.* at 364; *see also* NTP, Inc. v. Research in Motion, Ltd., 418 F.3d 1282, 1317 (Fed. Cir. 2005) (finding software code on a foreign web server to be "used" in the United States where U.S. consumers routinely interacted with the corresponding foreign network by manipulating handheld devices in their possession in the United States).

195. *Renchol*, 548 F. Supp. 2d at 362 (citing epicRealm, Licensing, LLC v. Autoflex Leasing, Inc., 492 F. Supp. 2d 608, 614–15 (E.D. Tex. 2007)).

196. *Id.* at 360 n.3.

197. Cardiac Pacemakers, Inc. v. St. Jude Med., Inc., 576 F.3d 1348, 1365 (Fed. Cir. 2009) ("We therefore overrule . . . our decision in *Union Carbide Chemicals & Plastics Technology Corp. v. Shell Oil Co.*, 425 F.3d 1366 (Fed. Cir. 2005), as well as any implication in Eolas or other decisions that Section 271(f) applies to method patents."); *see also Renhcol*, 548 F. Supp. 2d at 361.

198. *Renhcol*, 548 F. Supp. 2d at 361.

199. *Id.*

200. *See generally* Microsoft Corp. v. AT&T Corp., 550 U.S. 437, 442–45 (2007).

There is no doubt that online game environments are created by graphics-intensive computer programs that may have been created as the result of a multinational workforce. Under *Microsoft Corp.*, a foreign entity may be held liable in the United States for an infringing foreign-based product used in connection with a foreign-based virtual environment if the product implements code that was entirely developed in the United States, or if copies of the code were obtained in the United States and later modified overseas to create the product. For example, uploading a script created within the United States to complete an infringing device abroad may invite a court's further inspection.

Under *Renhcol*, one could contend that, due to the highly interactive nature of an online game or other virtual reality-based environment, portions of its hardware and software may be controlled by U.S. users, and thus "used" in the United States for the purpose of showing infringement of certain method or apparatus claims directed to performing software functions. On the other hand, when evaluating a virtual environment-related method claim, a plaintiff may find it more difficult to prove that each step of the method claim is performed by a single entity within the United States.

Indeed, as the economics of online virtual environments expand, litigants will undoubtedly use creative strategies to hold foreign online virtual environment providers responsible for overseas activities that would not normally be considered to be within the purview of U.S. patent law.

IV. Jurisdictional Issues in the International Enforcement of Intellectual Property Rights

Whether U.S. courts will adjudicate disputes arising between members of, or relating to, an online virtual environment may depend on a number of factors, including the physical location of the online virtual environment servers. Although many servers that host online virtual environments reside within the United States or are operated by U.S. companies, not all of them do, and many of the individuals and organizations that inhabit these online virtual environments access the Internet from abroad.[201] While some scholars have proposed that at least some disputes arising among members of a global virtual environment should be adjudicated within that virtual environment pursuant to established procedures and conditions,[202] it is unlikely that all parties would willingly forego the protections of their nation's laws (or their right to file suit) to instead adhere to the terms of the virtual environment.

One could foresee an online virtual environment requiring acceptance of an arbitration provision before allowing a user to become a member of the virtual environment. These voluntary agreements may be effective regarding certain activities and transactions that occur within the virtual environment. However, whether such an agreement could require a member to provide an "international" license to his or her intellectual property or submit to a foreign jurisdiction for activities that fall, at least partially, outside of the virtual environment remains unclear and would be fact dependent. Even so, patents and other intellectual property that pertain to the creation of the virtual environment or its components therein would remain subject to traditional jurisdictional principles.

U.S. courts have indicated that defendants "should not be permitted to take advantage of modern technology" via the Internet or other electronic means to "escape traditional notions of jurisdiction."[203] With respect to jurisdictional analysis, the nature and quality of commercial activity within an online virtual environment may be viewed as analogous to that of a traditional Internet website. In this regard, factors that may implicate jurisdiction may

---

201. North America representing 8.2 percent of world Internet users, compared to 49.7 percent from Asia, 17.0 percent from Europe, 10.4 percent from Latin America/Caribbean, 10.0 percent from Africa, 3.8 percent from the Middle East, and 0.7 percent from Oceania/Australia. *See* Internet World Stats, *Internet Usage Statistics*, http://www.internetworldstats.com/stats.htm (last updated June 2, 2018).

202. *See, e.g.*, Farnaz Alemi, *An Avatar's Day in Court: A Proposal for Obtaining Relief and Resolving Disputes in Virtual World Games*, 11 UCLA J.L. & TECH. 1 (2007); F. Gregory Lastowka & Dan Hunter, *The Laws of Virtual Worlds*, 92 CAL. L. REV. 1, 71 (2004); Ethan Katsh, *Bringing Online Dispute Resolution to Virtual Worlds: Creating Processes through Code*, 49 N.Y.U. L. REV. 271, 285–91 (2004).

203. Cybersell, Inc. v. Cybersell, Inc., 130 F.3d 414, 419 (9th Cir. 1997).

include, among other things, the level of interactivity of the online world and the effects of any cross-border transaction from which the dispute arises. Accordingly, questions involving personal jurisdiction are likely to follow Internet principles, including the "sliding scale" developed by *Zippo Manufacturing Co. v. Zippo Dot Com, Inc.*[204] and many U.S. courts to distinguish "interactive" and "passive" websites.[205] The "sliding scale" of *Zippo* takes into consideration "the likelihood that personal jurisdiction can be constitutionally exercised is directly proportionate to the nature and quality of commercial activity that an entity conducts over the Internet."[206]

The relationship between an online virtual environment and its participant may be considered highly interactive in ways that many websites are not. Moreover, online virtual environment providers are responsible for creating and maintaining user accounts, ensuring the proper functioning of the virtual environment, resolving low-level disputes between users, facilitating monetary transactions between members, and, in some cases, creating and selling virtual content and advertising. Under U.S. law, these activities may be enough to tilt the scales towards a finding of general jurisdiction over a provider in each jurisdiction the online virtual environment is made available to users.[207] When general jurisdiction is not present, inducement of members to visit the virtual environment, communications between the provider and its members,

---

204. Zippo Mfg. Co. v. Zippo Dot Com, Inc., 952 F. Supp. 1119 (W.D. Pa. 1997).

205. *Id.* at 1124.

206. *Id.; see also, e.g.*, ALS Scan, Inc. v. Digital Serv. Consultants, Inc., 293 F.3d 707, 712–14 (4th Cir. 2002) (exercising jurisdiction when the person "(1) directs electronic activity into the State, (2) with the manifested intent of engaging in business or other interactions within the State, and (3) that activity creates, in a person within the State, a potential cause of action cognizable in the State's courts." In contrast, "a person who simply [passively] places information on the Internet does not subject himself to jurisdiction in each State into which the electronic signal is transmitted and received."); *Cybersell, Inc.*, 130 F.3d at 419–20 (referencing *Zippo* in finding insufficient "purposeful availment" from passive home page posting).

207. *See* Arista Records, Inc. v. Sakfield Holding Co., 314 F. Supp. 2d 27, 32–35 (D.D.C. 2004) (finding general jurisdiction sufficient to constitute "doing business" under the District of Columbia's long arm statute where a website provider allowed its users in the District to download copyrighted songs without authorization).

and selling and/or providing of virtual advertising may be seen by some courts as enough to give rise to specific jurisdiction.[208]

Online interactions between *individuals* do not necessarily take into account the interactive nature of the website through which the individuals connected. And, members of an online game or other virtual reality-based environment routinely interact (and transact business) with one another without any regard for real-world geographic borders, even more so than through traditional Internet web browsing. Members may be seen as mutually traversing geographic boundaries of their own sovereign states during a single transaction. The provider of the virtual environment may facilitate the transaction without directly encouraging it to happen.

In *Boschetto v. Hansing*,[209] the Ninth Circuit concluded that despite the highly interactive nature of a popular e-commerce website, a single sale of an automobile did not provide sufficient "minimum contacts" to assert personal jurisdiction in California over the Wisconsin-based seller.[210] The holding of *Boschetto* has been distinguished from instances where the e-commerce website was used regularly and systemically as a core part of continuing commercial activity within the forum state.[211]

Interactions between online participants may have an impact in their respective jurisdictions and thus, in some cases, subject one or more of the participants to personal jurisdiction based at least in part on whether the action from which the injury arose was sufficiently targeted at the forum state and the defendant's knowledge that the impact would be felt in the forum state.[212] In

---

208. *See* Bragg v. Linden Research, Inc., 487 F. Supp. 2d 593, 599 (E.D. Pa. 2007) (citing that if a defendant website operator intentionally targets the site to the forum state and/or knowingly conducts business with forum state residents via the site, then the "purposeful availment" requirement is satisfied. A court may consider the level of interactivity of the website and the defendant's related non-Internet activities as part of the "purposeful availment" calculus); *see also* Toys "R" Us, Inc. v. Step Two, S.A., 318 F.3d 446, 452–53 (3d Cir. 2003).

209. Boschetto v. Hansing, 539 F.3d 1011 (9th Cir. 2008).

210. *Id.* at 1017–19.

211. *Id.* at 1019; *see also* Guffey v. Ostonakulov, 321 P.3d 971, 977–78 (Okla. 2014).

212. *See, e.g.*, Calder v. Jones, 465 U.S. 783, 789 (1984); Metro-Goldwyn-Mayer Studios, Inc. v. Grokster, Ltd., 243 F. Supp. 2d 1073, 1088 (C.D. Cal. 2003).

Doe v. Geller,[213] the district court found that personal jurisdiction was lacking in California over a U.K. national who was sued by a resident of Pennsylvania for sending a cease and desist letter to YouTube.com seeking the removal of an allegedly infringing video from the California-based website.[214] The court concluded that asserting jurisdiction would be unreasonable given, in part, that both defendants had attenuated contact with California, a lawsuit was pending in Pennsylvania, and California did not have a strong interest in protecting people in other states from takedown notices.[215]

While U.S. courts may elect to hear a case that invokes foreign intellectual property law, U.S. courts also have discretion to dismiss an infringement action involving a foreign party and/or foreign issues based on the doctrine of *forum non conveniens.*[216] Whether a U.S. court would elect to dismiss an international dispute includes the weighing of multiple factors, including the United States' interests in the dispute (e.g., the interest in protecting rights of U.S. citizen(s), entity/entities, or the public), the law to be applied to the dispute, and the location of witnesses and evidence.[217] Thus, if the alleged injuries are to a plaintiff residing in the United States, with respect to works first published (or trademarks

---

213. Doe v. Geller, 533 F. Supp. 2d 996 (N.D. Cal. 2008).

214. *Id.* at 1011–12.

215. *Id.* at 1009 ("Such broad jurisdiction, premised solely on the happenstance that many internet companies . . . have offices in Silicon Valley, is unreasonable. The Northern District of California is not an international court of internet law."). *But see* Peridyne Tech. Solutions, LLC v. Matheson Fast Freight, 117 F. Supp. 2d 1366, 1371–73 (N.D. Ga. 2000) (finding defendants who "manipulated their way into private files" from their computers in California "deliberately directed their activities at Georgia" and were subject to personal jurisdiction in Georgia).

216. *See* P&D Int'l v. Halsey Publ'g Co., 672 F. Supp. 1429, 1434–35 (S.D. Fla. 1987) (denying dismissal for *forum non conveniens* where U.S. copyright law applies because the alleged infringement occurred in the United States, and the majority of contacts are in Florida).

217. *See* Boosey & Hawkes Music Publ'g v. Walt Disney Co., 145 F.3d 481, 491–92 (2d Cir. 1998) (finding doctrine of *forum non conveniens* did not warrant dismissal even though copyright claims were invoked in foreign jurisdictions where, in part, the case was filed in New York, the defendant is a New York corporation, and the contract at issue was executed in New York); Greenlight Capital, Inc. v. GreenLight (Switz.) S.A., No. 04 Civ. 3136(HB), 2005 WL 13682, at *6 (S.D.N.Y. Jan. 3, 2005) ("The U.S. trademark laws are primarily consumer protection laws, designed

or patents first registered) in the United States, and adjudicated under U.S. law, it seems appropriate to allow the plaintiff access to a U.S. court. By the same token, as each of these factors shifts away from the United States (e.g., if the plaintiff is a foreign resident, or if U.S. law does not apply to the dispute), the balance tilts in favor of the U.S. court using its discretion to decline to hear the dispute and dismiss on *forum non conveniens* grounds,[218] even if the controversy arises from an action that took place within a virtual environment hosted on a server located in the United States.

Accordingly, whether a specific commercial transaction in an online virtual environment would subject an actor to personal jurisdiction in the United States will likely include an analysis of many jurisdictional factors, including whether that transaction, in combination with broader e-commerce activity in the forum state via the virtual environment, provided enough evidence that the actor purposely availed him- or herself of the privilege of doing business in the forum state and that the forum state has an interest in the controversy.

Conclusion

As in any good television show or movie, virtual reality systems come to life through the cinematography provided by their various members and screenplays composed by resourceful computer programmers. An inventor's reasons for wanting international protection for his or her inventions and intellectual investments in online virtual environments are no less compelling than in other aspects of traditional intellectual property. Indeed, modern companies often rise and fall on their global reach to the consumer market, and online games and online virtual environments provide a substantial mechanism for economic opportunity.

---

to shield domestic consumers from fraud and deception in the marketing and sales of products. . . . This Court has an interest in protecting those[ ] who create intellectual property in this jurisdiction.") (internal citations omitted).

218. *See* Creative Tech., Ltd. v. Aztech Sys. PTE, Ltd., 61 F.3d 696, 699–701, 704 (9th Cir. 1995) (granting motion to dismiss on *forum non conveniens* grounds where claims arose from manufacture in Singapore).

It is not surprising that what makes a globally accessible virtual reality-based environment unique—a seamless global community—also raises many untested legal issues. In the context of copyright law, even determining where a work originated is a challenge, much less where that work is infringed. The international nature of an online virtual environment also poses many problems with patent and trademark prosecution and enforcement, particularly in securing global protection. Existing systems of registration and case law are arguably still not sufficiently developed enough even for the Internet (now fully commercialized and a part of mainstream and widespread daily life for more than two decades).

However, some international issues may be avoided or circumvented through the use of contracts, EULAs, or voluntary arbitrations within the context of online virtual environments themselves. EULAs may provide copyright notice-and-takedown provisions (whereby the host will remove material claimed to infringe a copyright), as well as choice-of-law and choice-of-venue provisions. The use of arbitration to resolve international disputes between online virtual environment users may make sense in some situations—as a lower cost and timelier resolution compared to traditional judicial alternatives—but not all situations.

As virtual and online environments continue to evolve beyond their current status as "closed" or tightly controlled systems—and as the concept of "ownership" within online virtual environments becomes more fully developed—it seems almost certain that courts will look beyond traditional concepts of jurisdiction, and that international organizations such as WIPO will ultimately address some of these issues. In the meantime, it remains to be seen whether the uncertainty concerning international law issues will spur or impede the growth of commercial activities within online virtual environments. It may just do both.

Table of Cases

Aalmuhammed v. Lee, 202 F.3d 1227 (9th Cir. 2000), 90, 90 n.133, 95 n.156, 97

Abdul-Jabbar v. Gen. Motors Corp., 85 F.3d 407 (9th Cir. 1996), 207 n.184, 260 n.14

Abercrombie & Fitch Co. v. Hunting World, Inc., 537 F.2d 4 (2d Cir. 1976), 177 n.15, 179 n.26, 179 n.30

ABS Entm't, Inc. v. CBS Corp., No. CV-15-6257 PA (AGRx), 2016 U.S. Dist. LEXIS 71470 (C.D. Cal. May 30, 2016), *rev'd*, – F.3d – (9th Cir. Aug. 20, 2018), 74–75, 74 n.52, 74 n.55, 75 n.56

Activision Publ'g, Inc. v. Gibson Guitar Corp., No. CV 08-01653-MRP (SHx), 2009 U.S. Dist. LEXIS 21931 (C.D. Cal. Feb. 26, 2009), 143–44, 143 n.86, 143 n.89, 157 n.117

Adidas-Am., Inc. v. Payless Shoesource, Inc., 546 F. Supp. 2d 1029 (D. Or. 2008), 183 n.52

Adkins v. Labor Ready, Inc., 303 F.3d 496 (4th Cir. 2002), 25 n.110

A.E.I. Music Network, Inc. v. Bus. Computers, Inc., 290 F.3d 952 (7th Cir. 2002), 44 n.207

Affiliated Hosp. Prods., Inc. v. Merdel Game Mfg. Co., 513 F.2d 1183 (2d Cir. 1975), 81–82, 81 n.83

Agee v. Paramount Commc'n, Inc., 853 F. Supp. 778 (S.D.N.Y. 1994), 73 n.51

A.J. Canfield Co. v. Honickman, 808 F.2d 291 (3d Cir. 1986), 178 n.19

Akamai Techs., Inc. v. Limelight Networks, Inc., 797 F.3d 1020 (Fed. Cir. 2015), 159–60, 159 n.125

Alexander & Alexander Benefit Servs., Inc. v. Benefit Brokers & Consultants, Inc., 756 F. Supp. 1408 (D. Or. 1991), 252 n.114

Alexander v. Haley, 460 F. Supp. 40 (S.D.N.Y. 1978), 85 n.101

Alice Corp. Pty. Ltd. v. CLS Bank Int'l, 134 S. Ct. 2347 (2014), 122–24, 122 nn.8–11, 123 n.13, 131–33, 170, 333, 333 n.162

Ali v. Playgirl, Inc., 447 F. Supp. 723 (S.D.N.Y. 1978), 259 n.12

Allard Enters. v. Advanced Programming Res., Inc., 249 F.3d 564 (6th Cir. 2001), 326 n.125

Allen v. Lloyd's of London, 94 F.3d 923 (4th Cir. 1996), 27 n.119

ALS Scan, Inc. v. Digital Serv. Consultants, Inc., 293 F.3d 707 (4th Cir. 2002), 342 n.206

ALS Scan, Inc. v. RemarQ Cmtys., Inc., 239 F.3d 619 (4th Cir. 2001), 102 n.186

Am. Broad. Co. v. Aereo, Inc., 134 S. Ct. 2498 (2014), 102 n.183

Am. Dairy Queen Corp. v. New Line Prods., Inc., 35 F. Supp. 2d 727 (D. Minn. 1998), 196 n.135

Amdocs (Isr.) Ltd. v. Openet Telecom, Inc., 841 F.3d 1288 (Fed. Cir. 2016), 332 n.158

AMF, Inc. v. Sleekcraft Boats, 599 F.2d 341 (9th Cir. 1979), 181 n.45

Am. Family Life Ins. Co. v. Hagan, 266 F. Supp. 2d 682 (N.D. Ohio 2002), 183 n.54

AM Gen. LLC v. Activision Blizzard, Inc., No. 2:17-08644 (S.D.N.Y. Nov. 7, 2017), 216, 223

Am. Online, Inc. v. Superior Court, 90 Cal. App. 4th 1 (Cal. Ct. App. 2001), 38, 38 n.178

A&M Records, Inc. v. Napster, Inc., 239 F.3d 1004 (9th Cir. 2001), 103, 103 n.190, 112 n.253, 317 n.79

Am.'s Best Family Showplace Corp. v. City of New York, 536 F. Supp. 170 (E.D.N.Y. 1982), 193–94 n.121

Am. United Logistics, Inc. v. Catellus Dev. Corp., 319 F.3d 921 (7th Cir. 2003), 44–45 n.208

Anascape Ltd. v. Nintendo of Am. Inc., 601 F.3d 1333 (Fed. Cir. 2010), 167–69, 167 nn.151–57

Andrew Greenberg, Inc. v. Svane, Inc., 36 A.D.3d 1094 (N.Y. App. Div. 2007), 251 n.108

Anheuser-Busch, Inc. v. Balducci Publ'ns, 28 F.3d 769 (8th Cir. 1994), 196 n.135

Anti-Monopoly, Inc. v. General Mills Fun Group, Inc., 611 F.2d 296 (9th Cir. 1979), 177 n.13

Anti-Monopoly, Inc. v. General Mills Fun Group, Inc., 684 F.2d 1316 (9th Cir. 1982), 177 n.13

Apollo Techs. Corp. v. Centrosphere Indus. Corp., 805 F. Supp. 1157 (D.N.J. 1992), 252 n.111

Apple, Inc. v. Samsung Elecs. Co., No. 11-CV-01846 (N.D. Cal. Aug. 24, 2012), 154 n.109

Apple Computer, Inc. v. Franklin Computer Corp., 714 F.2d 1240 (3d Cir. 1983), 65, 65 n.8, 311 n.52

Apple Inc. v. Samsung Elecs. Co., 786 F.3d 983 (Fed. Cir. 2015), 160 n.129

Apple Inc. v. Samsung Elecs. Co., No. 11-CV-01846-LHK, 2017 WL 4776443 (N.D. Cal. Oct. 22, 2017), 164 n.140

Arista Records, Inc. v. Sakfield Holding Co., 314 F. Supp. 2d 27 (D.D.C. 2004), 342 n.207

Aristocrat Techs. v. Int'l Gaming Tech., 543 F.3d 657 (Fed. Cir. 2008), 145 n.96

Arma v. Buyseasons, Inc., 591 F. Supp. 2d 637 (S.D.N.Y. 2008), 310 n.48

Armendariz v. Found. Health Psychcare Servs., Inc., 24 Cal. 4th 83 (Cal. 2000), 26 n.111

Armstrong v. Virgin Records, Ltd., 91 F. Supp. 2d 628 (S.D.N.Y. 2000), 320 n.92

Ass'n for Molecular Pathology v. Myriad Genetics, Inc., 569 U.S. 576 (2013), 122 n.12

Atari, Inc. v. N. Am. Philips Consumer Elec. Corp., 672 F.2d 607 (7th Cir. 1982), 65 n.13

Atari Games Corp. v. Nintendo of Am., Inc., 975 F.2d 832 (Fed. Cir. 1992), 166 nn.146–47, 248–49, 248 n.100, 249 n.104

Atari Games Corp. v. Nintendo of Am., Inc., Nos. C 88-4805 FMS & C 89-0027 FMS, 1993 WL 214886 (N.D. Cal. Apr. 15, 1993), 166 nn.146–47

Atari Games Corp. v. Oman, 979 F.2d 242 (D.C. Cir. 1992), 65 n.13

AT&T Mobility LLC v. Concepcion, 563 U.S. 333 (2011), 21 n.84, 32 n.142, 33 n.148, 34 n.157

Au-Tomotive Gold, Inc. v. Volkswagen of Am., Inc., 457 F.3d 1062 (9th Cir. 2006), 182 n.46, 193 nn.117–20

A.V.E.L.A., Inc. v. Estate of Marilyn Monroe, LLC, 131 F. Supp. 3d 196 (S.D.N.Y. 2015), 180–81 n.40, 269–70, 269 n.59, 270 n.62, 282 n.132, 283

A.V.E.L.A., Inc. v. Estate of Marilyn Monroe, LLC, 241 F. Supp. 3d 461 (S.D.N.Y. 2017), 283 n.137

A.V. v. iParadigms, Ltd. Liab. Co., 544 F. Supp. 2d 473 (E.D. Va. 2008), 50 n.236

Baker v. Seldon, 101 U.S. 99 (1879), 80–81, 80 n.78

Balt. Bedding Corp. v. Moses, 34 A.2d 338 (Md. 1943), 221–22 n.261

Baxter v. MCA, Inc., 812 F.2d 421 (9th Cir. 1987), 101 n.180

B. Braun Med. Inc. v. Abbott Labs., 124 F.3d 1419 (Fed. Cir. 1997), 145 n.95

B.C. Ziegler & Co. v. Ehren, 414 N.W.2d 48 (Wis. Ct. App. 1987), 233 n.29

Belfiore v. Summit Fed. Credit Union, 452 F. Supp. 2d 629 (D. Md. 2006), 27 n.119

Bell Helicopter Textron, Inc. v. Elec. Arts, Inc., No. 4:06-0841 (N.D. Tex. Dec. 6, 2007), 188 n.83, 210–11, 211 n.200

Bell Helicopter Textron, Inc. v. Elec. Arts, Inc., No. 4:06-0841 (N.D. Tex. Feb. 15, 2008), 188 n.83

Bell Helicopter Textron, Inc. v. Elec. Arts, Inc., No. 06-841 (N.D. Tex. May 1, 2007), 211 n.200

Berkic v. Crichton, 761 F.2d 1289 (9th Cir. 1985), 110 n.245

Bissoon-Dath v. Sony Computer Entm't Am., Inc., 694 F. Supp. 2d 1071 (N.D. Cal. 2010), 85–86, 86 n.109, 110–11, 110 n.241

Blizzard Entm't, Inc. v. Lilith Games (Shanghai) Co., No. 3:15-CV-04084-CRB, 2017 WL 2118342 (N.D. Cal. May 16, 2017), 71, 71 n.35, 71 n.40, 72 n.44, 96–97, 96 n.166

BMG Music v. Gonzalez, 430 F.3d 888 (7th Cir. 2005), 317 n.79

BMG Rights Mgmt. (US) LLC v. Cox Commc'n, Inc., 881 F.3d 293 (4th Cir. 2018), 116, 116 nn.272–74

Boosey & Hawkes Music Publ'g v. Walt Disney Co., 145 F.3d 481 (2d Cir. 1998), 344 n.217

Boschetto v. Hansing, 539 F.3d 1011 (9th Cir. 2008), 343, 343 n.209

Boston Athletic Ass'n v. Sullivan, 867 F.2d 22 (1st Cir. 1989), 218 n.244

Boston Duck Tours, LP v. Super Duck Tours, LLC, 531 F.3d 1 (1st Cir. 2008), 177 n.18, 179 n.29

Boyds Collection, Ltd. v. Bearington Collection, Inc., 360 F. Supp. 2d 655 (M.D. Pa. 2005), 89 n.127

Bragg v. Linden Research, Inc., 487 F. Supp. 2d 593 (E.D. Pa. 2007), 3 n.4, 20–31, 20 n.78, 20 nn.82–83, 21 n.86, 22 nn.87–88, 22 n.90, 23 n.97, 24 nn.100–102, 25 n.103, 26 nn.111–12, 28 nn.123–24, 30 n.128, 31 n.138, 34–35, 34 n.156, 34 n.158, 35 n.159, 35 n.163, 40, 40 n.188, 54–55 n.247, 54–56, 55 n.251, 57, 57 n.260, 343 n.208

Bridgeman Art Library, Ltd. v. Corel Corp., 25 F. Supp. 2d 421 (S.D.N.Y. 1998), 307 nn.26–27, 315 n.76

Broderbund Software, Inc. v. Unison World, Inc., 648 F. Supp. 1127 (N.D. Cal. 1986), 64 n.7

Brother Records, Inc. v. Jardine, 318 F.3d 900 (9th Cir. 2003), 204 n.165

Brower v. Gateway 2000, 246 A.D.2d 246 (N.Y. App. Div. 1998), 19 n.77, 28 n.122

Brown v. Elec. Arts, Inc., 724 F.3d 1235 (9th Cir. 2013), 180 n.40, 190–91, 190 n.104, 210 n.199, 213 n.214, 286 n.159, 292 n.197, 294 n.208

Brown v. Elec. Arts, Inc., No. 09-1598 (C.D. Cal. July 22, 2009), 190 n.104

Brown v. Elec. Arts, Inc., No. 09-1598 (C.D. Cal. Mar. 6, 2009), 190–91, 190 n.104

Brown v. Entm't Merchs. Ass'n, 564 U.S. 786 (2011), 194 n.122

Buck v. Jewell-LaSalle Realty Co., 238 U.S. 191 (1931), 103 n.189

Burck v. Mars, Inc., 571 F. Supp. 2d 446 (S.D.N.Y. 2008), 268–69, 268 n.53, 269 n.56, 269 n.58

Burrow-Giles Lithographic Co. v. Sarony, 111 U.S. 53 (1884), 91 n.135

Cable/Home Commc'n Corp. v. Network Prods., Inc., 902 F.2d 829 (11th Cir. 1990), 103 n.195

Calder v. Jones, 465 U.S. 783 (1984), 343 n.212

Calvin Klein Indus., Inc. v. BFK Hong Kong, Ltd., 714 F. Supp. 78 (S.D.N.Y. 1989), 329 n.145

Capcom Co. v. MKR Group, Inc., No. C 08-0904 RS, 2008 U.S. Dist. LEXIS 83836 (N.D. Cal. Oct. 10, 2008), 109–10, 109 n.234, 176 n.9

Capcom U.S.A. v. Data E. Corp., No. C 93-3259 WHO, 1994 WL 1751482 (N.D. Cal. Mar. 16, 1994), 86, 86 n.111

Capitol Records, Inc. v. Naxos of Am., Inc., 4 N.Y.3d 540 (N.Y. 2005), 74 n.54

Capitol Records, Ltd. Liab. Co. v. Vimeo, Ltd. Liab. Co., 826 F.3d 78 (2d Cir. 2016), 116 n.271

Cardiac Pacemakers, Inc. v. St. Jude Med., Inc., 576 F.3d 1348 (Fed. Cir. 2009), 339 n.197

Cardtoons, L.C. v. Major League Baseball Players Ass'n, 95 F.3d 959 (10th Cir. 1996), 272 nn.68–69

Cargill, Inc. v. Sears Petroleum & Transp. Corp., 388 F. Supp. 2d 37 (N.D.N.Y. 2005), 231 n.20

Carnival Cruise Lines, Inc. v. Shute, 499 U.S. 585 (1991), 27 n.119

Carol Barnhart, Inc. v. Econ. Cover Corp., 773 F.2d 411 (2d Cir. 1985), 87–89, 87 n.124

Carter-Wallace, Inc. v. Procter & Gamble Co., 434 F.2d 794 (9th Cir. 1970), 179 n.24

Caterpillar Inc. v. Walt Disney Co., 287 F. Supp. 2d 913 (C.D. Ill. 2003), 182 n.47, 196 n.134

CCC Info. Servs. v. Maclean Hunter Market Reports, 44 F.3d 61 (2d Cir. 1994), 71, 71 n.37

Celebration Int'l, Inc. v. Chosun Int'l, Inc., 234 F. Supp. 2d 905 (S.D. Ind. 2002), 87 n.118

Century 21 Real Estate Corp. v. Lendingtree, Inc., 425 F.3d 211 (3d Cir. 2005), 204 n.163

Chamberlin v. Uris Sales Corp., 150 F.2d 512 (2d Cir. 1945), 81 n.82

Childress v. Taylor, 945 F.2d 500 (2d Cir. 1991), 95, 95 n.157

Circuit City Stores, Inc. v. Adams, 279 F.3d 889 (9th Cir. 2002), 26 n.111

Civility Experts Worldwide v. Molly Manners, LLC, 167 F. Supp. 3d 1179 (D. Colo. 2016), 80 n.77

Cliffs Notes, Inc. v. Bantam Doubleday Dell Publ'g Group, Inc., 886 F.2d 490 (2d Cir. 1989), 209 n.194

Cmty. for Creative Non-Violence v. Reid, 490 U.S. 730 (1989), 90–91 n.135, 92, 92 n.140, 93 n.144, 312 n.54

Columbia Pictures Indus., Inc. v. Aveco, Inc., 800 F.2d 59 (3d Cir. 1986), 103 n.193

Comb v. PayPal, Inc., 218 F. Supp. 2d 1165 (N.D. Cal. 2002), 25 n.108, 26 nn.113–14, 30, 30 n.130

Comedy III Prods., Inc. v. Gary Saderup, Inc., 25 Cal. 4th 387 (Cal. 2001), 276 n.100, 278–80, 278 n.108, 290 n.185

Confold Pac., Inc. v. Polaris Indus., Inc., 433 F.3d 952 (7th Cir. 2006), 220 nn.254–55

Corcovado Music Corp. v. Hollis Music, Inc., 981 F.2d 679 (2d Cir. 1993), 310, 310 n.45

Crawford v. Midway Games Inc., No. 2:07-cv-00967-FMC-JCx (C.D. Cal. Dec. 3, 2008), 109, 109 n.228

Creative Labs, Inc. v. Cyrix Corp., No. C 97-0912 CW, 1997 U.S. Dist. LEXIS 14492 (N.D. Cal. May 7, 1997), 102 n.182

Creative Tech., Ltd. v. Aztech Sys. PTE, Ltd., 61 F.3d 696 (9th Cir. 1995), 345 n.218

Cruz v. Cingular Wireless, LLC, 648 F.3d 1205 (11th Cir. 2011), 37 n.168, 37 n.172

Curb v. MCA Records, Inc., 898 F. Supp. 586 (M.D. Tenn. 1995), 319 n.94

Custom Vehicles, Inc. v. Forest River, Inc., 476 F.3d 481 (7th Cir. 2007), 178 n.20

Cybersell, Inc. v. Cybersell, Inc., 130 F.3d 414 (9th Cir. 1997), 341 n.203, 342 n.206

CyberSource Corp. v. Retail Decision Inc., 620 F. Supp. 2d 1068 (N.D. Cal. 2009), 125 n.33

Dalessio v. Kressler, 6 A.D.3d 57 (N.Y. App. Div. 2004), 266 n.43

Dann v. Johnston, 425 U.S. 219 (1976), 137 n.70

Dastar Corp. v. Twentieth Century Fox Film Corp., 539 U.S. 23 (2003), 180 n.39

Data E. USA, Inc. v. Epyx, Inc., 862 F.2d 204 (9th Cir. 1988), 85, 85 n.105

Davidson & Assocs., Inc. v. Internet Gateway, Inc., 334 F. Supp. 2d 1164 (E.D. Mo. 2004), 19 n.77, 22, 22 n.87, 23, 23 n.96, 40 n.187, 40 n.189

DaVinci Editrice S.R.L. v. Ziko Games, LLC, 183 F. Supp. 3d 820 (S.D. Tex. 2016), 82–84, 82 n.87, 84 n.99

Davis v. Elec. Arts, Inc., 775 F.3d 1172 (9th Cir. 2015), 292 n.197

Davis v. Elec. Arts, Inc., No. 10-cv-03328-RS, 2017 U.S. Dist. LEXIS 216505 (N.D. Cal. Dec. 11, 2017), 77–78, 77 n.68, 314 n.66

Dean Witter Reynolds, Inc. v. Superior Court, 211 Cal. App. 3d 758 (Cal. Ct. App. 1989), 24 n.99

de Havilland v. FX Networks, LLC, 21 Cal. App. 5th 845 (Cal. Ct. App. 2018), 260 nn.15–18

Demetriades v. Kaufmann, 690 F. Supp. 289 (S.D.N.Y. 1988), 103 n.191

Dep't of Parks & Recreation v. Bazaar del Mundo Inc., 448 F.3d 1118 (9th Cir. 2006), 179 n.24

Diamond v. Chakrabarty, 447 U.S. 303 (1980), 122 n.7

Dickerman Assocs., Inc. v. Tiverton Bottled Gas Co., 594 F. Supp. 30 (D. Mass. 1984), 247 n.91

Diller v. Barry Driller, Inc., No. 12-7200, 2012 U.S. Dist. LEXIS 133515 (C.D. Cal. Sept. 10, 2012), 203 n.154

Dillinger, LLC v. Elec. Arts, Inc., 795 F. Supp. 2d 829 (S.D. Ind. 2011), 189, 189 n.94, 189 n.97, 213 n.210

Discover Bank v. Superior Court, 113 P.3d 1100 (Cal. 2005), 21, 32–33, 32 n.145, 33 n.147

Disney Enters. v. VidAngel, Inc., 224 F. Supp. 3d 957 (C.D. Cal. 2016), 102 n.184

Dobson v. Dornan, 118 U.S. 10 (1886), 162–63, 162 n.135

Doctor's Assocs. v. Casarotto, 517 U.S. 681 (1996), 34 n.158

Doe v. TCI Cablevision, 110 S.W.3d 363 (Mo. 2003), 276 n.98, 277, 277 n.101, 286 n.161, 343–44, 344 n.213

Dreamland Ballroom, Inc. v. Shapiro, Bernstein & Co., 36 F.2d 354 (7th Cir. 1929), 103 n.189

Drill Parts & Serv. Co. v. Joy Mfg. Co., 439 So. 2d 43 (Ala. 1983), 233 n.29

Durham Indus., Inc. v. Tomy Corp., 630 F.2d 905 (2d Cir. 1980), 73 n.51

Egyptian Goddess, Inc. v. Swisa, Inc., 543 F.3d 665 (Fed. Cir. 2008), 129 n.50

EKCO Group, Inc. v. Travelers Indem. Co. of Ill., 273 F.3d 409 (1st Cir. 2001), 220 n.255

Elec. Arts, Inc. v. Textron, Inc., No. 3:12-0118 (N.D. Cal. May 7, 2012), 188–89, 188 nn.83–85, 189 n.88, 189 n.93, 212, 212 n.206

Elec. Arts, Inc. v. Textron Inc., No. 3:12-0118, 2012 U.S. Dist. LEXIS 103914 (N.D. Cal. July 25, 2012), 196, 196 n.135, 206–7, 206 n.174, 212 n.207

Elliot v. Gouverneur Tribune Press, Inc., No. 7:13-CV-00055(MAD/TWD), 2014 WL 12598275 (N.D.N.Y. 2014), 309 n.39

Enfish, LLC v. Microsoft Corp., 822 F.3d 1327 (Fed. Cir. 2016), 333 n.165

Eng'g & Distribution, LLC v. Shandong Linglong Rubber Co., 682 F.3d 292 (4th Cir. 2012), 316 n.77

epicRealm, Licensing, LLC v. Autoflex Leasing, Inc., 492 F. Supp. 2d 608 (E.D. Tex. 2007), 339 n.195

Epic Sys. Corp. v. Lewis, 138 S. Ct. 1612 (2018), 28 n.121, 33, 33 n.149

Erie R.R. v. Tompkins, 304 U.S. 64 (1938), 220 n.254

Eros, LLC, v. Leatherwood, No. 8:07-cv-1158-T-24TGW (M.D. Fla. filed July 3, 2007), 240 n.66, 245 n.85, 250 n.107

Esquire, Inc. v. Ringer, 591 F.2d 796 (D.C. Cir. 1978), 88 n.126

E.S.S. Entm't 2000, Inc. v. Rock Star Videos, Inc., 444 F. Supp. 2d 1012 (C.D. Cal. 2006), 187–88, 187 n.79, 209 n.194

E.S.S. Entm't 2000, Inc. v. Rock Star Videos, Inc., 547 F.3d 1095 (9th Cir. 2008), 206–13, 206 n.170, 209 nn.194–95, 210 n.197, 286, 286 n.156

Essex Group v. Southwire Co., 501 S.E.2d 501 (Ga. 1998), 253 n.116, 253 n.118

ETW Corp. v. Jireh Publ'g, Inc., 332 F.3d 915 (6th Cir. 2003), 272 nn.68–69, 275–76, 275 n.92

Evans v. Linden Research, Inc., 763 F. Supp. 2d 735 (E.D. Pa. 2011) [Evans I], 20–21, 20 n.83, 23 n.95, 24 n.102, 30 n.134, 35, 35 n.160, 38 n.176

Evans v. Linden Research, Inc., No. C 11-01078 DMR, 2012 WL 5877579 (N.D. Cal. Nov. 20, 2012) [Evans II], 20–21, 20 n.83, 29, 29 n.126, 30–31, 30 n.132, 30 n.135, 38 n.176

Expediters Int'l of Wash., Inc. v. Direct Line Cargo Mgmt. Serv., Inc., 995 F. Supp. 468 (D.N.J. 1998), 319 n.93, 320 n.97

Facenda v. N.F.L. Films, Inc., 488 F. Supp. 2d 491 (E.D. Pa. 2007), 268 n.52

Fahmy v. Jay-Z, 788 F. Supp. 2d 1072 (C.D. Cal. 2011), 310 n.43

Federal-Mogul-Bower Bearings, Inc. v. Azoff, 313 F.2d 405 (6th Cir. 1963), 180 n.39

Feist Publ'ns, Inc. v. Rural Tel. Serv. Co., 499 U.S. 340 (1991), 72 n.45, 73 n.47

Ferguson v. Countrywide Credit Indus., 298 F.3d 778 (9th Cir. 2002), 26 n.111

Ferrari S.P.A. Esercizio Fabriche Automobili E Corse v. Roberts, 944 F.2d 1235 (6th Cir. 1991), 193 n.119, 198 n.140

Festo Corp. v. Shoketsu Kinzoku Kogyo Kabushiki Co., 535 U.S. 722 (2002), 137 n.69

Fighters Inc. v. Elec. Arts, Inc., No. CV 09-06389 SJO(VBKx), 2009 WL 10699504 (C.D. Cal. Oct. 30, 2009), 286 n.159

Filias v. Gateway 2000, No. 96-CV-75722-DT, 1997 U.S. Dist. LEXIS 7115 (E.D. Mich. Apr. 8, 1997), 28 n.122

Fonovisa, Inc. v. Cherry Auction, Inc., 76 F.3d 259 (9th Cir. 1996), 103 n.188, 184 n.59

Frosty Treats, Inc. v. Sony Computer Entm't Am., Inc., 426 F.3d 1001 (8th Cir. 2005), 178 n.22

Fuller v. Berger, 120 F. 274 (7th Cir. 1903), 121 n.5

Funky Films, Inc. v. Time Warner Entm't Co., L.P., 462 F.3d 1072 (9th Cir. 2006), 108–9, 108 n.226

Game Power Headquarters, Inc. v. Owens, No. 94-5821, 1995 U.S. Dist. LEXIS 5998 (E.D. Pa. May 4, 1995), 179 n.27

GamerModz, LLC v. Golubev, No. 8:10-CV-1466-T-27TGW, 2011 U.S. Dist. LEXIS 116608 (M.D. Fla. Aug. 3, 2011), 179 n.24

Garcia v. Google, 786 F.3d 733 (9th Cir. 2015), 95–96, 95 n.159

Gates Rubber Co. v. Bando Chem. Indus., Ltd., 9 F.3d 823 (10th Cir. 1993), 80 n.77, 247 n.91

Gatton v. T-Mobile USA, Inc., 152 Cal. App. 4th 571 (Cal. Ct. App. 2007), 24 n.99

Gen. Motors Corp. v. Lanard Toys, Inc., 468 F.3d 405 (6th Cir. 2006), 198 n.140

Gen. Motors Corp. v. Urban Gorilla, LLC, 500 F.3d 1222 (10th Cir. 2007), 193 n.119

Geophysical Serv. v. TGS-NOPEC Geophysical Co., 850 F.3d 785 (5th Cir. 2017), 320 n.98

Gershwin Publ'n Corp. v. Columbia Artists Mgmt., Inc., 443 F.2d 1159 (2d Cir. 1971), 103 n.191

Gibson Guitar Corp. v. 745 LLC, No. 3:11-0058, 2012 U.S. Dist. LEXIS 4177 (M.D. Tenn. Jan. 11, 2012), 144 n.93

Goldman v. Breitbart News Network, LLC, 302 F. Supp. 3d 585 (S.D.N.Y. 2018), 317 n.80

Goodridge v. KDF Auto. Group, Inc., 209 Cal. App. 4th 325 (Cal. Ct. App. 2012), 28–29 n.125, 35 n.162

Gorham Co. v. White, 81 U.S. 511 (1871), 129 nn.50–51

Gottschalk v. Benson, 409 U.S. 63 (1972), 131 n.55

Gravano v. Take-Two Interactive Software, Inc., 142 A.D.3d 776 (N.Y. App. Div. 2016), 291–92, 291 n.195, 292 n.196

Gray v. Rent-A-Center West, Inc., 314 Fed. Appx. 15 (9th Cir. 2008), 27–28 n.121

Greenlight Capital, Inc. v. GreenLight (Switz.) S.A., No. 04 Civ. 3136(HB), 2005 WL 13682 (S.D.N.Y. Jan. 3, 2005), 344–45 n.217

Green Tree Fin. Corp.-Ala. v. Randolph, 531 U.S. 79 (2000), 27 n.120

Griffith v. Fenrick, 486 F. Supp. 2d 848 (W.D. Wis. 2007), 183 n.54

Grupo Gigante SA de CV v. Dallo & Co., Inc., 391 F.3d 1088 (9th Cir. 2004), 327 n.133

Guffey v. Ostonakulov, 321 P.3d 971 (Okla. 2014), 343 n.211

Guidiville Band of Pomo Indians v. NGV Gaming, Ltd., 531 F.3d 767 (9th Cir. 2008), 47 n.219

Haelan Labs., Inc. v. Topps Chewing Gum, Inc., 202 F.2d 866 (2d Cir. 1953), 258–59, 258 n.7

Halo Elecs., Inc. v. Pulse Elecs., Inc., 136 S. Ct. 1923 (2016), 161 n.131

Hamilton v. Speight, No. 2:17-cv-00169-AB (E.D. Pa. Apr. 14, 2017), 296–97, 296 n.215, 297 n.216

Hamrick v. Hosp. Servs. Corp. of R.I., 110 R.I. 634 (R.I. 1972), 50 n.234

Hard Rock Cafe Licensing Corp. v. Concession Servs., Inc., 955 F.2d 1143 (7th Cir. 1992), 184 n.58

Harper & Row, Publishers v. Nation Enters., 471 U.S. 539 (1985), 113 n.257

Harrington v. Atl. Sounding Co., 602 F.3d 113 (2d Cir. 2010), 20 n.78

Harris v. Quinn, 134 S. Ct. 2618 (2014), 183 n.55

Hart v. Elec. Arts, Inc., 717 F.3d 141 (3d Cir. 2013), 292 n.197, 297 n.220

Hasbro Bradley, Inc. v. Sparkle Toys, Inc., 780 F.2d 189 (2d Cir. 1985), 315 nn.72–73

Hernandez v. Internet Gaming Entm't, Ltd., No. 07-21403 (S.D. Fla. May 30, 2007), 37 n.169, 38, 38 n.174, 38 n.177, 43, 43 n.202, 45 n.212

Higgins v. Superior Court of L.A., 140 Cal. App. 4th 1238 (Cal. Ct. App. 2006), 19 n.76

Hilton v. Guyot, 159 U.S. 113 (1985), 306 n.21

Hilton v. Hallmark Cards, 599 F.3d 894 (9th Cir. 2010), 267 n.44

Hoffman-LaRoche, Inc. v. Yoder, 950 F. Supp. 1348 (S.D. Ohio 1997), 236 n.49

Home Builders Ass'n v. L & L Exhibition Mgmt., Inc., 226 F.3d 944 (8th Cir. 2000), 177 n.16

Hustler Magazine, Inc. v. Falwell, 485 U.S. 46 (1988), 274–75, 275 n.87

I.B. *ex rel.* Fife v. Facebook, Inc., No. C 12-1894 CW, 2012 WL 5303297 (N.D. Cal. Oct. 25, 2012), 48 n.226

Idenix Pharm. v. Gilead Scis., Inc., C.A., No. 14-cv-00846-LPS (D. Del. Nov. 16, 2016), 160 n.128

I.Lan Sys., Inc. v. Netscout Serv. Level Corp., 183 F. Supp. 2d 328 (D. Mass. 2002), 40 n.189

Illustro Sys. Int'l, LLC v. Int'l Bus. Machs. Corp., No. 3:06-CV-1969-L, 2007 WL 1321825 (N.D. Tex. May 4, 2007), 320 n.98

Imi-Tech Corp. v. Gagliani, 691 F. Supp. 214 (S.D. Cal. 1986), 252 n.112

Immersion Corp. v. Sony Computer Entm't Am. Inc., No. C 02-0710 CW, 2005 WL 680026 (N.D. Cal. Mar. 24, 2005), 166 n.149

Incredible Techs., Inc. v. Virtual Techs., Inc., 400 F.3d 1007 (7th Cir. 2005), 186–87, 186 n.68

Ingle v. Circuit City Stores, Inc., 328 F.3d 1165 (9th Cir. 2003), 25–26 n.111

In re Abele, 684 F.2d 902 (C.C.P.A. 1982), 132 n.61

In re Beauregard, 53 F.3d 1583 (Fed. Cir. 1995), 125 n.33, 133–34, 133 n.64

In re Bilski, 545 F.3d 943 (Fed. Cir. 2008), 125 nn.32–33, 131–32, 131 n.56, 132 n.60, 132 n.63, 133

In re Florists' Transworld Delivery, Inc., 119 U.S.P.Q.2d 1056 (T.T.A.B. 2016), 325 n.120

In re Hercules Auto. Prods., Inc., 245 B.R. 903 (Bankr. M.D. Ga. 1999), 237 n.52

In re Kappa Alpha Order, 2011 TTAB LEXIS 191 (T.T.A.B. June 3, 2011, re appeal of S/N 77/463,997), 176 n.11

In re NCAA Student-Athlete Name & Likeness Licensing Litig., 724 F.3d 1268 (9th Cir. 2013), 292–96, 292 n.197, 294 n.206, 295 n.213

In re Wyer, 655 F.2d 221 (C.C.P.A. 1981), 335 n.173

In re Zappos.com Inc., Customer Data Sec. Breach Litig., 893 F. Supp. 2d 1058 (D. Nev. 2012), 42, 42 n.197

Int'l Info. Sys. Sec. Certification Consortium, Inc. v. Sec. Univ., LLC, 823 F.3d 153 (2d Cir. 2016), 204 n.163

Int'l News Serv. v. Associated Press, 248 U.S. 215 (1918), 218 n.244, 219–22, 219 nn.247–48, 219 n.251, 221 n.260

Int'l Order of Job's Daughters v. Lindeburg & Co., 633 F.2d 912 (9th Cir. 1980), 193 nn.117–18

Inwood Labs., Inc. v. Ives Labs., Inc., 456 U.S. 844 (1982), 178 n.23, 184 n.59

Itar-Tass Russian News Agency v. Russian Kurier, Inc., 153 F.3d 82 (2d Cir. 1998), 306 n.21, 307, 307 nn.22–23, 307 nn.25–27, 310–12, 310 n.42, 310 n.44, 311 n.51, 314, 314 n.69

ITC Ltd. v. Punchgini, Inc., 482 F.3d 135 (2d Cir. 2007), 327 n.131

ITSI T.V. Prods., Inc. v. Cal. Auth. of Racing Fairs, 785 F. Supp. 854 (E.D. Cal. 1992), 316 n.78, 318 n.86

James Varga v. Twitch Interactive, Inc., No. CGC-18-564337 (Cal. App. Dep't Super. Ct. 2018), 43, 43 n.200

Johns-Manville Corp. v. Guardian Indus. Corp., 586 F. Supp. 1034 (E.D. Mich. 1983), 237 n.52

Johnson & Johnson v. Am. Nat'l Red Cross, 552 F. Supp. 2d 434 (S.D.N.Y. 2008), 176 n.11

Jordan v. Jewel Food Stores, Inc., 743 F.3d 509 (7th Cir. 2014), 183 n.55

Kellogg Co. v. Nat'l Biscuit Co., 305 U.S. 111 (1938), 178 n.23

Kernal Records Oy v. Mosley, 794 F. Supp. 2d 1355 (S.D. Fla. 2011), 308–10, 308 nn.31–35

Kewanee Oil Co. v. Bicron Corp., 416 U.S. 470 (1974), 230–31 n.19

Kieselstein-Cord v. Accessories by Pearl, Inc., 632 F.2d 989 (2d Cir. 1980), 87, 87 n.122

Kirby v. Sega, 144 Cal. App. 4th 47 (Cal. Ct. App. 2006), 288–91, 288 n.168

KI Ventures, LLC v. Fry's Elecs. Inc., 579 Fed. Appx. 985 (Fed. Cir. 2014), 148–52, 149 n.103

Knitwaves, Inc. v. Lollytogs Ltd., 71 F.3d 996 (2d Cir. 1995), 87 n.121

KSR Int'l Co. v. Teleflex Inc., 550 U.S. 398 (2007), 126–28, 126 n.39

Lahiri v. Universal Music & Video Distrib., Inc., 513 F. Supp. 2d 1172 (C.D. Cal. 2007), 307 n.26

L.A. Printex Indus. v. Aeropostale, No. CV 08-07085 DPP (Ex), 2010 U.S. Dist. LEXIS 46951 (C.D. Cal. May 5, 2010), 98 n.172

L. Batlin & Son, Inc. v. Snyder, 536 F.2d 486 (2d Cir. 1976), 73 n.46

Lee v. Cercoa, Inc., 433 So. 2d 1 (Fla. Dist. Ct. App. 1983), 236 n.50

Leicester v. Warner Bros., 232 F.3d 1212 (9th Cir. 2000), 87 n.120

Lemmon v. Hendrickson, 559 N.W.2d 278 (Iowa 1997), 252 n.115

Levi Strauss & Co. v. Abercrombie & Fitch Trading Co., 633 F.3d 1158 (9th Cir. 2011), 180 n.34

Levitin v. Sony Music Entm't, 101 F. Supp. 3d 376 (S.D.N.Y. 2015), 320 n.98

Lewis Galoob Toys, Inc. v. Nintendo of Am., Inc., 964 F.2d 965 (9th Cir. 1992), 67 n.21, 77, 77 n.64, 79

Lewis v. Activision Blizzard, Inc., No. C 12-1096 CW, 2013 U.S. Dist. LEXIS 149784 (N.D. Cal. Oct. 17, 2013), aff'd, 634 Fed. Appx. 182 (9th Cir. 2015), 93–94, 93 n.145

Lilith Games (Shanghai) Co., Ltd. v. uCool, Inc., No. 15-CV-01267-SC, 2015 U.S. Dist. LEXIS 128619 (N.D. Cal. Sept. 23, 2015), 66, 66 n.15, 247–48, 247 n.92

Liquid Glass Enters., Inc. v. Dr. Ing. h.c.F. Porsche AG, 8 F. Supp. 2d 398 (D.N.J. 1998), 198 n.140

Litchfield v. Spielberg, 736 F.2d 1352 (9th Cir. 1984), 67 n.21, 70 n.33, 108–9, 108 n.227

Liu v. Price Waterhouse LLP, 302 F.3d 749 (7th Cir. 2002), 98 n.171

Lohan v. E*Trade Sec. LLC, No. 601016/2010 (N.Y. Sup. Ct. Apr. 20, 2010), 259 n.13

Lohan v. Take-Two Interactive Software, Inc., 31 N.Y.3d 111 (N.Y. 2018), 291–92, 291 n.195, 292 n.196

Lois Sportswear, U.S.A., Inc. v. Levi Strauss & Co., 799 F.2d 867 (2d Cir. 1986), 193 n.119

Lory v. Fed. Ins. Co., 122 Fed. Appx. 314 (9th Cir. 2005), 45 n.210

Lugosi v. Universal Pictures, 25 Cal. 3d 813 (Cal. 1979), 284–85, 284 n.138

Luv N' Care, Ltd. v. Regent Baby Prods. Corp., 841 F. Supp. 2d 753 (S.D.N.Y. 2012), 182–83 n.52

Lyng v. Nw. Indian Cemetery Protective Ass'n, 485 U.S. 439 (1988), 208 n.186

MacGreal v. Taylor, 167 U.S. 688 (1897), 49 n.231

Magnavox Co. v. Activision Inc., No. C-82-5270-CAL, 1985 WL 9496 (N.D. Cal. Dec. 27, 1985), 165 n.145

Magnavox Co. v. Chi. Dynamic Indus., 201 U.S.P.Q. 25 (N.D. Ill. 1977), 164, 164 n.141

MAI Sys. Corp. v. Peak Computer, Inc., 991 F.2d 511 (9th Cir. 1993), 102 n.182

Major v. McCallister, 302 S.W.3d 227 (Mo. Ct. App. 2009), 20 n.81

Malden Amusement Co. v. City of Malden, 582 F. Supp. 297 (D. Mass. 1983), 193 n.121

Mariniello v. Shell Oil Co., 511 F.2d 853 (3d Cir. 1975), 176 n.9

Martin v. Teletech Holdings, Inc., 213 Fed. Appx. 581 (9th Cir. 2006), 25–26 n.111

Marvel Enters., Inc. v. NCsoft Corp., No. 04-9253 (C.D. Cal. Jan. 25, 2005), 191–92, 191 n.108, 191 n.112, 192 n.113

Marvel Enters., Inc. v. NCsoft Corp., No. 04-9253, 2005 U.S. Dist. LEXIS 8448 (C.D. Cal. Mar. 9, 2005), 191 n.112, 216–17, 216 n.233

Master Corp. v. Aluminium Ltd. Sales, 4 N.Y.2d 403 (N.Y. 1958), 266 n.43

Mattel, Inc. v. MCA Records, Inc., 296 F.3d 894 (9th Cir. 2002), 183 nn.54–56, 209 n.193

Maxwell Commc'n Corp. v. Societe Generale, 93 F.3d 1036 (2d Cir. 1996), 306 n.21

Maxxim Med., Inc. v. Michelson, 51 F. Supp. 2d 773 (S.D. Tex. 1999), 253 n.117

Mayo Collaborative Servs. v. Prometheus Labs., Inc., 566 U.S. 66 (2012), 122–23, 122 n.2, 122 n.10

Mazer v. Stein, 347 U.S. 201 (1954), 87 n.117

McBee v. Delica Co., 417 F.3d 107 (1st Cir. 2005), 330, 330 n.147

McCallum Highlands, Ltd. v. Wash. Capital Dus, Inc., 66 F.3d 89 (5th Cir. 1995), 41 n.194

McKenzie Check Advance of Fla., LLC v. Betts, 112 So. 3d 1176 (Fla. 2013), 37 n.172

McRO, Inc. v. Bandai Namco Games Am. Inc., 837 F.3d 1299 (Fed. Cir. 2016), 170–71, 170 n.173, 171 n.176

MDY Indus., LLC v. Blizzard Entm't, Inc., 629 F.3d 928 (9th Cir. 2010), 3 n.5, 29 n.127, 41 n.191, 43, 43 n.203, 47, 47 n.218, 47 n.221, 48 nn.223–24, 53–54 n.242, 78–79, 78 n.71

Med. Instrumentation & Diagnostics Corp. v. Elekta AB, 344 F.3d 1205 (Fed. Cir. 2003), 145 n.95

Meshwerks, Inc. v. Toyota Motor Sales U.S.A., Inc., 528 F.3d 1258 (10th Cir. 2008), 314 n.65

Metalurgical Indus., Inc. v. Fourtek, 790 F.2d 1195 (5th Cir. 1986), 231, 231 n.21

Metro-Goldwyn-Mayer Studios, Inc. v. Grokster, Ltd., 243 F. Supp. 2d 1073 (C.D. Cal. 2003), 343 n.212

M Gen. LLC v. Activision Blizzard, Inc., No. 2:17-08644 (S.D.N.Y. Nov. 7, 2017), 215–16, 216 n.232

MGM Studios, Inc. v. Grokster, Ltd., 545 U.S. 913 (2005), 104, 104 nn.196–97

Microsoft Corp. v. AT&T Corp., 550 U.S. 437 (2007), 338, 338 n.185, 338 nn.187–88, 339 n.200

Micro Star v. FormGen, Inc., 154 F.3d 1107 (9th Cir. 1998), 8 n.28, 67 n.21, 70, 70 n.31, 76 n.63

Midler v. Ford Motor Co., 849 F.2d 460 (9th Cir. 1988), 262 n.31

Miles Inc. v. Cookson Am., Inc., No. Civ. A. 12,310, 1994 WL 676761 (Del. Ch. Nov. 15, 1994), 228 n.8, 232 n.26

Miller v. Facebook, Inc., No. C 10-00264 WHA, 2010 WL 2198204 (N.D. Cal. May 28, 2010), 64 n.6

Mil-Spec Monkey, Inc. v. Activision Blizzard, Inc., 74 F. Supp. 3d 1134 (N.D. Cal. 2014), 214, 214 n.221, 215

Milton H. Greene Archives, Inc. v. CMG Worldwide, Inc., 568 F. Supp. 2d 1152 (C.D. Cal. 2008), 281–83 nn.130–34

Milton H. Greene Archives, Inc. v. Marilyn Monroe, LLC, 692 F.3d 983 (9th Cir. 2012), 282 n.132

Mine O'Mine, Inc. v. Calmese, No. 2:10-CV-0043-KJD-PAL, 2011 WL 2728390 (D. Nev. July 12, 2011), 267 n.47, 268 n.54

M. Kramer Mfg. Co. v. Andrews, 783 F.2d 421 (4th Cir. 1986), 73, 73 n.48, 76, 76 n.60, 76 n.61

Morrisey v. Proctor & Gamble Co., 379 F.2d 675 (1st Cir. 1967), 82 n.86

Morrison v. Circuit City Stores, Inc., 317 F.3d 646 (6th Cir. 2002), 27 n.121

Motown Record Corp. v. George A. Hormel & Co., 657 F. Supp. 1236 (C.D. Cal. 1987), 281 n.126

Nahom v. Blue Cross & Blue Shield of Ariz., Inc., 180 Ariz. 548 (Ariz. Ct. App. 1994), 45 n.210

Nat'l Basketball Ass'n v. Motorola, Inc., 105 F.3d 841 (2d Cir. 1997), 84 n.98, 220 n.255

Nat'l Conference of Bar Exam'rs v. Multistate Legal Studies, Inc., 495 F. Supp. 34 (N.D. Ill. 1980), 64 n.5

Nat'l Football League v. PrimeTime 24 Joint Venture, No. 98 CIV. 3778(LMM), 1999 WL 163181 (S.D.N.Y. 1999), 319 n.93

Neal v. State Farm Ins. Co., 188 Cal. App. 2d 690 (Cal. Ct. App. 1961), 22 n.89

Net Global Mktg. v. Dialtone, Inc., 217 Fed. Appx. 598 (9th Cir. 2007), 25 n.107

New Kids on the Block v. News Am. Publ'g, Inc., 971 F.2d 302 (9th Cir. 1992), 203–5, 203 nn.156–58, 204–5 nn.164–65, 217 n.242

Nintendo of Am., Inc. v. iLife Techs., Inc., 717 Fed. Appx. 996 (Fed. Cir. 2017), 169–70, 169 nn.163–70

No Doubt v. Activision Publ'g, Inc., 192 Cal. App. 4th 1018 (Cal. Ct. App. 2011), 266, 266 n.42, 289–91, 289 n.176, 291 n.194

NTP, Inc. v. Research in Motion, Ltd., 418 F.3d 1282 (Fed. Cir. 2005), 339 n.191, 339 n.194

Nucar Consulting, Inc. v. Doyle, No. Civ.A 19756-NC, 2005 WL 820706 (Del. Ch. Apr. 5, 2005), 228 nn.8–9, 232 n.26

Oakville Hills Cellar, Inc. v. Georgallis Holdings, LLC, 826 F.3d 1376 (Fed. Cir. 2016), 181 n.44

O'Bannon v. Nat'l Collegiate Athletic Ass'n, 7 F. Supp. 3d 955 (N.D. Cal. 2014), 293 n.199

Octane Fitness, LLC v. ICON Health & Fitness, Inc., 134 S. Ct. 1749 (2014), 162 n.133

Oracle Am., Inc. v. Google, Inc., 750 F.3d 1339 (Fed. Cir. 2014), 246 n.90

O'Shea v. Direct Fin. Solutions, LLC, No. 07-1881, 2007 WL 4373038 (E.D. Pa. Dec. 5, 2007), 28 n.124

PACCAR Inc. v. TeleScan Techs., L.L.C., 319 F.3d 243 (6th Cir. 2003), 204 n.163

Pac. & S. Co. v. Duncan, 744 F.2d 1490 (11th Cir. 1984), 76 n.59

Palmer/Kane LLC v. Gareth Stevens Publ'g, No. 1:15-cv-7404-GHW, 2017 WL 3973957 (S.D.N.Y. 2017), 309 n.40

Parks v. LaFace Records, 329 F.3d 437 (6th Cir. 2003), 209 n.193, 285–86, 285 n.149

P&D Int'l v. Halsey Publ'g Co., 672 F. Supp. 1429 (S.D. Fla. 1987), 344 n.216

PepsiCo v. Redmond, 54 F.3d 1262 (7th Cir. 1995), 253 n.116, 253 n.118

Perfect 10, Inc. v. Amazon.com, Inc., 508 F.3d 1146 (9th Cir. 2007), 317 nn.81–82

Perfect 10, Inc. v. Giganews, Inc., 847 F.3d 657 (9th Cir. 2017), 102 n.185

Perfect 10, Inc. v. Visa Int'l Serv. Ass'n, 494 F.3d 788 (9th Cir. 2007), 184 n.58

Perfect 10, Inc. v. Yandex N.V., No. C 12-01521 WHA, 2013 WL 4777189 (N.D. Cal. Sept. 6, 2013), 318 n.84

Peridyne Tech. Solutions, LLC v. Matheson Fast Freight, 117 F. Supp. 2d 1366 (N.D. Ga. 2000), 344 n.215

Pesina v. Midway Mfg. Co., 948 F. Supp. 40 (N.D. Ill. 1996), 261–62, 261 n.25, 291–92 n.195

Phillips v. Audio Active, Ltd., 494 F.3d 378 (2d Cir. 2007), 310 n.48

Pivot Point Int'l, Inc. v. Charlene Prods., 372 F.3d 913 (7th Cir. 2004), 87 n.117

Playboy Enters., Inc. v. Dumas, 53 F.3d 549 (2d Cir. 1995), 94 n.152

Playboy Enters., Inc. v. Frena, 839 F. Supp. 1552 (M.D. Fla. 1993), 102 n.181, 112 n.253

Playboy Enters., Inc. v. Welles, 279 F.3d 796 (9th Cir. 2002), 204 n.164

Playtex Prods., Inc. v. Georgia-Pacific Corp., 390 F.3d 158 (2d Cir. 2004), 182 n.46

Polaroid Corp. v. Polarad Elecs. Corp., 287 F.2d 492 (2d Cir. 1961), 182 n.46

Pollstar v. Gigmania Ltd., 170 F. Supp. 2d 974 (E.D. Cal. 2000), 42 n.199

ProCD, Inc. v. Zeidenberg, 86 F.3d 1447 (7th Cir. 1996), 20 n.79, 23 n.98

Qualitex Co. v. Jacobson Prods. Co., 514 U.S. 159 (1995), 176 n.12, 177 n.14

RCTV Int'l Corp. v. Rosenfeld, No. 13-23611-CIVSIMONTON, 2016 WL 6818955 (S.D. Fla. Sept. 30, 2016), 307 n.24, 310 n.47

Religious Tech. Ctr. v. Netcom On-Line Commc'n Servs., Inc., 923 F. Supp. 1231 (N.D. Cal. 1995), 234, 234 nn.33–34, 235–36, 236 n.47

Renhcol Inc. v. Don Best Sports, 548 F. Supp. 2d 356 (E.D. Tex. 2008), 338 n.190, 339–40, 339 n.192, 339 n.195, 339 nn.197–98

Rice Researchers, Inc. v. Hiter, 512 So. 2d 1259 (Miss. 1987), 231 n.19

Riensche v. Cingular Wireless, No. C06-1325Z, 2006 U.S. Dist. LEXIS 93747 (W.D. Wash. Dec. 27, 2006), 25 n.110

Rogers v. Better Bus. Bureau v. Metro. Houston, Inc., 887 F. Supp. 2d 722 (S.D. Tex. 2012), 309 n.39

Rogers v. Grimaldi, 875 F.2d 994 (2d Cir. 1989), 208–16, 208 n.189, 214 n.219, 276 n.99, 285, 285 n.147

Romantics v. Activision, 574 F. Supp. 2d 758 (E.D. Mich. 2008), 263 n.37

Rosa & Raymond Parks Inst. for Self Dev. v. Target Corp., 812 F.3d 824 (11th Cir. 2016), 261 n.23

Rosetta Stone Ltd. v. Google, Inc., 676 F.3d 144 (4th Cir. 2012), 204 n.163

Ross v. Roberts, 222 Cal. App. 4th 677 (Cal. Ct. App. 2013), 272 n.69

Russo v. Ballard Med. Prods., 550 F.3d 1004 (10th Cir. 2008), 239 n.61

R.W. Beck, Inc. v. E3 Consulting, LLC, 577 F.3d 1133 (10th Cir. 2009), 69 n.25

Sadhu Singh Hamdad Tr. v. Ajit Newspaper Adver., Mktg. & Commc'ns, Inc., 503 F. Supp. 2d 577 (E.D.N.Y. 2007), 330 n.151

Samsung Elecs. Co. v. Apple Inc., 137 S. Ct. 429 (2016), 163–64, 163 n.137

Sanford v. RDA Consultants, Ltd., 535 S.E.2d 321 (Ga. Ct. App. 2000), 236 n.50

Saregama India Ltd. v. Mosley, 635 F.3d 1284 (11th Cir. 2011), 307 n.26

Schiller & Schmidt, Inc. v. Nordisco Corp., 969 F.2d 410 (7th Cir. 1992), 94 n.152

Schrock v. Learning Curve Int'l, Inc., 586 F.3d 513 (7th Cir. 2009), 98 n.170

Screen Gems-Columbia Music, Inc. v. Mark Fi Records, Inc., 256 F. Supp. 399 (S.D.N.Y. 1966), 103 n.194

Sealectro Corp. v. L.V.C. Indus., Inc., 271 F. Supp. 835 (E.D.N.Y. 1967), 337 n.181

Sega Enters., Ltd. v. Sabella, No. C 93-4260, 1996 WL 780560 (N.D. Cal. Dec. 18, 1996), 102 n.181

Sega Enters. v. MAPHIA, 948 F. Supp. 923 (N.D. Cal. 1996), 103, 103 n.192

Shaffer v. ACS Gov't Servs., Inc., 321 F. Supp. 2d 682 (D. Md. 2004), 31 n.138

Shapiro, Bernstein & Co. v. H.L. Green Co., 316 F.2d 304 (2d Cir. 1963), 102 n.187

Shaw Family Archives, Ltd. v. CMG Worldwide, Inc., 589 F. Supp. 2d 331 (S.D.N.Y. 2008), 282 nn.130–32

Sherry Mfg. Co. v. Towel King of Fla., Inc., 753 F.2d 1565 (11th Cir. 1985), 73 n.46

Shroyer v. New Cingular Wireless Servs., Inc., 498 F.3d 976 (9th Cir. 2007), 24 n.99

SI Handling Sys., Inc. v. Heisley, 753 F.2d 1244 (3d Cir. 1985), 231 n.19

Softel, Inc. v. Dragon Med. & Sci. Commc'n, Inc., 118 F.3d 955 (2d Cir. 1997), 231 n.19, 238 n.59

Sojuzplodoimport v. SPI Spirits Ltd., 726 F.3d 62 (2d Cir. 2013), 310 n.44

Specht v. Netscape Commc'n Corp., 306 F.3d 17 (2d Cir. 2002), 40 n.189

Splitfish AG v. Bannco Corp., 727 F. Supp. 2d 461 (E.D. Va. 2010), 312, 312 n.55, 312 n.57

Spry Fox, LLC v. LOL Apps, Inc., No. C12-147RAJ, 2012 U.S. Dist. LEXIS 153863 (W.D. Wash. Sept. 18, 2012), 106–8, 106 n.209

Square Enix Co. v. Wholesale Gallery, Inc., No. 08 00875 (C.D. Cal. Feb. 8, 2008), 186–87, 186 n.72, 193

Square Enix Co. v. Wholesale Gallery, Inc., No. 08-0875 (C.D. Cal. Jan. 16, 2009), 187 nn.77–78

Star Atheletica v. Varsity Brands, 137 S. Ct. 1002 (2017), 87 n.121

Starbucks Corp. v. Wolfe's Borough Coffee, Inc., 736 F.3d 198 (2d Cir. 2013), 180 n.34

State Farm Mut. Auto. Ins. Co. v. Sharon Woods Collision Ctr., Inc., No. 07-457, 2007 U.S. Dist. LEXIS 86651 (S.D. Ohio Nov. 26, 2007), 204 n.163

Steele v. Bulova Watch Co., 344 U.S. 280 (1952), 329 n.142

Stern Elecs., Inc. v. Kaufman, 523 F. Supp. 635 (E.D.N.Y. 1981), 179 n.28

Stern Elecs., Inc. v. Kaufman, 669 F.2d 852 (2d Cir. 1982), 65 n.13, 76 n.60, 194 n.121

Stix Prods., Inc. v. United Merchs. & Mfrs. Inc., 295 F. Supp. 479 (S.D.N.Y. 1968), 179 n.26

Streetwise Maps v. Van Dam, Inc., 159 F.3d 739 (2d Cir. 1998), 69 n.25

Subafilms, Ltd. v. MGM-Pathe Commc'ns Co., 24 F.3d 1088 (9th Cir. 1994), 315 nn.74–75, 319–20, 319 nn.87–88

Summit Mach. Tool Mfg. Corp. v. Victor CNC Sys., Inc., 7 F.3d 1434 (9th Cir. 1993), 220 n.253, 222 n.263

Swarovski Aktiengesellschaft v. Bldg. #19, Inc., 704 F.3d 44 (1st Cir. 2013), 204 n.163

Swift v. Zynga Game Network, Inc., 805 F. Supp. 2d 904 (N.D. Cal. 2011), 19 n.76, 23 n.95

Synopsys, Inc. v. Nassda Corp., No. C 01-2519 SI, 2002 WL 32749138 (N.D. Cal. Sept. 16, 2002), 246 n.90

Tabs Ass'n, Inc. v. Brohawn, 475 A.2d 1203 (Md. Ct. Spec. App. 1984), 231 n.20

TC Heartland LLC v. Kraft Foods Group Brands LLC, 137 S. Ct. 1514 (2017), 148, 148 n.101

Techs., Inc., v. Virtual Techs., 400 F.3d 1007 (7th Cir. 2005), 85, 85 nn.101–2

Telex Corp. v. IBM Corp., 510 F.2d 894 (10th Cir. 1975), 247 n.91

Tetris Holdings, LLC v. Xio Interactive, Inc., 863 F. Supp. 2d 394 (D.N.J. 2012), 65, 65 n.11, 104–8, 104 n.200, 311 n.52

Texaco Inc. v. Pennzoil Co., 729 S.W.2d 768 (Tex. Ct. App. 1987), 47 n.220

Thane Int'l, Inc. v. Trek Bicycle Corp., 305 F.3d 894 (9th Cir. 2002), 182 n.52

Therasense Inc. v. Becton Dickinson & Co., 649 F.3d 1276 (Fed. Cir. 2011), 159, 159 n.122

Thorner v. Sony Computer Entm't Am. LLC, 669 F.3d 1362 (Fed. Cir. 2012), 157 n.118

Tiffany (NJ) Inc. v. eBay Inc., 600 F.3d 93 (2d Cir. 2010), 203 n.155

Times Mirror Magazines, Inc. v. Las Vegas Sports News, L.L.C., 212 F.3d 157 (3d Cir. 2000), 182 n.52

Ting v. AT&T, 319 F.3d 1126 (9th Cir. 2003), 26 n.111

Toffoloni v. LFP Publ'g Group, LLC, 572 F.3d 1201 (11th Cir. 2009), 274–75, 274 n.82

Tommy & Tina, Inc. v. Dep't of Consumer Affairs of the City of New York, 117 Misc. 2d 415 (N.Y. Sup. Ct. 1983), 194 n.121

Toyota Motor Sales, U.S.A., Inc. v. Tabari, 610 F.3d 1171 (9th Cir. 2010), 202–3 n.154, 204 n.164

TrafFix Devices, Inc. v. Mktg. Displays, Inc., 532 U.S. 23 (2001), 177 n.14

Trenton v. Infinity Broad. Corp., 865 F. Supp. 1416 (C.D. Cal. 1994), 76 n.63

Twentieth Century Fox Film Corp. v. iCraveTV, No. CIV.A 00-120, 2000 WL 255989 (W.D. Pa. Feb. 8, 2000), 112 n.254, 316–17 n.78

Twentieth Century Fox Television v. Empire Distribution Inc., 875 F.3d 1192 (9th Cir. 2017), 196 n.134, 215 n.231

Twin Peaks Prods. v. Publications Int'l, 996 F.2d 1366 (2d Cir. 1993), 113 n.258

Two Pesos, Inc. v. Taco Cabana, Inc., 505 U.S. 763 (1992), 177 n.15

205 Corp. v. Brandow, 517 N.W.2d 548 (Iowa 1994), 232 n.28

Uhlmann Grain Co. of Tex. v. Wilson, 68 S.W.2d 281 (Tex. Ct. App. 1933), 49 n.233

Ultimate Creations, Inc. v. THQ, Inc., 2008 U.S. Dist. LEXIS 8224 (D. Ariz. May 9, 2007), 217, 217 n.241

Ultimate Creations, Inc. v. THQ Inc., No. 05-1134 (D. Ariz. Apr. 14, 2005), 189–90, 190 n.99

Ultimate Creations, Inc. v. THQ Inc., No. CV-05-1134-PHX-SMM, 2008 U.S. Dist. LEXIS 8224 (D. Ariz. Jan. 24, 2008), 189–90, 190 n.99, 190 nn.102–3, 196 n.135, 217, 217 n.240, 220–22, 220 n.256, 222 n.262

Ultramercial, Inc. v. Hulu, LLC, 772 F.3d 709 (Fed. Cir. 2014), 132 n.59

UMG Recordings, Inc. v. Veoh Networks, Inc., 718 F.3d 1006 (9th Cir. 2013), 114 nn.261–62

Union Carbide Corp. v. Tarancon Corp., 742 F. Supp. 1565 (N.D. Ga. 1990), 237 n.52

United Rentals, Inc. v. Pruett, 296 F. Supp. 2d 220 (D. Conn. 2003), 227 n.4

United States v. Cox, 73 F. Supp. 2d 751 (S.D. Tex. 1999), 246 n.90

United States v. Sandoval-Lopez, 122 F.3d 797 (9th Cir. 1997), 208 n.186

United States v. United Foods, Inc., 533 U.S. 405 (2001), 183 n.55

United States v. W3 Innovations, LLC, No. CV11-03958 (N.D. Cal. Sept. 8, 2011), 49 n.228

Universal City Studios, Inc. v. Nintendo Co., 578 F. Supp. 911 (S.D.N.Y. 1983), 185–86, 185 nn.62–63

Universal Commc'n Sys., Inc. v. Lycos, Inc., 478 F.3d 413 (1st Cir. 2007), 203 n.157

Universal Furniture Int'l, Inc. v. Collezione Europa USA, Inc., 618 F.3d 417 (4th Cir. 2010), 88 n.126

Univ. of Ala. Bd. of Trs. v. New Life Art, Inc., 683 F.3d 1266 (11th Cir. 2012), 286 n.159

Update Art, Inc. v. Modiin, 843 F.2d 67 (2d Cir. 1988), 316 n.77

U.S. Auto Parts Network, Inc. v. Parts Geek, LLC, 692 F.3d 1009 (9th Cir. 2012), 92 n.142

Valco Cincinnati, Inc. v. N & D Machining Serv., Inc., 492 N.E.2d 814 (Ohio 1986), 231 n.20

Vanity Fair Mills, Inc. v. T. Eaton Co., 234 F.2d 633 (2d Cir. 1956), 325 n.122, 327 n.134, 329 nn.144–45

Vasquez-Lopez v. Beneficial Or., Inc., 152 P.3d 940 (2007), 28 n.121

Viacom Int'l, Inc. v. YouTube, Inc., 676 F.3d 19 (2d Cir. 2012), 114 n.261, 116 n.277

Video Pipeline, Inc. v. Buena Vista Home Entm't, 342 F.3d 191 (3d Cir. 2003), 112 n.254, 317 n.78

VIRAG, S.R.L. v. Sony Computer Entm't Am. LLC, 699 Fed. Appx. 667 (9th Cir. 2017), 196 n.134, 215 n.227, 215 n.230

VIRAG S.R.L. v. Sony Computer Entm't Am. LLC, No. 3:15-cv-01729-LB, 2015 U.S. Dist. LEXIS 111211 (N.D. Cal. Aug. 21, 2015), 215, 215 n.227

Virginia v. Black, 538 U.S. 343 (2003), 194 n.125

Virtual Marilyn, LLC v. Estate of Marilyn Monroe, LLC, No. 1:14-cv-07938-SAS (S.D.N.Y. 2014), 269–70, 270 n.62

Waits v. Frito-Lay, Inc., 978 F.2d 1093 (9th Cir. 1992), 262 n.31, 262 n.33

Wales Indus. Inc. v. Hasbro Bradley, Inc., 612 F. Supp. 510 (S.D.N.Y. 1985), 103 n.194

Wal-Mart Stores, Inc. v. Samara Bros., Inc., 529 U.S. 205 (2000), 174 n.3, 178 n.20, 179 n.25, 180 n.37

Washington v. Take-Two Interactive Software, Inc., No. B232929, 2012 WL 5358709 (Cal. Ct. App. Oct. 31, 2012), 290–91, 290 n.187

Water Servs., Inc. v. Tesco Chems., Inc., 410 F.2d 163 (5th Cir. 1969), 236 n.50

WCVB-TV v. Boston Athletic Ass'n, 926 F.2d 42 (1st Cir. 1991), 217 n.243

WEC Holdings, LLC v. Juarez, No. 07-0137, 2008 U.S. Dist. LEXIS 13841 (D. Nev. Feb. 5, 2008), 183 n.52

Weseley Software Dev. Corp. v. Burdette, 977 F. Supp. 137 (D. Conn. 1997), 246 n.86

Westchester Media v. PRL USA Holdings, Inc., 214 F.3d 658 (5th Cir. 2000), 209 n.193

Wham-O, Inc. v. Paramount Pictures Corp., 286 F. Supp. 2d 1254 (N.D. Cal. 2003), 199–200, 199 n.143, 200 nn.147–48

Whimsicality, Inc. v. Rubie's Costume Co., 891 F.2d 452 (2d Cir. 1989), 87 n.121

Whist Club v. Foster, 42 F.2d 782 (S.D.N.Y. 1929), 81 n.82

White v. Samsung Elecs. Am., Inc., 971 F.2d 1395 (9th Cir. 1992), 263 n.38, 268 n.52, 268 n.55

White v. Samsung Elecs. Am., Inc., 989 F.2d 1512 (9th Cir. 1993), 264 n.41, 272 n.68

Williams Elecs., Inc. v. Artic Int'l, Inc., 685 F.2d 870 (3d Cir. 1982), 76 n.60

Winston Research Corp. v. Minn. Mining & Mfg. Co., 350 F.2d 134 (9th Cir. 1965), 231 n.20

Winters v. New York, 333 U.S. 507 (1948), 195 n.129

Winter v. D.C. Comics, 30 Cal. 4th 881 (Cal. 2003), 287, 287 n.162

Wolk v. Kodak Imaging Network, Inc., 840 F. Supp. 2d 724 (S.D.N.Y. 2012), 114 n.261

Woodall v. Grant & Co., 9 S.E.2d 95 (Ga. Ct. App. 1940), 49 n.233

Xfire, Inc. v. IGN Entm't, Inc., No. C 06-6475 SI, 2006 WL 2990203 (N.D. Cal. Oct. 19, 2006), 234–35, 234 n.39

Xoom, Inc. v. Imageline, Inc., 323 F.3d 279 (4th Cir. 2003), 69 n.25

Zacchini v. Scripps-Howard Broad. Co., 433 U.S. 562 (1977), 271 n.67, 273–74, 273 nn.70–73

ZeniMax Media, Inc. v. Oculus VR, LLC, 166 F. Supp. 3d 697 (N.D. Tex. 2015), 248, 248 nn.97–99

Zippo Mfg. Co. v. Zippo Dot Com, Inc., 952 F. Supp. 1119 (W.D. Pa. 1997), 342, 342 n.204, 342 n.206

Index

Absolute novelty, 126
Activision, 123, 143–44, 214–16, 289–90
Administrative law judge (ALJ), 152–53
Adults Only (AO) rating, 16
Advertising, 36, 103, 178–79, 183, 197, 216, 257–58, 303, 324, 330, 342
Ali, Muhammad, 259
America Invents Act (AIA), 126, 154, 169–70
American Arbitration Association, 28
Apple, 65, 124, 140, 163, 179
Arbitrary marks, 177–79
Ariadne's Thread, 142
ARMA 2, 69
Art, First Amendment and, 275–76
Article of manufacture, in utility patents, 133–34
Associated Press (AP), 219
Astaire, Fred, 278
Atari, 164, 166, 248–49
Augmented reality, 79–80, 97, 124, 140, 142, 257, 265, 285, 301
Augmented/virtual reality (AR/VR) games, 175
Authorship and ownership, 89–101
  contributions, 95–97

employee-created works, 92–94
EULAs, 97–101
game mods, 98–99
joint works, 95
specially commissioned work, 94–95
virtual property, ownership of, 99–101
works for hire, 91–95
Avatars, 77–78, 88, 101, 233–34, 240, 249, 257, 289–91, 297–98, 318, 320, 334
A.V.E.L.A., 269–70, 283

Band Hero, 289, 290
Bank Secrecy Act, 13
Battle.net, 41
Battle royale, 70
Beauregard claims, 133–34
Benoit, Nancy, 274–75
Berne Convention, 306–13
BioShock, 195
Blizzard Entertainment, 7–8, 18, 23, 38, 41, 43, 47, 78, 93–94, 100, 215–16, 250
Board of Patent Appeals and Interferences (BPAI), 127 n.44
Breach of contract, 264–66
Brown, Jim, 190–91, 294–96
Burck, Robert, 268–69

Call of Duty, 63, 214, 216
Children's Online Privacy Protection
Act (COPPA), 48–49
China, proposed copyright reform
in, 321–24
Choice of law/conflict of laws
issues, 305–14
City of Heroes, 191, 216
Claiming considerations, in design
patents, 142–46
Clone games, 104–8
Collegiate Licensing Company, 293
Competitive advantage requirement,
230–31
Compilations, 71–72
Compositions of matter, in utility
patents, 137–38
Concepcion ruling, 37–38
Confidentiality provisions, 25, 27,
232–33, 235–36
Consumer confusion, 174, 180–82,
185, 187, 190, 192–93, 195–96,
198, 201–22
Consumers Legal Remedies Act
(CLRA), 38–39
Continuation-in-part (CIP)
application, 168–69
Contracts. *See* Terms and
agreements
Contributions, 95–97
Copycat games, 104–8
Copyright, Designs, and Patents Act,
311 nn.52–53, 313 n.61
Copyright Act, 63, 64–65, 68, 74, 76,
78, 91, 306, 308, 310, 313, 315,
319
Copyright infringement, 101–17
*Bissoon-Dath v. Sony Computer
Entertainment America, Inc.*,
110–11
Capcom Co. v. MKR Group, Inc.,
109–10
claims, 108–11
clone games, 104–8
copycat games, 104–8
Crawford v. Midway Games, Inc.,
109
DMCA, 112–17

*Funky Films, Inc. v. Time Warner
Entertainment Co., L.P.*, 108–9
international considerations,
314–21
Let's Play video, 111
Litchfield v. Spielberg, 108–9
machinima video, 111
place of infringement in online
virtual environment, 315–18
secondary liability for foreign
actions, 318–20
streaming of games, 111–17
takedown procedures for
minimizing, 320–21
Copyright issues, international
considerations, 299–346
choice of law and conflict of
laws, 305–14
conflicts in copyright ownership,
305–10
fixation as requirement for
copyright, 313–14
in online games and virtual
environments, 304–24
proposed copyright reform in
Europe and China, 321–24
territoriality of copyright
infringement, 314–21
works for hire, 311–13
Copyright law, 61–117
authorship and ownership,
89–101
clone games, 104–8
compilations, 71–72
contributions, 95–97
copycat games, 104–8
copyright infringement, 101–17
derivative works, 67–69
DMCA, 112–17
EULAs, 97–101
fixation, 75–80, 313–14
game mods, 69–71, 98–99
game rules, 81–83
idea/expression dichotomy,
80–82
in-game items, 88–89
joint works, 95
Let's Play video, 111

limitations on scope of, 80–89
literal/nonliteral aspects of
    computer games, 64–72
machinima video, 111
merger doctrine, 80, 82 n.86, 86
originality, 72–75
overview, 62–63
requirements for, basic, 64–89
right of publicity, 270–71
scènes à faire doctrine, 84–85
stock expression doctrine, 85–86
streaming of games, 111–17
trade secrets, 237–38
traditional infringement claims,
    108–11
useful articles, 86–89
video-sharing, 111–17
virtual property, 99–101
works for hire, 91–95
Copyright preemption, 270–71,
    280–96
    post-mortem right of publicity
        law, development of, 281–83
    predominant use test, 286–87
    right of publicity after death, 281
    Rogers test, 285–87, 295–96
    transformative use test, 287,
        289–90, 294–96
    variations in state law and call
        for federal law, 284–96
Counter-Strike, 69
Criminal actions, 253–54

Damages, 160–64
    additional, 161–62
    basic, 160–61
    design patent, 162–64
    misappropriation, 253
DayZ, 69
D.C. Comics, 287
Deceptive and Unfair Trade
    Practices Act, 37
Declaratory Judgment Act, 147–48
Defend Trade Secrets Act (DTSA),
    226–27, 237, 252
Defense of the Ancients (DotA), 97
De Havilland, Olivia, 260
Derivative works, 67–69

Descriptive marks, 177–79
Design patents, 138–46
    claiming considerations,
        142–46
    damages, 162–64
    U.S. patentability requirements,
        128–29
Diablo III, 41
Dickie Roberts: Former Child Star,
    199–200
Digital Millennium Copyright Act
    (DMCA), 112–17
Digital rights management (DRM),
    58 n.262
Dillinger, LLC, 189
Dilution, 179–80, 182–83, 218
Direct liability, 187–91
    Brown v. Electronic Arts, Inc.,
        190–91
    *Dillinger, LLC v. Electronic Arts,
        Inc.*, 189
    *Electronic Arts, Inc. v. Textron,
        Inc.*, 188–89
    *E.S.S. Entertainment 2000, Inc. v.
        Rock Star Videos, Inc.*, 187–88
    *Ultimate Creations, Inc. v. THQ,
        Inc.*, 189–90
Donkey Kong, 185–86, 192
Drama, First Amendment and,
    275–76
Duke Nukem 3D, 70

Economic Espionage Act, 253–54
Electronic Arts, Inc., 188–89,
    190–91
Electronic Communications Privacy
    Act, 235, 254
Employee-created works, 92–94
End-user license agreements
    (EULAs)
    copyright ownership, 97–101
    defined, 3
    future of, 17–18
    history of, 4–10
    international copyright issues,
        304–5, 346
    international trademark issues,
        329, 346

End-user license agreements (cont.)
limitations on, 38
minors, 50–51
privity of contract, 47–48
provisions in, 10–14
scholarly criticisms of, 14–17
trade secret laws, 241–45
unconscionability, 23, 27
E.S.S. Entertainment 2000, Inc.,
187–88
E*Trade, 259–60
Europe, proposed copyright reform
in, 321–24
European Patent Office (EPO), 333
EVE Online, 240, 243, 245
Everquest, 12, 18, 131

Fair Labor Standards Act, 33
Fair use, 276–80
predominant use test, 276–77
Rogers test, 278
transformative use test, 278–80
False endorsement/false designation
of origin, 268–70
Falwell, Jerry, 275
Fanciful marks, 177–79
Federal and state consumer
protection limitations on
terms and agreements, 36–39
Federal Arbitration Act (FAA), 21,
31–35
Federal district courts to enforce
patent rights, 146–52
Federal Trade Commission (FTC),
36, 49
Federal Trade Commission Act, 36,
37
"Feud: Bette and Joan," 260
FIFA International Soccer, 195
First Amendment
art and, 275–76
drama and, 275–76
Lanham Act and, 208–9, 213–16
newsworthy exception, 272–75
parody and, 275
right of publicity, 272–76
satire and, 275
trademark issues, 208–16
Fixation, 75–80, 313–14

Fixed in a tangible medium of
expression, 313
FormGen, 70
Fraudulent inducement, 266
FX Networks, 260

Galaxian, 62
Game design, 245–49
Game Genie, 77
Game mods, 69–71
ownership of, 98–99
Gameplay, 239–45
in-game trade secrets developed
by players, 242–45
real-world trade secrets revealed
in-game, 240–42
Game rules, 81–83
Generic marks, 177–79
Gibson Guitars, 123
Ginger and Fred, 278
Global Positioning System (GPS), 79
Golden Tee Fore!, 186
Grand Theft Auto, 188, 195, 206, 209,
210, 212, 286, 290–92
Grand Turismo, 100
Gravano, Karen, 291–92
Gwent, 100

Half-Life, 69
Hallmark, 267
Hamilton, Lenwood, 296–97
Haptic feedback, 166
Harmonix, 123
Hart, Ryan, 293–94
Hearthstone, 82, 100
Heroes of the Storm, 100
Hilton, Paris, 267
Hololens, 142
Hustler Magazine, 274–75

Idea/expression dichotomy, 80–82
Identity, right of publicity to
protect, 263–64
IGN Entertainment, Inc., 234–35
Image, right of publicity to protect,
260–62
Incredible Technologies, Inc., 186
Industry practices to remove TOU
limitations, 52–56

Index

Infringement
copyright, 101–17
patent, 157–60
In-game
direct liability use, 187–91
items, 88–89
real-world trade secrets revealed, 240–42
secondary liability use, 191–92
trade secrets developed by players, 242–45
Injunctive relief, 251–53
Innocence of Muslims, 96
Intellectual property (IP)
international enforcement of, 340–45
protection, 236–39
International Commercial Court (ICC), 28
International considerations, 299–346
copyright issues, 304–24
intellectual property rights, enforcement of, 340–45
overview, 300–304
patent law issues, 330–40
trademark issues, 324–30
International News Service (INS), 219
Inter partes review (IPR), 154–57
Invaders, 194
Invention patents, 129–30
Inventorship, international, 337
iPhone, 73, 104, 163

Joint works, 95
Judicial intervention to remove TOU limitations, 56–58

Kardashian, Kim, 260–61
Kirby, Kierin, 123–24, 288–91
Konami, 123, 139
Kozinski, Alex, 264

Lady Miss Kier, 288–91
Lanham Act
copyright preemption, 271
direct liability, 187–91
false endorsement/false designation of origin under, 190, 262, 268–70, 295

First Amendment rights, 208–9, 213–16
foreign defendants, 329–30
misappropriation, 220–21
overview, 176–79
physical products, 185–87
post-sale confusion, 193
protection from dilution, 179, 182–83
protection from infringement, 179–82
right of publicity, 181, 267–70
Rogers test, 285, 295, 296
secondary liability, 191–92, 218
trademark defined by, 176–77
trademark infringement under, 267–68
trademark protection, 179–83
League of Legends, 54, 63, 100, 301
Legislative action to remove TOU limitations, 58–60
Let's Play video, 111
Likeness, right of publicity to protect, 260–62
Lilith Games, 247–48
Limitations on terms and agreements, 19–60
industry practices to remove, 52–56
judicial intervention to remove, 56–58
legislative action to remove, 58–60
modifications, 39–43
privity of contract, 43–48
resolutions to TOU, 51–60
unconscionability, 19–39
Literal/nonliteral aspects of computer games, 64–72
compilations, 71–72
derivative works, 67–69
mods, 69–71
Lohan, Lindsay, 259–60, 291, 292

Machines, in utility patents, 134–37
Machinima video, 111
Madden NFL, 77–78, 190–91, 213, 292
Madrid System, 327–28
Malcolm X, 90

Marketing, 181, 193, 246, 257, 264, 268

Mars, Inc., 268–69

Martin, Scott, 199–200

Marvel Enterprises, Inc., 191–92

Massively multiplayer online (MMO), 4 n.6, 300

Massively multiplayer online role-playing game (MMORPG), 191

McCarthy, J. Thomas, 198, 222, 259

McFarlane, Todd, 277

Merger doctrine, 80, 82 n.86, 86

Microsoft, 124, 142, 174, 184–85, 197

Micro Star, 70

Midler, Bette, 262

Midway Games, 123

Midway Manufacturing Co., 261–62

Minecraft, 14, 63, 98, 300, 305, 314

Mine O'Mine, 267–68

Minors, 48–51

Misappropriation
  criminal actions, 253–54
  damages, 253
  injunctive relief, 251–53
  trademark, 219–22
  trade secrets, 251–54

Modifications, game. *See* Game mods

Modifications to terms and agreements, 39–43

Molinaro, Melissa, 261

Monroe, Marilyn, 269–70, 282–83

Moral Majority, 275

Multiplayer online battle arena (MOBA), 100

Mythica, 184–85

Name, right of publicity to protect, 259–60

National Collegiate Athletic Association (NCAA), 292–94

National Football League (NFL), 292

National Labor Relations Act (NLRA), 33–34

NCsoft Corp., 191–92

Newsworthy exception, 272–75

Nintendo, 77, 124, 166–67, 169, 174, 185–86, 248–49

Nintendo Entertainment System (NES), 166

No Doubt, 266, 289–91

Nominative fair use, 202–8

Nondisclosure agreements, 232, 233, 236, 238, 241–42

Nonliteral aspects of computer games. *See* Literal/nonliteral aspects of computer games

Oculus VR, 124, 140, 248

Odyssey game, 164–65

Old Navy, 260–61

O'Neal, Shaquille, 267–68

Originality, 72–75

OutKast, 285–86

Overwatch, 7

Pac-Man, 62, 94, 194

Paris Convention, 328, 336

Parks, Rosa, 261, 285–86

Parody, First Amendment and, 275

Patent Cooperation Treaty (PCT), 336

Patent law issues
  enforceability against foreign defendants, 338–40
  filing issues for online virtual environments and Internet-related inventions, 335–37
  foreign inventions, eligibility of, 332–34
  international considerations, 330–40
  issues involving international inventorship, 337

Patent lawsuits, video game, 164–71
  Anascape Ltd. v. Nintendo of America Inc., 167–70
  haptic feedback, 166
  Magnavox Co. v. Chicago Dynamic Industries, 164–66
  McRO, Inc. v. Bandai Namco Games America Inc., 170–71
  vibrating controller, 166–67

Patent protection, 119–71
  CIP application, 168–69
  damage issues, 160–64
  design patents, 128–29, 138–46
  infringement issues, 157–60
  inter partes review, 154–57
  invention patents, 129–30
  overview, 120–30
  patent rights, enforcement of,
    146–57
  trade secrets, 238–39
  utility patents, 120–28, 130–38
  video game lawsuits, 164–71
  video game patents, 130–46
  virtual world patents, 130–46,
    146–71
Patent rights, enforcement of,
  146–57
  federal district courts, 146–52
  USITC, 152–54
  USPTO, 154–57
Patent Trial and Appeal Board
  (PTAB), 127–28, 127 n.45
Peer-to-peer networks, 101, 309
Persona, right of publicity to
  protect, 263–64
Pesina, 261–62
PGA Tour Golf, 186
Physical products, 185–87
  *Incredible Technologies, Inc. v.
    Virtual Technologies, Inc.*, 186
  *Square Enix Co. v. Wholesale
    Gallery, Inc.*, 186–87
  *Universal City Studios, Inc. v.
    Nintendo Co., Ltd.*, 185–86
Picture, right of publicity to protect,
  260–62
PlayStation, 174
Pong, 62, 164–65
Post-mortem right of publicity law,
  281–95
  development of, 281–83
  variations in, 284–95
Post-sale confusion, 193
Predominant use test, 286–87
  copyright preemption, 286–87
  fair use, 276–77

Privity of contract, 43–48
  circumventing privity through
    tort, 46–48
  in digital games, 43–44
  third-party beneficiary clauses,
    44–45
Procedural unconscionability,
  21–24
Project Gotham Racing 3, 197
Provisions in terms and
  agreements, 10–14

Rainbow Six Vegas, 197–98
Registered marks, 180, 188–89
Regulations on Computers Software
  Protection, 312
Restatement of Torts, 229–30
*Restatement (Third) of Unfair
  Competition*, 228, 229, 243
Right of publicity, 255–98
  breach of contract, 264–66
  claims overlapping with, 264–71
  copyright, 270–71
  copyright preemption, 280–96
  defenses, 272–96
  development of, 258–59
  in *Dillinger, LLC v. Electronic Arts,
    Inc.*, 189
  elements, 259–64
  fair use, 276–80
  false endorsement/false
    designation of origin under
    Lanham Act, 268–70
  First Amendment, 272–76
  fixation, 77
  fraudulent inducement, 266
  overview, 256–58
  post-mortem, 281–95
  protection of likeness/image/
    picture, 260–62
  protection of name, 259–60
  protection of persona/identity,
    263–64
  protection of voice, 262–63
  trademark infringement under
    Lanham Act, 181, 267–68
  variations in state law, 271

Rock Star Videos, Inc., 187–88, 286
Rogers, Ginger, 278
Rogers test
  copyright preemption, 285–87,
    295–96
  fair use, 278
Rush, Rick, 275–76
Ryan Murphy Productions, 260

Samsung, 263–64
Satire, First Amendment and, 275
Savings clause, 32
Scènes à faire doctrine, 84–85
Scholarly criticisms of agreements
    and terms, 14–16
Secondary liability, 191–92, 216–18
  for international copyright
    infringement, 318–20
Secondary meaning, 178–79
Second Life, 14–15, 18, 23, 26, 29, 34,
    57, 240–42, 250, 305
Secrecy requirement, 232–36
Sega, 123–24, 288
Shaqtus Orange Clothing Co.,
    267–68
Simpsons Game, 195
Sleekcraft factors, 181–82
Slip 'N Slide, 199–200
Software code, 134, 247
Source code, 65–66, 92, 128, 228,
    230, 246–47, 251, 322
Space Invaders, 194
Specially commissioned work,
    94–95
Spry Fox, LLC, 106–8
Square Enix Co., 186–87
Star Wars, 72, 138
Statutory bar to patentability, 126
Stefani, Gwen, 266
Stock expression doctrine, 85–86
Stockholm Act, 327 n.135
Strategic lawsuit against public
    participation (SLAPP) motion,
    260
Streaming of games, 111–17
Subafilms, 319–20

Substantive unconscionability,
    24–31
Suggestive marks, 177–79

Tagging, 159
Takedown procedures, 320–21
Target, 261
Teaching, suggestion, or motivation
    (TSM) test, 126–27
Technical Board of EPO, 333
Terms and agreements
  federal and state consumer
    protection limitations, 36–39
  future of, 17–18
  history of, 4–10
  limitations, 19–60
  minors, 48–51
  modifications, 39–43
  overview, 2–3
  privity of contract, 43–48
  provisions in, 10–14
  purpose and scope of, 4–18
  scholarly criticisms, 14–16
  unconscionability, 19–39
Terms of service (TOS)
  defined, 3
  Federal Arbitration Act, 34–35
  future of, 17–18
  history of, 4–10
  industry practices, 55–56
  provisions in, 10–14
  scholarly criticisms of, 14–17
  unconscionability, 22–23, 29, 30
Terms of use (TOU)
  defined, 3
  Federal Arbitration Act, 31–32
  future of, 17–18
  history of, 4–10
  industry practices to remove
    limitations, 52–56
  judicial intervention to remove
    limitations, 56–58
  legislative action to remove
    limitations, 58–60
  limitations, resolutions to, 37,
    51–60

minors, 48–49
modifications, 40–43
privity of contract, 43, 46–47
provisions in, 10–14
scholarly criticisms of, 14–17
unconscionability, 22, 25
Tetris Holding, 104–6
Textron, Inc., 188
Third-party beneficiary clauses,
44–45
THQ, Inc., 189–90, 217, 220–21
Tort, circumventing privity through,
46–48
Trademark
categories, 177–79
consumer confusion, 174,
180–82, 185, 187, 190,
192–93, 195–96, 198, 201–22
defined, 176
global exposure, protecting
against, 327–28
predominant function of, 174
registered, 180, 188–89
secondary meaning, 178–79
unregistered marks, 180, 188–89
Trademark Dilution Revision Act,
182 n.52
Trademark infringement
misappropriation and, 219–22
right of publicity under Lanham
Act, 267–68
Trademark issues, 184–216
analysis of, 192–216
Brown v. Electronic Arts, Inc.,
190–91
*Dillinger, LLC v. Electronic Arts,
Inc.*, 189
direct liability, 187–91
*Electronic Arts, Inc. v. Textron,
Inc.*, 188–89
*E.S.S. Entertainment 2000, Inc. v.
Rock Star Videos, Inc.*, 187–88
First Amendment, 208–16
foreign defendants, 329–30
*Incredible Technologies, Inc. v.
Virtual Technologies, Inc.*, 186

international considerations,
324–30
*Marvel Enterprises, Inc. v. NCsoft
Corp.*, 191–92, 216–18
nominative fair use, 202–8
ownership and territoriality,
325–27
physical products, 185–87
protecting marks subject to
global exposure, 327–28
secondary liability, 191–92,
216–18
*Square Enix Co. v. Wholesale
Gallery, Inc.*, 186–87
*Ultimate Creations, Inc. v. THQ,
Inc.*, 189–90
*Universal City Studios, Inc. v.
Nintendo Co., Ltd.*, 185–86
Trademark law, 173–223
design features, 177
eligibility for protection, 177–79
issues in video games and virtual
worlds, 184–216
Lanham Act for protection,
179–83
overview, 176–84
product packaging, 176–77
secondary liability, 216–18
unfair competition, 219–22
Trademark Law Revision Act, 180
n.39
Trade-Related Aspects of
Intellectual Property Rights
(TRIPS), 314
Trade secret, defined, 226–27
Trade secret law, 225–54
competitive advantage
requirement, 230–31
copyright protection, 237–38
game design, 245–49
gameplay, 239–45
IP protection, 236–39
issues in video games and virtual
worlds, 249–51
misappropriation, 251–54
overview, 226–39

Trade secret law *(cont.)*
  patent protection, 238–39
  secrecy requirement, 232–36
  UTSA, 227–30
  in video games and virtual
    worlds, 239–49
Traditional infringement claims,
  108–11
Transformative use test
  copyright preemption, 287,
    289–90, 294–96
  fair use, 278–80
Twist, Tony, 277
Twitch, 43, 111–12, 113, 115
Twitchcasts, 111–12

Ultimate Creations, 189–90, 217,
  220–21
Ultimate Warrior, 190
Uncharted, 63
Unconscionability, 19–39
  FAA, 31–35
  federal and state consumer
    protection limitations, 36–39
  procedural, 21–24
  substantive, 24–31
Unfair Business Practices Act,
  38–39
Unfair competition, 219–22
Uniform Trade Secrets Act (UTSA),
  227–30
  Restatement of Torts, 229–30
  *Restatement (Third) of Unfair
    Competition*, 228
U.S. Copyright Office, 64–65, 114,
  166, 238, 249, 270
U.S. International Trade
  Commission (USITC), 152–54
U.S. patentability requirements
  for design patents, 128–29
  for utility patents, 120–28
U.S. Patent and Trademark Office
  (USPTO), 154–57
Universal City Studios, Inc.,
  185–86
Unregistered marks, 180, 188–89
Useful articles, 86–89

Utility patents, 130–38
  article of manufacture, 133–34
  compositions of matter, 137–38
  machines, 134–37
  processes, 131–33
  U.S. patentability requirements,
    120–28

Vampire: Bloodlines, 70
Vibrating controller, 166–67
Video-sharing, 111–17
Virtual Marilyn, LLC, 270
Virtual Technologies, Inc., 186
Voice, right of publicity to protect,
  262–63

Waits, Tom, 262–63
Warcraft III, 71, 97
Warner Home Video, 319–20
Wearable technology, 140
Wham-O, 199–200
White, Vanna, 263–64, 268
Wholesale Gallery, Inc., 186–87
Wii, 169, 174
Winter, Johnny and Edgar, 287
Woods, Tiger, 275–76
Works for hire, 91–95
  employee-created works, 92–94
  international considerations,
    311–13
  specially commissioned work,
    94–95
World Intellectual Property
  Organization (WIPO), 336, 346
World of Warcraft, 14–15, 18, 38, 41,
  43, 45, 78–79, 93–94, 131
World Wrestling Entertainment, 190

Xbox, 73, 174
Xfire, 234–35
Xio Interactive, 104–6

Yellow Submarine, 319
YouTube, 8, 96, 113, 114, 116, 344

Zacchini, Hugo, 273–74
Zeta-Jones, Catherine, 260

About the ABA Section of Intellectual Property Law

From its strength within the American Bar Association, the ABA Section of Intellectual Property Law (ABA-IPL) advances the development and improvement of intellectual property laws and their fair and just administration. The Section furthers the goals of its members by sharing knowledge and balanced insight on the full spectrum of intellectual property law and practice, including patents, trademarks, copyright, design, and trade secrets. Providing a forum for rich perspectives and reasoned commentary, ABA-IPL serves as the ABA voice of intellectual property law within the profession, before policy makers, and with the public.

ABA Section of Intellectual Property Law (ABA-IPL)
Order today! Call 800-285-2221
Monday-Friday, 8:00 a.m. – 5:00 p.m., CT
or visit www.ambar.org/iplbooks.

Qty	Title	Regular Price	ABA-IPL Member Price	Total
____	ADR Advocacy, Strategies, and Practices for Intellectual Property and Technology Cases, 2nd Ed. (5370231)	$149.95	$119.95	$____
____	ANDA Litigation, 2nd Ed. (5370223)	$369.00	$289.00	$____
____	Antitrust Issues in Intellectual Property Law (5370222)	$149.95	$119.95	$____
____	Arbitrating Patent Disputes (5370229)	$89.95	$74.95	$____
____	Careers in IP Law (5370204) (The ebook is complimentary with ABA-IPL Section membership)	$24.95	$16.95	$____
____	Chinese Expansion in the EU (5370224)	$169.95	$134.95	$____
____	Computer Games and Immersive Entertainment, 2nd Ed. (5370239)	$89.95	$69.95	$____
____	Copyright Litigation Strategies (5370228)	$369.00	$285.00	$____
____	Copyright Remedies (5370208)	$89.95	$74.95	$____
____	Copyright Termination Law (5370226)	$139.95	$109.95	$____
____	Crash Course on U.S. Patent Law (5370221)	$39.95	$34.95	$____
____	The DMCA Handbook, Second Edition (5370234)	$79.95	$64.95	$____
____	The Essential Case Law Guide to PTAB Trials (5370233)	$249.95	$199.95	$____
____	Fundamentals of Intellectual Property Law (5370218)	$89.95	$69.95	$____
____	Intellectural Property and Technology Due Diligence (5370236)	$219.95	$179.95	$____
____	The Intellectual Property Law Handbook, 2nd Ed. (5620154)	$139.95	$109.95	$____
____	IP Attorney's Handbook for Insurance Coverage in Intellectual Property Disputes, 2nd Ed. (5370210)	$139.95	$129.95	$____
____	IP Protection in China (5370217)	$139.95	$109.95	$____
____	IP Strategies for Medical Device Technologies (5370238)	$149.95	$119.95	$____
____	IP Valuation for the Future (5370237)	$89.95	$59.95	$____
____	A Lawyer's Guide to Section 337 Investigations before the U.S.International Trade Commission, 3rd Ed. (5370219)	$129.95	$99.95	$____
____	Legal Guide to Video Game Development, 2nd Ed. (5370227)	$74.95	$59.95	$____
____	A Legal Strategist's Guide to Trademark Trial and Appeal Board Practice, 3rd Ed. (5370220)	$169.95	$139.95	$____
____	Marketing Your Invention (5370165)	$20.00	$15.00	$____
____	Music & Copyright in America (5370201)	$97.95	$67.95	$____
____	New Practitioner's Guide to Intellectual Property (5370198)	$89.95	$69.95	$____
____	Patent Freedom to Operate Searches, Opinions, Techniques, and Studies (5370230)	$139.95	$109.95	$____
____	Patent Neutral (5370232)	$89.95	$69.95	$____
____	Patent Obviousness in the Wake of *KSR International Co. v. Teleflex Inc.* (5370189)	$129.95	$103.95	$____

ABA Section of Intellectual Property Law (ABA-IPL)
Order today! Call 800-285-2221
Monday-Friday, 8:00 a.m. – 5:00 p.m., CT
or visit www.ambar.org/iplbooks.

Qty	Title	Regular Price	ABA-IPL Member Price	Total
_____	Patent Trial Advocacy Casebook, 3rd Ed. (5370124)	$149.95	$119.95	$_____
_____	Patently Persuasive (5370206)	$129.95	$99.95	$_____
_____	The Practitioner's Guide to the PCT (5370205)	$139.95	$109.95	$_____
_____	The Practitioner's Guide to Trials Before the Patent Trial and Appeal Board, 2nd Ed. (5370225)	$159.95	$129.95	$_____
_____	Pre-ANDA Litigation, Second Edition (5370235)	$349.00	$220.00	$_____
_____	Preliminary Relief in Patent Infringement Disputes (5370194)	$119.95	$94.95	$_____
_____	Right of Publicity (5370215)	$89.95	$74.95	$_____
_____	A Section White Paper: A Call for Action for Online Piracy and Counterfeiting Legislation (5370213)	$25.00	$25.00	$_____
_____	Settlement of Patent Litigation and Disputes (5370192)	$179.95	$144.95	$_____
_____	Starting an IP Law Practice (5370202)	$54.95	$34.95	$_____
_____	The Tech Contracts Handbook, 2nd Ed. (5370216)	$39.95	$34.95	$_____
_____	The Technology Transfer Law Handbook (5370211)	$220.00	$176.00	$_____
_____	Trademark and Deceptive Advertising Surveys (5370197)	$179.95	$134.95	$_____
_____	Trademark Surveys (5370207)	$269.95	$239.95	$_____

* Tax
DC residents add 5.75%
IL residents add 10.25%
CA residents add local sales tax
(between 7.5% and 10%)
MN residents add 6.25%
TX residents add local sales tax
(between 6.5% and 8.25%)
Tax includes applicable shipping costs
in IL, MN, and TX.

Payment
❑ Check payable to the ABA
❑ VISA
❑ Mastercard
❑ American Express
❑ Discover

Credit Card #_____ Exp._____

Signature_____

* Tax	$_____
** Shipping/Handling	$_____
TOTAL	$_____

**Shipping/Handling
Up to $49.99 .... $8.95
$50 to $99.99 .... $10.95
$100 to $199.99 .... $12.95
$200 to $499.99 .... $15.95
$500 to $999.99 .... $18.95
$1,000 and above .... 3% of
order value

Name_____

Firm/Organization_____

Address_____

City_____ State_____ Zip Code_____

Phone_____ E-mail_____
(in case of questions about your order)

Please allow 5 to 7 business days for
UPS delivery. Need it sooner? Ask
about overnight delivery. Call the
ABA Service Center at 800-285-2221
for more information.

Guarantee: If—for any reason—you are
not satisfied with your purchase, you
may return it within 30 days of receipt
for a complete refund of the price of
the book(s). No questions asked.

Please mail your order to:
ABA Publication Orders, 321 N. Clark St., 16th Floor, Chicago, Illinois 60654
Phone: 800-285-2221 or 312-988-5522 • Fax: 312-988-5568
E-mail: orders@abanet.org

Thank you for your order!